AFTER THE REVOLUTION

Lessons From Local Government On
Designing A Dynamic Democracy

Clive Stevens

Collectors' Edition (Copies 1 to 200)

After The Revolution: Lessons From Local Government On Designing
A Dynamic Democracy
Original edition of 200 copies first published 2020 by Tangent Books

Tangent Books
Unit 5.16 Paintworks, Bristol BS4 3EH
0117 972 0645
www.tangentbooks.co.uk
richard@tangentbooks.co.uk

ISBN 978-1-910089-94-1
Author: Clive Stevens

Publisher: Richard Jones

Design: Joe Burt

Cover illustration: Grace Kress

A CIP record of this book is available at the British Library.
Printed on paper from a sustainable source

CONTENTS

9   About The Author

10   Acknowledgements

11   A Simple Guide To A Council

INTRODUCTIONS OF ALL SORTS

15   A1 – Greetings Good Citizens! The Prologue... Up Bristol!

18   A2 – Before The Beginning

22   A3 – My Diary – The Days Leading Up To The Beginning

24   A4 – October 2016 – Five Months After The Beginning; Wanting To Make A Difference (1)

29   A5 – Wanting To Make A Difference (2) (Biodiesel Generator)

32   A6 – Cock Up In The Council's Chamber

35   A7 – Councillors' (Members') Code Of Conduct

39   A8 – We Start Off In Court

42   A9 – Extinction Rebellion Face A Small Rebellion

WHY IS DEMOCRACY IMPORTANT?

45   B1 – The Mathematics Of Power

48   B2 – The Impact Of This Mathematical Truism Today

53   B3 – The Mathematics Of Power As Played Out In Bristol (Example)

57   B4 – If The Representatives Don't Know What's Going On, How Can The Electors?

59   B5 - So Who Does Run The Council?

63   B6 – As Officers Take Decisions, Can We Trust Them With The Big Ones?

67   B7 – Openness And Opaqueness

72   B8 – We Do Sometimes Make Some Progress

75   B9 – The Rent Is Going Up By How Much?

78   B10 – Finance Scrutiny, The Task And Finish Way

83   B11 – A Brief History Of Scrutiny

HAND-ME-DOWNS FROM GOVERNMENT

89   Introduction

91   C1 – I Blame The Government Or Should I Blame The King?

95   C2 – Universal Credit – A Credit To Anyone?

99   C3 – A Tale Of Two Caps – More Harmful Consequences

102   C4 – Licensing Of Bars And Clubs (1)

105   C5 – Licensing Bars And Clubs (2) – Should I Stay Or Should I Go?

109	C6 – £37m Of Losses Are Hidden Somewhere
113	C7 – Bristol Energy – The Money Is Hidden Behind The 1972 Act
119	C8 – Council IT Systems
122	C9 – Buses And Lack Of Service
125	C10 – More On Buses, But Fewer Buses
128	C11 – Post Legislation Scrutiny: Licensing, Local Government Scrutiny And Universal Credit

WHAT IS FAIRNESS?

135	Section D Intro
136	D1 – Being A Fairness Warrior (Part 1)
140	D2 – Being A Fairness Warrior (Part 2)
143	D3 – Being A Fairness Warrior (Part 3, Final)
146	D4 – @SageAndOnion Seeks Answers
150	D5 – Where @SageAndOnion Seeks Firmer Pillars For Equality And Freedom
153	D6 – I'm Now Free To Explore Freedom
157	D7 – Economists Should Study Different Types Of Economies
160	D8 – So To Reconstruct The Economy But To Do What?
163	D9 – Relating This Definition Of Fairness To The Real World
165	D10 – The Future Of Libraries
169	D11 – Opening Up Opportunities With A Better And Fairer Bus Service
174	D12 – Council Tax Reduction Scheme – Taxing The Poor Takes Away Their Freedom Of Opportunity
177	D13 – Freedom Of Opportunity And Avoidance Of Harm – It Gets Complicated

THE EXTRACTION ECONOMY

184	E1 – @SageAndOnion Rides Again.
186	E2 – Capitalism, Markets And Their Failings (1)
189	E3 – Marketplace Failings (2)
193	E4 – Earning A Profit Is Not The Same Thing As Creating Wealth
197	E5 – Four Stories ; The Economy Isn't Working For Any Of Them
201	E6 – Aligning Personal And Business Profit With Wealth Creation
205	E7 – Where We Have Ended Up With All This – Summary Of D And E
209	E8 – Competing Local Authorities
212	E9 – Market Shaping In Adult Social Care (1)
215	E10 – Market Shaping In Adult Social Care (2)
218	E11 – Commercialisation: Should Councils Go Into Business?
222	E12 – Children In Care

THE FUNDING BLACK-HOLE OF ADULT SOCIAL CARE

227 Interlude

228 Introduction

229 F1 – ASC – Blowing Up Bristol's Budget – Task And Finish

232 F2 – The Situation In 2017

236 F3 – Better Lives (For Older People)

239 F4 – The Bite Back From The Market Place Management System Used For Care Homes

242 F5 – Marketplace Analysis For Residential Care Homes

246 F6 – Oh Dear. The Council Says Its Doing Lots Of Good Things But The Costs Keep Going Up.

250 F7 – Different Types Of Homes For Older People

254 F8 – Getting Helen Two Million Pounds.

256 F9 – What Have We Learned From All This? Apart From Lack Of Leadership From Government.

257 F10 – Re-running 2010

260 F11 – For The Prime Minister – It's Not Rocket Science

262 F12 – Changing The Marketplace For Adult Social Care In Bristol (1)

265 F13 - Changing The Marketplace For Adult Social Care In Bristol (2)

THE USE AND ABUSE OF LAND

269 Interlude (2) – Land And Housing

274 G1 – Homelessness In 2020 (Prior To And Probably Post Covid-19)

277 G2 – Homelessness Continues

279 G3 – Affordable Housing, The Battle Was Going On Long Before I Entered The Fray

282 G4 – Viability Statements; The Developers' New Weapon

284 G5 – Chocolate Factory 15/06400/F

286 G6 – It Wouldn't Melt In Their Mouths

290 G7 – Back In The Hot Chocolate

293 G8 – The Capture Of The Planning System

296 G9 – A Tall Storey

299 G10 – A Solution? Suggested In 2017

302 G11 – Joint Spatial Plan – 1/8/2019 – RIP ?

305 G12 – University Expansion

309 G13 – The Numbers Behind The Lack Of Affordable, Rented Housing

CONCLUSIONS AND RECOMMENDATIONS

313   Dear Revolutionary (Or Reformer)

315   H1 – The Price Of Land

320   H2 – The Planning System

323   H3 – Land: Is It Suited For A Market (With Competition) Or Some Other Method Of Provision?

329   H4 – And What About Democracy?

332   H5 – Balancing Freedom Of Opportunity With Avoidance Of Harm

335   H6 – How To Drain The Swamp (1)

338   H7 – How To Drain The Swamp (2) – Up On The Podium

342   H8 – How To Drain The Swamp (3) ?

344   H9 – Failing All That

346   H10 – Local Interventions:

350   H11 – National Changes (If The Pact / Alliance Doesn't Form)

APPENDICES

353   App1 – Bundred And Trees (1)

356   App2 – Bundred And Trees (2)

357   App3 – Business Plans And Colston Hall (1)

360   App4 – Business Plans And Colston Hall (2)

362   App5 – Business Plans And Colston Hall (3)

364   App6 – Trees Within The Planning System

366   App7 – Neighbourhood Partnerships (1)

369   App8 – Neighbourhood Partnerships (2)

371   App9 – Neighbourhood Partnerships (3)

374   App10 – Love Letter To Mariana

376   App11 – Bristol Arena At Brabazon (1)

378   App12 – Bristol Arena At Brabazon (2)

380   App13 – Bristol Arena At Brabazon (3)

383   App14 – Commercialisation Around The UK

386   App15 – Is Bristol For Its People Or For The University? (1)

389   App16 – Is Bristol For Its People Or For The University? (2)

391   App17 – Is Bristol For Its People Or For The University? (3)

393   App18 – The Battle Of Belgrave Hill (The Craziness Of Planning?)

396   App19 – The Maths Of Affordable Rented Housing

409   App20 – A Summary Of Things That Need Changing

417   Bibliography (And Reviews)

425   Epilogue

Clive has had a varied career, mainly in business, starting out in his father's shop in East London in the 1960s (probably underage) then setting up an impromptu car wash in a car park in Shenfield, Essex. Jobs at Marconi, Courtaulds, De La Rue and Sealed Air Corporation saw him move from electronics product development, sales and marketing of marine paints, production management in the packaging sector, technical service of cash machines and eventually to become managing director of a 120-person security packaging business. A career of sorts, which took him from: Brentwood; London to Newcastle upon Tyne; London again; Bristol; the West Midlands and ending up near Cambridge.

Then a break from "big business" aided by a big row with his boss: he moved with family back to Bristol to set up his own business in 1998 (and with entrepreneurship the order of the day, that led to lecturing in business and a limited amount of angel investing).

Education wise: Clive went to Woodford Green, then Brentwood, then off to Emmanuel College Cambridge (Nat Sciences); in 1987, a year at INSEAD in Fontainebleau (MBA) with a short internship at Goldman Sachs. He continued a lifelong learning approach and adding post graduate diplomas at UWE in Teaching (Further and Higher Education) and then Law.

As well as running a business, Clive taught business at the University of Bath (for 18 years, and wrote his first book) as well as shorter stints at UWE and one year at Bristol University.

Not much time in politics; he joined the Green Party in January 2015 and was elected Councillor for Clifton Down ward, Bristol in May 2016. He is also a fellow of the Royal Society of Arts wanting to develop social enterprise ideas to enhance themes covered in this book.

Two lovely daughters to whom this book is dedicated, he says, "it's your world now; my generation has messed up, enjoy fixing everything…"

ACKNOWLEDGEMENTS

As to all the people who have helped towards this book, there's too many, there's all my ex-students that's over 1,000. I should also add the lady whom I bumped into at a garden party last summer (2019), she asked for my advice about what foods to stock up on before Brexit, I said you could do with tomato soup, cream crackers, long lasting stuff, if nothing else it would help the food banks. She said oh, changed the subject and left to talk to someone else!

Far too many, but there are some who deserve special thanks: My Green Councillor colleagues; Carla Denyer; Charlie Bolton; Cleo Lake; Eleanor Combley; Fi Hance; Jerome Thomas; Jude English; Martin Fodor; Paula O'Rourke; Stephen Clarke as well as Paul, Anya and Sue who have provided part-time support and advice to all of us. Thanks to all of you for helping develop the thinking and being drivers of the ideas of Social Value and Citizens' Assemblies which are in this book. And not forgetting the campaigns for clean air, carbon neutrality and all the others; I hope my contrary nature helped as a sort of internal scrutiny.

Thanks to all the other Councillors in Bristol, the Mayor and officers without whom this book wouldn't have been possible.

Thanks to the LGiU (Local Government Information Unit) who have provided a most excellent daily newsfeed over the years and which has formed one whole strand to this book showing that the issues facing Bristol are similar to those throughout the country (in cities). The LGiU have given permission to reproduce part of this newsfeed.

Thanks especially to Richard Jones of Tangent Books for providing lots of encouragement especially in the early days and all the work you have put in latterly and for publishing. And to Grace Kress for the cover artwork, and to my youngest daughter who did much of the proof reading and some questioning.

And thanks to everyone else who deserves thanks but whom I have forgotten. Let me know.

A SIMPLE GUIDE TO A COUNCIL
(JUST ENOUGH TO GET YOU STARTED)

A Council, also called a local authority (LA), can, in general, only do what it has been given powers or duties to do by Government. Broadly a LA has three roles:

- Regulatory (planning and licensing approvals)

- Processing locally of national provision e.g. payment of housing benefit, school places etc

- Funding and provision of local services like adult and children's care, roads, parking, waste and recycling, noise pollution, council houses, libraries, parks and infrastructure etc

REGULATORY ROLES

For planning it is called the Local Planning Authority (technically a separate body to the LA). A person or business applying for planning permission in order to build or change a structure will engage with their LPA. The process is usually to file a pre-application which gets advice back from an officer, then put in an application for permission. This might be granted or refused by an officer or if it is big or controversial (or both) it will go to a Planning Committee (of 11 elected councillors) to decide. In each case the decision is based on whether it meets, on balance, local planning policy. If the application is refused then the applicant can appeal to a Planning Inspector (employed by the Secretary of State). In really big developments the SofS might decide themselves.

Local Planning Policy (The Local Plan) is set every five years (or so) also by the LPA. This involves incorporating any new national, top level policies and targets (for homes for example), any regional policies and developing new policies that are a local response to evidenced harm. Such harm must relate to an issue already included in one of the higher level policies. Neighbourhoods in Bristol can also produce their own plans and some have. They have to pass a local referendum.

Licensing of bars, clubs, taxis etc follow a similar process with the Council acting as the Licensing Authority (LA for Bristol).

NON REGULATORY ROLES

The other roles come under the Executive. In Bristol this is an elected Mayor and Cabinet. The Cabinet comprises up to nine elected Councillors chosen by the Mayor (sometimes taken from different parties). The remaining 61 Councillors are supposedly to help with scrutiny and other roles including the regulatory functions above. In Bristol we have elections every four years (except 2020, which was delayed a year).

There are some roles which are reserved for a Full Council vote (all 71 of us including the Mayor). The budget and constitutional matters are Full Council votes. In Bristol, like many cities, there is one party with a majority of Councillors on Full Council (and happen to be from the same party as the Mayor) so opposition parties can't stop the constitution being changed. In Bristol we had (July 1st 2020) a Labour Mayor, 35 Labour Councillors, 14 Conservative, 11 Green and 9 Lib Dems (one is Lord Mayor so abstains in votes). That adds to 70 as one Labour Councillor has just retired; Labour therefore have 36 votes, the opposition have 33 maximum.

A few quick points:

- Bristol is part of a combined authority of three councils (Bristol, Bath & North East Somerset and South Gloucestershire). It is called WECA (West of England Combined Authority) and has its own Mayor and an increasing budget and regional responsibilities for; business growth, transport, adult education/skills and house building. It has no Councillors and comprises the three leaders of the Councils (including Bristol's Mayor) plus the WECA Mayor (or Metro Mayor).

- In Bristol the Mayor's decisions can be challenged by a call-in from a scrutiny body which needs to find a flaw in the process and then can only ask that the decision be taken again. Additionally, there is the ultimate recourse of Judicial Review by an aggrieved party.

- Elected councillors have four roles: to scrutinise; to sit on committees so the LA fulfils its statutory roles; to represent residents impacted by issues within Council control and to represent Bristol on some outside bodies like the Port, Airport and Fire Authority.

I think that's enough. Don't you?

SECTION A
INTRODUCTIONS
OF ALL SORTS

CHAPTER A1
GREETINGS GOOD CITIZENS! THE PROLOGUE[1]...
UP BRISTOL!

The person who first coined the term revolution was clearly a cynic: proceed in one direction, then rotate 360 degrees and continue on in the same direction! That's not what I'm after at all. I'm after a political earthquake. Pressure builds up over time, sometimes released with a tremor, often nobody gets hurt, similar to a reform perhaps; but sometimes you get a massive earthquake along with death and destruction. In most

---

1   Title inspired by the late great Frankie Howerd

instances the aftermath of a quake is the land changes position not a jot or just a centimetre or two, occasionally though, the change is metres, very, very rarely the level changes so much the land ends up under the sea. Although the build-up of seismic pressures can be predicted the release and outcome is unpredictable. If this book achieves a small tremor I'll be happy. And that's down to you.

This is not a book about the next revolution. That is assumed and there are plenty of books[2] and articles to read up about that, the reasons they occur, searching for patterns and studying the lessons learned from previous ones. No doubt some are advising investors where to put their money. This book describes some of the pressures I have witnessed first-hand mainly during the years of 2016 to 2020 when I was an elected Councillor in Bristol. These haven't been written up elsewhere and I think and I hope you will see there are lessons to be learned.

This book documents some of what I saw as an opposition Councillor in Bristol City Council watching the struggles of a Labour Mayor trying to seek justice for those living in deprivation and suffering injustices. And balance that with the needs to reduce carbon emissions, at a time when Central Government was going through a nervous breakdown[3] (according to a former UK MI6 Chief), cutting the budgets from under his feet and cutting us all off from the EU. What the Conservative Party were undergoing was... Well, I'm sure you have your own views and describing Tory misadventures is not the prime focus of this book either.

"So get to the point," I hear you say.

The focus of this book is to provide learning points for those fighting for reform, or if that has failed, to advise those who have successfully achieved a revolution on what to do next. There are always points that can be learnt from how people and groups behave in certain situations. Future governance should be informed by the mistakes of today. My speciality, if you can call it that, is observation in depth[4] of some

2   The one I liked the best is George Lawson's *Anatomies Of Revolution* 2019 Cambridge University Press. It covers a whole range in geography and time and shows that many can be peaceful. It also attempts to forecast the likelihood for the future.
3   https://www.theguardian.com/uk-news/2019/jul/06/ex-mi6-chief-uk-going-through-political-nervous-breakdown I think that the description is unfair on people undergoing mental health difficulties.
4   As Councillor between 2016 and 2020

specific issues like adult social care, housing and inappropriate use of confidentiality and teasing out any lessons, morals even. We discover that the foundations of the UK's form of democracy suffer from systemic weaknesses, somewhat like a green and pleasant land sited over a geological fault or magma chamber.

There are recommendations near the end in section H for you to think about, discuss and then dismiss or implement in part or in whole. I won't spoil the surprise and you do need to read the evidence I present to help you with your consideration. If book groups are still going after your revolution then don't discuss the quality of my writing, discuss the evidence and recommendations. It's for you to decide, because you will be building the new system, not me.

Each of the stories or extracts[5] from speeches gives an insight into the consequences of decisions, often by Government; as well as the economic and political system that underpins them (underpinning implies stability, nothing of the sort). Hopefully when the reform comes it will not be violent, politics will reach a tipping point through ideas and memes spreading out; perhaps a benign contagion crossing to other countries. It needs to be enough to change our systems to remove the systemic problems that have caused these social injustices, climate change and other assorted environmental disasters.

On this latter point, inequality is becoming corrosive and undermining the premise of a modern liberal democracy. My solution is not to increase taxes, sure they need reform, but other changes are more fundamental. Read on and see if you agree. If your revolution is minor, you can buy this book online or in a bookshop. If it is major then rest assured I have buried three copies in waterproof deposit boxes (time capsules) which can be found by post revolutionaries. Readers of early editions might like to suggest where these copies should be buried, I stress, buried so they can be found and not buried so they are never read!

Each chapter is short, just right for a bus journey, if buses still exist. Each chapter exists to raise a point, often it's a story I experienced. A

---

5   Most of the stories and speeches are in response to a specific Council paper coming forward for a decision so if you really want to go to town you can check the documents on the Council's website.

number of chapters comprise a theme (section) and each theme is summarised at the end to illustrate the learning point. Oh yes, sorry, as an ex-lecturer at three universities[6]; learning outcomes were the order of the day. But don't worry, there is no theory exam, just the practical one of constructing a new and better society. And I doubt if I will be marking that.

The main university I taught at was Bath, the one up the hill. I taught in business and it involved reconciling the business profit motive with good outcomes for society. I eventually reached an economic understanding that guided me in my lecturing plus my many statements to the Mayor[7] of Bristol City Council. It took a while but I managed to resolve the cognitive dissonance you get from holding two contradictory ideas or beliefs at the same time. If you don't like the economic framework I arrived at, just ignore that bit and continue. Towards the end of this book a solution becomes clear, but then there's a twist. And then another. Not quite a whodunnit but more of a "whosgonnadoit".

I do hope you enjoy it.

Clive Stevens 06.08.2020

PS: This book was mainly written before and during Covid-19 lockdown. There are some references to the immediate impacts of the virus and actions needed to lift it. I'm mainly describing life pre-Covid-19 as I fear we will go back to the same problems when the virus is under control.

CHAPTER A2
BEFORE THE BEGINNING[8]

I woke up in 2014. Like some disagreeable, sleeping beauty awakening from fifty five years of bliss. Except that it hadn't been total bliss what with two children and an unhappy wife. My life had been spent earning

---

6   University of West of England (3 years), University of Bath (18 years) and University of Bristol (1 year)
7   I doubt if Marvin appreciated all the efforts I went to!
8   Beginning is defined by me as Monday May 9th 2016, the day I was sworn in as Councillor for Clifton Down, Bristol.

money, ferrying children to and fro, reading school reports, the usual quota of family discord plus going down the pub with mates and some five-a-side.

An awakening in 2014 and surrounded by thorny issues too: my wife felt it necessary to leave me, the children were well on their way to becoming adults, I needed to think about their future and not just their present. The prospect I saw alarmed me; the impact of four years of austerity: homelessness, foodbanks, UKIP, stagnant wages, increased student fees, and also rising house prices fuelled by quantitative easing[9] with some people getting very rich. Plus an uncaring and out of control big business, polluted air, carbon dioxide emissions unabated and the downsides of technology like the use of antibiotics on animals and the potential acceptance of GM foods[10] from America.

My children were soon going out into this cruel world. How had it happened and how had I not seen it coming? Surely I'd done the right things, I'd voted Labour and lately Lib Dem, that was the right thing to do wasn't it? I had been generally sympathetic to the Lib Dems and yet they were enabling the very austerity that seemed to be creating a world so dreadful, unwelcoming and uncaring, the one that my darling children would soon be entering. So what to do?

The only answer I could think of, to protect and prepare them for a world of student debt and housing deposits, was for me to go and earn some more money.

So I applied for and gained a teaching contract at Bristol University on the back of the reputation of the business course I taught at Bath (which had been going for some fourteen years back then). Bristol contracted me to teach their engineers about business and sustainability. I was good at teaching business to engineers but apart from sustainable earnings

---

9   Quantitative Easing was introduced after the 2008/9 banking crash. It is where the Bank of England creates money and buys primarily government debt (gilts). Government can then borrow more as there is a level of demand for gilts and normal banks who hold gilts can sell them to the Bank of England in return for cash which they are then supposed to lend out for useful purposes like business loans. But it is less risky for them to lend into the property market, so those wanting to buy land or other property can borrow cheaply, this increases demand and prices (for land) and other assets. It does seem to cause a form of inflation but not in everyday goods.
10   It's not the genetically modified food that I specifically object to; it's the business models that go with it, making the farmers beholden to the chemical industry.

and the term "sustainable competitive advantage" I was ignorant about the wider meaning of sustainability. But five months of deep research, listening, discussion and work on the subject and I was ready.

And by the way, it's not just students who learn from a good university course, the lecturers do too; for me this had been a five-month journey into the causes of some of society's problems. In the first month I blamed the engineers for not coming up with sustainable solutions, then I accused the businesses that employ them, but they just operate within the rules set by politicians. So I then blamed the politicians, many of whom owe their positions to money and prestige from big business, some in the press, rich individuals and the unions. Economic players nudge, lobby or even pay to preserve the status quo because they gain from it; extracting as much money from national prosperity, leaving the rest of us relatively less well off. And worse, they even convince themselves that they are doing right thing. I should know, I was teaching my students how to do it!

Sustainability is ensuring you have enough resources to keep going: people, money and materials. But it is also about doing minimal harm to others. Too much damage, then they could and should get you shut down unless you change your ways. It is not sustainable to continue arguing with your neighbour year in year out. It is not sustainable for a hundred thousand people to drive diesel cars in a city centre and kill hundreds of people every year due to traffic fumes. Either way something will eventually make the situation stop; that's why those are unsustainable behaviours.

Those harmed may be those who are alive now or others yet to be born. If your acts are threatening the lives of future generations it is more difficult for them to get you to stop, after all they haven't been born yet and they don't have legal recourse not even to the vote. So it is down to us, the present generation, to protect them.

In October 2019 I heard about The Well-Being Of Future Generations Act (Wales 2011). The speaker was Lord John Bird – founder of the Big Issue magazine – today's problems are caused by a failure in the past, in the 1980s, back then they laid their plans for the future and this is what we got! He said,

"Politicians, even royalty said congratulations for thinking outside the box, but if the box is not working you have to think inside the box to fix it, so get in the box".

Comment: I see that he is bringing a Future Generations Bill to the House of Commons, as of 24th March 2020 it had passed its second reading in the House of Lords. I hope it gets on the Statute Books.

Having had to listen to and learn from my own lectures, I decided it was a system issue; politicians are trapped by vested interests. I gave up on Labour and the Lib Dems and joined the Green Party, primarily to help get a second Green MP into Parliament. The Greens are quite strong in Bristol and in the General Election of May 2015 the Green, Bristol West candidate, Darren Hall, with a little help from my canvassing, came second with 17,000 votes a creditable 28%. Labour won with 35%, so I think Greens did well, as we had just 2,500 votes five years previously.

Late in 2015, I was asked if I would like to run for Councillor in a Bristol ward. I accepted and was elected, with a majority of ten votes, it took two recounts. I didn't know what I was letting myself in for and this book is a series of stories from my time as a Councillor which may make you consider whether our entire political and economic system is broken and that we are hurting people presently and those yet born. And if do you come to that conclusion I may also give you some motivation and ideas about how we fix it.

My own view is that the UK's current political and consequently its economic approach is unsustainable. In the past that has sometimes led to revolution, these things creep up on you, I'd prefer that not to happen, revolutions have unintended consequences, ask any French person. So please view the lessons from the stories that follow as an input to peacefully avoiding chaos.

CHAPTER A3
MY DIARY – THE DAYS LEADING UP TO
THE BEGINNING

Monday 2nd May 2016 – Tempting fate.

If I don't start this diary now I never will. The next three days are to be the same as all previous days that I can remember: canvassing, canvassing and… Which means knocking on doors and smiling to people, some of whom even smile back. The vote is on Thursday.

I've been canvassing and manning stalls since the end of February and trying to fit in a job and family too. Why am I doing this?

Friday 6th May – The calm before the storm?

It's the day after the vote but two days before the count. A limbo; quantum[11] state where I might or might not be a Councillor. It's good to unwind though, I can rest my smile muscles too.

I catch up on some work. Work is actually calming. Plus I have saved up some tree felling applications to object to. Both are easy compared to walking the hundred and fifty miles, talking to nearly a thousand people on doorsteps and the stalls plus the nine hours of telling yesterday.

Telling is a quaint old custom, quite legal, where you stand outside the polling station smartly dressed, in your rosette and ask each voter for their registration[12] number as they go in or leave the booth. These numbers are then tallied, taken away to a makeshift office and compared with the list of voter registration numbers of those who we think might vote Green. Then later in the day our "knocker uppers" pop round to the homes of those who haven't yet voted and politely remind them to vote, some then do, of course but we don't know if they will vote Green or not, we hope. It's what other parties do too and supposedly key to winning elections. I'm not convinced and it's a dated system that is rapidly being outmoded by new, modern ways of voting. Modern approaches like the postal vote. I can be quite sarcastic sometimes.

---

11   As in Schrödinger's Cat (Neither Councillor nor not a Councillor until the vote is counted).
12   Voting registration numbers not car registrations although some gave me that too.

Objecting to planning applications that include tree felling has been a part of my life since 2012. Not only does it save some trees, but if I can convince a Planning Officer to enforce the rules then it brings in money for new planting because other rules mean developers have to pay for replacement trees. There's a third reason too: I find it empowering. A few hours a week, equipped with detailed knowledge of a couple of planning policies and I can beat those with power and money, a win for the underdog, well sometimes.

But back to now, in this indeterminate quantum state, I can't do anything regarding getting more votes so now I'm relaxed. It feels so good... time for a beer?

Monday 9th May (am) – The day after the count
The count was yesterday, I am to be sworn in this afternoon. I had a nightmare the Saturday night; you know the type where you wake up in a sweat thinking you haven't revised for your exams?

The count took eight and a half hours for the ward I'm standing in, Clifton Down. Two Councillors will be elected. The favourite, Carla Denyer, is also a Green and already the existing Councillor albeit only one year. Time spent watching all those piles of paper shift around in front of the counting staff, then the first news came through after about four hours and it was worrying, there were just nine votes between second place, i.e. being the other Councillor, and third, i.e. being the loser, so was I second and in? Or third and out? Or just overly optimistic and completely thrashed? More counting and paper shuffling; an hour later all candidates were called to a huddle and I discovered I was the one in second place and still just nine votes ahead. Labour immediately asked for a recount, fair enough but it was all rather draining[13].

What to do now? Pace up and down the converted open plan office in Hengrove, South Bristol where all the counts were taking place, Forrest Gump like except the building, large though it was, didn't stretch the width of America. The counters counted piles of papers, entered numbers into a laptop, exchanged puzzled looks, un-piled piles of paper,

---

13   And not just for me, those poor tally uppers too.

counted again and still looked puzzled. It was now 6.30pm and I was apologising to the other Greens who were staying on, "just go to the pub, I'll come later". But they hung on in there, then a second official huddle and my vote had gone up by two. Labour's vote? That went up too, but crucially only by one, so hugs all round – I was a Councillor for Clifton Down along with Carla who'd known already, her vote count was determined some four hours earlier. But what did it all mean?

It took someone to hold me still and say "Clive you are now a Councillor!" It might have been Carla. No time to think about that, taken over to the stage for the official declaration. Not many people were left, nearly everyone else had gone home. I think I gave the biggest smile of my life (nobody remarked on it, so maybe I don't smile very well). I hung around another ten minutes for the very last declaration, it might have been Horfield. Claire, a Conservative, won by just one vote! Then off to the pub with the Greens. Celebration tinged with commiseration because our party had won two seats but lost five, meaning eleven Councillors, the third largest party.

Next morning, and off to my first Council meeting, the first of possibly three thousand meetings over the next four years. Still I'd walked about a hundred and fifty miles during the canvassing and talked and smiled to perhaps a thousand people so what's three thousand council meetings?

And I must remember to work for the people in the ward and not get sucked into the Council bubble of self-importance and the dreaded chamber.

I was sworn in this afternoon, signing the Councillors' Code of Conduct.

CHAPTER A4
OCTOBER 2016 – FIVE MONTHS AFTER THE BEGINNING; WANTING TO MAKE A DIFFERENCE (1)

People go into politics at this level wanting to make a difference. It means you care. But then again caring opens you up to emotional highs and lows, some get close to, even surpassing, the intensity of experiences of bringing up children; well, that's how it hit me. The other thing I discovered was the unfairness of it all...

Here are some highs and lows taken from my diary five months into the role.

"A month since my last post; the Last Post is played in honour of the dead? I feel I've been there and back. In fact managing the ups and downs is probably the biggest problem I have. And the IT problems haven't helped.

"Ups: The best has to be getting the biodiesel generator planning application rejected when it came back to Committee. It was still recommended for approval by Planning Officers, it had been deferred in July 2016, when it came back to Committee the Councillors voted to reject it by eight to two. Well done Labour, Lib Dems and Green[14]. I gave my best speech to date (still much room for improvement of course) and my co-Councillor Carla Denyer who was on that Committee excelled by pulling together all the relevant material planning reasons made by objectors in their statements. Some were filtered out: reasons have to be based on issues that are relevant to planning law, which she then summed up. Even the Chief Planning Officer was impressed and didn't give his usual warning speech about going against Council advice and calmly noted the reasons and summarized. But will the applicants appeal? That's the $64,000 question. Greens had a press release ready by 16.30 and got good coverage, it even made national planning journals... definitely an up I'd say.

The story of those biodiesel generators continues in the next chapter. Back to the ups and downs..

"Downer: I have decided to resign as Non-Exec Director of the Port. What's the Port got to do with being Councillor for Clifton Down, you might ask. Bloomin' good question, but Councillors have to do some adhoc activities. I took on the role naively hoping I'd influence the Port's approach to environmental matters, like you take on a new partner hoping they will change.

---

14   But Conservatives what on earth were you thinking of voting for a scheme that causes cancer, lung disease and death.

In this book we have a whole section on Planning. The use of land, especially in a city, is of critical importance. It is truly the one scarce resource, especially if the city is surrounded by Green Belt. You can build down, up and in-between but you can't sprawl. Yet National Planning policies allow all sorts of speculative proposals, relying on the market which increases land prices to make sure the most economically productive ideas are implemented (rather than need). In the case of the biodiesel, the land was designated for industrial, industry is declining and so the land was relatively cheap. There's no consideration of the need for homes, the cost of pollution nor the fact that the generators could have been installed outside the city where the air pollution harms less people. Planning Law doesn't properly take account of any such things. Wait until section G when I really lay into it.

Conflict emerged straight away, the Councillor's Code of Conduct[15] says I must be open and transparent and represent all the people of Bristol. However, as a Non-Exec, I had to represent the Port and abide by their confidentiality clause. As a Green we attract lots of campaign groups and every port with people living nearby has more than its fair share of environmental problems. Worse still, the board meetings were on Fridays (I lecture in Bath on Fridays) so this combination caused many sleepless nights about secrecy and letting people down; all too much. I decided to resign and immediately found I could sleep again (obviously a good decision). I might perhaps have made a small difference in my five months there, I'll suggest a future Councillor takes more time to learn before attempting change. Perhaps the Port will take Corporate Social Responsibility more seriously too.

"Ups: My economics blog[16] called "The Elephants Of Austerity" was well received, I decide this should become part of a series and I have just written a second piece entitled "Entrepreneurshit".

---

15   More on this in Chapter A7.
16   This is my @SageAndOnion blog which helped me to clarify my learning from some of the world's best economists and apply their principles to current problems. More in sections D and E.

"Downer: The Council is going ahead with nine hundred plus job cuts and the budget cost gap has now widened to £32 million in this financial year. Next year it is predicted to be another £30 million more, it's being described as a black-hole, it's worse than that. If the Council were a business it would have been shut-down for insolvency, failing the going concern test[17]. Apparently Bristol is being hit hardest[18] of all the core cities as funding switches from Government grants to business rate funding. Teresa May has to do something surely? And now some Councillors are saying the way out is to reduce the Council Tax subsidy for the poorest. Tax the poor; that sounds like Tory policy[19]? I thought we had a Labour Mayor. Alternatively, how about increasing the new Council Tax: the Adult Social Care Precept by a significant amount, it would need a referendum, but it's social care costs that are blowing the budget, that and Government cuts. Government has completely left this to Local Authorities with inadequate funding, a hangover from the Osborne years of hitting the vulnerable because it plays well with Tory voters".

"Another downer, yet more IT problems."

> One of the purposes of the diary was to let off steam and help cope with stress. I stopped it in October, it didn't do either. All it seemed to do was highlight the failures in the system. A system people seem to keep voting for. I guess if 37% are happy with their lot then that's enough to control Parliament. I develop this idea in Section B calling it the mathematics of power.

Updates... Those diary clips were from October 2016, what follows is an update written during 2019:

1. Firstly the IT issues: In July 2019 I was asked whether I had any

---

17   This is something that accountants need to assess of any business when auditing their accounts. A business if it is likely to continue to trade has one value but if it is likely to shut down then it's a different calculation.

18   With hindsight this wasn't true, whether it seemed true at the time, maybe.

19   I have developed a more sophisticated understanding of various policies now, but my Oct 2016 diary said, "Tax the poor, that's Tory policy surely", so that's virtually what is being reproduced here.

comments about the new IT proposed for Councillors? This was my reply.

> *"I've told you before, for me the damage was done in 2016. I had iOS updates deleting my PDF files and we discovered no back up. Links didn't work. Emails going missing and reappearing, iPad crashes and being told I could only have access to one month's worth of emails – so I can't do my job. There was no folder system. And there is still no system for casework, some emails from .bristol.gov.uk go into the spam system and so I have to email the release email to my personal address because the link doesn't work on the iPad. I already have Outlook on my iPad, but it picks up Sth Glos Council and my Gmail. I don't want BCC's mail on Outlook, I wouldn't be able to cope. Joining BCC as a Councillor in May 2016 was so traumatic, partly due to the appalling IT support and systems that I just want to leave. I care for my residents and it was obvious BCC didn't care for me, nor my stress levels.*

The next question the email questionnaire asked was, "How could we improve the way we review and update your IT"? I said

> *"Keep leaving me alone[20], which you have been doing quite well up to now – thank you".*

IT sent someone to see me, they were very sympathetic and decided to leave me alone.

2. The Council's Non-Exec Directorship at the Port has now become a two year role, I was able to hand over to another Green Councillor and he did a much better job than me.

3. My economics blog continues, it has shaped much of my thinking and

---

20   My daughter gave me a right telling off for this attitude. I mollified her by saying most other Councillors were providing good feedback so that IT could improve. The problem I have now is it's May 2020 and I have to stay on another year. They are sure to change the IT in the next eleven months and I can't keep putting them off.

statements. Bits are used in various chapters, mainly in f

4. Bristol's 2016 Budget Black-hole: The May
some swingeing cuts to parks, libraries (reprieved), public
neighbourhood partnerships, grants and much more. Additionally there
was a big program to improve efficiency and some investment into
productivity leading to further job cuts, of course. The Government
allowed extra increases in Council Tax (and Adult Social Care Precept
increases) which over three years increased bills by nearly 12%. They
didn't cut the Council Tax Reduction for the lowest earners, although
a consultation came out suggesting they might do just that. Fortunately
we mobilised residents and tenants to ensure that it never happened. In
Bristol we can be proud that we look after our poorest (at least in relief
from Council Tax) see chapter E7.

Later on in 2016 there was an investigation into the causes of the
Black-hole; called the *Bundred*[21] *Report*, it was quite scathing. Lessons
from this appear throughout this book.

5. But what about those biodiesel generators, did they appeal? Yes they
did and what happened then comes next.

CHAPTER A5
WANTING TO MAKE A DIFFERENCE (2)
(BIODIESEL GENERATOR)

Extract from Statement to Planning Committee B (DCB) – Biodiesel
generator Appeal Decision – July 2017 – from Councillor Clive Stevens

> *"Quite often in our jobs as Councillors we feel powerless, it is easy to slip
> into a mindset just thinking of the futility of it all... and then something
> like this happens.*
>
> *I am referring to the Appeal Decision on the Avonbank biodiesel*

---

21   I'm sure Steve Bundred would be amazed that his work has been referred to in this way.

generator scheme and the fact that your Committee's decisions of deferral and then refusal, both against officer advice, were upheld by the Planning Inspector. So well done DCB you should give your colleagues a pat on the back as you have really made a difference and undoubtedly saved lives.

But as always the devil is in the detail. I will talk about the officer's error[22] and the lack of pollution data in the engine specs. That seems to leave the opportunity for someone to reapply with the extra information about the pollution levels and abatement techniques for diesel generators.

The Inspector's report has a tiny mention of the nursery, no mention of inequality, no mention of the fact that any level of air pollution kills. It doesn't talk about the fact that the legal levels are chosen by The World Health Organisation as a "balance" between the costs of loss of health and life versus the economic benefits from transport and other polluting activities i.e. some deaths are acceptable. You can't ask the dead what they think.

So despite this decision we live in a planning environment where we get occasional victories like this or perhaps on levels of affordable housing, but overall the system is stacked against those living in cities especially those in areas of deprivation.

But it isn't futile and as the new Local Plan is being developed I urge those of you working on it to reflect on the power imbalance between developers, industry and our residents who are just trying to stay alive and so I ask you please to do what you can to even it up."

As you can see I had a lot of emotional commitment to this project. Perhaps I shouldn't have, it was in a different ward, not even a Green ward, but the local Councillors had started off pretty ill equipped to protest. The planning officers were recommending these 32 death machines for approval, there was a local group organising a protest and a nearby nursery school. They needed help from a Councillor, me. It just seemed so unfair. We delayed the application the first time by sowing seeds of doubt; questions on noise and how to reduce it. They came back with the answers and officers still recommended approval

22   The inspector said the officer should have included the impact on the workers during the day too.

(because they couldn't think of a reason not too). Councillors refused it. The applicant took it to the Appeal Inspector; I wrote to the Inspector, the Council opted for a Written Representations process to save money if they lost. I felt a Public Enquiry or Hearing would be more likely to stop the development but it was more expensive and the Council was in a financial crisis at the time.

The Inspector's decision was announced in July 2017.

All the time the health evidence against diesel fumes was mounting. The Appeal Inspector considered the impact of air pollution on the workers at the industrial estate, something that the Council's officers hadn't. Indeed we must remember that officers had recommended this application for approval not once but twice. The Inspector decided the impact of the pollution and noise would be too much. Appeal dismissed, three cheers! And in 2019, in the draft Local Plan, this patch of land is to be allocated for much needed housing; six cheers!

I still don't know why I was so involved. It was certainly a David and Goliath (the community being David not me) and an example of uncaring capitalism, I see all too many of these nowadays. Writing this in 2019, the draft Local Plan now has controls for all applications for diesel generators whether in hospitals, road works and certainly no standby generators for the grid. That was the problem, when the previous planning documents were written there was no consideration about mini power stations fuelled by diesel in the centre of the city; a city like so many others with air already polluted due to Dieselgate and caused in part by Volkswagen's[23] cheat mechanisms. So no planning policies; no policies mean people and business can in theory do what they like because harm hasn't been defined. Such is life in a liberal democracy.

---

23   I understand that Volkswagen are still denying aspects of this. I hope I don't have to retract this bit in future print runs.

CHAPTER A6
COCK-UP IN THE COUNCIL'S CHAMBER

We are all human. It's time to admit it. I am too. This is an apology to those who voted for me in 2016 believing I would defend what's right, here is how I got things completely wrong:

Long before I had to get to grips with being a Councillor I had been finding in class that students' questions were getting more and more muffled and indistinct. I put this down to the increasing shyness of the youth of the day and the rapidly increasing class and thus room sizes.

My family also noticed and especially my wife, they badgered me to go down to St Michael's Hospital and get my ears tested. Their two complaints were that I always had the television on too loud and they had to keep repeating their questions to me. "You should speak more clearly then" was my usual reply. But eventually I did go and lo and behold the audiologist said I needed hearing aids.

In denial, I didn't wear them for six months, eventually I did for the following year's lectures. Strangely the students spoke loud and clear this time, no shrinking violets.

I wear the aids much more now, sometimes they are helpful, but occasionally, like in the pub, they make things worse; high pitched chatter, laughing and clinking glasses create a background noise so loud that it's impossible to hear. Audiology have turned up the gain and I've had to start thinking about strategies on how to cope with my disability.

One-to-one conversations are fine, especially if I can see the other person's lips moving. I did an experiment once while watching the news. Turning the volume down so I could just hear the newsreader when she was to camera, but the moment they cut away, her voice became inaudible. So assuming the BBC don't deliberately muffle their sound, I'd discovered I was partially lip reading, no lessons but watching lips move boosts clarity. So in meetings I try to position myself where I can see most people and concentrate on their lips, this has an unintended, positive consequence that the speaker thinks I am unusually interested in what they are saying which of course I am – always. But it also means

I get tired more quickly, so much concentration on lips, hearing and watching what they are saying that after fifty minutes my brain needs to relax for a minute or two. I can't stop it doing that, and during this respite sometimes I miss something, occasionally important. I should of course ask for a repetition but I often don't and that can lead me into trouble.

My colleagues are getting more used to me zoning out after an hour or so. And as I have learned how to cope with poor hearing I feel more secure with them so I ask daft questions with less awkwardness to get back on track. If I don't ask and it was something important then I have to work it out from subsequent conversation; that risks me getting it wrong, and I do. One approach is to offer to take the minutes, or chair the meeting. Both give me an excuse to confirm what was said and correct any misunderstandings. I don't make the offer often enough.

It's not always possible to do that in the Council; chairpersons are chosen a year in advance and the minute takers are officers not politicians. An event happened during a Planning Committee which prompted me to write this piece and think again about better coping strategies.

We were in a fairly tense Planning Committee meeting in 2017 about allowing the Zoo to continue to use a section of the Downs as a temporary overflow car park for 30 or so days per year; bank holidays that type of thing. This is not permitted by the Act of Parliament that created and protects the Bristol Downs but a temporary arrangement has been in place since the 1960s to allow parking on pre-designated days. This temporary permission was formalised in the 1990s and is renewed every three years at a planning meeting; the number of days allowed has slowly been reduced.

So an hour and a quarter into this meeting we came to the vote on this application. There was an amendment put forward to ask the Zoo to do certain things and then the actual vote. I followed the proceedings carefully and planned to vote against the amendment, then for the actual permission. The Zoo needed a warning shot across their bows that this parking has to stop, but they deserve time to plan alternatives.

Something was said, the proposer, let's call her H, forgot to switch on her microphone, but that was OK as we'd only recently been reminded that amendments[24] are voted on first and then the actual permission is voted on second. So I voted against the first and for the second, as per my plan.

Next morning I was badgered on Twitter and told in no uncertain terms, there's not much room for subtlety in the 140 characters allowed back then, that I'd voted against the application itself. How dare I try to shut down the Zoo and prevent car drivers from exercising their God given rights to park on the Downs. I also got some emails saying "well done Clive, you stuck to your principles".

Of course I denied I'd voted to stop the car parking and kept quiet on those congratulatory emails. I skimmed the local newspaper, they must have reported it wrongly too, no wonder the Twitterverse was confused.

Later on, I thought I'd better check with the horse's mouth, the horse being the Council's minute taker. He confirmed that it was I who was mistaken and the newspaper was right. I was quite taken aback, especially as this was during the 2017 General Election campaign and it didn't do for a party to have a complete idiot as a Green Councillor when trying to win a seat.

How could this have happened? Well it seems it was agreed to include a "message to the Zoo" that this was the last time it would be allowed, I missed that, presumably due to the switched off microphone, poor hearing, tired brain and not asking. I still recall my confusion in front of all those objectors. Fortunately, my mistake didn't change anything as it was my vote versus the other six, but more importantly what about those tweets of denial I'd sent out earlier on? Had I just become yet another lying politician? So to those on Twitter I apologise, I did publish a version of this on Facebook back in 2017 with a link and to those who wrote to me saying well done, sorry too.

---

24   This procedure was changed in 2019. The Committee incorporates minor amendments into the vote for the officer's recommendation. If that fails then we vote for a deferral asking for more work on an issue or the potential for adding amendments or conditions. Rarely are we allowed to vote against the officer's recommendation and if we do then it comes back again with an amended officer's report. That change was brought in to control legal costs and overturns by Planning Inspectors. Some committee members have said that it is virtually a rubber stamping exercise now.

Many millions of people have disabilities and disadvantages, lots are hidden like mine. My experiences have helped my awareness of the more general problem and built an empathy with all those who have fought for better understanding by wider society. Like all things though there needs to be a balance and fairness.

And what have I learned? I wrote the Facebook draft in May 2017, it helped me reflect on the journey of coping with worsening hearing loss. I am much more open about it now and most chairs ask people to speak up, I wear headphones in the Chamber, looking like I'm listening to music, maybe I am.

I even deliberated about resigning but then it would mean the system has beaten yet another person of disability, we have to fight the unfairness, so I will continue to work at this and develop better strategies. Oh and H, if you read this, it wasn't your fault, it was mine, I should have asked you to repeat the proposal.

This is all just part of getting old. I know someone who is losing their sight, that seems really scary; and going deaf isn't painful[25] either so I should be thankful for that. And thanks to all at Bristol City Council for being so understanding.

CHAPTER A7
COUNCILLORS' (MEMBERS') CODE OF CONDUCT

You'd think that one of the benefits of being a Councillor is that you'd be able to hold council officers to account for their decisions. Well not only are we told that we should follow their advice (to minimise the chances of judicial review in the courts), but we can't robustly hold them to account either! Not directly anyway. This ties one of our hands behind our backs, (the other is tied by the Law), there's no Parliamentary Privilege[26] here

---

25   Not physically, not to me anyway.
26   Parliamentary Privilege includes freedom of speech (to members of either House of Parliament) without interference from outside (like being sued).

and we are all told to sign up to "The Councillors' Code of Conduct" which governs how we should behave. There is a sister document called the "Member Officer Protocol" on how we should treat officers and how they should treat us. Officers, in theory, are independent and work quietly in the background, it's Councillors and the Mayor who take the decisions. My arse it is. There are hundreds of decisions taken daily by officers and only a tiny minority are subjected to public scrutiny. The Code of Conduct tempers Councillor tempers (sometimes usefully) but the end result is that residents have more freedom to say what they think about officers than Councillors.

Here's an example from January 2019 when I was referred to Legal for a potential breach of the Code. The Code of Conduct had been recently revised and voted through by Full Council, I helped revise it but I never thought it would be applied to mild mannered me!

It all relates to a fence being installed to cordon off land designated as a school playing field. Installation required digging in and around the roots of valuable and veteran trees. In 2018 officers had decided that the works were fine and there was no need for the school to apply for any planning permissions because the works wouldn't harm the trees, some of which were nationally recognised. I took what the officers said in good faith.

But then it started: emails from residents and tweets with camera footage of lorries driving over the root zones and photos of cut roots all of which convinced me that due process was not being followed. So pen to paper on 29th January I scripted a short statement to the relevant Planning Committee whom I hoped would instruct officers to change their decision.

Here it is:

"The minutes of the last planning meeting describe the decision you took on the planning application for extra signage at Stoke Lodge. One extra sign was refused. You considered the impact on trees amongst other things just for one signboard.

"But in this instance, today, about the new fence, you didn't consider

possible damage to trees regarding the new fencing even though, if installed in an uncontrolled way, it would cause far more harm. That's because your Planning Department decided that national, primary legislation regarding Tree Preservation Orders (TPOs) could be bypassed using their powers of discretion.

"Even if it's true, which I doubt, this reminds me of the Monty Python scene in the Holy Grail with the French soldiers replaced by planning officers up on the battlements hurling dung, rubble and dead cows at plucky residents and Councillors in the field below. Picture the scene... If anything could bring the Council's reputation into disrepute that could. It is for the good of the Council's reputation that the decision regarding damage to the trees by this fence is open, transparent and ideally democratic."

Apart from the factual inaccuracies in the third paragraph; it was actually live animals, ducks, chickens and a live cow that were hurled over the ramparts by the taunting Frenchmen. I checked. The cow became dead and somewhat plastic in the next frame after it had landed on the knights, so that error aside, I turned to thinking how my written statement could be turned into a persuasive speech for the meeting the next day. So persuasive that the Councillors on the Committee would ask, nay demand, that a planning application be brought forward for this fence.

The written statement (as per above) was circulated along with all the others from the public so they could all be read in advance of the meeting. That was enough to trigger another Councillor to refer me to Legal about a possible breach of our wretched Code of Conduct.

Was I bringing the Council into disrepute?

Jan 30th, 17.55pm. I walked towards the entrance of the Council Chamber thinking of rotten eggs, tomatoes and other suitable visual descriptions to embellish my speech. At the door I passed one of the Council's legal team seated right outside, I stopped and said, "strange to see you here tonight?" they smiled, a genuine one but mixed with a watch your step. That triggered a neuron which jumped a synapse, causing a tiny cascade[27] which led to a thought, all this in 200 milliseconds. The brief conversation ended with the Legal replying, "that depends on what you say Councillor Stevens".

Ummm… quick thinking needed, so this is what I actually said;

"Chair and Committee, I am one of the many Councillors who loves trees. I took it on good faith that the fence and trees didn't need planning permission. But last weekend I watched the videos showing the vehicles driving over roots and the cut roots of TPO'd trees.

"I snapped, I felt betrayed, the Council was bringing itself into disrepute, this whole process is wrong.

"This process now needs to be open and transparent otherwise the disrepute will worsen. Committee you can correct this. Perhaps the answer is to ask for a TPO application, then we will see openness, enforcement and conditions.

"I have considered the Code of Conduct and apologise if my taunting Frenchmen analogy was inappropriate but the message is openness. I have no plans to play King Arthur, in fact I think Councillor Eddy has taken on that role already."

Councillor Eddy by the way is an outspoken Conservative Councillor, with a speech impediment, which he has adjusted to so that you end up hanging on every word he says. Unfortunately, it means you listen to him carefully and that can sometimes be unhealthy. He was on the Committee that night and agreed with me this time.

And what happened next…

The Committee listened to public statements, it was all getting a bit heated, Councillor Richard Eddy chipped in following a similar line of reasoning to me, without the dead cows. We then received what was presumably a pre-prepared brief from the very same planning officers I was bemoaning about explaining that they had decided to take no further action. The Chair closed the debate down. So that was that.

---

27   *A Day in the Life of the Brain* by Susan Greenfield 2017 Penguin Books. Susan describes this process by calling the collection of neurons that fire close together as a neuronal assembly.

"Democracy" stifled, Councillors then proceeded, with the officer's reasons to ignore us.

I did receive a very nice email from the Councillor who had referred me earlier saying he was happy with my speech. He's a nice chap, no political shenanigans; he just cares for the reputation of Planning Dept. So do I but we have different ways of voicing it.

The Planning Department did make better efforts to engage with the community after that bit of pressure but refused to budge on asking for a planning application. Ten months later we got sight of the Ombudsman's report (following an official complaint from residents) which said the Planning Officers were within their rights to take the decisions they did.

OPENNESS AND TRANSPARENCY

Many times we will come back to the need for more openness and transparency, combine it with good scrutiny and you get better decisions. Scrutiny involves a combination of challenging the ideas, interpretation of the data, playing devil's advocate and constructively suggesting different approaches and view-points. As you will discover it is of major importance to good decision making. But it is avoided too often which is why we get so many bad decisions from politicians.

In chapter A9 we see an example of scrutiny internal to the Bristol Green Party. To get there we must first start off in court...

CHAPTER A8
WE START OFF IN COURT

Scene opens. We are sitting in Bristol Magistrates Court late morning one fine day in Spring 2018.

Let's call him Sam, when I arrived he was in the dock, well dressed and confident even though he was facing charges of criminal damage which can carry a prison sentence. His friends and my co-Councillor

Carla Denyer were sat at the back. I joined them. It was laid out like on the TV shows except no cameras and nobody saying cut. Fairly soon after, the three magistrates stood, we had to stand too, they left the room to decide Sam's fate.

The first thing you notice about Carla when you meet her is that she is well, small, but I'd never dare call her petite, packed in there is a mind that sees the detail, an almost photographic memory and a desire to be respected. She doesn't suffer fools gladly. That is combined with a determination to get things done. She must have wondered what she did in a past life to deserve me as a co-Councillor. We rapidly found our different areas to specialise in and concentrated on them. Carla is a mechanical engineer and worked in the wind turbine industry before switching to politics. She was elected in May 2015. I arrived a year later and always felt I was the new boy.

Back to the story...

A few months earlier before that day in court, Carla received a request for support from one of our constituents; would she write a character reference to help justify the actions that Sam had recently taken? He had been caught daubing divestment slogans in black washable chalk all over Barclays Bank. Divestment means moving your investments away from fossil fuel companies like Shell and BP to other companies in unrelated industries. It's a way of making the oil company acknowledge, even agree to, the call for change due to the climate crisis as highlighted in the Paris Accord.

Painting the walls of Barclays Bank didn't convince them and they promptly asked the Crown Prosecution Service to bring charges against this group of people which included Sam. I offered to write a reference too arguing a defence of necessity.

As it turns out the magistrates refused to even accept our statements but Sam's barrister kindly said she welcomed them as an extra source of information.

So back in court, the magistrates return looking very stern faced.

"We pronounce you... not guilty. You have convinced us of your good

character and that you did not know that you were causing the damage, by your choice of washable materials... blah blah".

Phew well done Sam and well done his barrister.

Some months afterwards, Sam invited me to a talk he was giving on behalf of his group called Rising Up. I entered the small room, within the University and along with six other people, we politely listened and watched. He described the climate emergency and said if politicians aren't listening this is how to make them listen. It turns out the whole purpose of the group was to get arrested and locked up in sufficient numbers so that the cause becomes a major issue in the press, living martyrs so to speak. The idea came from America and I wasn't convinced whether thousands would actually get incarcerated in the UK but above all I left feeling cheated. I'd written a statement[28] to the magistrates explaining why Sam had not done intentional damage when some months later he openly admitted to me and others in the room that his group's intention was now to be caught and tried. It wasn't his fault, I'd offered to do a statement, didn't check and assumed differently.

It seems my reaction was quite unusual, Rising Up were catching the headlines all over the UK for protests and acts linked to raising the issue of climate change. Needless to say I didn't join but some of my colleagues got thoroughly involved. By then the police had realised the solution was to allow the protests, they were peaceful and in a good cause. I'm sure many of them were concerned about inaction to climate change too. Closed roads and closed bridges, the only one which got a reaction was Lambeth Bridge in London which police ensured remained open – I've wondered why.

---

28   I'd better stress that I have no evidence that Sam's motivation at the time of the trial or more importantly at the time of the act many months earlier was malicious.

CHAPTER A9

EXTINCTION REBELLION FACE A SMALL REBELLION

Rising Up morphed into Extinction Rebellion (XR) who now had political demands; for councils there were two. The primary one was to declare a climate emergency along with setting a carbon neutrality target for 2025. The other was to supplement[29] Government who had so miserably failed (on climate change) with peoples' assemblies[30] made up of hundreds of carefully selected people to be representative of the population. In September they wrote to Carla with a draft letter asking if we Greens would turn their demands into a motion to be discussed and voted on in Full Council in November 2018. Carla drafted a motion asking that the Council declare a climate emergency and asking the Mayor to come up with a plan not just for the Council but for the whole city to become carbon neutral by 2025.

As always draft motions are circulated and discussed among the rest of us Green Councillors to agree or modify. Carla worked immensely hard gathering the data and support for this but being a stubborn old mule I said I wouldn't vote for it.

"2025 is not a credible date, we'd have to rebuild half of Bristol to achieve it."

was one of my more flowery statements.

I'd recently come back from Cambridge where they had put on a series of lectures about climate change. It was certain there were some major problems building up and some potentially catastrophic irreversible changes. Three examples they covered in depth:
• if the Siberian permafrost loses its "perma" so releasing mega tons of methane,

29   If not wholly replacing Government then getting them to embrace Citizens' Assemblies as the way of taking important and urgent decisions. Not enough progress had been made and Government was and is beholden to vested interests.
30   To be held in different locations around the UK. People would be paid and chosen from different walks of life to be demographically representative. The conclusions from the different assemblies would then inform Government; more on this later.

• or the arctic ice melts darkening the surface colour of the polar region and thus causing more solar heating (the sun reflects off white, not off dark blue),

• or sea water getting under one of the massive ice sheets in Antarctica melting it from underneath as well as from the top.

If any of those three events happened then others would be triggered and tip the climate irreversibly warmer for thousands of years. Runaway climate change would cause mass starvation, migration and inevitably war. Hence the threat of extinction that Extinction Rebellion were and are campaigning to avoid.

I had also seen forecasts from energy consultants showing that energy was on track to become carbon neutral by 2080. Which although encouraging that it was actually predicted to improve, was obviously not quick enough. Green Party policy nationally was neutrality by 2030 and I was on one of the working groups looking at how that change could be financed by the state and private sectors. But by 2025? I didn't think it could be done within a democracy. Government would have to declare a state of war and with no real prospect of that I told my Green colleagues that I considered that 2035 was likely the best date to choose for the motion but I'd agree to 2030 as a really ambitious target.

You know it's difficult to stand up to your friends and colleagues. It's tiring, coming up with counter arguments and data to stand steady. But I did and time was running out as the motion had to be submitted. I would vote against 2025. It seemed Carla and others had stopped talking to me, perhaps I shouldn't be so pig headed. Our Political Assistant Paul, wise beyond his years, brokered a deal with hours to go. The motion would be for carbon neutrality for 2030.

It came to Full Council, it was passed unanimously, Carla was interviewed by the national press, voted Politician of the Year by one magazine and was and still is inundated with requests on how to get motions passed up and down the country.

To date I think over one hundred councils have declared climate emergencies with 2030 carbon neutrality targets.

Bristol's Mayor who voted for the motion has embraced the goals and with the help of a Green budget amendment in February 2019 has extra money to help coordinate plans. Bristol University are developing their own 2030 neutrality plans. There are the stick in the muds, the airport (if you include flight emissions) and the port, but you always get laggards in any change program.

Will this succeed? I don't know. Was it better to have the 2030 target instead of 2025? I think so, I think 2025 might not have been voted through. Then and now in 2020 more people think 2030 is closer to achievable whereas 2025 definitely wasn't. But was 2030 a better choice than 2025? You have my view on that. Time will tell. Maybe I will become public enemy number one.

WHAT IF XR FAIL?

The story of Extinction Rebellion, Carla's and Bristol Councillors' active parts in it needs writing up. That is their story, not mine. Progress on bringing environmental issues to the fore is to their immense credit. If climate change is halted at three degrees centigrade then that's better than four or five degrees. I don't believe the world is capable of delivering on two degrees.

Because of that, my worry has been and still is whether our democratic and economic systems are up to the challenge of coping with the inevitable disasters, migrations, disputes and more that a three degree increase in climate will bring.

Therefore this book is about having a fit democracy that can cope with that. Currently I would describe our democracy as a couch potato, unfit in the extreme, read on and decide for yourself.

SECTION B
WHY IS DEMOCRACY IMPORTANT?

CHAPTER B1
THE MATHEMATICS OF POWER[1]

In 2017, at the height of Corbynmania, many Greens were worried for the party's existence. It seemed to many of us and to me too that his manifesto was almost green. So I did what I often do on such occasions: I wrote a lecture. This one was delivered three times. Don't worry I won't reproduce the whole lot but the section below is salient. And so to a three-quarters full room in Bristol in September 2017, with an

---

1   This term is used differently to its existing use describing voter power. I use it to mean political power.

audience comprising one half concerned Green Party members and the rest interested non-Greens I sallied forth.

The following is about a manifesto that says it was for the many and not the few. Labour's mantra at the time…

Clive's Lecture September 2017: A political system for the many? Slides 38 to 52.

"Corbynomics is supposedly aimed at an economy that works for the many and not the few. And yet they still support first past the post. These two ideas are incongruous and we shall journey back to 16th-century Florence to find out why.

My definition of an economy is, and I hope you will agree, a truism for all time.

"An economy is an economic system to provide for the needs and wants of… those in power and their friends." Think of that, not everyone, just the friends, families and supporters of those in power.

Hunter-gatherer economic systems worked fine until another tribe encroached on their patch and fought them off. The Roman Empire worked "fine" as they could expand and get more slaves, they even gave their slaves the hope that their descendants might become citizens of Rome. Feudalism was about providing for the lords, royalty and their courts; the Industrial Revolution was about the capitalists gaining from their investments (and sometimes their employees) and Thatcher and Reagan launched the latest example; their friends being the lobbyists, some newspaper owners, big business and those with money. Unfortunately, I think this will always be the case with power, it is human nature (of those that need power) so the answer is to have an electoral system that maximises the number of friends that the leaders must embrace.

Five hundred years ago in Florence and a thought experiment: A newly elected ruler takes his crown and mansplains[2] to his partner that the next thing to do is to reward all the people that got them into power. If it was a small number he can afford to pay them off with quite a lot, if it's a high

2   Meant tongue in cheek but he might have done in those days, even as a Renaissance man! Mansplaining: When men explain things in a condescending or patronizing manner.

proportion it is difficult to afford to give them much each.

After the ceremony they both descend the marble stairs and with guards go straight to the basement of the palace, the treasury, where all the silver is stored. There are a thousand bags. He calculates he can afford fifty bags for "thank yous" to those that put him in power. He will need to earn an extra fifty bags for next year as well, so determines to raise taxes for everyone else.

This can be shown mathematically. For example, if he budgets on allocating 5% of the state's tax take to thank the 10% of the population who put him into power (e.g. the army and the wealthiest citizens) then the ruler can afford to use the money to benefit[3] those loyal to him so they stay steadfast in the future. This might take the form of a wage increase to the army and concessions, tax breaks or land to the wealthy nobles. 5% of the tax take allocated across 10% of the population means an increase of 50% to his supporters."

So how did I arrive at the result of 50% as the uplift to the lucky 10% then? Study the table over the page. The duke can afford to give supporters differing levels of benefit depending on how many he has to thank. Our ruler needs to be careful of course to ensure the wealthiest citizens get enough to notice. Someone else might promise more.

These are just averages so maybe he considers a smaller pay increase to the army and much more to the wealthy. However it is divvied up, he has a budget of 50% to share out over 10% of the population. The remaining 90% get nothing or maybe even have to pay increased tax to their new duke. At these levels the system is called patronage and even in a republic with elections the voters would likely be only the wealthy landowners.

But if the number of supporters that our ruler has to pay off is 20% of the population then the budget he can afford is not 50% but a 25%

---

3   Nowadays the benefits that supporters get include peerages; low tax and tax breaks that they can take advantage of; defence of offshore banking; policies to help their specific industry and more. The worst example I have ever read (in recent times) was in 1980s Junta-ruled Argentina, where political enemies of the new regime were being arrested. But note, if they were pregnant they were stripped of their child (at birth) then murdered and the babies were given to those members of the army who wanted to adopt a child: From *The War on Women* by Sue Lloyd-Roberts 2016 Simon Schuster.

uplift on average per person to the 20% he has to thank. By the time he has paid off the nobles then there's not much left for the army. That could store up problems for the future. But that is his problem not ours.

THE MATHEMATICS OF POWER

Tax to be redistributed to say thank you to supporters = 5% of £100 million tax take = £5 million.

Total population = 50,000. Currently all getting public benefits from taxes of £100 million = £2,000 worth each person as an average (public benefits = police, parks, pageants, etc.).

If he needs to thank 5,000 supporters i.e. 10% of the population, then that £5 million is divided among supporters to give £1,000 each. That's a 50% improvement on top of what they got from the state before (£1,000 more on top of the £2,000 of benefit previously gained).

If he needs to thank 20% of the population then he can only afford an average of £500 per supporter and so on, the amount becoming less the higher the % of supporters to thank.

% to thank=	People	Thank yous	% of £2,000	Rest of population get
10%	5,000	£1,000 each	50%	45,000 get nothing (or pay more)
20%	10,000	£500 each	25%	40,000 get nothing "
30%	15,000	£333 each	17% approx.	35,000 get nothing "
40%	20,000	£250 each	13% approx.	30,000 get nothing "
50%	25,000	£200 each	10%	25,000 get nothing "
60%	30,000	£167 each	8% approx..	20,000 get nothing "

CHAPTER B2
THE IMPACT OF THIS MATHEMATICAL TRUISM TODAY

Our problem now is to apply this mathematical truism to a democratic system where the leader is elected and "everyone" has the vote. In the UK a party can't win an election with 20% of the vote, but one might win with 30% and certainly 40%. Allow for those who don't vote at all.

The uplift[4] that the victor owes his or her voters calculates to 17% or 13% respectively. In the UK we can observe that pensioners and the wealthy have gained about that percentage over time relative to the rest of us. A coincidence probably as it spanned both Labour and Conservative regimes, but to me, someone who has watched the desires of those in power to stay in power the mathematics would predict that level of gain.

In a country with a voting system where you can win an election with 30% or a bit more, the leading party does not have to reward the very many, just enough. Around the world there are systems[5] where the leaders need 50% or more of the votes and there are other places where voting is compulsory[6].

Corbynomics[7] didn't seek to address changing the UK's first past the post voting system, one that allows 30% of the electorate to have their party in power; still slaves to a system that almost forces the politicians to reward their supporters. Corbyn's approach would have cut the pie differently, more fairly[8] possibly, but benefit a different 30 or 40% of society. Only when you get to needing to reward 51% or more people do the percentages that the ruling party can afford get so low that you might as well reward everyone.

In Florence, five hundred years ago, the duchess too knows that this is a truism and however "nice" her husband might be to everyone she knows that to keep in power he has to reward the people who got him there and their friends.

Comment on above: So to reward the many you need to be elected by the many in a system that means you need the votes of the many. My point here is not to critique Corbynomics but to explain a truism of staying in power using simple mathematics. In my opinion, this will always be true of leaders everywhere at every time, whether dictators,

---

4   Uplift as in a gain or benefit you or your business gains from having this leader compared to current; can be monetary, status or well-being.
5   I'm talking about free and fair elections. Someone winning 99% of the vote is probably rigging the election.
6   To minimise this you need as many voters as possible to vote (even if they say none above) and of those 51% or more to be needed to choose their leader.
7   For the many not the few.
8   Whatever fairness is. We come to that in section D.

elected or appointed. The maths shows that the more people you need to get you into power the less you can afford a system of patronage that pays off those who put you there.

Thomas Hobbes wrote about the anarchy of the English Civil War, his book called *Leviathan* can, I think, be summarised as follows: "having any leader is better than having no leader". Three hundred and a bit years later, American economist, Mancur Olsen (pronounced Mansour), in his posthumously published book *Power and Prosperity* demonstrated that life under a bandit who has settled (e.g. a mafia) is better than life under bandits who raid your lands from time to time (stationary bandit versus a roving bandit). So combining the ideas, life under a static leader is better than under bandits who come in trash and rob you and then move on. Our maths shows if a leader is beholden to many for his position it's even better for the general population.

Olsen had an earlier work published in 1982[9]; in there he presented his studies on the power of collective organisations such as trade unions and cartels. It was, I'm told, one of the ideas that inspired Margaret Thatcher in her war on the unions. As a darling of the right, his economic thoughts apply anywhere to collective power and attempts to amass income. Trade unions and cartels were successful at extracting money from markets with higher prices for labour or their goods respectively so robbing others of the economic gains. Using Olsen's insights I argue that the collective power of the rich and global business is now successful at extracting money from the economy, this time by ensuring markets work to their advantage and encouraging governments to keep taxes low. When this gets excessive this also brings harm, just in the same way as out of control cartels and trade unions did in the past.

Here is an example:

9   Around about the same time a young Michael Porter of Harvard Business School and also of McKinsey was developing his theory of Five Forces which described the negotiating power of different business players within an industry. One of the many lessons was the power of joining a collective whether it be a labour union or a business oligopoly. I find it interesting that studies from economics (Olsen) and business (Porter) came out with theories that agreed and at about the same time.

"The impact of the superrich on the London housing market is pricing locals out and creating barriers to young people". BBC, Sean Coughlan, 22 Jan 2020

So far we have talked about participants influencing their leaders and expecting returns. Business can act as one of the beneficiaries of "handouts or favours" They don't have a vote but their money and more often their main shareholders' money is highly influential.

Here is another example of lobbying, in the EU. From an article published in *Photovoltaic* magazine in 2019 written by Max Hall

"Non-profit organisation, the Corporate Europe Observatory, which publicizes the effects of corporate lobbying on EU policymaking, joined forces with sustainability charity Food & Water Europe, the European branch of Friends of the Earth and Greenpeace to produce a report which claimed Exxon Mobil, Shell, Total, BP and Chevron – plus the industry associations they belong to – between them spent €251 million lobbying the European Union on fossil fuel policy from 2010 to 2018. The figures were reportedly drawn from the EU's transparency register, in which companies can voluntarily declare meetings held with EU organizations and policymakers.

The spokeswoman for Shell said the report unfairly assumed "we are lobbying against renewable energy targets" when, she said, "we discuss day to day business". She said there could, for instance, be examples of meetings where Shell representatives, given a suggested clean energy-related target, might feel it was not sufficiently ambitious and could lobby policymakers for a more demanding target."

Comment: on article above: It seems to me that this form of lobbying is trying to get elected representatives to give you an advantage in business; a sort of money-go-round, rich people and organisations supporting a political party who will benefit their interests[10]. This should be of no surprise to anyone, as we know it's money that makes the world go round but this does impact on democracy and I would argue it directly or indirectly extracts money on behalf of the rich at the expense of those less fortunate, more on that in the next chapter.

The news (below) just came in before going to press; it shows the Maths of Power at work. Fortunately the travesty was spotted and stopped just in time. First reported in *The Times* on 27th May 2020.

Housing Secretary Robert Jenrick (Conservative) accepted that he showed "apparent bias" in giving planning approval to billionaire Richard Desmond for a £1 billion pound development in London. Mr Desmond's company, Northern & Shell, has donated to the Conservative Party in the past.

The approval would have saved Northern & Shell £40 million because it was given the day before a Planning Levy was set to increase. In doing this, Mr Jenrick MP overturned the Appeal Inspector's decision[11] to refuse. He accepted that his decision showed "apparent bias," because it looked like it was timed to avoid the new levy. His admission of "apparent bias" was allegedly because Mr Jenrick could avoid sending full disclosure documents to the Court. He doesn't have to send them now[12].

---

10   There is a 2003 paper about how electoral rules shape government coalitions and economic policies by Persson, T, Roland,G and Tabellini, G (Stockholm, Berkeley and Bocconi Universities respectively). It concludes that coalitions (from PR systems) end up with a higher overall Government spend. In my view that's not necessarily a bad thing as it indicates the desire to benefit more sections of society, rather than minimise spend so the economy could just tend to benefit the wealthy. I'd be fascinated to hear of more research in this area. The authors claim this kind of research is unusual because it crosses the divide between politics and economics. That also backs up a separate point I make later in this book (end of section D and into E) about politics and economics being inexorably linked.
11   Refused by the Inspector, because of the impact on views of historic London and not enough affordable housing.
12   The story continued a few weeks later. It emerged that a couple of weeks after the planning approval was given that a sizeable donation was given to the Conservative Party. https://www.bbc.co.uk/news/uk-politics-53011728
And following that, on 15th June 2020 the LGiU news stream brought another revelation that Boris Johnson supported Mr Jenrick's behaviour. There you have it. The PM reinforcing my point that behaviour predicted by the maths of power is "doing the right thing". Indeed it is Boris, because of the UK's current electoral system and that's how you retain power.

CHAPTER B3

THE MATHEMATICS OF POWER AS PLAYED OUT IN BRISTOL (EXAMPLE)

Even closer to home I witnessed this money go round effect at the Port of Bristol. In September 2019, I had to research it in detail to debate against the idea of Freeports. It is an idea from Conservative Government, linked with Boris Johnson, their newly elected leader. It is something the Conservatives in the Council wanted the Bristol's Labour Mayor to support, they claimed allegedly it was going to benefit the people of Bristol.

In that Full Council meeting the Conservative speaker was to be Councillor Mark Weston, who was also selected as the 2019 Tory candidate for the constituency of Bristol North West, the constituency in which sits the Port. As both the Greens and Conservatives are in opposition to Labour we sit on the same side of the Council Chamber. In fact I sit only four seats away from him on the front row. Mark is an imposing figure with lots of presence and convinced of the veracity of his message. I sometimes jokingly think of him as a political ogre dressed up as a big teddy bear. I would love to really debate with Mark, it's a shame that I didn't get many chances. There are an example or two later in the book of me jousting with Mark. It was always a bit unfair because he got to speak first[13]. Despite my image of him as a teddy bear with form, Mark is fun to be around, helpful and insightful on various working groups we attended together. He is leader of the Bristol Conservative Group of Councillors and I think pretty ambitious.

Here is the speech I never gave. Full Council in September 2019 ran out of time for the debate. Maybe I should send Mark a copy?

"Thank you Lord Mayor
Councillor Weston, this really is a rubbish idea. Rubbish for 2 reasons.
Freeports make sense only when tariffs generally are high, a Freeport

---

13   The order you speak is determined by the number of Councillors you have. Mark spoke before us as the Conservatives had three more Councillors than us Greens.

will have none and then they support imports more. That's the EU and USA experience. Also they often take jobs from nearby areas. To be successful they need to be big and part of a low tax regime. The most successful have VAT, Corporation Tax and Duties all set at 0% and they use cheap labour too.

And that leads us to the second reason why this is rubbish.

This motion exposes the Tory system of fundraising in return for favours for all to see.

Your party is funded by rich people and in return you create situations for the rich people to get further rewards.

It is well documented that the Port and its owners donate big money to the Tories (and climate change denial too). £600,000 at the last count. I'm sure they will continue to do so and indirectly some of that money might indirectly end up funding Mark's campaign to become Conservative MP in Bristol NW, the very same constituency that the Port sit in.

And so what does Mark do, he puts forward a motion that would benefit the owners of the Port. Business would increase on their land, they'd earn more rent and their land value would go up.

Shame on you. So Mark why have you made this issue so visible, your colleagues must be cringing, I thought many were one nation Conservatives, not the mad, megalomaniac Conservatives we see in Parliament and you seem intent on joining.

And it gets worse, whilst the Port were funding the Tories, we, the Council, as part owners of the Port were indirectly funding the Tories too because of that shareholding. So the Council has been implementing Tory Austerity and cuts whilst funding that very same party. Funny if it wasn't so sad.

Mark - a plague of Avonmouth flies on your house.

The rest of you Conservatives, to maintain any credibility you should abstain."

The references I used to research the above are listed in the footnotes[14].

Comment on the script above: Avonmouth is locally famous for its flies[15], which come from the Port and surrounding areas due to the forms of waste cargoes that are processed. We are only allowed three minutes for our speeches so I left out the fact that EU freeports are being investigated for money laundering and tax avoidance. I left out the fact that one of the main owners put in £60,000 into the Tory leadership campaign earlier in the summer. And I left out the fact that one of the advisors to the select committee Drewry (Shipping Consultants) also said something to the effect that because the word free was within Freeport[16] it had become a popular idea in some circles.

> Like any equation, the Maths of Power works both ways. As rulers you can use it to guide your behaviour to stay in power and equally as voters we can use it to predict the type of behaviour we will get from rulers based on the percentage of the electorate needed to form a majority Government.
>
> 51% would be fairly democratic and benefitting the many, whereas 10% would lead to autocratic rule, rife with nepotism and corruption. 30% is what we have in the UK, a bit of both and you have just read about the behaviour we get from our leaders.

14   References to Bristol Port story (apologies if any prove to be wrong). Nobody is doing anything illegal, in fact that's my very point. All this is within the law.
https://www.opendemocracy.net/en/dark-money-investigations/revealed-climate-change-denier-makes-big-donation-boris-johnson-and-jeremy-hunt/
http://powerbase.info/index.php/Terence_Mordaunt
https://www.desmog.co.uk/terence-mordaunt
https://parliamentlive.tv/Event/Index/29699801-8d72-40a1-aa80-7d476d51ad1e#player-tabs
http://www.sussex.ac.uk/broadcast/read/47945
https://www.portstrategy.com/news101/world/europe/free-ports-wont-help-brexit-britains-economy
https://www.instituteforgovernment.org.uk/explainers/freeports-and-free-zones
https://www.gov.uk/government/news/trade-secretary-announces-freeports-advisory-panel-will-ensure-uk-is-ready-to-trade-post-brexit
https://assets.publishing.service.gov.uk/government/uploads/system/uploads/attachment_data/file/762200/port-freight-statistics-2017.pdf
15   The flies came back in 2020 as well.
16   The key thing politically is Freeports might be necessary in the event of a no deal Brexit to have free trade for the automotive industry. These seem to be the way Boris wants to pursue it. There are lots of problems too as you have read. It encourages lower tax regimes in the area surrounding ports, need I say more

This book works on the premise that the best forms of democracy require the votes of as many of the people as possible. Their democratic systems are less prone to being "hijacked" by a smaller grouping within the population who keep their leader(s) in power and thus extract more benefits from the economy. There is a phrase used by some leading economists who call it "state capture". In 2020 there are concerns that state capture has been allowed to occur in a number of leading democracies because of weaknesses in their democratic systems.

51% doesn't make it perfect, you still need openness and scrutiny.

Updates on Freeports (thanks to the LGiU for all their news summaries).

Government advisers warn of freeports dangers

The Times reported on 20th January 2020, Government advisers have warned that plans to create 10 freeports - low-tax zones around selected sea and airports that remove certain tariffs and checks - after Brexit risks distorting markets and creating "a lot of losers" around the country. British Ports Association chief Richard Ballantyne, a member of the freeports advisory panel, said: "There may be areas who have just as much an operational reason to get a port zone, but it may not tick a box because it may not be in part of the UK that the Government has targeted for growth and regionalisation". He also added that freeports could be a "very attractive" proposition for ailing coastal communities, if combined with a package of incentives such as fast-tracked planning permission, grants and reduced business rates. UK Major Ports Group boss Tim Morris said: "It seems to be one of the most fashionable phrases in the Westminster village that everything in the North needs regeneration and everything in the South is paved with gold. That is not the case."

Freeport advisory panel members raise concerns

And on 18 Feb 2020, The Times published, After the Government last week published proposals on the introduction of freeports as part of its post-

Brexit economic strategy, it has emerged that the advisory committee for the plans met just once in six months. Some members of the committee have also privately questioned their role, and they have raised concerns that ministers could grant freeport status on political, rather than economic, grounds. One panellist said: "I don't think members feel completely involved in the process... What's the point of having an advisory group if you're not going to consider its advice"?

Even if our democracy does get to the stage where leaders are elected by the majority of voters, those voters need to be able to make an informed decision when they choose. They and their elected representatives need to know what's going on. This requires openness and transparency in all levels of Government and the organisations dealing with them. The following are some stories where this didn't happen and later on in this section where it did happen.

CHAPTER B4

IF THE REPRESENTATIVES DON'T KNOW WHAT'S GOING ON, HOW CAN THE ELECTORS?

Judge Kotter called us irrational. Irrational, how dare he. It was late on a Friday evening in the summer of 2018 after yet another long week of work. My summer holiday of a few weeks ago long forgotten. Irrational, I'm never that. Testy, moody, grumpy, yes perhaps, but irrational? So that was the start of a long, long weekend digging and investigating.

This judgment was sent to me by one of the parents who had just won their Judicial Review against Bristol Full Council's decision in February 2018 to cut £4 million[17] of spending on school children who have special educational needs (SEN or SEND, the D standing for disabilities).

Bristol City Council oversees the quality of local school education as is usual of Councils throughout the UK. One area of high spend is

---

17   About 8% of the High Needs Budget for Education. At a time when numbers were increasing and the cost of specialist support was increasing.

the extra support given to those children who are dyslexic, autistic, disabled in some way or other or have ADD, ADHD and a whole host of other characteristics which make it difficult for them to follow the teacher in a class of thirty or more without extra help. We all feel like that some days but these kids need help every day and the statistics are that if they don't get help when they are young then the taxpayer often spends much more money caring for them during adulthood. Dyslexia being a major example where with early assistance the child can grow up to be a genius and fulfil their potential and more, diagnose it much later and they already have dropped out and are potentially en route to the criminal justice system. So from a moral, fairness and financial point of view supporting SEND makes sense. Except to Full Council apparently, who voted for that budget cut. Irrational of course but that's not the type of irrationality the judge meant.

The judicial review judgment created a local Twitter storm that weekend but it was being called irrational that really piqued me. I read the judgment and then I read the budget papers from February, the Cabinet papers, the Schools' Forum papers and much else.

Most of the judgment was about lack of consultation and why the £4 million cut had to be reversed, but near the end the judge also stated that when Full Council voted (70 Councillors plus the Mayor) it wasn't making an informed decision, the judge implied that most, if not virtually all, of us didn't know about the cut. I certainly didn't, that only came out weeks after the budget vote when we found out that some parents were taking us to court. In fact I was the Green lead for the budget, with an MBA from one of the world's best business schools and having sat on budget scrutiny all the previous autumn I thought I knew it inside out. But we didn't look at the education budget, it is directly funded from Government, it didn't need scrutiny as we were told needs were catered for. They evidently weren't.

As it turns out I voted against the budget, but for other reasons relating to Austerity and lack of control of spend on areas like adult social care. It was the Labour Councillors who dutifully voted for the SEND budget cut, I can't blame them, they almost certainly weren't informed either, I doubt the new Cabinet Member (Labour) Councillor Anna Keen had been briefed properly as well. And there was no scrutiny, so if I were to make a bet I think officers worked out this "financial wheeze" to save money unaware of the real harm it would cause some of the most vulnerable people: children with special needs. Fortunately some of them have pushy parents. The Cabinet Member for Education had been changed in November 2017 by the Mayor and the new one, Anna, was a part time teacher and dropped in it big time.

But back to that busy weekend, digging and asking. A Lib Dem Councillor Tim Kent was very helpful, his child is SEND and his wife was one of the parents who took the Council to court, and I must say that I would not have uncovered half of this without his help. Anyway by the Sunday night I'd come to the conclusion that the Cabinet Member should consider resigning. Unfair you might exclaim, and yes it would be unfair, but politicians in power need to be in control of their officers, and because Bristol's scrutiny wasn't working at that time she didn't get help from that front. The administration didn't seem to like scrutiny; more on that later.

So I penned a letter to the local paper. "Dear Editor..."

CHAPTER B5
SO WHO DOES RUN THE COUNCIL?

In that letter to the *Post* I wrote,

"I feel sure that Councillor Anna Keen, Cabinet Member for Education, will be considering resigning from her post."

A few days later I got a phone call and the journalist asked me if she could use some of the contents of my letter in a piece she was writing. The key issue for her was whether I was calling on Cllr Keen to resign, a headline was needed. I said no. We agreed a compromise that appeared in the paper the next day "Calls for cabinet member to 'consider her position'" were the headlines. Technically correct but putting a slant on it that sells newspapers. Interestingly there was already a response from the Labour Machine and reported in the Post further down was,

> *"Like a cheap opportunist, Councillor Stevens is trying to score political points for himself by misrepresenting half a sentence from a five minute speech at a cabinet meeting, rather than reaching out to support important ongoing work for Bristolians' benefit.*
>
> *"Unlike Labour members, he did not raise the issues in advance and, as normal, he's attacking Bristol's progressive Labour administration rather than the Tory Government who are responsible for funding in this area."*

Given I had worked most of the weekend and much of the Monday, my efforts didn't seem cheap to me! Plus I was agreeing with the judge, I bet he wasn't a cheap opportunist. The fundamental problem was that officers stitched Councillor Keen up, but us Councillors, we can't criticise officers (see next chapter), I can now by the way as I've stood down[18], so any potential joint working between Councillors to solve the problem is destroyed with officers running a divide and rule approach. And how do I know it was officers[19]?

You may be wondering why I was irritated at being called irrational especially as I voted against that budget in Feb 2018. Well, perhaps mistakenly, I feel some camaraderie and pride with fellow Councillors even Labour ones. There are only seventy of us representing four hundred and fifty thousand people and we all get treated badly by some residents, possibly by some officers and maybe by the Mayor too. It sort of forms a bonding and if some judge says "Councillors were irrational" then I take that to heart, probably proving that I am irrational in the normal sense of the word.

Coincidentally I had been chosen to Chair the budget scrutiny process that autumn of 2018 leading to the 2019/20 budget. Also luckily the Lib Dem Councillor Tim Kent who had helped me navigate that

---

18   Except I haven't because the elections were cancelled for a whole year. So publish and be damned.
19   A combination of discussions and a particularly useful tip off.

SEND legal judgement a month earlier was to be on the budget scrutiny commission too. I asked if he wanted to be vice chair. And go on have a guess at what budget line received the most scrutiny that year. Twice it came to us, only one other budget item came twice and that was adult social care which was heading towards a £15 million overspend that year.

So armed not only with a better understanding and a healthy mistrust of the Education Department I went about making sure I knew more than they did. I'm Governor of a Local School and they kindly invited me to a private meeting of all the SEND Coordinators for about twenty four schools. It was so good to hear the facts from those who were starved of funding, they had to fight the Council's bureaucracy too and the effects of the funding limits on the rest of their schools. I can write here, for the first time, that inadequate support for the special educational needs of one, two or three children in a class means disruption for all children, stress for the teachers and almost certainly worse outcomes for the whole class of thirty which is a massive cost to society. It took me one meeting to learn this, officers must have known this too but the system had long trod them down.

Back to budget scrutiny, with me much better informed, the Judicial Review rebuke of irrationality now transformed into a beacon for change, and my Vice Chair a SEND parent: officers didn't stand a chance. The judge had forced the Council to add £4 million back in, we then upped the budget by a further £3 million which would have to come out of future Government funding. If they don't stump up it will need to come out of business rates and council tax. So be it, I nearly said "I will pay for it myself". But I'm sure and would hope that most Bristolians would understand the need to support SEND, teachers and the better education of the whole class.

But can you believe this, at the very same time[20], Education Officers wrote to schools saying that there was now going to be a limit of three children per funding review. For example at the school I was Governor for, if six SEND children joined in one year, they could only apply for top up funding for just three of them; madness and presumably

20   Autumn 2018.

illegal. My Lib Dem colleague spotted this first, spoke at Full Council and the new policy was dropped immediately and explained to us as a misunderstanding[21].

Had they told the Cabinet Member? Still Councillor Anna Keen, who, by the way made an excellent "I hold my hands up, I made a mistake" speech about the original issue. She won us over that day.

2020 update: SEND funding still isn't enough even though it's now £12 million higher than when the judge forced the reversal of the 2018 cuts. The children coming in have more complex needs, there is no specialisation[22] at schools. Bristol has a system where as many SEND children as possible are integrated into mainstream schools. That's good, it is good for them and especially good for the other children who can make friends with and interact with differently brained people, so important for inclusivity in later life and in secondary education. But such an approach costs more and without extra funding becomes self-defeating.

> The point I draw from these two chapters on SEND is not to revolutionise the provision of education. It's not even to say I'm right, I can't be sure, I'm not enough of an expert, but it is to illustrate the question, "who runs the Council, officers or elected representatives?" Even if the democratic system works but if your representatives can't take informed decisions then what's the point of a fantastic voting system!

By the way I have found more examples[23] of things hidden in that fateful budget of 2017, they are in Section F.

---

21 I have an opportunity I can't resist; it's to say "my foot" in a footnote. I've said it.
22 Specialisation is a route that often leads to better efficiency and quality in other fields. An example: a school could specialise its mainstream SEND provision to a particular problem say hearing problems or another in mild autism, that way each school can provide and equip for specific needs.
23 Adult Social Care; money that hadn't been allocated to the care budget but was held centrally, also underfunded (almost every year running).

CHAPTER B6

AS OFFICERS[24] TAKE DECISIONS, CAN WE TRUST THEM WITH THE BIG ONES?

May 2019, in a small top floor meeting room; the minutes of the March 2019 HR meeting had been diligently recorded and were handed out to us on paper, we were given a couple of minutes to read them, then they were collected back and the officer ordered them to be destroyed along with the computer record. So nothing of that previous meeting would exist without a forensic inspection of the hard disk on the server.

Jumping back eight months; for me the issue of whether I could trust senior officers came to a head around October 2018. You might ask why did it take me so long? Maybe I'm a slow learner. We were in Audit Committee listening to all the reasons why the Council's Accounts were late for sign off. One of the excuses given was that the Council hadn't given the Auditors sufficient information for them to make a decision on how to categorise the ex-Chief Executive's payoff. Despite the fact that the payoff was in September 2017 and we were now in October 2018.

Previously I had phoned the External Auditors to get at the facts, as Vice Chair I had some status and was independent of the ruling regime too. Armed with information, off the record, I then diligently listened to fiction at the meeting. Well possibly fiction is tad unfair, "truth economy" would be more accurate. It was claimed by the Auditors that key sections of her contract, emails and legal advice hadn't been passed on to them even now. Senior Officers and the Auditors were very guarded in what they were saying and deflected Councillor questions extremely skilfully; it was getting most frustrating and nowhere near the truth. And we weren't even allowed to see the documents. Time went on, more questions, more deflections and then it was my turn to speak.

So looking down the table, at a long line of council officers, I said

---

24 Officers have delegated powers to take decisions up to £500k and sometimes more if approved by Cabinet. They must refer to Cabinet if the decision is "political". There are so many decisions to take, the Mayor and Cabinet can't take them all some have to be delegated.

something along these lines,

"I don't know who of you to trust, there is a cover up going on here which is worse than the fact of the severance payment".

As these Audit meetings aren't recorded, lack of resource I've been told, but I can think of other reasons too, then the only record is in the minutes and the local paper. The *Post's* reporter said I was nearly in tears when I was saying this, she was right. If you cannot trust senior officers you can't do the job as a Councillor because 90% of all the information you get is from officers.

This all relates to the, infamous in Bristol, payoff to the ex-Chief Executive, Anna Klonowski[25], which is the subject of the next chapter. The manner of her payoff and the cover up just rumbled on and on despite officers' and Labour's attempts to cover up.

First, some more on lack of trust; in January 2019, a different meeting this time, the HR Committee. I had just entered and was waiting for the agenda item I was involved with but heard the closing remarks of their previous discussion about staff appraisals. "And so the Mayor now does the appraisal of the Executive Directors". Umm...I thought, I'll save that one.

I discussed the implications of this factlet with other colleagues a day or two later. Some of us were horrified and others thought, so what? I said,

"If the Mayor sets the objectives for the Executive Directors then the Mayor is the boss."

When you are the boss, if you tell someone to do something, then the director will do it. And they in turn will pass those objectives down to her staff and so on, that's how management by objectives works, it cascades down the whole organisation. So any dream and pretence I held that

---

25   Anna seemed to me to be a very pleasant, intelligent woman. But I didn't have to work with her much. She is referred to as the Ex-Chief Executive in most Council documents of the time.

officers were independent (like in the Civil Service) was sunk. In such an organisational structure, officers are there to do the Mayor's bidding. If the Mayor says he wants something done then they do it, if he says, "I want this made difficult to find", then as long as it's not illegal to do so, it will be covered up. The confidential stamp comes down. Thump.

I managed to voice my concerns to officers at the March 2019 Value and Ethics Committee where fortuitously we were discussing the Member Officer Protocol and the need for mutual trust. Perfect, just the topic I wanted to pour my heart out about. Again no recording but our newly appointed Local Democracy Reporter Amanda Cameron was there and she wrote the following,

> "When asked for feedback on the protocol, three of five Councillors said mutual trust was in short supply. "They blamed the new Council power structure that was introduced last year after the role of chief executive was scrapped. "Green Councillor Clive Stevens said that he started off with a huge amount of trust in officers but slowly and surely it's declined. "He'd tried to think through why, and it's not the people, it's the structure of having an all-powerful Mayor controlling the head of paid service, so the Mayor is the boss. And if the Mayor says I want an arena built at Filton then the Head of Paid Service has to follow that, so due to this structure Councillor Stevens would find it very difficult to trust whoever was in the role of Head of Paid Service."

This newish structure means the Mayor reviews the performance of the person who oversees important democratic functions of the Council like finance, HR, legal and democratic services. The article continued,

> "It's nothing to do with the actual people, it would be the same even if Mother Theresa[26] or whoever is the most trustworthy person in the world was doing that job"

26   Later on I remembered that Mother Theresa had been dead for twenty years so I ran to Google and apparently the most trusted people of 2019 were David Attenborough, Tom Hanks and Michele Obama. So if any of them were Head of Paid Service reporting into the Mayor I wouldn't be able to trust them either. (Also there are now criticisms of Mother Theresa's whole approach).

A Lib Dem Councillor added that this lack of trust extended to access to meetings or information.

> "It is understandable if information is made exempt because of commercial sensitivities but it is not a reason to protect the reputation of individuals. "We depend on the good judgment of officers to make sure there is no infringement." And I would have added if I had thought of it at the time," But if officers are subject to this reporting and appraisal structure the pressures to keep quiet must be high."

Amanda's article in the *Post* continued by quoting a Labour Councillor, it wasn't so rare back then to find one brave enough to criticise the Mayor's decisions.

> "I don't think the current system is working, any mistakes by the Mayor risk tarnishing the whole Council and so end up costing the taxpayer, what sort of rights or powers do officers have if they are actually concerned that something is wrong?"

In May 2019 the staff appraisal feedback came out which revealed that about 48% of staff were not confident that they could raise an issue about poor behaviour or practices and if they did that it would be responded to effectively. This was about the same level of confidence as in 2016. And that was back when Steve Bundred's investigation [27]uncovered a management culture of council officers hiding bad news from leadership and possibly even lying to them.

So I bring you back to where and when we started this chapter, May 2018 high up in City Hall and the ordered destruction of those minutes. On its own, perhaps just over-diligence, but set into this context, what do you think?

Officers have an interest in making sure the Council has a good reputation because that reflects on them and their job prospects if they

---

27   Investigation into the mistakes made in 2015, during the previous administration, that led to the financial black-hole.

move to other authorities. With the extra pressure of the appraisal system and reporting structure direct[28] into the Mayor I think that it is damaging for democracy and destroys trust in senior levels.

The next chapter looks into the Ex-Chief Executive's payoff and the one after that covers the battle for openness and transparency of Council documents versus the "need to know" brigade.

CHAPTER B7
OPENNESS AND OPAQUENESS

Anna Klonowski came in as an interim executive around 2016, initially as Director of Resources, and then interviewed by the Selection Committee and appointed to the role of Chief Executive of Bristol City Council in March 2017. Five months later she was gone.

Rumours abounded, but then they always do. The Selection Committee who apparently wanted someone else was overruled; and then, allegedly when she was in her role there were clashes and even accusations of bullying at top level meetings about how to react to the Austerity funding cuts, to save jobs and services. It would be difficult times for anyone. Those closer to the gossip suggested that Anna was on her way out anyway. In early September we were told that her parents were ill, she had resigned and was leaving to care for them. I wished her well and thought nothing more of it.

A few weeks later it got into Private Eye that she had received a payoff, a big one too, big even by Bristol's standards. Now companies do this all the time when they want to get rid of senior managers. They agree a deal (often called a compromise agreement) so that the person

---

28   On May 7th 2020 (The day elections were supposed to be held) The Mayor announced he was reverting to the previous structure of having a Chief Executive (CE) and all officers report in to the CE. The CE still reports into the Mayor. This was a recommendation of the External Peer Review held in 2019 and was the public reason for the change. So two and a half years after the last CE left we now have a new one. I think this is better, not perfect, but perfection might not be possible. On May 21st A Full Council debate was held on whether the CE should receive their annual appraisal, not by the Mayor alone, but by a cross party panel (including the Mayor). The vote was 30 for and 35 against. Lost, but close. The Labour Chair of HR said the proposal will be considered later in the year and the CE's Terms and conditions changed if appropriate.

leaves, says nothing and the business can move on. It's good for both parties, but in the state sector with responsibility for appropriate use of public money there is a value for money test for decision making and for something like this any payoff should be justified against that test. Perhaps it was justified[29], but nobody made the justification public.

Some Councillors followed up, those who sat on that Selection Committee back in March 2017, the one that had been overruled; they smelled blood and wanted to show that the original mistake by the Mayor to hire Anna, against their recommendation, had badly backfired.

We all know that recruitment decisions go wrong, possibly the majority at senior roles, and it is often best to come clean and agree a break. A negotiated severance would have involved a compromise agreement between the Council and the departing officer. Typically an investigation into whether it was value for money might be done by the External Auditors. This all came to light late in 2018 and we were never told whether an investigation was done and if so what the outcome was.

(In the last chapter we covered the impact of the Mayor's reorganised senior management, removing the role of Chief Executive altogether; and claiming to have saved over a million pounds in salaries with everyone reporting in to him[30] but at what cost to the effective running of the Council?).

The External Auditors did their investigation and found that the payment was not contractual, they recommended some changes but crucially we, including me the Vice Chair of Audit Committee, weren't allowed to see key documents held by officers. These were the same documents that the External Auditors hadn't yet seen either and their absence delayed the sign off of the Council's accounts by over six months. The officers in the know kept quiet despite protestations and local press articles. It was only when the Annual Accounts were announced as delayed in August 2018 that we started to find out what was going on. The External Accountants refused to believe the Council's claims

---

29 The public will view this as a matter of fairness. Why should she have got such a big payoff. As far as I'm aware there is no Fairness Act applying to Local Government. Perhaps there should be?
30 Reporting into the Mayor

that all of the ex-Chief Executive's payment was contractual. Their audit revealed that part of the payment she received in 2017 was contractual and that some of it was discretionary, as if it were via a compromise agreement. £98,000 worth of discretionary payment including £18,000 pension top up. Was the decision to pay that amount value for money?

From my perch on Audit Committee I watched and contributed to the questioning on this at every meeting from September 2018 through to the Full Council debate in January 2019. As Vice Chair I was party to a very revealing document prepared by the previous (Interim) Legal Officer that I was sworn to secrecy about, but it explained a lot. Others didn't even know I had this information and as I watched and listened further, I continued to lose trust in what some of the officers were saying.

They said there was no compromise agreement. Everyone asked why was an ex-Gratia Payment made to the ex-Chief Executive? I knew why.

They asked what was it that officers were covering up? They denied a cover up. I knew there was.

They asked whether the Mayor had signed off this payment? No answer, even the Mayor said in public that there were no Human Resources (HR) procedures to cover such an eventuality. Can you believe that, no procedures to cover the sacking of a senior director, something done with too much regularity and in Bristol it had also occurred the year before too[31], in 2016!

The Mayor received a very public grilling that January 2019, he sounded like a scratched record, needle jumping, running over and over the same refrain.

So what did I know all that time? The document I saw had been prepared I think to inform the External Auditors. They would want a timeline of events around September 2017. It didn't cover the recruitment but did cover the decision to make a payment. There were multiple versions of the employment contract on file and the advice regarding any payoff was given by two separate external legal advisors, they gave differing advice, based presumably on different contract versions. Also much of the paperwork was found to be missing and decisions were not

31   Nicola Yates that time.

recorded. (That last bit by the way was found to be common practice in those days on many issues not just this Klonowskigate cover-up as it was now being called).

If you took the document I saw at face value it was simply describing incompetence[32]. Not by the external legals, but by the internal and interim council officers most of whom had long since left. If you prefer a conspiracy theory; say one suggesting this document was created to provide the external auditors with something that would convince them it was just ineptitude; thus hiding some real reason, then the document wasn't convincing because of who the author was. He was of high integrity, leaving of his own accord and had a reputation to protect to take into his next job. There was a clear line of poor decisions and lack of record keeping that was just too incompetent to be believed, you couldn't make it up.

So the officers who did this have left, the payoff cost £98,000. The legal advice must have cost too. It included a pension payment that shouldn't have been made on any of the versions of the contract. There is an argument that the ex-Chief Executive resigned, left without working her notice which means legally she was due nothing.

But someone took the decision to cover this up[33], presumably in the interests of the Council's reputation and so that added further cost. The External Auditors charged £21,000 for their report, we had meeting after meeting with 20 or more people in the room, the press had a field day so the Council's reputation, such that it was, emerging from the Bundred Report and the financial black hole, a reputation already well sullied just got worse. Many Councillors lost trust in officers and vice versa I'm sure.

The document I saw was confidential and eventually classed as exempt. That means only members of Audit and HR Committees could see it but then we had to return it. But as Vice Chair of Audit

---

32   Assisted probably by poor record keeping; if you are in an interim role and the records you inherit are poor it's not easy to get it right.

33   It's the cover up that gets me. Sure we all make mistakes but the cover up was deliberate. And as far as I was concerned those officers who I diligently listened too but who said things that disagreed with the documents I had.

I'd had it emailed to me a few months earlier labelled confidential so I didn't return it. It was on my iPad and easy to find. I would argue it shouldn't have been exempt at all, there was no personal information in there, even a very twitchy lawyer could have deleted a few words, i.e. redacted them. But as it had been written by a lawyer it was subject to something called "Legal Privilege". Any legal document is confidential unless decided otherwise. It could have been released but it was clear that it was only confidential to save the Council's face. I have explained why the Mayor's reputation, which now the Chief Executive's position is gone[34], is seen as synonymous with the Council's reputation, and so would want it suppressed. And even if he didn't ask for that to be done, then officers who report to him would automatically seek to protect him and their own reputations which affects their own career prospects.

So Klonowskigate has nearly been shut but the battle continues. JRR Tolkien would have loved this as a sequel to Return of the King. Middle Earth is saved but real earth or Bristol at least, descends into a cloud of opaqueness. The battle for openness and transparency begins….

So not only do officers take lots of decisions but then they cover up to protect their reputations. If the structure means they report to the Mayor that further emphasises in their minds the need to protect the Mayor and the Council's reputation. This is public money and Councillors are there to ensure it is spent well. But when push comes to shove documents are kept confidential, people keep stumm and trust is lost. How do Councillors take the right decisions, or input usefully if they can't trust those who provide the information and analysis?

All is not lost. There is a process called Scrutiny and we will look at that over the next few chapters, next up though is the guidance managing Councillor and officer interactions.

34   As we know from May 2020 the role is back again.

CHAPTER B8

WE DO SOMETIMES MAKE SOME PROGRESS

In May 2019 they (Legal) tried this on us. We were reviewing the Member Officer Protocol which governs how officers should interact with Councillors and how Councillors should behave with officers. In theory Councillors (in Bristol, primarily the elected Mayor) take decisions and officers make recommendations upon which the decisions are made. If Councillors (including the Mayor) ignore officer recommendations then a Council is more open to legal challenge, called judicial review, by parties who have lost out. Normally, but not always, the fear of judicial review comes from harming the opportunities of a wealthy business, party or group. The public, if they lose out are less able to organise, but if they can, then the judge might be more understanding as in the Judicial Review of the SEND budget cuts described in an earlier chapter.

The section the Legal Officer tried to tie us up in was called: Access to Information. The new draft document was to read as follows:

"All Members have a right to view Council documents so far as their access to the document is reasonably necessary, to enable the exercise of their duties as a member of the Council. This is known as the 'need to know' principle. A Member's 'need to know' will normally be presumed where the information clearly relates to the discharge of a function of Bristol City Council. The need to know depends on the member's role at that time."

Cabinet member, scrutiny member, ward member, party group leader are all different roles. Access to exempt or confidential information will depend on each role's need to know.

It's a bit tricky to get your head around, but my main point is the clause completely misses the presumption to be clear and transparent. One of the seven duties detailed in the Nolan Commission's principles of public life. A presumption that is clearly shown in official Council documents, ones that the public can read but is so clearly missing in real life workings?

We sent Legal away to check their law books. Back they came a month or so later. Not good enough so they had to work on it more. These cancelled meetings were visible to the public, out of the nearly 400,000 adults in Bristol just two[35] expressed an interest in what was going on, asking why the cancellations.

Then the third meeting and progress; my political leader, Councillor Eleanor Combley spoke on this, as eloquently as always. Here is her brief speech to November 2019's Full Council when the new Member Officer Protocol was voted through:

"One of the great joys of being a Councillor is the opportunity to work alongside such talented and committed officers. We have some extraordinary expertise amongst Council staff, and some passionate individuals who put their all into providing the best service they can for the people of Bristol.

It is not all plain sailing though, and Councillors have an important role in holding officers to account, in bringing the voice of the ordinary people they represent into City Hall, and ensuring transparency and openness. It is really important to have a set of rules by which we operate so that this work can happen as smoothly and effectively as possible.

That is the purpose of the member officer protocol, and so I welcome the work that has gone into this revision.

The first thing to note is that it is shorter, and clearer, than the previous version, which in my book is always a good thing.

The second thing I note is that the requirement for members to trust officers has been removed. In a way this is negative, as it reflects a sense that trust is not possible. When we have a reporting structure with the Mayor at its head, it is hard to trust that officers can remain politically neutral. When we have had experience of obfuscation, such as over the pay out for the previous Chief Exec, it gets hard to trust officers full stop. However, I don't see removing the requirement as entirely a bad thing. Blind trust should not be necessary, because Councillors should have access to enough information to know that what they are being told is true.

Which brings me on to another welcome change, which makes it clearer

---

35   Still two is better than nought.

that there is a presumption of openness - that information should be made public unless there is a reason to conceal it, rather than hidden unless there is a need to know. I really hope that this tone of greater transparency translates into real cultural change.

So, thanks to all those Councillors and officers who worked to produce this improved protocol as part of ongoing work to make sure our Constitution and other documents are fit for purpose. There is still a glaring omission: after seven years as a Mayoral Authority we still have no protocol governing the behaviour of the Mayor or his office. I look forward to seeing this gap filled in the next episode!"

I hope you noted Eleanor's tactful wording in her first paragraph. At the time I couldn't have said that or even have agreed with the sentiment. But on reflection I think hardworking and committed applies to all officers. Sometimes they are compromised due to instructions from above or perceptions of what the Mayor wants. In February 2020 I witnessed this first hand when three officers shared with me some very interesting information.

I said, "you know, if I reveal this you might lose your jobs".

The next day, about an hour before my speech I returned, they had back tracked and suggested I say something else[36].

Comment: So we did get access to information changed from need to know to presumption of openness. Whether this will make any difference only future Councillors in Bristol will see. But why are we, at a time of increasing homelessness, cost overruns and poor outcomes for SEND children and overspends for adult social care having to waste time fighting for openness and transparency simply so Councillors can do their jobs? That should be a national dictate surely. All Councils should have the same Member Officer Protocols and open access to information. It is the public's money, we are the representatives of the public. More on this further into the book.

This obsession with secrecy (for reputation often) isn't just at

---

36   I did, I didn't want my sources sacked.

Councils. BBC journalist Rianna Croxford wrote on 12th February 2020:

> *"UK universities are using "gagging" clauses to stop students from going public with complaints of sexual assault, bullying and poor teaching.*
>
> *Students said they felt pressured to sign non-disclosure agreements and one was told she would be expelled if she broke her contract.*
>
> *Nearly a third of universities have used NDAs for student grievances since 2016, data obtained by BBC News shows. Universities UK said NDAs should not be used to silence students.*
>
> *Non-disclosure agreements, which were designed to protect business secrets, are legal contracts that stop people from sharing private information."*

Referring to the above article; it seems that instead of fixing the problem, the obsession to protect their reputation leads universities to gag student complaints. Universities aren't democratic institutions but something is seriously wrong if they need to cover up too.

I did promise you some positive examples.

CHAPTER B9
THE RENT IS GOING UP BY HOW MUCH?

The bastards, how on earth could they do this and just before Christmas too. Not only was the roof leaking, but the landlord had just put in a rent increase and timed it as the tenant was organising improvements to the landlord's property; improvements using public money (and donations) that I had supported, if fact I led on it just a few weeks earlier. How can this be fair?

Who are the bastards? The Council are of course; and the tenant? A community group running a dance and activity centre in my ward. Not for profit. Part of their "deal"[37] with me was if I proposed the funding for better insulation and disabled access then they would promote the use of the building and add extra activities so it was available to a wider audience. The only other community building[38] we have in the ward is the library. And its future is uncertain even though it's been deemed safe from closure before the upcoming mayoral election.

What takes priority? Roof or rent? Leaky roof above the wooden, parquet dance floor; just before Christmas, it's not a good blend. The roof was in the process of being improved but a very wet December and roof contractors who didn't seem to worry too much weren't a good mix. I decided to worry about the proposed rent hike in January. Hike, more like a mountain climb. 200% increase was the claim. Market rates, can you believe it?

January 2020 and Growth and Regeneration Scrutiny meeting was scheduled. I was preparing for this anyway and then saw a paper called Corporate Property Strategy where the very same people were claiming to the Councillors on Scrutiny that they were going to become professional landlords, extract market rents but also respect social value. Lying sods I thought. I rang one of the directors of the establishment in my ward, the flooring had survived Christmas, the rain held off. I asked for permission to reveal this "rent demand" into the full face of public scrutiny. Some thought and discussed it with the other director(s). It is very difficult and worrying for tenants to take action against their landlord. But I hoped that faced with a 200% mountain and no hope of paying that they would say, "go for it". They did. Here is an extract from my question to Scrutiny.

"Here is, what seems a disgraceful example, from our very own Council.
In my ward the Council is landlord of a three room community building called Redland Club. A not for profit community group has leased

37 Although you might say, "Clive, here's an example of you giving favours", the benefit was to the community and a not for profit group who as far as I know don't fund the Green party (one admitted they voted Labour). Councillors help locals navigate access to grants. I wanted this group to become more inclusive.
38 Community buildings are important in this context to provide opportunities for voluntary or socially beneficial work that's not able to be provided by business, often services to the poorer of our area.

the building since 2009. The rent has been £3,600 a year. The community group provides exercise classes, dance and play activities for all sorts of social groups and therefore adds much social value.

In October 2018 they had notice that their lease would be renewed in 2019 for another five years at the same terms. On that basis, the community group organised a large investment in improving the disabled facilities, energy efficiency and roof repairs paid via S106 developer payments, external grants including some from other community groups and the roof paid for by the Council. This totals to £110k of investment. The group is now wedded to this building.

Then in Dec 2019, Rachman[39] like, the Council's Property Services wrote to them to say that they made a mistake a year earlier and the rent should be £10k pa not £3.6k. This has thrown the whole refurbishment and upgrade into question and the future of the group. It has also caused me to challenge the Officers' report you have before you. On this piece of evidence it seems a sham.

My question is: how can the Council claim to be a professional property landlord when it sends a 200% rent increase demand out of the blue. It didn't seek to evaluate the social value either (as it should do per the corporate property strategy). Can the Council please reset the rent review and discuss with the Councillor[40] a proper Corporate Landlord Approach so as to get best value taking into account social value[41] from the uses? Thank you. And if property services come back to us before the meeting then I will update you on the day."

That was submitted five days in advance. I was given a written answer from officers before the meeting and that just made my mood worse. I walked in to give my speech, the press were there. A more senior officer for property services asked if I wanted to discuss this outside the meeting and looked at me with doey eyes. I hesitated.

Despite that I did say my piece; the officer publicly offered a meeting

---

39   Peter Rachman, a notorious bad landlord from the 1960s
40   i.e. me
41   Social Value is explained more in chapter E6

the very next day. I was prepared with all the evidence. Two meetings later and enough compromises to allow officers to save face. The lease was formally renewed at the old rate. £30,000 of the improvements were deemed enough by officers to offset five years of £6,400 pa of "lost rent". The problem is postponed until 2024 when hopefully Social Value is better accepted and the Redland Club has widened its user base.

I reported back to Scrutiny in February as follows:

"Well it's good news. After some hardball negotiations from both sides over the past weeks it was decided by officers that the value increase of the improvements being undertaken by the group to a Council building were enough to offset the £30k of extra rent demand, so the lease has been renewed at the old rent until 2024."

Everyone is happy.

Until 2024 of course, when we fully expect another attempt at a 200% or more rent increase.

I fully understand the need for the Council to obtain best value from its buildings, but please realise the social value created by not-for-profit businesses can be large. In this case improving health and community cohesion are worth a lot. Please make sure that letting policies to outside tenants fully take account of the social value the tenants provide.

Comment: In the example above direct, in yer face, public scrutiny worked a treat; but that's often not the case. You have to be more subtle.

CHAPTER B10
FINANCE SCRUTINY, THE TASK AND FINISH WAY

"We love scrutiny but when we engage with what seems like an innocent question we find that later on it comes back as an attack. That's why we get upset, that is just like the first part of your question"

Above: So said Councillor Craig Cheney Cabinet Member for Finance, on 21 Jan 2020 (approx. 1hr, 43mins and 30 seconds into the recording).

Comment: Nobody likes to be scrutinised. It may remind them of their childhood or school. In this quote above, Craig was voicing what many administrations must feel. And yet as you will see in the coming chapters the right type of scrutiny, ideally early on can improve policy and with Councillors reflecting a wide cross section of society it is critical to good decision making.

One of my favourite council officers wrote,

"It was the Head of Consultancy for Centre for Public Scrutiny (CfPS). I attended a workshop in December that he ran on Getting Finance Scrutiny Right and he was very impressed with what Bristol is doing and described it as Best Practice and told all the other Local Authorities who were there to 'follow Bristol's lead.'"

She was explaining why Bristol's Finance/Budget Scrutiny (part done in secret, part held in public) was best in class.

I take some comfort in this, I was chair of the Finance Task and Finish Scrutiny group in both 18/19 and 19/20. Like most successful things it was down to teamwork and Councillor Graham Morris chaired the all-important first year (2017/18). The idea to scrutinise the budget using a task and finish group approach (where some is done in secret, earlier on in the process, and it enables you look at some topics in great detail) came out of some soul searching by Councillors in early 2017. This idea of doing some scrutiny behind closed doors (or even smoke filled rooms without the smoke) was and still is quite controversial.

Being held in secret gives officers and the party in power (and a Mayor) the comfort that they can reveal issues of concern early on and these can be debated, thrashed out between officers and other Councillors including opposition ones like me without us running to the press every five minutes to say what a dreadful job the Mayor is doing. Bristol's budget scrutiny process is therefore a hybrid approach of confidential meetings and then a summary paper for public consumption and wider discussion. This is repeated three times; a shuttle between private and public.

Firstly in September looking at the Medium Term Financial (Five Year) and Capital Plans in confidence, critiquing them, pointing out where assumptions might be weak, like the impact on wage rates for agency staff because of Brexit and discussing implications like the new limit on borrowing. Then that gets written up (in the two years I chaired, written up by me) and sent to officers for approval. The report might be tweaked a bit and it then becomes public so can then be discussed and questioned widely at Resources Scrutiny in early November.

Then we repeat the process, this time looking at the one year budget assumptions, again firstly in confidence and then a report comes out in December for public view and scrutiny.

Finally in January the Mayor then publishes his budget proposals and the third stage starts, which is to ensure Councillors understand what they will be voting for in February to avoid any legal charges of irrationality (the budget stretches to well over a hundred pages of numbers). The members of Finance T&F discuss points and issues in private with officers. We then publish a list of questions in public for officers to reply to in public. These questions and replies are discussed in public[42] scrutiny and then used to explain the issues to all Councillors, the press and the public. The aim is that all Councillors can take an informed vote in February.

So three times this shuttle between confidential and then public. Is that a model for scrutiny? The meetings held in secret include a smattering of Councillors from all political groups, we are the representatives of the public. It is clear from surveys that the public don't trust politicians but there is some evidence that Councillors are trusted[43] more than MPs. Perhaps that is because relatively more people have met us? Each time,

---

42   By now we are reporting to the top scrutiny body, the Overview and Scrutiny Board.

43   A June 2020 poll by the Local Government Association shows a rising measure for local Councillors (trust at 71%), exceptional times indeed: https://www.local.gov.uk/polling-resident-satisfaction-councils-june-2020

within a month or two, the financial information comes into the public domain for further discussion and with better understanding all round.

So that process seems to work for Bristol. I wanted to get this point across to other scrutiny members (in case they didn't understand the process). So I wrote a statement to Bristol's Overview and Scrutiny Board hoping to pass on this insight.

2/3/20 Statement - Agenda 11 - work program - Councillor Clive Stevens

Dear OSMB - I realise four years isn't really a long time in politics, despite what Prime Minister Wilson once said, but it's been long enough for me! And with 66[44] days to go I am starting on a process of reflection about my experiences working in the Council and would like to share some initial thoughts about scrutiny.

It seems to me we have an administration that is overly sensitive to criticism. Perhaps that's the way it is everywhere nowadays in this press release dominated world. So I think we should consider how scrutiny can be more effective at bringing a better deal for the people of Bristol if such an environment were to exist after May.

My thoughts....

Scrutiny works better the earlier we can get involved, months, years even, well before the forward plan[45] shows something is coming up on the agenda for Cabinet.

Scrutiny that helps inform and develop policy works better if some or maybe most aspects are undertaken in a task and finish group involving "deep dives" of analysis of the detail and injecting comments to officers and Cabinet to help them consider different approaches and options early on.

Scrutinies I attended that I would say worked particularly well were the Better Lives T&F in 2017/18, Finance/Budget Scrutiny (I would say that of course) and the recent SEND evidence day. There were others I'm sure, it's just I didn't attend them (or have simply forgotten - so apologies in that case). Some of these three were fully public and some half public.

---

44 Little did I know...
45 The forward plan only has to show decisions to be taken in the next twenty eight days.

So I don't think it's whether something is in the public eye or not, I think it's having time to understand the detail and contribute to decisions early on so nobody loses face if unfortunate discoveries are made or U turns considered.

Don't get me wrong there is still a place for holding the administration to account for Value for Money or Lack of Process for example, so I'm talking about the mix of effort between scrutiny of Cabinet decisions versus that done much earlier on."

I then added a little verbal flourish saying we need to take account of whether we have an overly sensitive Labour administration or a cold and heartless Tory one.

"So in conclusion, depending on the sensitivity of the next administration, you might wish to tailor the 2020-24 approach to scrutiny to reflect that sensitivity (or not) as a reality of the culture you will be working in. If you do, then I would hope the administration in turn would help you and tell you the longer term projects it is working on so you can inject worthwhile effort much earlier on."

Comment: I made a mistake in my approach, did you spot it? It was the verbal flourish; I pissed off both the Conservative and Labour members on this scrutiny group, the highest in Bristol, and since Greens are only the third biggest party my point didn't get the traction I was after. But whether the next administration will be cold and heartless or over sensitive, good local scrutiny comes early on when it can really influence policy....

TAKEAWAYS

Summary[46] (of Section B) In this section we have covered the nature of power, leaders in power and their supporters and why and how they capture the economy for their benefits. In a democracy this dynamic should be balanced by having as many people vote as possible so that to form a government a leader should need fifty percent or more of the electorate.

To have a meaningful vote the public need to know and that starts with their elected representatives knowing what's going on. Ideally decisions are not being taken by unaccountable officers, or information withheld, this destroys trust and corrodes democracy.

The press play an important role[47], their impact is referred to throughout this book and we look specifically at the Local Democracy Reporting role in Section H.

Information on emerging policy when available should be scrutinised, we explored an approach where it was discussed early, initially in secret and then brought into the public domain for further debate. It needs to be done early to improve the quality of decisions. In fact I've decided that scrutiny is so important[48] it deserves a special, bonus chapter. So here it is...

CHAPTER B11
A BRIEF HISTORY OF SCRUTINY

Autumn 2017; at the same time that Bristol's Councillors were navel gazing about how to do better local scrutiny[49], so the Government[50] were doing the same nationally. They launched an inquiry into the operation

---

46   This isn't quite the end. I've added a bonus chapter after this called a brief history of scrutiny.
47   The Centre for Public Scrutiny thinks so too. www.cfps.org.uk/scrutiny-and-local-journalism/
48   If for no other reason that this is public money: Tax payers need to know and be confident that there are checks and balances on power to invest or waste their taxes.
49   Due to budget cuts from the Mayor (due to Government cuts).
50   The House of Commons Communities and Local Government Committee

of local government scrutiny in January 2017 and at the end of the year they were receiving evidence about its workings and non-workings.

Local government scrutiny is a relatively new invention, introduced in The Local Government Act 2000. Before then, Councils operated a committee system (no Mayors, no executive, no cabinet) but the Blair government felt that introducing some accountability (someone to blame?) was a good idea. With that change bringing in an executive (cabinets with or without Mayors) but limited to nine, that left "backbench Councillors" needing something to do. The idea was they would scrutinise the executive.

It was clear quite quickly that things weren't working properly, changes were planned in 2008 but didn't progress. In 2011 two academics[51] David Wilson and Chris Game reported that three conditions were required for overview and scrutiny to realise its full potential: New skills[52] for Councillors: both technical and learning how to work together[53] and thirdly dedicated officer support.

On to 2012[54], there was now an option for Councils to go back to the old committee system (scrapped in 2000). By 2017 we had this new Inquiry[55] a real serious look taken at local government scrutiny.

Some snippets from the evidence submitted:

The Government's Cabinet Member at the time, Marcus Jones MP, said[56]:

"Overview and scrutiny committees have two functions. The first, as you say, is holding the executive to account, but in many ways it can be equally important that scrutiny develops policy in a particular area".

---

51   De Montford University and University of Birmingham respectively
52   Assessing and probing, working collaboratively to draw out evidence and views from witnesses, and understanding performance indicators, comparative data and financial processes in a way that few will have done previously.
53   Party 'whipping' and tight disciplinary regimes need to be relaxed, something that does not come easily to members who may have spent their entire lives opposing just about everything their political opponents stand for.
54   Via the Localism Act 2011.
55   https://www.parliament.uk/business/committees/committees-a-z/commons-select/communities-and-local-government-committee/inquiries/parliament-2017/local-authority-scrutiny-17-19/publications/
56   Oral evidence at 6/11/17 Q110

Comment: I agree whole heartedly with Marcus about the two different functions. They are quite dissimilar. It is a shame they are both called scrutiny.

a) Holding the executive to account is about discussing the proposals about to come for a decision and if things look bad or there is poor process, scrutiny has the power of "call in" after a decision has been made (so it has to be remade perhaps with more information).

b) Policy development is different, it should occur months, years even before implementation. It is the one in my view that adds most value and is most neglected. Why? Because, if you have for example, a Labour administration they don't want other parties messing with their policies. What's the point of people voting Labour and them winning if they don't then get Labour policies. The fact that a Labour (or any other administration) can get into power with 35% of the vote seems to get forgotten. What about the other 65%? In Bristol policy development does happen occasionally. These are termed working groups and are kicked off by an enlightened Cabinet Member or Officer.

In evidence submitted to the Inquiry in 2017. Professor Copus[57] said,

"Executive accountability is absolutely vital. It is an area where some overview and scrutiny committees struggle, because you are asking members of the majority[58] political party to challenge in public an executive they put in place. Often that area is fraught with some difficulty, but it is a prime role for an overview and scrutiny committee.

The other role is policy influencing through evidence collection. One of the complaints I often hear from Councils is, "We cannot make decisions in overview and scrutiny". No, that is right: you cannot. However, you can shape and influence policy if you develop an evidence base either aimed at some internal service the Council itself provides or, more often, aimed at some external policy area.

---

57   Professor Colin Copus, Director of the Local Governance Research Unit, De Montfort University, submitting evidence on 16/10/19 at Q8.
58   In Bristol it means you are asking whipped Labour members to criticise (constructively) the Labour Mayor.

The good professor continues at Q12.

> *"The place to look at is something like Select Committees here or, indeed, Select Committees in the US Senate. Irrespective of whether there is a President or Prime Minister of your political colour, your job is to scrutinise.*

Comment: There are two types of scrutiny: holding to account which is aggressive questioning, party political often. It is necessary. This is the type that in my experience cabinet, Mayors and their press release obsessed advisors hate.

Then there's the policy development type which should happen well before and requires cross party working, open minded officers and cabinet members. It's rarely news worthy but is what's needed to make better policy.

As a result of this Inquiry the Good Scrutiny Guide came out in 2019. One interesting bit is access to information which you will know is one of my hobby horses. Scrutiny members now have slightly broader[59] rights (than Councillors and the public), not wide enough for my taste but it is progress. Statutory Guidance[60] came out too. I'll pick just four clauses and comment directly underneath each one. Clause 11(c): asks for early and regular engagement between the executive and scrutiny – especially regarding the latter's future work programme.

> **Re above**: *In Bristol the Forward Plan (future work programme) regularly gave Scrutiny less than 30 days' notice of what was coming to Cabinet (and then just a few words or a title). Deliberately designed in my view to make it difficult to scrutinise and hold them to account. It's a little better now.*

---

59 The provisions permitting information from being withheld (Exempt) do not apply to overview and scrutiny committees regarding information which relates to: (i) an action or decision that that member is reviewing or scrutinising; or (ii) any review contained in any programme of work of such a committee or sub-committee of such a committee; or (b) of a document or part of a document containing advice provided by a political adviser or assistant.
60 www.gov.uk/government/publications/overview-and-scrutiny-statutory-guidance-for-councils-and-combined-authorities

Clause 12: A strong organisational culture that supports scrutiny is particularly important in mayoral authorities. To ensure there are the checks and balances to maintain a robust democratic system.

Re above: *I read this that mayoral authorities were taking the worst liberties with scrutiny. A Mayor has enormous power over all in the organisation.*

Clause 68: The results from Evidence Sessions should be fed into Cabinet Members for comment.

Re: above. *Evidence gathering and task and finish groups relate to policy development, the type I like.*

And below, the most important clause of the whole lot; how the public fit in (also about collecting evidence). Although clause 53 is limited to the work programme, it leads me to consideration of the use of citizens' assemblies and juries to look at issues too. This in my view is part of the solution.

Clause 53: Gathering evidence requires conversations with the public. Asking individual scrutiny members to have conversations with individuals and groups in their own local areas can work better that formal consultation.

In Bristol and bringing us to April 2020 UWE and UofB issued a joint report[61] which Amanda Cameron[62] reported on and said in Bristol, Councillors are being side lined and opportunities to hold the Mayor to account with good scrutiny have plummeted. They recommended residents should get involved. I agree, especially in policy development scrutiny.

---

61   https://www.bristolpost.co.uk/news/bristol-news/elected-mayor-bristol-harder-hold-4079631 UWE; University of West of England and UoB is University of Bristol
62   One of Bristol's BBC funded local democracy reporters (started 2019)

LOCAL GOVERNMENT SCRUTINY

Summary of B11: Local Government Scrutiny. Councillors have to fight for their seats every four years, they have an electorate with limited attention spans so it's a press release dominated world. Scrutiny work is rewarded by the press coverage occurring around the Cabinet meeting papers. There are no political rewards for policy development, except the personal feeling of, "yes, I made a difference".

The solution? Professor Copus suggested to model scrutiny on Parliamentary Select Committees. We shall look at that in the next section. My own view is to involve the public in policy development, in a big way. We pick up Citizens' Juries and Assemblies later in the book. Bristol City Council are looking to pilot these but they have so far given the job to the department tasked with consultation. I think that needs changing. CJs and CAs are tools to improve policy development. Without more open policy development processes I question whether CJs and CAs will work. We shall see.

Comment: Perhaps lowly Local Authorities can learn from their Lords and Masters up in the Lords and the Commons. Scrutiny in Government starts off the next section, C.

SECTION C
HAND-ME-DOWNS
FROM GOVERNMENT

INTRODUCTION

"Scrutiny is shocking"
"The scrutiny of legislation here is very bad"

These quotes come from page 84 of *Why We Get The Wrong Politicians* by Isabel Hardman[1]. Isabel isn't talking about Bristol City Council. She is talking about the Houses of Parliament. Here are some other quotes from the same page:

"Scrutiny in Parliament is terrible, you definitely get bad legislation coming out."

And back in 2015 Frank Dobson MP apparently said,

"Even if you don't agree with the laws, at least the bloody things ought to work, and so frequently they don't"

You'd think that the elected chamber, The Commons, the one that's chosen by the people, sort of democratically, would be the good scrutineers. It must be that unelected chamber, The Lords, the one many voters want to totally remove[2]; surely it's the Lords who get in the way of good scrutiny, good law and instead favour themselves, fat cats and rich landowners?

Isabel's book quotes Wes Streeting, a Labour MP in 2015,

"I think the Lords is much better for scrutiny than the Commons. Patronage is so strong (in the Commons) and the executive dominates in the Commons, we don't really have time for scrutiny."

We learned from the last section it is good scrutiny, the earlier the better; that ensures good decisions. And surprise, surprise, without good scrutiny the laws are not so good. If you want to see how not good they can really get, then read Isabel's book.

In the next few chapters we will see the bad intended and unintended consequences of national law-making and how they have impacted upon us in Bristol (and presumably most other places). One role of us Councillors is to sweep up Governments' mess.

---

2   And many of those who don't want it shut down say they want elected members in the House of Lords.

CHAPTER C1
I BLAME THE GOVERNMENT OR SHOULD I BLAME THE KING?

January 2020: She[3] nabbed me in the street. I knew she was going to, she had that determined look on her face. I also sensed the topic was going to be the very same thing that Poppy, who lives opposite, had tackled me about the night before. Oh to be so popular with the ladies! But I was on the home run[4] of my Councillorship and I thought it was time to tell some truths and this chapter is in one way an apology to both these charming women.

Their complaint, that's the only reason I'm nabbed by anyone at the moment, was about fly-tipping in and alongside a builder's skip next to a pizza takeaway right on a main shopping road. The builder is refurbishing some conservation grade buildings and needs somewhere to store the waste before it's collected. And just opposite is a small patch of land with uncertain ownership rights, perfect for a skip.

Some history is needed: The builder had originally organised a half container so it could be locked up and fenced off so it didn't attract fly-tipping. Despite his best intentions it did attract some and attracted quite a few residents' complaints too, including from Carol and Poppy who decided the container was an eyesore. And to support my residents, we complained to Planning Enforcement. Six months later the Enforcement Department decided it had been there long enough to be classed as a permanent structure without planning permission and so asked that it be removed. It was and what was the builder to do instead? He hired a skip which he knew would attract fly-tipping, and it did. Residents complained and when it was full it was removed, emptied, a new one put in its place, more fly-tipping and so the cycle went on.

Back to being nabbed: Carol then asked me why can't he put the skip in the builders yard another 50m up the road (a different builders).

3   Let's call her Carol.
4   Or so I thought

"They're a private company",

I said, beginning to lose patience (from hunger, probably). I added,

"So you ask them. It's their private land but they can only say no".

Perhaps she thought I should ask them? Not now with just four months to go. I explained the least worst option was a half container like he had had before, or of course he might actually finish the building work which seemed never ending. What's the builder doing? A nuclear bunker?

The laws afforded to Councils don't allow the resolution of such a problem. The skip is permitted, it attracts fly-tipping, it gets complained about and then eventually cleared away. And a new cycle starts. Maybe that's how it's meant to be. People are free to do what they want unless there are powers to stop them. If so, and I think that's broadly right in a liberal democracy, then stop complaining to us Councillors as we can't and perhaps shouldn't do anything?

And another thing: This is where my rant to Carol starts properly. She has lived in the area a while and is part of the local community group. She doesn't use the internet so communicates to me either by nabbing me on my way to or from Sainsbury or sending a message to Poppy who then emails me. But that didn't stop my rant building up, moving to the latest initiative to do with recycling. (The Council have introduced a blue bag for residents to help improve recycling rates of cardboard, it can be folded and importantly doesn't take up much room so is ideal for use in a flat).

"But what if it's wet?"

She asked. I had an answer to that,

"The main problem is all the student houses, they don't have space for recycling boxes and bins, a bag is better,"

Carol considered that. Now it was my turn,

"And what about bicycles? Residents don't allow us to put bike racks on the roads or pavements, insurance companies don't allow bikes to be stored in the communal areas of these multiple occupancy houses. We want people to cycle but refuse to give them anywhere to store their bikes".

My arms were waving quite animatedly now. Carol was looking alarmed and took a step back.

I could have talked on and on: about parking spaces, litter, noise, overdevelopment, not clearing away leaves, blocked drains, student parties and much more. These are the important things that those who have a home, an income and aren't in need of social care worry about around here. I didn't talk about them, I jumped quite a few steps of logic and moved the topic straight onto the person to blame.

I'd clearly lost the plot by now. I got onto an emerging hobby horse of mine; the need for more local powers in cities. To illustrate that the laws and rules needed in cities are nowadays quite different to those needed in rural areas, I jumped to blaming King John. Actually I should have attributed King Henry II, for it was he, in 1154, who started the process of unifying[5] the laws of this land and gave us common law too. It is clear to me that in 2020 that city problems and rural problems are so different, we need different rules. So my apologies to the much maligned King John.

Carol glanced down at my shopping, decided I was going mad and allowed me to continue my walk home.

Comment: If you think I was "cracking up" in January then by March 2020 my emotional state was getting worse. I think writing this book wasn't helping, it brought home the futility of it all; then came Bristol Energy (see chapter C6).

So on Friday 20th March I told my colleagues I was intending to

---

5   In those days the King was the Executive and the barons were Government. As explained recently by Lady Hale, she of the spider brooch.

stand down during this imposed fifth year, I wasn't going to last much more. It would be at a date to be determined, so long as the by-election it would trigger could be held at a safe time. Just telling them was tough, we rely on mutual support and now one was dropping out. The strain of Covid-19 was telling.

Then when it couldn't get more futile I got an email a bit later from a Tree Planning Officer about an application to fell a small tree. The tree wasn't that great, but it seemed the Officer was giving permission without insisting on a replacement. It was a development site, therefore it should have been against the planning conditions. That was something I'd worked on since before I was elected. Meetings had been held with Officers in 2015, 2017 and 2019 to reiterate policy. I was so angry that I couldn't take the call. I emailed to wait until Monday maybe I'd calm down. I sent an email to that effect. His boss then contacted me to complain about my behaviour.

It's a recurring idea within this book as to whether some laws should be different in cities and in rural areas.

In 2018, Bristol hosted an International Conference with about 80 Mayors from different cities across the world. One quote I recall from the press coverage was that they decided they had more in common with one another than they had with villages possibly just ten or twenty miles away from them. That seems so true. Cities need the rural areas of course for food if for nothing else but also countryside, recreation, country pubs and much more. Do rural areas need cities? Presumably yes, they are a source of jobs, a market for their products and food and much more. They live in a symbiotic[6] relationship. But why should they have the same laws?

As there are so many problems with law making, asking for two sets might compound the problem. To follow is an example of the mess caused by Universal Credit; one system across our land.

---

6   I have been advised the exact term is a mutualistic symbiotic relationship, so there.

CHAPTER C2
UNIVERSAL CREDIT – A CREDIT TO ANYONE?

Below is a briefing that I gave to my fellow Green Councillors in December 2019. I wrote it following a meeting with officers and it was approved by officers. I shall not name them to keep them out of trouble, they work very hard within a poorly designed system. I have edited it to make it a bit more understandable but it illustrates the detail needed to understand what's going wrong. And as it has affected so many people, especially since Covid-19 threw millions onto Universal Credit, it might be of interest to many of you. One would hope there was good scrutiny from those in Westminster in advance to ensure it wouldn't go wrong. Decide for yourself whether that scrutiny was effective.

"We have heard much about the hardships that UC brings to recipients: the famed five-week delay, mitigated by applying for a two week cash advance that must be paid back within the year (that way you only receive 49 weeks' benefit cash in the first year and from that you need to save up two-weeks' worth to pay the cash advance back). The amount changes each month if your income varies, as it would for example, if you are on zero hours contracts or do irregular overtime. UC is now replacing housing benefit too and unless direct payment to the landlord is requested, the recipient needs to manage their money so, so carefully, just one domestic disaster away from spiralling debt problems leading to homelessness.

"And that's before the dreaded sanctions (which are not the subject of this briefing).

"Many, many people on UC are working hard, it's just the economic system doesn't pay them enough to live on.

"This struggle can be alleviated by Local Crisis Funds, but there is more and more call on these. Often the staff in the centre have to point the increasingly desperate and presumably hungry "service users" to food banks, a 39% increase in referrals when compared to 2018 at the last count. Some local authorities have closed down their Local Crisis Prevention Funds altogether, people fall, some are lucky and land in the hands of charity, others drop into the jaws of loan sharks. It's whoever gets them first. Others move, often to cities like Bristol where there is still some compassion.

"Bristol is granted, from Government, a discretionary housing payment allowance of £1.1m/year to help those in most need. It's fully used up each year.

"UC was supposed to reduce administration. It does in part. Centrally; the Real Time Tax information that employers fill in is collected by HMRC (Tax) and communicated automatically to the benefits IT system at the Department for Work and Pensions (DWP). This means the UC benefit calculation responds to week by week changes in income. This is communicated to local authorities (who administer all benefits). But the local authorities use different software than DWP. Local authority software is provided by Capita or Northgate or another of the four main providers. Their software is not connected into this great new system. Information is input by hand. So although the caseload of old housing benefit in Bristol has fallen by some 14% because of UC, the workload per case keeping up with the changes each week and inputting by hand has gone up and overall the amount of work has remained the same whilst funds for staffing have fallen. Government don't recognise this lack of joined up IT and so have cut the staff funding payment to Bristol Council by £270,000 per year to cover the "falling administration costs" of Housing Benefit, UC and Council Tax Reduction. This drop in funding is set to continue until those left on Housing Benefit are either pensioners or those living in exempt or temporary accommodation. That will be about a 68% drop. That will mean a fall in payments from Government of over £1 million per year and until Capita, Northgate and friends integrate with the DWP software then it will all rely on human inputting. Does anyone know their plans?

"As less and less people claim housing benefit (because UC replaces it) there will be a stage where Councils aren't able to easily collect overpaid housing benefit, this currently stands at £8 million. Housing benefit is often overpaid and was easy to claw back. You might fairly ask why some housing benefits are overpaid? The most common reason is someone gets a job and delays telling the Local Authority which then with its own delays takes time to reduce or stop payments. This wasn't an issue as it could be clawed back slowly.

"But not in the future, because LAs won't be dealing with the UC payments themselves, they are just a conduit for a direct payment and won't be able in future to deduct say a fiver a week to slowly recoup the overpaid money. There is no agreement with the DWP how to resolve any remaining debts once someone is moved across to UC. And how many years has UC been running now?

"By 2023[7] all those of working age not in exempt or temporary accommodation should have transferred.

"In future local authority debt (for overpaid housing benefits) will rank alongside water bills or other dues which will involve more collection costs, less money recovered and dare I say more bailiffs?

"Bristol also operates a fully funded Council Tax Reduction Scheme CTRS, the only core city left still operating to the original Council Tax Benefit rules. Whilst this has to be maintained for pensioners by law, it can be changed or even abandoned for people of working age. Bristol hasn't changed it, but could modify it to make it administratively easier to operate in a world of UC. This was attempted in 2017 but done so clumsily that a campaign forced no change at all. Changes are needed, for instance not processing fluctuations in claims for amounts less than £1. As working age people are migrated to UC, the administration that was shared across benefits and Council Tax Reduction will only be doing the latter throwing a disproportionate admin cost onto that scheme. It is thought it might cost £1.5 million/year in admin just to run a scheme of about £38 million. With Government funding being reduced, some suggestions need to come forward for consultation in the next Mayoral term, perhaps even June 2020[8].

"Finally tapers[9] (also called benefits traps). As we earn more we pay tax

7　This date was delayed again and then there was Covid-19 so who knows?
8　The Mayoral elections have been delayed to 2021 now
9　A taper is the rate at which you lose your benefit as your earnings increase. If your after tax earnings increased by £100 you'd lose £63 of Universal Credit and another £20 of Council Tax Reduction. That leaves you with £17.

and national insurance, typically someone earning £200 a week would pay 20% tax and 12% NI on the final bit of pay (after their allowances) and on any extra earnings. So if they had the chance to earn another £100 gross[10], by working say 10 more hours, they would see £68 after tax and national insurance deductions in their payslip. Tapers work on the net income. HMRC would inform the DWP and the UC payment claws back 63% of extra net income and also Council Tax Reduction drops by 20%. So if you were in receipt of both then out of that £68 net income you would see in the following month a deduction of 83% (£56.44) less in benefit. Overall you'd be left with a little less than £12 for those 10 hours of work, before you pay the bus fares and for any other extras. That's about £1.20 an hour. Hardly worth it especially if the job is meaningless. I suggested to the officers that they consider a 15% CTRS taper rather than 20%. The difference would be worth another £3.40 to the person in that instance. Not much, the real improvement would come with a lower taper rate for UC to say 40% but that's for the Government. Interestingly a Universal Basic Income[11] could help, if structured right, to reduce the benefit taper problem even with UC. UC has reduced some of worst[12] traps that occurred with the old system of six separate benefits plus Council Tax Reduction.

Comment: So in summary; there's only so much a LA can do. The Council Tax Reduction Scheme needs to be looked at (assuming UC continues) from a taper and administration cost point of view. June 2020 could be a good time to do it. Efficiencies in administering UC await software from Northgate and Capita etc. And there's a risk to being too compassionate an authority, it attracts those in need from other areas. Or perhaps this is something Bristol should be proud of?"

10   Gross i.e. pre-tax and NI.
11   Also called a Citizens' Income and a Universal Income. Where everyone receives the same amount from the State.
12   Negative marginal income. This means if you worked 10 hours, earned £100 gross paid £32 tax and NI so leaving £68 after tax but then had benefits cut by more than the £68 so effectively you earned negative income. So in that respect UC is an improvement but keeping £12 out of the £100 before tax still isn't much of an incentive.

As reported by BBC News, Financial Times, The Independent, The Times, The Daily Telegraph, Daily Mail, Daily Express:
4th Feb 2020 Further delays to full UC rollout.
Full rollout of universal credit (UC) is being delayed again, adding £500m to its overall cost. The system was meant to be fully live by April 2017, but the new delay will push it back to September 2024. Welfare delivery minister Will Quince claimed that claimants will not lose money as a result of the change.   All these news clips with thanks to LGiU.

Update: July 2020. It seems that the software automation needed to link to the DWP system has progressed somewhat.

Comment: Perhaps someone has now realised the problems with UC? The Conservatives started planning all this fifteen years ago, in the Blair years. Was it properly scrutinised early on by people who understand what it's like to be on low and irregular wages? And by people from a wide range of backgrounds so as to bring in different perspectives? You probably guessed right. And why didn't the Civil Service identify these issues in 2010?

CHAPTER C3
A TALE OF TWO CAPS – MORE HARMFUL CONSEQUENCES

Housing is a basic need, perhaps not as high on the scale as air, water and food but it would come next on my list. Bristol, like many cities, suffers from expensive housing, when I last looked average house prices were ten times average wages. In my day[13], to get on the housing ladder you could get a mortgage for three times salary and needed a deposit of a thousand pounds or so, that was not so easy to cobble together even then. Now you need a deposit of maybe £100,000 or more.

Back in the 1980s, in middle class circles, rising house prices made

13   In 1980

for popular chat, for those on the ladder anyway, and especially when they were going up which was nearly all the time. Conversation was about how much money you "made" this year,

"Oh do you know next door sold for £34,000, I've earned more on my home this year than from working".

And so we chinked our glasses and moved on to the next topic of conversation, before we were married that would be football or women. After marriage I can't recall.

Looking back, it's all a bit embarrassing, but that's how it was, can't deny it. Nearly 40 years on, house prices are clearly unsustainable[14]. Our whole economy seemed and seems to run off rising house prices, re-mortgage and pay for your extension, new car and holidays. And for some youngsters it is still the case. Children whose parents were on that gravy train will be able to ride it until it finally hits the buffers, but what about those left at the gravy station? It is unfair.

All Governments have created schemes that usually involve subsidies for first time buyers (paid from our taxes). More recently, as they have become more desperate, often due to actions of their own making, they have asked property developers to subsidise housing. About time, but Government has added a requirement that developers only have to provide "affordable housing[15]" if they are going to make profits in excess of 20% on a building site. This latter requirement is policed via Local Authority Planning Departments and their Committees on which Councillors preside including me.

In 2012, at the beginning of the Austerity years, the coalition Government did two sudden, and in my view, quite stupid things. Firstly they took the cap off student numbers at universities. At £9,000 a student, the more students a university can capture the better, for the university and for vice chancellor salaries, which of course rocketed. Some universities expanded like crazy. University of Bristol was one

---

14   Why rising house prices is long term unsustainable is explained in more detail later.
15   This is discussed in depth at section H.

of these and added some 10,000 new places. These students are most welcome of course, they add to the vibrancy of the city, but Bristol as a city had to find 7,000 bed spaces for them after they moved out of their first year hall of residence. Private enterprise found a way, landlords upped existing rents, evicted poorer families who became homeless and filled their properties with higher paying students.

Stupid Government act number two was to cap the amount of money Councils could borrow to build new Council houses. So on top of losing affordable housing stock to right to buy (a slight aside: I've recently been told of a beneficiary of right to buy advertised their home at over £600,000. It had been bought from Bristol City Council a few years ago at a quarter of the price). Councils were further hamstrung and couldn't even build enough homes to plug those losses. I won't mention the other stupid acts by Government like: reducing the rental income from Council houses so that the whole business model of Council house provision began to fail. I also won't mention that much of the income to a Council from Right to Buy is returned to Government so it's almost impossible to fund the building of new ones[16]. And the result of stupid act number two? We are left with 10,000 families on the housing list. Was the Government stupid, not interested in the poor, or just simply uncaring for people that don't vote for them? – You decide.

> My take on this is it's due to poor scrutiny, yet again. It is obvious what would happen taking the cap off student intake per university would do. You might not be able to predict which ones would expand, but some would, that's presumably why some asked for the cap to be removed. And what about the consequential impact and costs to the public of that housing loss?
>
> The Council housing borrowing cap was to keep the lid on the deficit which was mushrooming at the time following the bailout of the banks. So let's work this through, fewer Council houses leads to more

16   The Ministry of Housing, Communities and Local Government released the following information (written up in The Independent on 21 June 2020): "Since the Right to Buy policy was updated in 2012/13, 85,645 homes have been sold through the policy, while just 28,090 have been built to replace them using receipts earmarked for this purpose".

homelessness. Rocket science? Who was predicting this in scrutiny? Did the Government listen?

Strong stable Government is what we need, we are told, to me that means the ability to implement bad laws.

LICENSING OF BARS AND CLUBS (1)

I love going to the pub. But I never much enjoyed pub licensing and left most of the Councillor work to Carla who did an admirable job and is so good with follow up. But she couldn't make this particular licence review meeting, so after two and a half years of abstinence, in July 2019, I was dragged in to getting involved and representing residents versus the owners of a basement cocktail bar who wanted to have a licence to be able to use their outdoor terrace for serving drinks.

There needs to be a balance, we need a thriving night life economy, it brings enjoyment for the public, successful businesses for jobs and also to pay the rates which fund a third of Council activity, and Government[17] activity too. It's fine as long as they don't cause too much harm.

The then Prime Minister, Tony Blair, brought in the 2003 Licensing Act (enacted in 2005), some of you may remember him saying that he was trying to make Britain a more European society with bars open late, tables out on the pavement and engender a culture with a more mature approach to alcohol. Also, perhaps with a hidden agenda was to respond to the growing impact of the internet on traditional retail and so relaxing the laws for food, drink and entertainment, it was a way of helping sustain high streets too? One of the changes he brought in was that licences were to be granted by the Council and each case decided by three Councillors. These three sit in what's called a licensing sub-committee in a supposedly more relaxed process, before you had to apply to a magistrates' court and a more difficult process.

---

17   Bristol sends something like £80 million of its Business Rates to fund Government each year.

So roll on thirteen years to 2016, and my first few months as a Councillor; the impact of the 2003 Act was described by some residents as bringing vomit and food detritus to the pavements, hordes of youths late at night singing and shouting their way up the streets waking everyone up as they left establishments en masse at four am. Exaggeration? Possibly, but there had been a night club near our local station that apparently caused just that, it had temporarily closed in 2014 and there were rumours it might reopen. Panic was setting in.

My first experience of a licensing sub-committee was later that same year and it gave me the impression of mainly untrained new Councillors being told by the Council's legal advisor what to say and do. In this case they granted a four am licence to a takeaway; kebabs I think, and added new late night services of food and alcohol delivery to residents that wanted them at those hours. Other residents had visions of fleets of mopeds waiting outside at 3.30am ready to burn off down the streets waking up all those who had finally managed to get some sleep after a student party had kept them up until 3am. Suggesting that a delivery of kebabs at 4am might quieten everyone down was not appreciated by locals.

Not all the Councillors on the sub-committee were untrained (lack of training was actually permitted back then). At the hearing in City Hall, the applicant had their own solicitor, they, plus the Council's legal advisor made it feel like we were in a magistrates' court after all. But worse than that; it was without experienced magistrates who could at least give the Legal Advisor short shrift if they felt the advice was inappropriate. In City Hall the lawyers reigned supreme. Needless to say we lost and I went away licking my wounds and the takeaway has its 4am licence. At least the hordes of mopeds didn't materialise.

I suffered another experience a few months later, less painful as I then knew what to expect, but an equally dismal showing. I handed licensing over to Carla and I concentrated on planning.

Knowing what I wasn't good at, I worked in other areas and I added licensing to my list of allergies which already included dealing with the

Highways Department[18].

Right! Back to the basement cocktail bar, my third licensing experience and in July 2019, the licence review I couldn't avoid: the bar had been open a year and wanted (maybe needed) to offer a different experience; the local evening entertainment sector is pretty competitive around here and clientele, I'm told, are a bit flighty and are drawn to whichever bar is in fashion or open the latest or both. The entrance to their basement bar is up a few steps across a terrace/patio and then down to the underground level. Their perfectly natural idea was to apply for a drinks licence until 11pm for the patio (waiter service) so people could sit out on warm evenings, gaze across the Downs and watch the sun go down supping their sundowner. They said they'd close the terrace at 11pm and they calculated they could then shepherd their guests down into the cocktail bar until 2am to earn more money from them, sounds logical.

But they hadn't reckoned on the residents living next to and above in the nearby buildings (converted to multiple flats). The owners had invited residents over to discuss the plans and have a drink but people usually don't react kindly if they have already decided that there's an enemy next door, they won't negotiate, they want their fight, day in court and so it was to be.

I had sent in an email back in June suggesting the patio be completely cleared away by 11pm. One resident had contacted me, she put in a representation[19] as they are called in licensing. Statements are the description for everything else like planning, scrutiny, cabinet, Full Council. But that word is not good enough for licensing. Do you detect in me a hint of partisanship?

---

18   I had to cut the diary entry for 15th May 2016 due to space reasons. But in summary the first Highways closure report I got to see as a new Councillor was to close part of a main shopping road to traffic for 18 months. This brought flashbacks of the dreadful treatment that Highways had caused me on the Neighbourhood Partnerships and it seemed they wanted to do the very same in my first week as a Councillor. Fortunately once I got the detail it was a five week closure (sometime within that eighteen month period) and it was at the other end of the street so the traders would still get their passing trade. I never gelled with Highways at all. They don't care for the public in my view, just cars and tarmac.

19   If you put in a representation into a Licensing Review you then become "a person who has made a relevant representation", that status gives you access to the Licensing meeting and a chance to speak and discuss your issues. Putting in a statement to a planning meeting gives you a right to speak (usually one minute) but not to discuss any further.

Anyway as it was licensing and you know I am allergic to it, I decided not to attend the hearing, it all seemed simple enough. I had scheduled something else for that next morning.

But then late afternoon, I was contacted by phone and email by a rather distraught lady who said she'd been away, had just come back to read that there would be drinkers on the terrace staring down at her while she sat sunbathing in her garden and they would be able to stare in through her front window too. And worse she had just been told she was too late to submit a statement – no, I mean a representation. Fortunately the helpful licensing officer said I could add this new information to my written representation and so I duly did, I suggested a screen like a fence or hedge and closing the terrace at 10pm. I sent it off early evening.

I didn't sleep well, my mind in continuous loop,

"should I be present? Should I not show? No, I wasn't really needed. But what if I can make a difference?"

So with that circulating around my head combined with one of the hottest nights of the year and the after effects of a few beers as I confess I'd been out that evening too.

The next morning over breakfast I was still unsure, "should I go or should I stay?"

CHAPTER C5
LICENSING BARS AND CLUBS (2) – SHOULD I STAY OR SHOULD I GO?

Supping my cup of tea and with a mild headache I looked down at my diary, crossed an appointment out, put some sandals on and off. I was in shorts and tee shirt[20] as I hadn't planned to go and fight with the Legals. I set off somewhat dejected down to City Hall. I'd be late, it was going to be hot and no time to change there, but licensing committees always

---

20   At least I wasn't in my pyjamas.

start late anyway. One thing I haven't told you yet. The day before, I asked officers if I could see the other representations, those from the police, environmental health and if there were any from other neighbours. "No", came the reply, "we only send them to the applicant". My hackles rose, with licensing you wouldn't think there was more room for my hackles to rise higher, but they did.

"Do you mean that not only does the applicant have a right to a lawyer, but they can see all the representations and I, the democratically elected representative of the neighbours, cannot. What kind of justice is this, it's not fair, it's not democratic?"

And I shot off an email to Democratic Services with words to that effect. The reply,

"But we've always done it this way, it's what the Act says".

My follow up email was along the lines of "I'll get you when this is over". You being plural for the department and policy and not the officer, she was just doing her job.

I arrived ten minutes late, they hadn't started, so I sat down next to Adam, one of the local democracy reporters, paid for by the BBC apparently, he'd started in January 2019 he writes up these meetings for any local papers to pick up on. He had the unenviable job of sitting through three licence applications, so probably seven hours in total and then doing a write up which may or may not be published. I got to know Adam better over the coming months.

A Council Licensing officer came over to check we were alright and I let rip on lack of democracy, not being able to see the representations and thus not being able to do my job. He said he'd look into it afterwards.

We entered the room and to my horror that very same officer was there providing advice to the subcommittee. And sitting next to him was the lawyer too, I hoped, "he won't bear a grudge, will he?" I wasn't sure.

As it turned out the applicants appeared very reasonable and accommodating. They suggested changes themselves and they didn't have a solicitor. And the Council's lawyer was also equitable. Most lawyers dress in their tailored suits but the Council's one was more relaxed, not a tee shirt but apparel appropriate for Tony Blair's original, more informal plan for licensing sub committees.

It started, we all had our say, I heard that Environmental Health wanted a 9pm closure Sunday to Thursday and 10pm Friday and Saturday, "damn it", I'd asked for 10pm, if only I'd known.

An hour and a half later the meeting broke, the subcommittee of three Councillors, all trained this time, would make their decision in private. I asked Adam if he wanted a coffee, he did. On my return, we chatted; his son had just come back from an international chess tournament. He didn't win, but impressive all the same. Unsurprisingly we got back onto the subject of other neighbouring local authorities.

"You know Clive, they all publish the representations, it's only Bristol that doesn't".

And Adam then emailed me a link to licensing papers from the other three authorities with examples showing that what he said was exactly right. "Good on you Adam, I owe you a pint" I thought to myself. I offered him another coffee instead, it was only 11.30am.

With that evidence I thought, "right that does it". And I banged out this email to BCC's Head of Legal.

Here is some evidence why the default position for information has to be openness and transparency. I discovered yesterday that Bristol City Council is the only Local Authority (in our region) not to publish licensing representations for others to see. This is due to some mistaken interpretation of the 2003 Licensing Act.

I am getting this corrected (after 14 years of this information being hidden) so there is no need for you to do anything other than note that if BCC had a default of "openness and transparency" rather than "need to know" then officers would not have made what I think is a mistake.

I still feel parts of Bristol City Council operate in a culture of secrecy. We need to break this. The Member Officer Protocol is getting there but we must take this opportunity to make it clear across the whole organisation that information should be open unless there are reasons to keep it exempt[21]. At the moment there are pockets (like licensing representations) where the default is exempt unless the Law says it must be open. That is not acceptable in this day and age.

I finished it off more politely in writing than I actually wanted to, and then waited, I nagged and nagged and finally got an answer in March 2020, eight months later from the Council's top legal guy. It's all about Section 185 of the Licensing Act 2003 apparently.

His abridged response was,

"Section 185 states that information obtained must not be further disclosed except to a licensing authority or responsible authority for the purposes mentioned in subsection (2). That means it can only be seen by Council officers. And the Licensing Act 2003 (Hearings) Regulations of 2005 says that if representations are made then a notice of a hearing is sent out to the applicant and all others (residents, Councillors, officers) who have made representations. The applicant is provided with copies of all relevant representations including those from residents and Councillors. The applicant has a right to a fair hearing. Nobody else other than the Council can see the representations. Local residents will receive a notice of the hearing only, no details of what others have said."

So it seems Parliament deliberately intended that Councillors and residents would face a biased process when fighting for their rights to sleep and in some cases their mental health if you happen to have a night club open until 4am at the bottom of your road. Licensing decisions can be appealed to the magistrates' court by residents or Councillors but

---

21   The word Exempt can be used generally to mean confidential as is used hear but it has a specific meaning in Local Authority parlance that relates to the Local Government Act 1972 which lists the information that can only be revealed to a few people in the Council and never the public. Much more on that in Chapters C6 and C7.

without all the facts it's difficult to put together a case. And finally it seems the other three local authorities are not following the law although they are following natural justice and being fair to both sides. I knew I hated licensing in Bristol, now I know why!

Oh and you want to know what happened to the licence application? That's actually not the point of the story but if you insist. We were invited back into the room at around midday. The Councillors had decided. It was granted. But the bar owners have to put up a two metre high fence or hedge to protect the privacy of their next door neighbours and close the terrace by 10pm to protect all locals from late night noise. The applicants didn't seem too pleased. I hope it's still enough to make a success of their business. I'm not sure how pleased the residents are, hopefully they realise it could have been worse.

> I have previously wondered before whether we need different laws for cities where everyone is so crammed in, 500 people can easily be living within 100 metres of a venue. Compare that with a rural location. Additionally, this is yet another example where the public and in this case their elected representatives are at a disadvantage versus business, especially big business which runs chains of clubs and bars. The night economy is important, but it mustn't do excessive harm to people that live nearby.
>
> The system seems so unfair. But what is fairness? It seems that what's fair to the bar owner isn't fair to the resident.

CHAPTER C6
£37 MILLION OF LOSSES ARE HIDDEN SOMEWHERE

I was hit for six. The metaphorical batsman was an accounting company called Ernst Young. I read their exempt interim report. Wow. It was so bad it took me a while to recover my senses and much longer to be able to write about it. Anyone based in Bristol at this time (March

2020) might hazard a guess what I'm talking about. It combines secrecy, bad decisions, good intents and more bad decisions: a terrible failure, partially due to lack of scrutiny over five years certainly, possibly eight. Guessed it? No it's not about the arena; the subject is Bristol Energy.

Dreamed up in 2012[22] by the Lib Dem administration, then like any self-respecting volcano it lay dormant for a while, to let the brand new Mayor[23] settle in. It seems something was bubbling away under the surface, because in July 2015 came a full blown Cabinet paper to authorise the investment of £4.2 million maximum into a start-up retail energy business. All the maths was done, due diligence by PwC[24], their report was exempt then, few could see it and so couldn't discuss it widely. The PwC report is still exempt, presumably to save their embarrassment.

There are some highlights from the publicly available information of 2015. The business was predicted to make a 12% return on investment by 2021 (year 5) and 35% by 2026. Apparently it had the right governance structure and used prudent customer forecasts.

So let's take stock, this is a new retail energy business entering a highly competitive market against the big six suppliers who are vertically integrated (some generate their own electricity and some are into local distribution). A few Councillors asked questions, but you had to be privy[25] to the exempt stuff to ask difficult questions and it was you versus PwC. Others just trusted PwC's say so. The Mayor's role is "all powerful" and he was up for it. So were many others albeit less powerful.

The business was launched in early 2016, a new Mayor was elected in May that year and was briefed that the Council's finances were in a mess. He sacked one Chief Exec, found an interim, replaced many senior officers and at one stage about 80% of senior staff had been replaced. A

---

22   Papers refer to a 2010 document but this doesn't seem to be available to view – there is an exempt document!

23   Mayor George Ferguson, a report came to him early in 2015 before the full decision in July 2015.

24   One of the major consulting and accountancy firms.

25   This would generally be Cabinet Members who tend to agree with the Mayor (collective responsibility) and Overview and Scrutiny Members (about ten) upon everything rests. Sometimes exempt material was printed and held in a room. You could go in there, read it, make notes and then the paper was collected in and handed out at the meeting. That is no way to allow people to digest complex information. Also it required some of those Councillors to be familiar with business and probably the retail energy business. The chances of good scrutiny in those conditions get close to zero.

new Finance Officer and a probe into the Council's funding black hole (The Bundred Report) on lack of financial controls and overspends busy, busy, busy. The interim Chief Exec left, another took on the Chief Exec role in April 2017 but they had gone by September[26].

Meanwhile Bristol Energy had blown their original £4.2m, needing twice that, they were going for growth. Lower prices, winning business, year two losses of £11 million on sales of £50 million, year three losses were reported in August 2019 of £12 million on sales of £75 million. In August 2019 the new MD of Bristol Energy explained that the old approach of chasing retail customers wasn't sustainable and implemented a change in strategy that had been agreed by the Mayor and his Cabinet. That was to move away from low margin retail business to a more value-added approach, linking the business with Bristol's big energy plans for carbon neutrality (called City Leap): heat networks, generation, heat pumps, insulation and more, well over a billion in investment, mainly private sector. And Bristol Energy we were told was to play a major part in this.

Going back a bit, it was late 2017 and clearly something was going wrong, it attracted the Chief Finance Officer's attention as she came up for breath following twelve months of sorting out the Council's own financial chaos. Perhaps it was already too late. Councillors don't know, because the performance and business plans were cloaked in secrecy. Exempt you see, the Law (Local Government Act 1972 schedule 12a Part 1, Para 3) says that information belonging to a person or business should be kept secret (or in the jargon; be exempt) so all the businesses set up by every Council anywhere in England and Wales can be secretive about their plans. Once the trading year is ended then the accounts come out, we are allowed to see them, but nothing useful about their plans for the future.

The Localism Act (2011) enabled Councils to run businesses. But the

---

26   See Chapters B6 and B7 for the woeful tale of her payoff and the cover up.

clauses in the 1972 Act[27] weren't changed. So this country is in the bizarre state that most quoted businesses which have shareholders' meetings and publish their plans and strategies willingly (and give analyst briefings) are more open than local authority businesses which are investing and risking tax payers' money. Local authorities are supposed to be part of our democracy, open, transparent; plus, as we have learned, in order to make good decisions you need good scrutiny. Not if you are a business owned by a Council you are not, they can hide behind the 1972 Act.

Some Councillors had other suspicions; it was very convenient for the Mayor to hide behind this law and keep the information secret, and by 2020 as it was coming up to mayoral elections and it would have been a big embarrassment for Bristol's Mayor to have to go public. He was saved by Covid-19. Bristol's Council Tax payer continued to lose out.

It was mid-March 2020 when I first saw exempt information about Bristol Energy. I'd been a Councillor for nearly four years. Finally the chair of Overview Scrutiny, Geoff Gollop, who had been party to this stuff as Council's Observer bit the bullet and wrote to the external auditors and supported a motion to Full Council brought in by his colleagues in the Tories and Lib Dems. The trigger was a business plan that had come to Cabinet in January 2020 (exempt of course) it was approved I'm told and just ten days later it was junked. It was deemed not achievable any more. Whilst I applaud the honesty of dumping something that isn't going to work, it instils no confidence in management and systems whatsoever.

A question was asked in public at the Budget Full Council (late February) by Geoff but no information was revealed and we were all assured by the Chief Finance Officer and the Deputy Mayor for Finance that the budget would be fine. No one was the wiser so we continued and set a budget[28]. And then things really started to happen...

27   It had been amended in 2000 I think by the Freedom of Information Act. Indeed looking at Schedule 12a after the FOI Act it is much simpler and less reasons that information be withheld. I can't imagine what things were like before 2000. But then Councils were run by a Committee system, no Cabinets, nor Mayors. No scrutiny either, these were all introduced in the Local Government Act 2000. The Localism Act 2011 failed to take account of the emergence of Council run businesses and the need to have information in the open for scrutiny. Hansard may show whether it was debated. Maybe the omission was deliberate? Whatever, it was a mistake in my view.
28   I voted against the budget, mainly due to the under budgeting of adult social care costs, setting up a black hole for the incoming Mayor in May 2020, so I thought.

CHAPTER C7

BRISTOL ENERGY – THE MONEY IS HIDDEN BEHIND THE 1972 ACT

Poor Geoff, he's a Conservative but a very likeable one, with the patience of a saint, an accountant I believe and had been Finance Cabinet Member for the previous Mayor's reign. In theory he is my political enemy, in practice he is someone whose opinions I listen to. I say poor because he has been the only person outside of the senior Council Officers and Labour Cabinet members who knew[29] what was going on in this company burning twelve million spondoolies a year (about a £100 a year for each Council Tax payer).

A problem shared is a problem halved they say and I took on some of Geoff's pent up emotion he must have been harbouring for so many years. I'd spent much of the last two years chairing budget scrutiny, warning officers and Cabinet where the budget might go wrong. We knew Bristol Energy was losing money but I was told it was factored in. I was about to find out that all those hours of work were effectively wasted because of this big elephant in the room. Not quite invisible but shrouded in secrecy and calmly munching a million a month of tax payers fodder. I took it badly. Another "what's the point?" moment; but enough about me.

On Friday 20th of March 2020 we were scheduled to hold an Extraordinary Full Council[30] in an exempt session where all Councillors (who turned up) would be briefed on the position. An exempt briefing was published a week earlier. Oh my God. Bristol Energy was not only losing money but they were now losing customers, growth had gone into reverse[31]. The change in strategy announced last summer was being implemented but what a shock. Easy come easy go but what a cost: if

---

29   We have subsequently found out that information was hidden from him too.
30   This meeting finally happened on May 26th 2020, via Zoom. My own view is that the exempt motion was out of date. There was a new MD, a journalist (Adam again) had dug into his past and it seems he is a "company turn around" expert, perhaps preparing the company for sale. Relief, finally something has been done. The lack of transparency was still an issue and most of us focussed our ire on that.
31   This information had been exempt but it was revealed by Sky News in early May that customer numbers were about 100,000 (they had been higher some nine months earlier).

you target your business at people who are good at switching energy suppliers and then if you try to get better margins they will switch away, of course. Some rapid calculations and it wouldn't make so much impact on the losses, as the business they were losing was probably at or below breakeven prices anyway. But there is a second source of losses. The breakup value of an energy business is based on the number of meter points multiplied by an amount which has varied from £75 to £100 each. If you lose lots of customers with their precious one or two meter points each then your business value is reduced too. That will be a big hit on the accounts maybe five or even ten million quid alone, plus the cumulative losses.

Losing customers at such a speed and following their new strategy, my prediction would be they would continue losing them at a similar rate. That's basically no hope.

In theory those in the know were refashioning Bristol Energy to support City Leap (to carbon neutrality), and some of the bids for that apparently did want an energy retailer to help sell to Bristol customers. But Councillors already knew nearly 90% of Bristol Energy's customers were not in Bristol. I think you know enough, other stuff is still exempt. I prepared my speeches over the weekend.

These speeches were not given.

A quote from my notes,

"You claim you need to keep this exempt to protect shareholder value. The very fact this has not been subject to scrutiny by Councillors, but you have relied on officers who are not business experts has generated the biggest loss of shareholder value Bristol Council has known" And worse, at the time this was being set up, I was teaching my students at Bath University how difficult it was to make money from the retail energy market." Just twelve miles up the road. I knew and you relied on consultants who obviously didn't".

Monday 16th March 2020 was Audit Committee, the last meeting we held as Covid-19 was shutting everything down. Mark, the Chair, was self-isolating, I was suddenly Chair, something I usually hate in big rooms as I can't hear well. We rattled through the main agenda in twenty five minutes agreeing to deal with questions via email. Then we came to Geoff Gollop's exempt letter to the Council's external auditors. It was couched very politely but picked out some points about the management and systems at Bristol Energy, information that new consultants had uncovered. I let the others speak while I was building up a head of steam. Officers were saying that the actions they were taking were improving the situation and that we should be reassured. Officers do things, Councillors ask questions and in theory we are reassured by their answers that they are doing the right things.

It was my turn,

"I am totally not re-assured about this. I have no confidence in you at all. If this were a business, I would have you in my office tomorrow discussing the turnaround plan. But no this is a Council, things take a hundred times longer. This has triggered doubts in my mind that we are capable of running any business at all. And the main problem is lack of scrutiny".

I said my bit about Bath University and loss of shareholder value, it does no harm to practise I thought. And I wonder what the minutes are going to say.

It was agreed that a report would come back in a month, that was quick! A month, losing a million a month. What planet are these officers on? I wanted it the next day.

Two days later, Wednesday, I was walking past City Hall about four pm and lo and behold but Adam the Local Democracy Reporter emerged. I said,

"I thought all meetings were off".
"Planning is still going,"

he replied...

"Let's go to the pub".

We both said, simultaneously.

And so at 16.10 we were sitting in the Hatchet Inn, Bristol's oldest pub they claim, with human skin stapled to one of the doors. Guess what we were talking about? I made sure I didn't share any exempt information but Adam's sharp and worked some of the stuff out himself. I don't know if he will publish, but at least he is better informed.

And my carefully prepared speeches? The Extraordinary Full Council was postponed for two months. The scripts were in the fridge trying to cool down, but when or if I get to deliver them they will be white hot with anger and urgency. You see there is a public interest test to the Local Government Act 1972 Schedule 12A, Part 1, it is clause 10, nobody explained that, but if the public interest is sufficiently strong then exempt information can be released. I don't mean interest from the public, but the wider issue is about learning from mistakes.

I'm jumping back to my management training back in the 1980s. Good management courses in those days often started with this IBM story[32]:

> *Tom Watson Jr, CEO of IBM between 1956 and 1971; a key figure in the information revolution. Watson repeatedly demonstrated his abilities as a great leader, never more so than in this story.*
>
> *A young executive had made some bad decisions that cost the company several million dollars. He was summoned to Watson's office, shaking and fully expecting to be dismissed. As he entered the office, the young executive said, "I suppose after that set of mistakes you will want to fire me." Watson was said to have replied,*
>
> *"Not at all, young man, we have just spent a couple of million dollars educating you."*

Bristol Energy, its strategy, the consultants' reports and especially lessons of lack of scrutiny is Bristol City Council's £37.7 million mistake.

---

32 This is taken from https://the-happy-manager.com/articles/characteristic-of-leadership/

It should all be made public so Local Authorities in England, Wales and elsewhere can learn. Government needs to learn too to amend the 1972 Act that is so damaging: it is in the wider public interest. Bristol City Council please, please publish the information.

A few months earlier the *Sunday Telegraph* published the following about Nottingham Council.

8th December 2019, Council accounts delayed by energy firm hold-up

Accountancy firm BDO is yet to finish its audit of Robin Hood Energy, Britain's first Council-owned energy supplier, which in turn has caused a delay of three months to the publication of Nottingham City Council's accounts by Grant Thornton. The energy firm's finances have been under scrutiny since the Council lent it an extra £9.5m earlier this year so it could pay a bill due to the industry regulator to boost green energy schemes, having missed a deadline. Robin Hood's accounts are not legally due until the end of the year. A Council spokesperson said of Robin Hood Energy: "We are committed to its objectives of reducing fuel poverty and challenging the Big Six energy companies by putting people before profits." Report thanks to LGiU

Does this sound familiar? It seems Nottingham and Bristol both set up energy companies with the best of intentions, but did they have the skills and level of scrutiny needed?

Update: 18 June 2020. The Monitoring Officer is letting me read the second Ernst Young report tomorrow (As the topic is coming to Audit Committee – we have refused to sign off the 18/19 accounts unless we see it). I am writing this today so I don't accidentally reveal any exempt information (yes it's still exempt). In the public domain is the fact that it is up for sale and an article[33] by Adam Postans where he has interviewed a commercial lawyer saying that any buyer will just want the customers and won't care about how badly the business was run. I expect the Ernst Young report to reveal how badly it was run and implicit in that was

33   https://www.bristolpost.co.uk/news/bristol-news/warning-redundancies-bristol-energy-city-4217358

how mistaken Bristol City Council was to let things get this bad. I'll find out tomorrow if I am right. Maybe one day I can tell others.

I don't much care how embarrassing this is to the Mayor, I do care that the £37 million loss is learned from; by Bristol City and by other Councils. It is only by releasing all the exempt information that will enable learning to be done.

GOOD SCRUTINY

We started this section with quotes from Isabel Hardman's book *Why We Get The Wrong Politicians*, she lists about ten Acts of Parliament that haven't worked as intended and she suggests, and others agree, it is due to poor scrutiny. You have just read, I hope, about the Local Government Act 1972 and the secrecy it allows because it wasn't amended by the 2011 Localism Act that enabled Councils to set up businesses. And earlier on there were the problems with Universal Credit. Before then we looked at the impact of uncapping university growth and capping Council house borrowing. And the Licensing Act meaning information is kept secret from Councillors. There are more examples later on.

But Government makes mistakes by not doing things too. Adult Social care is a prime example, see Section F, but we are now going to take a brief foray into the world of Council IT...

CHAPTER C8
COUNCIL IT SYSTEMS

Statement from Cllr Clive Stevens to Cabinet – Item 16 – IT Future State Assessment - 3/7/18

"Dear Councillor Cheney,

It is good to see an IT strategy come to this Cabinet and I support the general goals. I have a few points that you might wish to quietly consider after you have approved this report (which, by the way, is for £20.3million, an awful lot of money and much of it un-budgeted).

Currently IT supports over 600 separate programs used within BCC (figure taken from the GDPR analysis). That has to be unsustainable, so rationalisation is the only way to go."

(I subsequently discovered it was 800), I continued...

"But....

1) I see that the no scrutiny box is ticked. So may I ask, have we budgeted for the likely consultancy and training costs that inevitably go with IT systems changes? Sometimes these can be as much or more than the software and licence costs themselves.

2) It says that HR advice is included within the report, but what I can't see and what really concerns me, is we need to understand early on how much retraining and redeployment of staff is actually possible and roughly how many redundancies this IT transformation will cause, all voluntary I hope? The statutory accounts show that we still have over £5 million in the business transformation reserve which in the past has been used for that purpose. That could cover about 200 or so redundancies.

3) At page 250 of this Cabinet report it refers to co-creation[34] of new solutions. My experience is that co-creation should be done carefully and

---

34 Co-creation in this case means the users have a chance to influence the design of the software system. If it has been written so it is flexible then this is often a positive thing as it gets commitment.

usually when it offers competitive advantage. Competitive advantage is a concept not really appropriate for the public sector and so I question whether it should be done at all. The difficulties are caused when it causes change deep in the structure of the system. Co-creation as configuration is one thing but when it affects the core modules it can go horribly wrong. Or does this section refer to process re-engineering before new software is implemented? In which case, it should say so. I await the first report that comes to Resources Scrutiny[35] which I sit on.

4) The objective of channel shift (moving as much activity as possible to BCC online services) should work well, have you considered it going hand in hand with modernisation of the libraries especially in the context of services for older people. For example people coming into a library to be trained/made aware and supported to use BCC online. If this seems appropriate, IT and service efficiency improvements could be one of the revenue streams supporting the redesign of our libraries in the future.

5) Big programs need quick wins to show success and keep commitment. Have you identified the quick wins within this strategy?

And then thinking more widely

6) Working with other core cities[36]: All core cities have similar IT needs I assume. And yet they are each doing their own thing regarding IT which must mean a large duplication of effort and consequent extra costs to each city amounting to millions if not tens of millions of pounds. Have you considered initiating a "Core Cities" IT strategy?

So six issues (at least). But I do want this IT strategy to succeed. BCC needs it for the future delivery of better, more cost-effective services. Some of the residents in my ward, those with IT experience, feel our systems are out dated and clunky. I won't say what some Councillors think. Let's show them we can become a 21st Century Council."

Update: I didn't get an answer. I didn't expect one and then the IT Director (who was an Interim anyway) left for some reason or other and

---

35   The report came but by a new officer and from what I remember didn't address any of these issues.
36   Government has identified about ten key cities in the UK but outside London that are the engines of growth. These are called the Core Cities.

was replaced with a new, equally confident chap. He rewrote the strategy to be suitable for cloud based IT and immediately got hauled over the coals by the Council's Audit Department who called in an external, specialist, IT systems auditor to help identify the issues. Although it's a budget of £20 million, the whole existence of some Council services depends on better IT to make processes more efficient. That frees up costs for investment into labour intensive activities like care (children's and adults'). During 2019 there were some problems between Bristol City Council and its IT supplier, the biggest IT company in the world I think, mainly around the scope of the project and what would and would not be delivered. I'm not sure the external IT auditor helped but his presence did mean it got agenda time, discussion and scrutiny (in exempt session of course).

One of the projects that wasn't included in this all embracing "IT Future State" program was termed "Mobile/Agile Working" for social workers and other staff within the care system, like occupational therapists. At that time they had to go back to a PC in an office and type up the notes and statutory forms for every single person in care they visited, about 5,000 adults and 600 children in care and probably many more.

The Agile Working objectives were to enable staff to fill out the forms and have discussions with the adults using an iPad or laptop all 4G enabled. It turned out that the supplier of the software wasn't privacy compliant (GDPR[37]) and so the software couldn't be transferred onto portable devices. The supplier was one of the main ones in the industry but its software still wasn't amenable to new data protection standards. The Mobile/Agile working project was abandoned. Fortunately not too much money was wasted but lots of time. Sections of the adult social care operation were running 10% or maybe even 20% less efficiently than they might have done had they had this software and hardware working. It is critical that costs are contained to maintain a good quality of care. Care costs though are always overrunning.

---

37   GDPR is the latest requirements to meet for data protection

So you have all these Councils doing basically the same thing but many using different IT systems. The suppliers are private businesses, who understandably don't respond quickly enough and when they do they charge the earth for changes because the cost of writing the software is enormous and private sector businesses need to know they are going to win the contract. A risk that can really only be taken on by the biggest. These enormous costs upfront mean that software production is subject to what's called large "economies of scale". That means the costs of developing software don't increase much whether it's just for one Council or for 100. For these reasons this is surely a task for a Government Department?

Just Google "Council IT projects", you will see a whole host of requirements out to tender and contracts being discussed. All of this is funded by the tax payer and many fail.

In cities good transport is critical. Government laws and regulations mess that up too.

CHAPTER C9
BUSES AND LACK OF SERVICE

Bristol has been ranked in UK's top three for traffic jams, presumably due to poor public transport arrangements. Most commuters rely on cars and consequently the city also has high levels of air pollution. This will really impact when life returns after Covid-19, as the cocktail of that plus air pollution is apparently really dangerous[38].

One answer is better buses (ensuring they are safe of course) to clear car congestion and air pollution; ideally with an integrated transport service of joined up ticketing and bus routes and timings serving the people that need them. This could have been arranged in the 2017 Bus Services Act. In fact the House of Lords wanted a clause that would allow

---

38   Various studies published in April 2020 show a correlation between levels of air pollution and the lethality of the virus. These studies are being verified and causation hasn't been proven yet.

Councils to run some or all bus services for the benefit of the people, less congestion for those not using buses, better, faster services for those that do use the buses, healthier air quality, safer roads for cyclists and more. But no, the Bill ping-ponged between the Commons and the Lords and eventually the Commons won. Not because the Lords gave up, but because Theresa May called a general election and Bills simply go through to become Acts in this eventuality. So buses are still at the whim of private operators creaming off the best routes and forcing Councils to subsidise the less profitable ones or to not have buses there at all. Therefore lots of people have to use their cars to the detriment[39] of everyone else in the city.

This next story doesn't look specifically at buses but at bus infrastructure so you can see the type of waste this approach causes.

Clive's Statement to Cabinet in January 2017
"At page 39 of the Council's business plan the officer says that money to invest in transport infrastructure is hard to come by, of course it is, which is why the infrastructure we do put in place needs to be effective.

In my ward we have four pretty new, raised platform, bus stops - some with the flashy led displays and all of which are now completely unused because the bus operator decided to reroute the buses because that route wasn't making enough profit.

Buses don't stop at them now at all. This must be £60,000 plus of stranded transport infrastructure, for which we are now looking for creative ideas to reuse.

I have since been informed there is a similar newly unused bus stop in the neighbouring ward of Clifton, so now we have five.

As this is a statement I can't ask questions, but if I could have, I would have asked please if the Cabinet Member for Transport could find out please whether there are many more stranded (expensive) bus stops in Bristol. And also I would have asked please, whether the Council could negotiate with the

---

39   So the economy is designed to run as private buses, private cars and lots of congestion and air pollution. Surely it would be more efficient and better if it were redesigned so we had (in cities) more buses, fewer cars, less congestion and better air? We do have a choice you know. The Bus Services Act put a stop to Councils doing this directly; hopefully there are indirect ways of achieving this.

private bus companies so they contractually use new stops for a reasonable time period after they have been installed – thank you."

You can see I was quite polite in those days. I even said thank you. My anger about the governance of the country was still quite muted.

As it was a statement I didn't get a reply. But it didn't matter as I knew the Cabinet Member for Transport was as frustrated with the system as I was. Buses are deregulated and the companies can do what they want. If routes are unprofitable then they can pull the route or part of it, and if socially necessary the Council could choose to bring it back using subsidies. But in 2018 and 2019 Government was continuing to suck the funding from Councils, so subsidies had to be reduced.

Bus companies pick and choose their routes to profit maximise, they just need to make sure that competition can't make enough money on the routes they don't provide, or even better make sure competition don't dare enter the market with potentially predatory acts like flooding a route with buses so the newcomer can't get enough business[40].

Having a local monopoly position should be quite profitable for bus companies. But it isn't, certainly not in Bristol. Costs were going up, wage rates up and buses were going slower, strangled by the congestion. Going slower means higher costs to the bus companies and that means either higher ticket prices or curtailed routes. Both of which mean more cars and more congestion and that means fewer buses and therefore more cars!

If I can explain that in a paragraph why can't the Government get it? It's as if they want more cars, more congestion and pollution. Maybe they do? Do car companies fund them in some way?

It must be pretty depressing being a bus passenger in Bristol, waiting at the stop, bus sign says it's due in five minutes and then the electronics flick over. That message just disappears and a new bus shows and is scheduled in twenty minutes. It's been rerouted, again. You look at your

---

40   We did a case study on this type of thing at Bath University; Firstbus and Wessex were fighting over the route up to the Uni. First won and the service and prices became so bad that the Students' Union decided to subsidise some Wessex services.

watch, you'll be late for work, maybe your boss won't forgive this third instance in two weeks. So you go home and hop in the car, if you have one. If not[41], you wait and maybe lose your job.

I rarely take the bus, from where I live it's quicker to get on the suburban train or simply walk. But as a Councillor, a lack of buses are a problem: in fact a job losing problem.

CHAPTER C10
MORE ON BUSES, BUT FEWER BUSES

The long overdue and dreaded email came in. The same impact as if news that a quiet local pub had finally sold out to Weatherspoons; an email so, so important and yet it only elicited the usual Outlook ping. It sat there calmly whispering, "Clive you are out of a job" waiting for me to read it.

This was the 3rd June 2019, just one of the fifty-seven emails I received as a Councillor that day, but this one was enough to bring me to tears. It wasn't simply a sad story, just a real crying shame.

The saga starts soon after I was elected in May 2016.

Firstbus are the company that has pretty much a monopoly of the routes in Bristol except the subsidised ones. Funding reductions meant that subsidised routes were being cut, only one of these passed through my ward of Clifton Down, the number 505. There is a separate non-subsidised route[42], the number 9. It ran from Bristol Temple Meads main station through the shopping centre, up the hill and then wiggled a lot: firstly around the not quite suburban areas, but not quite central areas either; called Cotham and Redland. Then at the top the bus shot off west to Clifton Down before making a straight, but congested run, down to the shops and eventually on to the main station.

---

41 Many have pointed out to me that people could take their bike. True and that is becoming a more popular mode of transport but not enough to cancel out the bus versus car choice for most, one day I hope.

42 There are lots of North South routes going up and down Whiteladies Road, but only the number 9 wiggles.

Wiggling around was one problem, combined with a private bus company's need for profit. To improve productivity bigger buses were being used. But when they came across roads laid out for Victorian times, productivity halted along with the bus. That impasse limited the availability of routes for the east to west run to Clifton. The roads were better going up, across, down, across and up which isn't that direct and is in all the traffic jams. The other problem was also congestion nearer the centre.

In May 2016 Firstbus announced that they were going to change the route of the number 9 and its mirror image route the number 8 so they would be more profitable. For most residents this would mean a quicker journey to the Centre but there is a smaller section of society, quite vociferous it turns out, who depend on the waggly bit.

They claim that Councillors had been informed just before the May 2016 elections. There was, I'm told, even a consultation, notices on the buses themselves and at bus-stops, but no meetings, nor emails so we didn't actually know until September. That's when Firstbus proudly made their change. Councillor Carla Denyer, I and other locals then started to receive horror stories of our charming old ladies and gentlemen waiting at the bus-stop on the Monday morning. Simply wanting to do their regular shop and they sat there and sat and nothing came. A half hour wait had always been quite common but it seems their wait could have been forever and that's quite some difference.

The consultation hadn't worked at all and this change of route is what led to the stranded bus-stops, the stars of the previous chapter. We managed to get in touch with the Managing Director of Firstbus (West of England). James is a very friendly chap who has worked his way up from being a bus conductor, indicating his heart is in the right place. He offered to come to a public meeting which we held one evening in the local library.

No problems with the consultation this time, the drums had been sounding and we think one hundred and seventy one of our precious voters attended. An average age of seventy I'm guessing, not just to hear James's story of bus franchises, the need to make money, consultation done in the usual way, but also to ensure James listened attentively to their feedback. Not only do older people vote at the ballot box but they give short shrift to ex-bus conductors if they get an inkling that he hasn't quite listened. Tales of melting ice cream, defrosting chickens and more as people waited at the interchange that Firstbus had created, an interchange where you wait ages to get a bus to take you 400 yards. But with heavy shopping and frail legs, 400 yards on foot is not possible.

We bundled James safely out of the library at the end and he clearly understood that a section of the public were not happy. I hoped that in him was still a small vestige of a public service mentality.

The Councillors for Clifton and Clifton Down met with James a few days later down at Brunel House (City Hall was being refurbished), profuse thanks to him for coming along and being so good with the mob. We knew that James had our futures in his hands. For historic reasons the public thinks the Council controls the buses. That stopped a long time ago. But the memory lingers.

We discussed his company's need for profit and how could he adapt the route to be more profitable for Firstbus and still provide a semblance of east/west connectivity. Jerome Thomas, Councillor for Clifton had a genius idea, a sort of hybrid route. James promised he'd look at it and I escorted him out. We looked at Jerome in awe, had he saved our bacon? (As Carla is vegan I exempt her from this metaphor).

A few weeks later we got a reply from James, "Yes it might work". And indeed it was announced at a public meeting that the number 9 would be rerouted in January 2017 and I still have all the emails of thanks. The bus stops were still stranded, but as Councillors we were local heroes (temporarily).

That was a positive end to the 2016 story, but due to Government legislation and the intended consequences of the 2017 Act of keeping buses private then that job ending email of 3rd June 2019 was always likely to come in one day.

The email was of course from Firstbus, they were planning on ending the number 9 altogether.

You may be asking why have I devoted two chapters to buses. Even if you aren't asking that I'm going to tell you. Firstly, it illustrates the Bus Services Act 2017 which was supposed to improve the ability of Local Authorities to get a better service for their citizens. It wasn't doing the job as far as I could see. That Act followed the disaster (from a users' point of view) that was the bus deregulation of the twentieth century. The House of Lords attempted to use their scrutiny powers to improve the 2017 Act. That was stopped, albeit a casualty of Theresa May's General Election.

But it also demonstrates that a service that brings so many benefits to non-users: less air pollution, less congestion, safer roads, less transport poverty is not suited to a market at all. Markets are for when the buyer gets most of the benefits, that's what he/she pays for. Buses; sure the user gets some benefits but the non-user does too, especially in a city.

This is a good lead into the next section which is the economic thought processes I had to develop as a Councillor to contribute my "good ideas". But one last story about Government scrutiny, in this case after the law has been made and implemented.

CHAPTER C11
POST LEGISLATION SCRUTINY: LICENSING, LOCAL GOVERNMENT SCRUTINY AND UNIVERSAL CREDIT

At the beginning of this section I included a quote reproduced from Isabel Hardman's 2019 book;

Wes Streeting, a Labour MP in 2015,

"I think the Lords is much better for scrutiny than the Commons".

You will be pleased to hear that there is a process called Post Legislative Scrutiny. An example is the House of Lords 2017 report about the workings and non-workings of the 2003 Licensing Act, the subject of the stories in chapters above C4 and C5. In those you will recall I was upset at the biased process caused by the inability of a Councillor (me) to see other representations. Therefore I didn't have all the information needed to put the case on behalf of residents.

I contributed to Lords' consultation during August 2016 and got two mentions in their write up[43] but more importantly for this book the summary from the Lords on transparency is at paragraph 113 (In 2016 I hadn't appreciated the issue fully, it just felt wrong). It starts;

"Transparency was another concern of Mr Gouriet's: (He was a special advisor) "I am concerned at the growing extent to which decisions are influenced (if not effectively taken) by the result of discussions taking place behind closed doors, at which not all interested persons are present ... there should be much greater transparency regarding these behind-closed-doors meetings. In particular, it is essential that reasons are given (by the relevant responsible authorities) for not making representations if there is an otherwise contested application ... pre-hearing consultation can sail too close to the equivalent of a hearing."

That was published in 2017, had anything happened by end of March 2020? I asked. This is the edited reply from Bristol's Top Legal bod (for Licensing),

"The actual decision making process is always undertaken by the committee. Some LAs may delegate some decisions to officers which may have given rise to that concern but in Bristol that is not the case.

In terms of conversations between responsible authorities and applicants, that is inevitable especially the more complex applications for events in an effort to agree conditions e.g. fully understanding crowd dynamics, capacity in area etc. I have never seen such matters that may

---

43   The Government did issue some new guidance in 2018 on the Licensing Act possibly incorporating input from the HofLs review. It didn't as far as I can see address the issue of transparency and information imbalance.

have compromised an application or the decision making process, the alternative would be for all of the matters to be played out in front of committee which members would not want and would certainly interfere with the efficiency of the hearing processes. I hope this helps".

So if we unpick the second paragraph, yes things are agreed before the committee, just as Mr Gouriet had said in 2016 and if we add the fact that Councillors and residents aren't allowed to see the representations or understand why some comments e.g. by the police, have been withdrawn then things are not transparent at all. The officer probably doesn't even realise the lack of transparency is a failing. I concluded it was a battle I couldn't win as a Councillor. It had to go in this book.

Although in 2016 I sent in three pages of evidence to the House of Lords, the two pieces included in their report only related to what I said about the night time economy:

At para 443 the HofL report says :

"Indeed, many respondents were highly critical of the Licensing Act 2003's provisions for 24-hour licences, and believed a reversion to blanket closing times should be considered. As one Councillor from Bristol put it, "the Licensing Act 2003 seemingly ignored the costs of enforcement, harm and tidying up. In these times of austerity, society can't afford the luxury of the 2003 Act."

And at para 497.

"Councillor Clive Stevens, of Bristol, informed us that while nightclubs could be a "catalyst" for public nuisance, in the early hours of the morning it was often large groups of people congregating around takeaways which were causing a greater public nuisance for local residents."

I hope you don't get the impression I'm a killjoy, as a Councillor one of my jobs is to represent the people who live in my ward. If they don't like being woken up at 2am nor like the litter on the streets the next morning then I have to put their case. Interestingly on 18th January 2020 the *Daily Telegraph* reported that a pub was increasing its prices after 10pm as the Local Authority had imposed a "Late night levy" on establishments open late. The summary as written in the LGiU update was

> *"Drinkers in the Ten Bells pub in Spitalfields, City of London, are being charged more for their drinks after 10pm, with the business thought to be passing on a Council "late night levy". Councils are allowed to charge a levy on businesses that supply alcohol late into the night in order to pay for the cost of extra policing and licensing".*

Moving from licensing to Local Government Scrutiny; we studied the Commons Inquiry into the workings of scrutiny in depth earlier in chapter B11. The resulting Good Scrutiny Guide did slightly improve Councillors' access to information but I think they missed the main issue about openness and transparency and could have developed public scrutiny better. I wonder why Government wants to keep information under wraps?

A third example, and switching from Local Government to Central Government, discussion about the potential post implementation scrutiny of Benefits Sanctions. I find the following news piece quite shameful (DWP is the department of work and pensions).

On 26 Jan 2020, The Independent wrote (quote from the LGiU):

DWP refuses to assess impact of benefit sanctions (DWP is the Department of Work and Pensions).

Campaigners have criticised the government for refusing to assess the impact of benefit sanctions on claimants' mental health, despite warnings from charities, doctors and academics that sanctions can lead to mental health problems, including suicidal tendencies. Employment minister Mims Davies has said that "no assessment has been made" of the impact of sanctions, claiming that the department takes "all the claimant's individual circumstances" into account before deciding they are warranted. Research as far back as 2016 by Salford City Council found that sanctions are "devastating" for claimants, and a year later Britain's leading psychologists urged ministers to immediately stop the practice or risk soaring rates of mental health issues. The Department of Work and Pensions (DWP) pledged to review the policy of suspending benefits "on an ongoing basis" in 2013, but the Committee found in 2018 that no such review had been carried out, and that as a result the Government had "no idea how many people are suffering."

And the Guardian and the Independent published two weeks later on 8th Feb 2020, (summarised by the LGiU):

Benefits failures linked to dozens of suicides:

The National Audit Office has found that at least 69 suicides could have been linked to problems with benefit claims over the last six years – and that the true number of deaths linked to claims could be much higher. The NAO also found that until recently, the Department for Work and Pensions failed to actively seek information from coroners and families, or investigate all of the cases that were reported to it. It also found that although the DWP said it sought to use internal investigations to improve the safety and quality of services, it has no idea whether lessons have been learned from these reviews, or whether their recommendations were ever implemented. Former MP Frank Field, the former chair of the work and pensions select committee, said the report "presents a catastrophic situation for vulnerable claimants and their families," and called for a "full investigation." Shadow disability minister Marsha De Cordova also called for an independent inquiry into the "heart-breaking" report.

So the Government are quite clearly not willing to undertake post legislative scrutiny on Universal Credit and benefits sanctions.

The 2003 Licensing Act was brought in by Labour and scrutinised recently, although the recommendations I was interested in haven't been implemented. Local Government Scrutiny was brought in by Labour in 2000 and was looked at recently. Benefit sanctions were brought in by the Conservatives and there is a refusal to do post legislative scrutiny.

Three examples, not statistically significant, but I wonder if the Party that brought the law in has anything to do with who decides to scrutinise it?

SUMMARY SECTION C

This section builds on the previous one (Mathematics of Power, who takes decisions, openness and need for early scrutiny...) and looked at the impact of legislation on sections of the population (in cities) and what Councillors can do to alleviate the harm caused whether the direct impact or the inability to scrutinise. The bigger issue is that many of these laws or decisions even with good intentions have bad outcomes.

The mechanism for ensuring good law lies in good scrutiny. (This is a dreadful weakness in the country's governance). Scrutiny is done in the House of Lords, the very chamber some want to get rid of. We have also seen that Government could do sensible things like common IT systems but doesn't and in many cases washes its hands by leaving it to "the market" when it is quite clear the market won't work.

Much of what we deal with is fighting for fairness. The predominant economic system in the UK is capitalism operating via markets, neither of which is designed to consider fairness. I've now got to the stage where I need to share with you my views on how the economy could be run to truly benefit us in a fair way rather than primarily for those who are the friends and supporters of those in power.

Section D will also introduce us to my Twitter alter ego @ SageAndOnion[44], set up a long, long time ago, the plan was I was going to say things wise and acerbic. That was after my experience on the Neighbourhood Partnership. But I couldn't think of anything to say so I stayed silent, but from 2015 I started to tweet, some wise, some silly but it did help refine my thoughts, not quite in a peer review way; well you read on and decide. So what is fairness?

---

44   Nobody has yet said I should get stuffed so I thought I'd get that in first.

SECTION D
WHAT IS FAIRNESS?

INTRODUCTION

One of the good things about being in the Green Party is the ability to be able to think and, within limits, be able to say what you please. Between us 11 Councillors we had a system where anything we proposed to put into the public domain was circulated amongst us first, normally to weed out possible misinterpretations or identify if it went against Green Party policy. In which case the procedure is you say what the policy is, and then go on to say if you think differently. I haven't done that with this book. And as far as I'm aware, this book is not Green Party policy[1].

I find the economic narrative that the Greens use quite difficult to explain to others and thus hard to relate to specific Council problems

1   Although there is plenty of overlap.

when it's to non-Greens, who I am trying to convince, as they don't read the same books. I found the concepts fine for the big picture, but the doughnuts[2], zero growth[3] and much more were difficult to apply to the nuts and bolts of communicating to others not versed in such language[4].

So I decided to develop my own approach[5] to help recommend local action, based on more traditional language combined with pragmatism. This section is the result. Thinking formulated from experience and reading so, so many books.

We start with fairness and what the word might actually really mean: the first three chapters are a case study on yet another unfair planning application. Then we progress through a journey defining fairness within a political environment and end up applying it to examples as wide ranging as libraries, buses, Council Tax and air quality.

CHAPTER D1
BEING A FAIRNESS WARRIOR (PART 1)

Sunday 5th May 2019 - I've learned something profound about myself today. It's beautifully sunny and yet I'm busy indoors at my Council iPad reading air quality reports. What on earth would make someone do that when I could be out on a walk or down the pub?

A clue: yesterday I tweeted a reply to: "What's happening?" Twitter always asks that first.

"Well I'm up to my ears in an air quality report for a gas powered generator to go into St Philips, and yes near the nursery school, you couldn't make it

2   I see that *Doughnut Economics* is to be applied in Amsterdam, its first test; I decided to reread the main points and felt that much of what I will be saying is similar but using different words – phew! Basically society should ensure needs are fulfilled first then allow some excess (for wants) as long as it's within the limits of nature's and society's ability to supply. Kate Raworth the author hasn't been asked to endorse this opinion of mine.
3   *Prosperity without Growth*, Tim Jackson, 2009 Earthscan
4   In fact one of the reasons for this section and the next is to try to "translate" some of those concepts into language that is understood by most of us. How do you apply "zero growth" to speaking about a grant that is to encourage growth? By the time you have explained it, you have run out of time.
5   My Twitter handle is @SageAndOnion and some early ideas are still up on line.

up. Officers are likely to recommend it. Today I decided to step down from Committee to fight it"

I have come to the conclusion that I'm a "fairness warrior"; most Greens are ecowarriors, I'm not, I'm a fairness warrior, that's someone who fights for the underdog, for the vulnerable, for those who don't have the training to fight back themselves.

But how has it taken me 60 years to realise all this?

Vague memories pop into my head from the distant past, I remember I studied law to become an environmental barrister, but only to be told I might have to represent big corporations too, the disappointment. That was the end of that venture. I used to fight for fairness for my employees ages ago and got into trouble with American Head Office, they eventually sacked me.

It also underpins why I find being a Councillor quite difficult. I have to represent everyone; a rich resident who complains about the Council tenant next door or their bins not being emptied on time. I've managed this[6] for three years, I can cope with a fourth but I don't think it's me long term.

I could actually be a fairness warrior without being a Councillor.

But today I am both. I am fighting for the residents and workers of Lawrence Hill, one of Bristol's most deprived areas and where land is less expensive. In the future it could be developed and used for lots of affordable housing, mixed in with other homes, a park maybe, business, shops, students even. But in the here and now a scrap yard is planning on closing and the land owner wants to make a profit by permitting a business that wishes to install three massive electricity generators, running off natural gas, slap bang in the area, right near a nursery school and where so many people work.

It seems like we are back to 2016 again but instead of biodiesel the fuel of choice today is natural gas. The pollution will be less than

6   I reconciled this by imagining the resident were a business customer and I was sorting out a problem for them, but the sense of purpose and drive comes from supporting those who are systematically being treated unfairly.

biodiesel but the carbon dioxide output will be massive, at least biodiesel is a renewable fuel. Yet in 2019 there still aren't the planning policies nationally or locally that can stop this type of thing. But don't despair, Clive the geek, is on the case.

First, let's go back five days to Monday 29th April: I was almost marching down Whiteladies Road and then Park Street on my way to the 10am Agenda Planning Meeting. I normally walk fast, but this was faster and with real purpose. I was thinking of Douglas Adams and his series *Hitchhiker's Guide to the Galaxy* and the Vogons. Assuming they exist; Vogons are the species of alien who write the third worst poetry in the Universe. They are also suitably disposed to become intergalactic planners. I was thinking of how Douglas Adams described their home planet and their upbringing, where if any young Vogon accidentally gets a creative thought, a root pops up from the ground and slaps them in the face. Thus after many years, every inhabitant has learned to eliminate creativity and common sense too from their minds. And with Vogons on my mind, I entered the Agenda Setting Meeting for Planning.

The particular application that reacquainted me with the Vogons was left until last. It was having an effect, I was already somewhat belligerent about the first two applications. But then these gas powered electricity generators came up, planning reference 18/05628/F, if you want to look them up. But don't, it's mind bogglingly boring.

Officers were concerned that I wasn't open minded enough to sit on the Committee to decide the application. You see, we Councillors mustn't be what's called predetermined. Well I probably was. I spent much of Tuesday morning reviewing the application and sent some carefully crafted questions to the officer. I thought if I could persuade them to refuse, then that would be OK, I could sit on the Committee.

Nothing back on Tuesday, nor Wednesday, nor Thursday. Perhaps my arguments had been decisive, so on that basis I chased up Friday morning.

But no, they just hadn't had time to look at them. And now they had my arguments, I hadn't persuaded them at all, not even a tiny bit.

How dare they, my points were perfectly crafted and so I wrestled with my conscience for a few minutes, it wasn't much of a bout, I emailed back saying I thought they should be looking after people in deprived areas and said I'd step down from Committee for that item. However, if I stepped down, we'd lose a Green vote; helpfully a Green colleague said she'd cover for me so I could speak against and we would still have our two votes. She said she wasn't predetermined. I decided to believe her.

The agreement with officers as I left that Monday Agenda Planning Meeting was that I'd send them my questions for clarification as early as possible. Well not now. I'd already sent them some and pre-warned officers of lines of argument. But now I was effectively a member of the public and as a fairness warrior any new discoveries would remain hidden until the day before. My aim is to create enough doubt in the minds of fellow Councillors sitting on Committee that they would defer, or even refuse it. That had worked with the biodiesels in 2016 so is worth a try now.

I tweeted that line from earlier, many replies came back. This was the best.

"Good decision. You're a politician not a bureaucrat's rubber stamp."
(from someone called Bristol Citizen)

Absolutely right whoever you are; so the afternoon of Friday 3rd afternoon and all of Saturday I spent slumped over the iPad, reading report after report. By 4pm, with the sun streaming in, overheating my back and almost hiding the screen, I'd done my draft objection on air quality grounds. I emailed it to myself so it wouldn't get lost (The IT systems we have are prone to losing drafts, I have found).

I also have a friend in the trade who would look at the noise assessment. I looked at the climate change impact and referenced a previous application, but the killer argument, in my view, was "inefficient use of land". Taking up 1,260sqm of important industrial land and only providing two jobs. I'd already sent in this point to the officers, so they would be ready with a riposte. The best approach would be to wait for their write up which they had to publish a week in advance to see how they argued against that.

No way were they going to get more out of me until it was too late. And this journey might now be recorded on video too....

CHAPTER D2
BEING A FAIRNESS WARRIOR (PART 2)

15th May 2019: It's Wednesday, the morning of the Committee meeting. I've rewritten my speech three times, timed it twice, it's 70 seconds. I have put "in conclusion" at 45 seconds in to buy me the extra 10 seconds I need before the Chair cuts me off. It's Don, he's strict on time.

I submitted my written statement on Monday first thing, a day and a bit early. A niggling suspicion that I'd missed something, you know the feeling when you've packed for holiday and are convinced you've left something at home, that type of doubt. It was eight pages, 3,000 words and two weeks of sweat under that hot sun; tears, not yet. Everything checked and double checked. I copied in the officers too, they had been helpful in answering questions and so I thought it only fair to give them some notice but not too much.

And within an hour I had a reply, I was told what I'd forgotten to pack, more accurately my mistake. I'd messed up the units for carbon monoxide (CO) concentrations. That meant it was now unlikely to be a pollutant. Shit, I need to resubmit this. And I'm on the train. How am I going to fix this?

But I have my laptop and iPad. I open up the laptop, edit the report, fortunately there are 15 other issues still wrong with the application, although I did think that carbon monoxide was one of the best. So with mouse ready, like a surgeon's scalpel, I excised CO from the report. 10 minutes later, OK it doesn't look too bad, write it to PDF, tether my laptop to the iPad hotspot and away. So version two was out, just a couple of hours later. Phew! I'd have looked an idiot at the meeting. Thank you air pollution officer, the very one whose report I was trying to rubbish. He's quite a good egg really.

Tuesday afternoon I received a reply to my 15 points or most of them. I flicked through them. Good, some of the answers seemed a bit weak like, "we didn't think it reasonable to..." that sort of thing. I wonder if members of the Committee will think it reasonable to pump all that CO_2 into their air with no mitigation. We now have an email warning us that Extinction Rebellion are due to turn up and do a mass die in; extra security. I hope after all this effort the meeting isn't cancelled.

Wednesday at 10.45am; meeting is at 1pm. I've made myself a coffee, filed the 180th email from the public telling me to vote against. They don't know I stepped down two weeks ago. Two from people I know so I write back.

"Hi, you know it's me you've written too?"
    The reply: "Hi Clive, no sorry it was one of these automatic forms I had to fill in."

Such is technological progress. I'm feeling nervous. Should I email my speech to Councillors and officers or just the Councillors? Too difficult, I'll decide when I get to City Hall. Last swig of coffee and I'm off. Damn, more emails.

It's now 12.55: I'm in the Council Chamber, sitting behind where the Councillors will sit, in fact on the bench which is right behind where I would have sat had I not stepped down from Committee.

The layout of the Chamber is a bit like the House of Commons but with the chair and officers high up at the front (where the Speaker would be), Councillors along benches either side of a central corridor and the public gallery at the back (to my left).

It's quiet, hardly anyone in the room, that's why I'm now whispering to you! A hail from the Chair breaks the silence,

"Clive you can't sit there, move back a row."

Slightly puzzled until it then dawns on me, I'm now a member of the public and if I were directly behind a Committee member I might be able to influence them. "Alright", I say, before "I always do what I'm told." Don laughed. And said something I didn't quite catch. It was good to see that, it is going to be a tough afternoon for him.

13.00: Still hardly anyone in the Chamber. I pop out to see why, and there's a massive queue where searches are being conducted. Someone's trying to take a group photograph, it's Acorn, the better deal for renters group. I stand straight and wait for the camera to click. He notices and takes it from another angle. Not unreasonable, I'm not even a member of Acorn. But where are the XR (Extinction Rebellion) people?

13.15: The meeting starts, procedure is explained, first a briefing from the Head of Planning on Appeals and he mentions that the massive student block in St Paul's, one that I was instrumental in getting turned down had gone to the Appeal Inspector. He read the reasons, they sound defendable.

Now it's the Planning Application. Firstly it will be Public Statements (including mine); the Planning Officer presents a summary of the application, followed by Councillor questions, then debate and then a decision. There is only one: 18/05628/F - Philip Street Scrapyard, St Philips. That is the three gas powered generators for the grid. There were 142 written statements (including my eight page one) and three sets of questions. If they all turn up and take their allotted sixty seconds that's nearly two and a half hours. I look around and there certainly aren't 145 people here.

13.45: Some of the statements are quite moving, parents with small children at the nursery school, really anxious about poor air quality, already on their little ones' lungs or asthma. For me, it is the sense of injustice that drove me to all this work and my objection, but for the parents it goes deeper. It's a real worry for the lives of their children. I think back to when my two offspring, now in their 20s, were three or four. Yes, highly understandable.

The Chair calls "Councillor Clive Stevens"

CHAPTER D3
BEING A FAIRNESS WARRIOR (PART 3, FINAL)

I stand, switch on two mikes, to really emphasise my points and say;

"I would like to thank officers for their quick and helpful answers.

"Two weeks ago I stepped down from Committee to fight this. It is clearly unsustainable development. The noise and NOx are certainly more pollution, above legal I don't know. Too many things modelled and assumed.

"But my main point is all these out-of-date policies. We are told that mitigation by 20% is not reasonable, the 2011 policy is out of date. Yes by 8 years and by 80%. The NPPF[7] tells you what to do about out-of-date policies. The impacts need to be made acceptable. Well how do you make the emission of 30 killer tons of carbon dioxide acceptable? 50%? More? Or move the location and use biogas?

"The Government's Energy Policy EN1 also dates from 2011, the Climate Change Commission in May 2019 says policies need updating and that energy in the 2020's needs to become carbon neutral. So write to the minister and ask them when new policy is coming out.

"In conclusion, this is a waste of important and central land. NPPF policies 117 to 123 apply to brownfield and tell you to make the optimum potential. These generators are not that.

"Please, please do not approve and instruct officers to get more modelling and use up-to-date policies".

A round of applause follows. Each speaker received a round of applause making the meeting good natured, that's except for the applicant's representative of course. I heard some stifled boos.

More speeches, some angry, some really anxious; mums holding their children asking how could the Council subject little ones to such high levels of pollution: very good question.

---

7   The NPPF is the Government's National Planning Policy Framework under which all local plans must sit, the one that must be obeyed.

14.15pm. No more statements, and the Councillors on the Committee start to ask their questions.

First up, Councillor Eddy,

"We heard Councillor Stevens claim that policy is out of date. Is that so?"

The officer replies,

"I think Councillor Stevens is referring to BCS13?"

She looks up, at me, I nod, she continues,

"That came out in 2011 before these standby generators were envisaged, the policy wasn't designed to cover them."

And Councillor Eddy says his thanks and moves to another line of questioning.

To me that sounds like an admission that the policy was out of date, but as we shall see that hadn't convinced Councillor Eddy.

Two hours in and Councillors are running out of questions. A few have kindly referred to my work, but I'm worried they are not landing knock out blows. I actually now wish I was on that Committee; I could have tried, barrister like, to drill down into what you do when policies are out of date? I know the answer. Why aren't they pushing that? I guess they have never come across the issue before. But if you can prove policies are out of date, then you use the NPPF rules (the overview document). Oh the frustration, I hope they aren't going to blow it. I was fairly confident they'd refuse or defer, but it's pointless if the reasons are no good. They, we, will get slaughtered if the applicant appeals.

15.15pm Councillors, the members of the Committee, are saying what they think. Many have been moved by the speeches, I was too. All but one is going to vote against, but still no rock solid planning reasons, plenty of moral reasons, plenty of common sense reasons but neither work in Planning Law[8].

And then the white rabbit; the very Planning Officer who had been defending this dreadful scheme suggests a reason for refusal. He whispers it to the Head of Planning who whispers it to the Chair.

"I propose we reject under policy DM14" he says aloud.

What on earth is DM14? I think.

"It's to do with health and well-being. So the reason for rejection, to be voted on and recorded is to prevent the perceived damage to mental health and anxiety of residents from this development".

Perceived? We are told that this type of reason has even been defended in Court before, so it has case law behind it.

The vote is taken to reject the application under policy DM14 (which dates from 2014 by the way). And it is 10 to reject and one to approve. Dear Councillor Eddy, who I neglected to tell you said something along the lines that we needed these gas generators or else the Greens would be having us all living in caves. Maybe, but the impact of climate catastrophe might have the same effect, or worse.

So the climax was an anti-climax, a rabbit pulled from a hat to support the rejection. I'm not confident it will stand up at appeal (if it is appealed). There was no process of discussing policy DM14. I think that will be its Achilles heel.

So we wait and the residents of St Philip's Marsh and the children at the nursery school continue to breathe bad air and continue to worry about it getting worse[9].

Comment: Not only was it unfair that the applicant could take advantage of a hole in the Council's Planning Policies, but to run to the

---

8   By the way there have only been two NPPFs and both were written under Conservative led governments.
9   They didn't appeal! In fact there is a new application to put in a massive bank of batteries. It will be decided in July 2020.

cheapest solution and pollute the environment and worry the hell out of the people living there. The new Planning Policies (being consulted on) were looking to re-designate some of this space from industrial use to housing. That would be fantastic as it would be low cost land and enable plenty of affordable housing except there would be a bloody great big gas powered power station (almost) in the centre. It would keep house prices cheap for sure but wasn't fair on future occupants either.

We now move on to what is fairness (in my fairness warrior world)

CHAPTER D4
@SAGEANDONION SEEKS ANSWERS

I thought I learned a lot about unfairness as a Dad to two wonderful but squabbly[10] daughters. Those lessons helped hone my "fight for the underdog" approach. I found I could apply it at the Neighbourhood Partnership meetings and follow ups. I'd been Chair of the local Neighbourhood Partnership, abbreviated BCR[11] NP, since 2010 and I'd seen it grow from nothing to a locally recognised greatness and then. Well no need to say more here. The story of its ups and downs is in the Appendix (7, 8 and 9) and a good lesson in devolved democracy.

That led me to taking a more serious interest in politics starting around about 2012 (You will recall from chapter A2 that I woke up in 2014), the two years prior to 2014 were a long political doze, pushing the snooze button so to speak. The only politicians I knew were those on BCR NP.

BCR NP had six Lib Dem Councillors plus some elected members of the public. I was one of the latter, a representative of the local community group RCAS[12]. I worked closely with three of the six Councillors: Neil

10   One daughter has suggested lively as a replacement word for squabbly.
11   BCR stands for Bishopston, Cotham and Redland which are three wards around where I live, when I became Councillor it was for Clifton Down ward which is next door, in this part of Bristol the wards are all close together as we are so densely packed in.
12   Redland and Cotham Amenities Society; a well-meaning bunch of people who have over 800 members and quite a lot of influence in the area and in the Council (Planning certainly).

Harrison, a lecturer in Sociology at UWE and a slow left arm spin bowler if I recall. Anthony Negus, who has remained a Councillor and I still count as a friend even though I joined the enemy and we became distant for quite a while; I hope he has forgiven me, it's difficult to tell. Anthony is a retired conservation architect. Over the last ten years, the time I have seen and worked with Anthony in the Neighbourhood Partnership and then on the Council (he is the only one of the three who has lasted) he has developed into a sort of political rhinoceros[13]. The way he charges on with his points in straight lines, head down metaphorically barging others out the way, unfortunately for him age has taken its toll, as it does to us all, for dear Anthony it's his eyesight, coincidentally rhinos are short sighted too[14].

The third of this gang of three was Councillor Bev Knott who is a retired Latin teacher and famous for his long sentences. He himself described his sentence structure as parentheses within parentheses, they could get so convoluted he would then forgot the point he was originally trying to make.

At that time all three had Cabinet roles and I helped them develop a planning policy for trees on development sites[15]. Protect them and if one or more has to come down then get lots of replacement trees planted on and off site. This tree policy became an example for other local authorities to follow and some did.

I also fed[16] the three of them direct input into how residents see the workings of the NPs themselves; they were the architects, but as Councillors they would hear what officers told them, so having a member of the public feed in the reality was useful. It was with mixed results as you will read in the appendix.

---

13   By the way rhinos are necessary in the Council, as you may have already concluded yourself. I'd watch Anthony in admiration when it was a situation when his qualities were needed and then I'd pick up the pieces.

14   And thick skinned!

15   At the time the policy was thought of as revolutionary, according to the Councillors the officers didn't think it could be done, but they ploughed on led probably by Anthony in his rhino like way, thick skinned too, and the policy was put in around 2012 and has stayed (apart from one glitch explained in C1).

16   Actually I used to feed Anthony, he would arrive at our NP meetings at 7pm following eight hours solid of Council meetings, or so he said, I can believe him. The only way to get him to work with us constructively was to bring him a cheese and pickle sandwich. He devoured it; then he was fine. If only it were so easy to calm real rhinos.

I sat down with Bev one day, not quite in the "nudge, nudge, wink, wink" mode but a similar question, "what's it all about then?" I was asking about politics. I chose Bev as he seemed the most approachable on this subject. I thought politics and economics were inextricably linked, I knew a lot about economics, or so I thought. I realise many others see economics as a separate subject, that's how it's taught in schools, but for me there was and always has been a clear choice of economic direction between a Conservative view of survival of the fittest versus Socialist ideas based on equality of opportunity with public services for all.

I thought different political goals and systems would require different economies. Back then I didn't understand how the UK could keep swapping and changing government every five or 10 years when it would take 10, 20, or even 30[17] years or more to have an economy working the way they wanted. And at that time I dismissed the Greens as a joke, how wrong I was, but what I wanted to know then was what approach the Lib Dems followed?

But could I get Bev to teach me? Even the offer of coffee and apple cake, delicacies served at the Coffee Number One that used to be on Gloucester Road, wasn't enough. But as a Cabinet member he was far too busy to give me what a degree course would have delivered. So after a while I decided I had to work it out for myself. And I slowly morphed from a light Lib Dem to a deeper Green with what became my own home-made economic point of view. My way of making sense of "what's politics all about then" and it has led to "what do we need to do then". To understand my statements and projects from now on you need to understand this view point. Let's hope my writing is up to the job.

By 2012, my political/economic views had progressed this far: a belief in the state's role in defence, policing, upholding the rule of law, democracy, freedom and fairness whatever that is, probably equality of opportunity and a mixed economy. I was a believer all the same, relying on faith, gut feel even and not really having much understanding

17   For example the Thatcher reforms of the 1980s really took effect in the Blair years and were one of the causes of the 2008 crash (in my view). Norman Tebbit's "My Dad got on his bike and looked for work" (Norman is often misquoted) but this policy undermined family support and led to the isolation and loneliness of elderly life nowadays (so that effect took 30 years to become clear).

of the facts or mechanisms underpinning the logic of it all. I was also developing a growing uncertainty that perhaps some of my beliefs were wrong; watching the events that followed the banking crashes of 2008 and seeing the rich get richer, nobody imprisoned[18] and the common person having to pay.

As a teacher of business at Bath University, I began to wonder if I was teaching them the right things. Essentially the message was, "get your business into a position where the competitive environment is under your control, if you can do this you make excess profits for shareholders, yourself and the business can afford innovation". Innovation is what the engineers, whom I was teaching, were interested in and that was what I was paid to teach them. Most enjoyed it and many got good jobs. They learned to understand about the business and economic system they fitted in to, that they had to innovate to keep their employer ahead of competition and so command the market and in return the business would provide secure, well paid and interesting jobs. That's what I'd been taught in 1987 (at INSEAD Business School) and had seen and experienced since then. But was it right?

To formulate my own view on the economic system I needed to discover my own political values[19], something I'd not really worried about ever before. One flows from the other, surely. I am taking you through this journey because I think the country needs to work out its own answer too, but I'm getting ahead of myself.

My first degree is in Physics[20] and I have this psychological need to go back to first principles, to really understand issues, that means needing to think deep and that takes time. This drives my colleagues crazy. I'm slow on the uptake and in a political world slowness means you miss the press release and making the news. And my deafness enhances that view I guess. But anyway that's me, "Clive, first principles, Stevens".

So what are the first principles, pillars if you like, of my desired

18 Apparently 47 went to jail but only one from the USA and none from the UK: https://ig.ft.com/jailed-bankers/
19 When and why the universities took the politics out of political economy I don't know but it was surely one of the greatest mistakes in history?
20 Actually Natural Sciences, specialising in Physics.

democratic political/economic system? Ways I might define fairness. I started with a list, it wasn't very long. In fact, there were only two things on it and I relied on thinkers greater than me to help me get that far.

The fairness list: Equality of Opportunity (not equality of outcome; that experiment[21] has failed) plus Freedom to do what one pleases as long as you don't harm others. That was my list, it has changed since and gotten even shorter. But first some words on each pillar.

CHAPTER D5

WHERE @SAGEANDONION SEEKS FIRMER PILLARS FOR EQUALITY AND FREEDOM

The Equality of Opportunity Pillar; long ago I'd bought into the ideal that any person should be able to start life in a situation where his or her future shouldn't be dictated by luck, and luck includes advantages[22] from parents, their advice, earnings and contacts. That's why we have free hospitals, free healthcare, dentistry and schooling up to the age of nineteen, surely. In theory we are all equal under the Law too. But EoO, if I may abbreviate it, unravels very quickly when you start to worry about hypocrisy.

I can buy into EoO for helping the disadvantaged but what about preventing gain to the already advantaged? If parents are successful why shouldn't they give their offspring advantages? And if you say, "well yes", if we still allow that, it quickly undermines equality of opportunity as a value. Is it in reality just a sham? Private schools for some, inheritances, parental help using their networks to get themselves, children or even extended family a good job, better legal help if you have money, and much more. If you stop all that then you are saying to parents that you should allow downward social mobility for their own children, that's not only unpopular but probably goes against human nature.

I think most of us can agree that those with disadvantage should be

---

21 With communism.
22 Blindly ignoring the advantages I had gained from my parents.

able to climb the ladder[23], but what about those who start off higher up, surely that means some need to fall down to make room for others to climb up? I wouldn't want that to happen to my children, not that they are particularly high up. I used to think that my values included a strong belief in equality of opportunity. But as a parent, I recall vividly the drive to help my children get a better start in life, it is very, very strong, it's probably evolutionary so perhaps the idea of equality of opportunity is not one that fits with human evolution and thus human nature. It's not one I can believe in without being a pretender.

Well that wasn't a very successful pillar! Let's try the other one.

What about the second principle on my list; The Freedom Pillar? Hopefully by the time you read this book we will have emerged from our house arrest imposed by Covid-19.

Ding dong. Older woman answers the door. Visitor asks, "Is Jean-Paul free?" "Oooh", she replies, "he's been asking himself that for years." (Abridged Monty Python sketch)

Freedom to do what you want as long as it doesn't harm others. This principle is often attributed to John Stuart Mill a political thinker of Victorian England; an atheist during religious times; freedom for yourself, in your local community, and as a larger group in a nation state. Democracy is a subset of freedom. Running a business in "free markets" is a subset of this freedom idea too. Freedom, liberty, as opposed to equality sit better with human evolution (in my view) and fit peoples' values more in my experience, certainly in the West[24]. We voluntarily give up some freedom if we get married for example and certainly if we have children. In most forms of employment we consent

23   This ladder implies status is important. Everything I've read says it is, to many of us anyway. If you can remove the need for status or perhaps you can change it; that is for someone else to research and write about. Or you can increase the number of activities that are socially recognised as worthy of status. I once suggested this at a Governors meeting for a local primary school. To create an awards ceremony with 60 categories so each child would be best at something: most friendly, best improved at, all sorts of things. It prompted some discussion. Someone said that parents who want their children to progress on to private school (at age 11) would not like this idea one little bit and in all likelihood move their children out early. I didn't push it any further.
24   But not exclusively the West. I have seen the residents of Hong Kong also value liberty highly. I'm sure other places too.

to a hierarchical system and give up some freedom in return for a wage packet to buy other forms of freedom. But what if you are poor, do you have as much freedom as someone who is wealthy? i.e. in debt, or at the whim of a landlord and increasing rent? I think many of us can agree that liberty is a good thing, something inherently desirable and probably based on human nature. However, for some of us, it can seem like a prison, not behind bars but similar, captivity due to lack of money.

And what about the "doesn't harm others" bit? If you lived in a village of a hundred people, any person you harmed would let you know and the village elders will help you to put it right. Run your diesel engine outside someone's house and you'd be told. But in a city of half a million, or a world of eight billion, is driving a polluting diesel car doing harm? It certainly is, but we don't know who it harms. Some other questions I asked myself; are taking flights and contributing to the world's excess of CO_2 doing harm? And who is going to tell you off? And how is sending your child to private school harmful? Does it harm freedom of opportunity for others? Harm just can't be any harm as that would stop everything happening, it has to mean significant harm surely?

I'd got to the stage of thinking, "If I now believe in freedom without doing significant harm to others, then surely I have to buy into the idea of not significantly harming the freedom of others too". And if that was my new belief perhaps I should add the word liberal in front the term democratic political system. And please don't say, "Clive you must be a Lib Dem then", although some might try to say just that!

So both pillars of my initial democratic political ideals, the ones I started with, are looking a bit shaky. The first one has crumbled altogether unless I'm happy to be a fraud, which I'm not. The second, freedom or liberty, is still just about there but limited to liberty without doing significant harm which crucially also means not harming the liberty of others. And if you agree with this logic and recognise that many peoples' liberties (freedoms) are constrained due to poverty or lack of opportunity then we should look to a system that views fairness as freedom of opportunity and look to help increase that freedom to take opportunities to other people too.

A short reminder of why I think this is important; because over time the economy will reflect the political viewpoint of the leaders. If, as we learned from chapter B1 (the Mathematics of Power) those leaders' values only support and represent a minority of the population then the economy will be guided, or captured, so that they and their supporters gain more. State capture as it is sometimes called.

If the political system is changed so that more voters support the leaders (51% or more) then the leaders need clear political goals that a majority can buy into. The values of the nation become important because the economic goals will follow. And if as a society we can't agree about fairness/equality of opportunity then we need to find an accommodation and then design an economy to reflect what we have chosen.

CHAPTER D6
I'M NOW FREE TO EXPLORE FREEDOM[25]

Back to my own trials and tribulations about fairness. I have lost the equality of opportunity pillar altogether. But what should replace it? This gave me a headache. I then checked out the writings of the philosopher John Rawls with his 1985 essay; *Justice is Fairness*. That gave me an even bigger headache. Wikipedia summarises his fair equality principle as;

> *"This principle maintains that "offices and positions" should be open to any individual, regardless of his or her social background, ethnicity or sex. It is stronger than 'Formal Equality of Opportunity' in that Rawls argues that an individual should not only have the right to opportunities, but should have an effective equal chance as another of similar natural ability"*

So now you know!

This is even stronger than equality of opportunity and I said that

---

25   Although I'm writing this as if it were a logical journey it wasn't at all and to a certain extent these ideas have become clearer as I've had to explain them to you. I'm sure your feedback will mess it up again!

didn't fit my beliefs now due to my experiences as a parent and the drive to provide my children with an advantage. In theory I can accept what John Rawls is saying and I'd be happy to adopt this, except for my children. I know others who would take exception to an even wider group, to close friends or members of a particular club.

The way the Rawls's approach plays out, and he has been very influential, can be illustrated by using an example of recruitment: some organisations redact the person's name, age and other details, school even that might reveal ethnicity or advantage from the CV. This is to allow those from disadvantaged backgrounds a better chance. It is especially important to do this to minimise the impacts of unconscious bias like racism or sexism. When it comes to interview many characteristics become visible, but at least there's an attempt at fairness in a recruitment system that follows these rules and giving the person the opportunity of an interview. Then training of the interviewers kicks in.

I can subscribe to doing that for recruitment and in a work setting but I keep coming back to the kids. I can't say I follow equality of opportunity for everyone, except my own kids; that rings a bit hollow. For some other people it's not what they can vote for at all, not what they have worked hard all their lives for; that's to afford a nice house, car, status and private education for their children and the best chances in life for them. In fact they might say, "What's the point of working hard and getting rich if I can't give that advantage to my children"? They use their network of friends to open up jobs, careers, some even go so far as to make sure their children mix in the right social circles so when they become young adults they meet the right type of persons to do business with and perhaps someone of the right standing to wed. I would love to be able to argue that people with these values are not true democrats but definitions of the word democracy rarely include fairness or equality of opportunity, so I can't. It is also the situation that the general ruling party in the UK is the one that represents such values.

It seems if you want society to adopt equality of opportunity you have to argue for it, get people to vote for it and win an election or referendum. Not enough do. I would struggle too I think.

So I'm now down to just one value (politically), one pillar, freedom. People should have the liberty to take opportunities so long as they don't do significant harm to others. This also means not harming the freedom of others to take up their opportunities; that broadens it enough, my strong definition of freedom. For me it is also a definition of fairness that I can live with. It can mean that if you are recruiting and you want to put in a system to not harm the freedom of opportunity of others then you might well redact specific information and conduct training of the panel in eliminating bias. But the fact it is linked to freedom rather than equality makes it easier to fit with giving advantages to one's own children. As long as those advantages don't significantly harm other people's opportunities then it's OK. If I sent them to Eton (which I didn't) then I'd have to decide whether such a school harms[26] the opportunities of others who don't and can't attend.

If you agree with this logic and recognise that many people's liberty (freedom) is constrained due to poverty or lack of opportunity then we should look to an economic system that views fairness as freedom of opportunity and helps to create more of it and reduce harm.

I agree it's a minefield. These are not just my issues, they have been thought and fought over for thousands of years in a long line of western political philosophy[27] as far back as Plato.

So armed with one wobbly pillar I needed to think how an economy could be tweaked to improve the opportunities of the people of Bristol. Back in 2016 I had sworn an oath to serve:

"I have a responsibility to represent all communities and the city of Bristol and work constructively with our officers, partner organisations and each other to secure better social, economic and environmental outcomes for all".

---

26   There's a great book called *Posh Boys, How English Public Schools Ruin Britain* by Robert Verkaik 2018 (One World) that argues just this issue.
27   I did try to consider non-western philosophy too but it all got just a bit too difficult. There is one book though which I can wholly recommend if you like this sort of thing: *How The World Thinks* by Julian Baggini published by Granta in 2018.

My foray into first principles has ended. You can see why my colleagues must have got so infuriated! It's taken until March 2020 and I'm sure my thoughts will develop further. I used to think I valued equality of opportunity but now I think that due to my experiences as a parent I actually have different values. I would sum them up now as "freedom of opportunity" and the issues that much of my politics revolves around are the "without doing harm to others and their own freedom of opportunity". What are the harms and how to reduce them? Later on I give four examples of how this can be applied: libraries, buses, Council Tax and air pollution.

This is the one value where society, even friends, have a divergence of views. Some people hold dear to equality of opportunity, others freedom and others to meritocracy. I have already discussed my problems with equality. I have settled on a middle ground for now. As for the third, meritocracy, it sounds great until you wonder if a person merits having wealthy parents and the advantage that brings; or if someone merits a disadvantaged upbringing and so less freedom. Meritocracy falls apart too. If UK society can sort out what it wants then we can all move forward together.

Nationally there is an answer out of this cul-de-sac, that's let the people decide. Democracy (whether liberal or not) is our system. If there is a desire to change it then let's do it. Some ideas[28] are suggested in section H.

---

28 Discussing this with my daughter she said, "if the country agrees on any one of these then that's the end of politicians". That sounded like a good result to me. Unfortunately her comment doesn't stand up to scrutiny as politicians would argue over the details. Still that might be a positive result and bring us better law making.

CHAPTER D7
ECONOMISTS SHOULD STUDY DIFFERENT TYPES OF ECONOMIES

I didn't go into this exercise (developing my own view of who the economy should serve and how) without reading up and I did plenty of reading. There's a bibliography[29] at the back. I also broke the task down into manageable chunks and used the opportunity of giving business lectures at both Bristol and Bath Universities to prompt further ideas aided by deadlines. So the Autumn of 2014 brought "Business And Sustainable Engineering" to over 400 students at Bristol University. Whilst it was mainly about technology, I did bring in some politics and told the engineers that they could influence the world in four ways whereas we mere mortals have only two controls. Mortals are limited to our voting and shopping choices. Engineers have those two devices and also have the innovations they develop which bring their businesses or organisations more success and can make them greener too. Those very same innovations can also make political choices easier too, so engineers can influence the heart of power. Make electric cars or solar energy cheaper and you create an easier decision for a politician. Whether the students listened to what I was saying I don't know. But I did and a month after that lecture at the end of 2014 I joined the Green Party.

The confidence coming from a focus group[30] review of those lectures and marking the answers I got back from a specific exam question I set at Bath encouraged me to continue. I gave some talks to the Bristol Green Party in 2015 called, "Money Or A Life" and added an evening optional lecture at Bath University called "Corporate Social Responsibility". I flagged it up as political, students were free not to attend and it was not examined. Most came though. That one continued for three years until I stopped teaching at Bath University altogether. Too much going on, too many students in the class and 18 years was a good innings.

29 Of the books I can remember reading, that have had an influence.
30 A focus group is a fancy way of saying a discussion group about a topic aided by a facilitator. I cheated and facilitated myself which might invalidate the findings.

My message: The economy is what we make it to be. It combines a series of social and technical innovations all meshed together into a system. The cogs, pipes and meshing can be changed. It could be changed to support the needs and wants of most people if their chosen leaders wanted to.

Many people, including some economists, suggest that the workings of an economy are cast in stone, a law of nature; they spend their energies justifying the current arrangements and writing or using their marvellous maths to recommend modifications to get even closer to an ideal: free market, free trade, small government world to seek ultimate efficiency. I'm going to show you why I think they have it all arse about face. Here goes…

There can be and are different types of economies. A part of economics should be the study of how different economies work to provide for the populations and support their social goals and values.

Before the invention of the plough, virtually all humans were hunter gatherers[31]. Hunter gathering itself is an economic system, roaming in small groups, dividing up skills into specialist tool users, meat and fish hunters, fruit collectors, honey gatherers, plus rituals to celebrate events, memorise where and when to find resources at different times of year and ways of trading with other groups. The study of this type of economy is by anthropologists and archaeologists, a good part of what they study are the economies but they aren't called economists.

Then the invention of the plough[32] changed everything.

With a plough, a group doesn't need such a wide ranging territory; just settle on some fertile land close to water and farm it. One person can now grow enough food to feed four or five people. And as Tim Harford writes, "what do the others do now?" And what they did was kick off a completely different type of economy. And in addition there

---

31   https://www.nytimes.com/2015/10/27/science/nothing-simple-about-hunter-gatherer-societies.html
32   According to Tim Harford's 2017 book "50 Things That Made The Modern Economy" (drawing from James Burke a respected scientist of the 1970's who no doubt drew from researchers before him).

was a new form of wealth. It used to be the territory they roamed over which needed some protecting. But with farmed land they have houses and livestock to protect too as it's all much more productive; you will need soldiers, perhaps armies and leaders, and so we sow the seeds of inequality of wealth; all coming from the plough.

Humanity didn't stop at the plough, further inventions helped build the modern economy. Some are key materials like steel and concrete, others are made from those materials like roads, wheels and cars to run on them; boats and ships to move all those materials. And then clay for cooking pots and clay tablets upon which to tally your possessions, write invoices and IOU[33]s.

Some inventions are not things at all. They are social constructs, social infrastructure which means getting organised as Wallace, our Bristolian with a Yorkshire accent would say, "get organised Gromit": Leaders, laws, police, judges, writing, numbers, companies, limited liability or not, contracts, IOUs, IOUs you can trade, money and on it goes. Slavery was invented long ago, it was a system that helped build many economies and despite attempts to eradicate it, it hasn't gone away so far. Not all inventions are good.

Many inventions have improved productivity, productivity is important for wealth creation. It is the amount of output that can be produced by one person. Prior to the plough it used to take a few hours each day for a person to find enough food to feed themselves and any dependents. Nowadays statistics show that it takes 2% of the UK population to produce enough food for the other 98% of us (although we don't all get our share). And about 15% of us make enough things for the rest of us, again not shared out equally and some is exported so we can buy in other things like foodstuffs not farmed locally. So the remaining 83% of us provide services to support agriculture, manufacturing and all the other wants like cappuccinos, meals out, haircuts, bank accounts, government, health care, holidays, pubs and more…Not all inventions directly improve productivity though. Here's one, you can probably

---

33   For any non-English speakers IOU is an "I owe you" a note you write out and give to someone where you confirm you have borrowed £10 or something.

think of many more. My example is computer games.

> The modern economy uses all these inventions but it is a man-made system itself. Because of that, it can be broken, or remade. It isn't like the laws of physics. It is what humanity has constructed.
>
> Changes in the economy have often been triggered by new technology. Technology can be new things or new social constructs. I suspect that's what will prompt transformation.

CHAPTER D8
SO TO RECONSTRUCT THE ECONOMY BUT TO DO WHAT?

Every economy started somehow, then was added to, evolved, improved and reinvented many times over. But what is it for? For a long time I thought it was a system to provide for the needs and wants of the people. I now realise it is a system to provide for the needs and many wants of the people in power[34] and their friends.

The plough brought the ability to generate excess food and so others are freed up to create further wealth some or all of which can be extracted by kings, leaders, and powerful individuals and groups. The extracted wealth (let's call it earnings) needs protecting so the leaders then need armies and police. It enables hierarchies and their masters. The top dog needs to pay for their support structure, usually by taxes[35] of some form, often to pay the army, police and the influential so as to maintain power from internal and external competitors. That is why the economy must work for them. And if they don't look after their friends and their supporters then they will surely be toppled.

And for everyone else? As long as the economy provides their needs,

---

34   Chapters B1 to B3 describe this in more depth.
35   This paints tax as a negative thing. It can be. It can also be positive if it assists an economy that is supportive of the people to achieve their goals.

just sufficient to live and work then that is enough (sometimes they get more – the great plague helped redress the balance in England for a while). They stay alive and work hard for the system, if the system doesn't supply their needs they die. And back to Tim Harford, he writes that the Roman Empire seems to have stretched the inequality model the most of any civilisation, anymore and the poor and slaves would have died and their economy would have collapsed.

I haven't yet explained the "many wants" of the people in power and their friends. A system can't provide everything and a hierarchy is best maintained if, by moving up it, you achieve more wants, status and trappings. Much of the system depends on social standing, which is a successful approach because status seems to be a basic human (and animal) want, possibly even an emotional need. There are many books about status and our desire for it, the harm it can bring (Robert Frank talks about positional goods[36]) and the biochemistry[37] that fuels a desire for status in humans and many animals and the impact, damage, to those who are bottom of the heap.

In Roman times the leaders had to keep the aristocracy plus armies happy, supported by a massive economy based on slaves and peasants. Nowadays many countries have universal franchise (vote), usually all adult men and women can vote. As leaders your "friends" are now the ones who vote for you. Keep them happy, provide for their needs and allow them hope that through hard work their standing will improve.

You will, I hope, recall that early on I showed that in the UK, with its first past the post voting system, a leader can get into power from the votes of just 30% of the voting population. If a party stays long enough in power to modify the economy it can mean that the rest, the 70%, end up being there to work within an economic system that favours the 30%.

36   R.Frank, *The Darwin Economy*, 2011 Princeton University Press: in chapter five Frank develops the impact of the work by Fred Hirsch on positional goods. Position can refer to both location and status. Positional goods are limited in supply. Living in a house in a catchment area of a good school or having a Ferrari on the drive to demonstrate your social status. One argument being that someone buying a positional good (so increases their status or opportunity) deprives someone else. So a trade is win-win for the buyer and seller but third parties lose out. See section E2.
37   *The Spirit Level* by Wilkinson and Pickett, 2009, Penguin; some detail has been criticised but the message is clear and confirmed by other studies. Continuous stress (from poverty) causes illness and early death. It also causes bad decision making (Mcgarvey, D. 2017 - *Poverty Safari*)

In countries with different voting systems and referendums, those in power have more "friends" to keep happy, it can be 51% or more that need to be "looked after". And if coalitions are required then it's not just your own voters but those of your coalition partners too. When you get up to keeping 50% or 60% of the population as friends you are operating in the region where the majority are the "supporters' friends" and so the wealth, hope, power and status is more spread out.

I will proclaim boldly that since the plough all economies have been about supporting power structures. Always have and always will do. If we have other goals for the economy then it still has to marry up with this truism. Different economic systems lead to a different percentage of the population benefiting. If the population wants a change in the economy and its distribution of wealth then the political system needs to change.

I think it is possible to reconcile the realities of human nature with the Maths of Power and design an economy that concords with liberal democratic goals of fairness, freedom of opportunity, liberty to do what we want without harming others? I think it is also possible to design a different economy to deliver something a bit closer to equality of opportunity, should it be so desired. But they would be different. In my view the current economy in the UK corresponds closely to one needed to support a system of meritocracy.

If you agree then those who see the downsides of the meritocratic system should look to get the nation behind a change in value system and a revised economy to deliver it. My assumption is achieving such a goal would improve average well-being, but it might upset[38] a few at the top.

I think I have found a small part of the answer how to do this. But you will have to wait until Section H for that. In the meantime, armed with these new insights (for me anyway) I put these thoughts to work for my constituents and for Bristol, though not always exclusively for the Greens.

38   This fact makes such a change difficult to achieve.

CHAPTER D9
RELATING THE DEFINITION OF FAIRNESS
TO THE REAL WORLD

FAIRNESS AS FREEDOM

To sum up the journey so far: I have dropped equality of opportunity. I thought hard about my experiences as a parent. I'll fight for the values of freedom, liberty, but without doing significant harm to others. And that includes not doing significant harm to their freedom of opportunity. It seems to be as close to a consistent approach as I am going to get. I can live with that. That's now my definition of fairness.

If you believe in freedom for yourself and your family but you don't worry if your actions harm the opportunities of others then I question your commitment to liberal democracy. If you believe in equality of opportunity which is built into socialist ideals then why do many left wingers and MPs pay to send their children to private school?

Fundamentally I think this is what elections are fought over, Labour, Greens, Lib Dems and Conservatives all with different stances: Equality of Opportunity versus Freedom versus Meritocracy. What's it to be?

If we could sort that out and get a national consensus then that would be huge progress. It is hugely wasteful and probably harmful to move the economy one way and then back again.

Footnotes for the above text box are at the bottom, private school[39] Labour equality[40], Conservative meritocracy[41] and move the economy one way and back again[42]

---

39   https://www.thesun.co.uk/news/9981131/labour-vote-abolish-private-school-hypocrites/
40   The 2019 manifesto (Corbyn) had a lot in it about equality and some was equality of outcome like women's pay, much more wasn't sufficiently specific to be able judge whether it was equality of outcome or equality of opportunity; nevertheless much more about equality than the other main parties.
41   Interestingly the 2019 Conservative manifesto didn't seem to include mention of meritocracy but there are still plenty of speeches from key members which say this is a core value: Priti Patel in 2018 and Dominic Raab in 2019. But if the Tories don't believe in meritocracy any more then please tell me and let me know what's replaced it.
42   In theory this should be a check on power but in practice it seems that on average we get Conservative rule forever.

Before you jump to judge me please read the next examples that I have pushed for as a Councillor in the later years that illustrate what I mean by freedom of opportunity. This term is used already and I see it can be used to underpin right wing views sometimes it is even presented as the exact opposite of equality of opportunity. I don't see it that way at all.

Please read the examples, see what I mean and decide for yourself.

Unless you persuade me otherwise, I've settled on the view that freedom of opportunity means helping those without the opportunity to help themselves, empowering them and giving them chances to take up opportunities if they want to. That, combined with a political system in Bristol where 34% voted Labour which resulted in a Labour Mayor and a Labour majority of Councillors, the other 66% needed representing[43]. I decided my role therefore was to give people a helping hand to help themselves; whether with problems dealing with a noisy pub, parking or especially children in Council care, or adults with social care needs. It seemed the right thing to do was to fight for the underdog and leave them with the tools and resources to continue the fight on their own.

To apply these views meant working closely even cooperating with Labour as they were the ones in power and could get things done, it meant not doing work related to putting out press releases criticising Labour all the time, even though they made their share of mistakes. To be honest I often felt I let my Green colleagues down. That's the power of tribal[44] think for you.

After four years as a Councillor I have come to the view that trying to get noticed by a busy public most of whom have limited or no knowledge of a particular topic means the messages have to be delivered more like adverts, repeated and repeated and ideally add a sprinkle of shock to get attention, repeat again and keep on the same theme and always find something critical of those in power.

But reality isn't like that, most issues are complex and sometimes

---

43   I was always conscious that I only won by 10 votes with just 28%; the ward of Clifton Down was a four way marginal. I sneaked it. I tried to represent the other 72% too, but as a Councillor I had nearly no power so don't worry.

44   I'm using the word tribalism to mean a very strong feeling of loyalty to a political or social group, so that you support them (almost) whatever they do. (*Cambridge English Dictionary*).

the ruling party gets it right, especially with a bit of nudging in the right direction. But politics as real-life, because of the tiny amount of time and attention that voters want to devote to understanding decisions and issues, means that press releases like adverts are what's needed to get elected. It's a competitive system, and so it continues with most people understandably ignorant of the details.

The following four stories are about working with Labour to help get the right things done for better freedom of opportunity for those who are poor. Labour didn't always agree with me! Chapter D10 is about using libraries to improve freedom, D11 on the buses to improve freedom for those without transport. D12 is about retaining the Council Tax discount for the poorest and D13 about air quality.

CHAPTER D10

THE FUTURE OF LIBRARIES... 3/4/18 TO ABOUT 40 CONSTITUENTS (ALSO SPEAKING WERE COUNCILLORS ANTHONY NEGUS AND CARLA DENYER)

I use the term social mobility a lot in this chapter; I'm meaning the ability for people to better themselves. If you are stuck in a low paying job, eking out your earnings to pay the rent then you are not socially mobile, and in practice have less liberty.

"Freedom's just another word for nothing left to lose"

Famously sung by Ms J Joplin, written by Kris Kristofferson and Fred Foster; I completely disagree, it's a great song but the line is 100% wrong. If you have nothing, in a city, you have no freedom.

Venue: Redland Library - April 2018 about 8pm, I was the final speaker (edited)

I started with how I voted for funding libraries in the recent Full Council motion, indeed who would vote against? As it turned out, it passed by one vote. Councillor Negus's speech there was electric. Unfortunately the video recording doesn't do it justice. He puffed himself up like a big handsome toad and gave a lesson in oration. The Mayor was saying the Council didn't have any money. Knowing the figures especially for adult social care, I was inclined to believe him. However, there is money in the city, the Combined Authority (WECA) has responsibility for adult education; the universities also have money "raking in one quarter of a billion a year in fees" I said and now here's where I come in with what I said to the assembled multitude:

"I've been your Councillor two years now. I'm also a businessman. It's clear where the money is and where it isn't. And I was thinking what could you do to attempt to plug into these sources?

Many libraries (and museums) were set up 200 years ago with the aim of providing opportunities for workers to engage in self-improvement. It is that sense of opportunity that makes many of us still love libraries to this day. Back then they were encouraging an activity that we today include within the term social mobility.

Social mobility or lack of it was a problem then and it is also today's problem and it is behind WECA's money for adult training as Government believes it will help increase worker productivity. The UK has the worst social mobility in the developed world according to David Cameron when he was PM[45] [46]. It means people fail to reach their full potential, it forms

---

45   https://www.independent.co.uk/voices/theresa-may-social-policies-cabinet-david-cameron-legacy-eocnomy-heal-broken-britain-a7133306.html

46   In 2020 The UK came 21st out of 82 countries so not too bad? Among the G7 economies, Germany is the most socially mobile, ranking 11th with 78 points followed by France in 12th position. Canada ranks 14th followed by Japan (15th), the United Kingdom (21st), the United States (27th) and Italy (34th).
Denmark topped the rankings with a social mobility score of 85.2 points, closely followed by Finland (83.6), Norway (83.6), Sweden (83.5) and Iceland (82.7).
https://www.weforum.org/reports/global-social-mobility-index-2020-why-economies-benefit-from-fixing-inequality
http://reports.weforum.org/social-mobility-report-2020/social-mobility-rankings/

a drag on the economy, on tax payers and on the individuals themselves. There's lots of effort going into reversing this.

So taking stock...we have a problem. The Council's pretty bust and the current administration doesn't seem to want to keep libraries open[47], not this one anyway. Some form of mutualisation could be the way but whatever overarching approach you need sources of income.

So I thought, "there seems to be income in improving social mobility".

Let's see what resources and advantages Redland Library has. It has great transport links. It's easy for people to get here. It is surrounded by helpful people who can help others learn skills like networking, cv writing, practical courses, coaching and simply give advice. I look around and see it full of books and computers. And it's linked to the Library Service

So in addition to being a library you might consider this facility becoming something I would call a "social mobility centre". Not mobility as in wheel chairs or bikes but a place with resources to help others escape inequality[48] caused by their roots.

In some places libraries are still thriving, as arts centres, or community hubs or just libraries. So I'm throwing another idea into the pot - a library as a social mobility centre.

Why? There's money in social mobility whereas there's not so much for arts nor for community hubs. Redland Library is superbly located. And the bonus, to be a social mobility centre you probably need to remain a library too with books, a service and computers.

Libraries started 200 years ago responding to the leisure society[49] and trying to offer workers opportunity for self-improvement and social mobility. Perhaps we should go back to the original mission? The problems are similar.

So I offer you this idea. A social mobility centre[50], it aligns with potential funding streams, exploits our superb location and there's a need to remain part library."

47 By late 2019 they'd changed their mind. Post Covid-19 we shall see.
48 I think I'd now replace the word inequality with lacking opportunities
49 First leisure choice back then was gin. That was the competition to libraries.
50 Darren McGarvey in his 2017 book, *Poverty Safari* describes libraries as the engine room of social mobility especially in communities characterised by poor education, low opportunities and high levels of stress.

Fairly soon after this and with lots of encouragement from me, the Bristol Libraries Forum was launched. Strength in numbers, to cancel out the Council's "divide and rule" approach, maybe not even deliberate but that's how it seemed. Their first meeting was 19th October 2018 and look at the trust they had in the Council;

> *"I have been told by the organisers of Bristol Libraries Forum that this really is confidential so don't tell anyone please.*
>
> *Please keep this quiet at the moment and I assume official invites will go out (not sure if all Councillors are invited at this stage - this is a people empowerment initiative) If we are invited we obviously don't all need to go. They are not inviting Asher[51] I'm told. They aim to get over 14 libraries groups represented (so over 50%) and then to agree a committee and a constitution (using Parks Forum as a model)".*

Update: 15 months later, Martin Booth the editor of one of Bristol's local journals B24/7 wrote[52]

> *Stephen Morgan (Labour shadow minister for local government) heaped praise on Mayor Marvin Rees for keeping all of Bristol's libraries open, but library campaigners are not convinced by the plaudits.*
>
> *Morgan said: "Since 2010, under the Tories, nationally some 100 libraries have closed each year. Here in Bristol, Mayor Marvin Rees' Labour administration have kept every single library open and are investing in the service".*

But so far I haven't seen any plan for libraries based on social mobility.

---

51 Councillor Asher Craig was the Cabinet member for Neighbourhoods which includes Libraries. As of 2020 she still is but has changed her tune and is keeping them open so that's good.
52 https://www.bristol247.com/news-and-features/news/shadow-minister-praises-rees-for-helping-save-bristols-libraries/

CHAPTER D11
OPENING UP OPPORTUNITIES WITH A BETTER AND FAIRER BUS SERVICE

This next story illustrates how I think an economic change regarding local transport can improve the freedom of opportunity for those living in deprived areas. The change doesn't do harm to others as it increases overall welfare. See what you think…

Autumn 2018: We Green Councillors meet most Friday mornings to discuss issues of the week. I had submitted a draft Council motion to the group; I was suggesting we put it forward for debate at the next Full Council. It was calling for a congestion charge (to make the roads clearer at peak times) and for all the money to go into bus subsidies. I suggested various groups whose freedom could benefit from cheaper travel: school children of course, those from poorer areas and so on. Basically to enable them more freedom to travel further and faster, so it would be easier to take up opportunities like jobs, training that type of thing and the congestion charge would clear the roads too so safer for cyclists and better bus schedules.

But, hold the bus; colleagues said nobody would vote for this, we need to change it so that the congestion charge is only paid by people living outside Bristol's boundaries when they commute in. It would be better if Bristolians had no charge but still benefited from the better buses. Better because the roads were clearer and buses weren't held up and better through subsidies to encourage commuters to take the bus. A different proposition to mine, mine was based on targeting low income groups and giving travel freedom. The second approach was aimed more at improving the environment and safety for cyclists, reducing congestion; plus some money for free travel for the young. It was important to get this right as it would likely become an issue for the Mayoral elections of 2020 (now May 2021).

Should we try it out as a Full Council motion or not? And if so which version? There was a third hot candidate too: "End indefinite detention for immigrants and asylum seekers". This motion was to ask the Mayor to write to Government and local MPs to ask for an end to the UK's disgraceful approach to refugees; an approach that treats asylum seekers fleeing[53] torture and threats as if they were potential criminals. In Government's eyes they were lumped in with economic migrants, people wanting to come here for jobs; and all viewed as villains. Seeking jobs is controversial but many would argue it doesn't make you guilty of anything. Nevertheless they are all lumped together as immigrants, and the time confined is often open-ended; that is inhumane[54].

So the Green Councillors debated and then voted.

The result was; Better Buses (paid for by out of town commuters): four and Asylum seekers: four (eight Councillors voted as three weren't there).

A draw, the solution to Bristol's greatest problem was stuck just like the buses themselves. More discussion and eventually I agreed to pull the buses motion as it could well become one of the Green mayoral candidate's manifesto ideas. The Asylum Seekers motion went to Full Council and was passed[55]. Hurrah! And what has happened? Zilch of course; I'm sure the Mayor did what he was asked to do but Theresa May was the arch villain. Asylum seekers still[56] have the threat of indefinite detention and our buses are still blocked, unreliable and expensive for some: A good policy seemingly waiting indefinitely at one of those stranded bus-stops we covered earlier.

Then just before Christmas, Bristol University asked the people of Bristol if they had ideas where research might help resolve some of Bristol's problems. On the off chance I wrote in suggesting that

---

53   Economic migrants are seeking a better life. Refugees are seeking to guard their life. The difficulty is deciding which is which as current Government policy is to prevent economic migrants. I don't agree with the Government's approach but that is not the scope of this book.
54   Victor Frankl (see bibliography), describes life in German concentration camps, he writes, "Former prisoners agree that the most depressing influence of all was that a prisoner could not know how long his term of imprisonment would be".
55   You can read the full motion at Bristol City Full Council 11 December 2018.
56   Indeed it failed in Parliament again in June 2020, detention is still indefinite. https://www.independent.co.uk/news/uk/politics/immigration-bill-vote-indefinite-detention-boris-johnson-a9594511.html

a student could collect data showing the harm that too much car use brings to those who live in cities; air pollution, safety risks, noise and more. And if enough people took the bus with help from subsidies then that harm would be reduced. Amazingly I heard that my idea was accepted; so I'd better prepare the talk...and Better Buses (my version, increasing freedom of opportunity if you are low income) was back on and starting up its engine. I had been given an hour's slot at the Bristol Forum scheduled for March 2019.

Meanwhile in January and February we tried to get the out-of-towners-pay version of Better Buses through as a budget amendment. It went in alongside four other Green Party amendment[57] proposals.

February 28th 2019 Full Council debate on the Budget started at 2pm and finished at 7.20pm, we Greens wound up in the pub celebrating. Three of our five amendments had passed. The other parties had all their amendments rejected, including the Lib Dems with their big investment plan for bus lanes.

But the Greens' Better Buses (out-of-towners-pay congestion charge) was rejected. It was our big ticket amendment, some £6 million pounds per year. Labour claimed it was illegal, later we found out the prior legal opinion and it wasn't. The local newspapers were all over this but it was positively framed as something to be discussed and so we had started the ball rolling. Ever optimistic me, yes you wouldn't believe it but I am an optimist at heart, reflected on how this had played out and decided it was good to get the issue out into the open, there must be a thousand ways to improve the buses with one form of road user charging or another, we had proposed one, there are bound to be better solutions so watch this space. And another thing:

Never ever give up.

Things moved forward within weeks.

You will recall my talk to the Bristol Forum (as invited by Bristol University), the one scheduled for the end of March 2019. What if I modified the talk to be about the harm that cars do in cities and explain why the car drivers should be charged for that harm and that money

57   As in amending the Mayor's budget proposals.

be used to support those who use buses. So idea in mind, I met the organiser and he said, "great idea" as long as it concludes with the point that cities require more devolved power from Government[58]. That's easy as it's true. So my Better Buses has had a time out and morphs into a research project proposal to collect the actual data in Bristol to show why congestion charging is economically better than just leaving the situation to free markets.

My lecture slides are not available now, but here is the gist of it without the mathematics:

"If you live in a sparsely populated area, buying a car benefits you and society. It brings you well-being, it brings profit to the car salesman and doesn't harm anyone else. If the area then becomes crowded say due to a housing estate being built, your car brings a small amount of downside to everyone else now living there: a little air pollution, risks to children on streets and noise. Once all those other houses have cars too then the downsides are magnified and a new factor is introduced; congestion, that reduces the benefit to you of the car you originally bought.

Now if there are enough people and someone introduces a bus service some will use it and it eases congestion a bit. The main beneficiaries though are those who still drive their cars due to the benefit that having a car brings. Congestion and pollution will be slightly less the main beneficiaries of the bus service will be the car users. That is the "free market optimum".

If this were a situation that could be managed by an authority, it would be possible to increase everyone's well-being. The authority could do it by charging all those using their cars at peak times at a price which still meant they benefit overall compared with the clogged up, polluted situation previously. They benefit as long as the costs remain less than the gains from less congestion and cleaner air. Those not using cars would benefit too, as bus users they wouldn't pay the congestion charge, they would get cleaner air and if the authority used the money to subsidise bus prices then more regular, cheaper services could be run. This would more likely appeal to the less well off in the community, subsidised by the wealthy.

58   Somebody else thinking that laws in a city could be different.

Even some well-off people would switch from cars to buses as they would be better off too, no need to run a car due to the cheaper fares. That is the "managed market solution".

But if a new party gets elected and the Authority then takes away the congestion charge and the subsidy, some people will revert back to using their cars and cause more congestion, pollution and danger to children, reducing the average well-being to everyone.

A question and answer followed and we agreed that exceptions needed to be made for people who actually really need their cars: the disabled or perhaps single parents with infants for example.

Are you convinced?

To do this requires powers from Government to assist cooperation between individuals. That creates more freedom of opportunity. Everyone is still free to choose either bus or car and all benefit over and above the unmanaged free market situation with its attendant congestion, pollution, accidents, noise and more.

Update March 2020: The University of Bristol have continued this idea and are working with Firstbus to improve their modelling by using real Bristol data. This is along my preferred freedom of opportunity to the poor lines by offering freedom of choice across better transport opportunities.

Better Buses was a key theme of the Green Party mayoral campaign and relied on the congestion charge for out of town commuters. It was a key difference between the Greens and Labour. The 2020 election was stopped by Covid-19 so we shall see how it all pans out.

Of course I'm disappointed that the alleviation of poverty version wasn't taken up as the prime goal of the Greens. But I'm told "politics is the art of the possible[59]", so there you go.

---

59   Otto von Bismarck apparently on 11 August 1867. He also said some rather nasty things about his neighbours the Poles so I'm not a fan of him.

CHAPTER D12
COUNCIL TAX REDUCTION SCHEME – TAXING THE POOR TAKES AWAY THEIR FREEDOM OF OPPORTUNITY

The 2010 Coalition Government removed funding from Councils to give Council Tax discounts to the very poorest. Actually that's not quite right, they kept the funding to support the poorest pensioners, maybe because most pensioners vote, but they reduced it for working age claimants. It was one of their many decisions to target the underprivileged to help the bail out of the bankers and the economy as a whole; yes you Lib Dems, I know your party stopped the Tories from being even worse, but honestly why did you let them make mistake after mistake for five years?

By 2017 Bristol was the only Core City[60] left fully funding Council Tax Benefit, now renamed Council Tax Reduction. In theory it was costing the Council £39 million, but £14 million for pensioners was fully funded and much of the rest was financed within the Local Government Settlement of 2015 which included 100% Business Rate Retention and the increasing income from that. Nevertheless the headline cost was shown as £39 million per year shared across about 38,000 people liable for Council Tax, but because of their low income they didn't have to pay it; saving in some cases over £1,000 per dwelling (£20 a week).

So just think about it, these are the poorest, most are on benefits and many on in-work benefits, which are being cut anyway. How much extra money do you think a Council can extract from people living from hand to mouth and many in constant fear of eviction if they miss a rent payment?

Officers considered that charging five pounds a week was not unreasonable, with some options for special cases. It was thought that taking that amount from around 25,000 working age people might bring in another much needed £6 million less the costs of collection,

---

60 https://www.corecities.com/ : Belfast, Birmingham, Bristol, Cardiff, Glasgow, Leeds, Liverpool, Manchester, Newcastle, Nottingham and Sheffield

bailiffs and the rest.

Unfortunately for Labour, so they say, the rules set in Bristol meant that if it looked like the headline cost might go over £39.5 million then the whole issue should go out to consultation along with options to save money. The Conservatives supported this action I'm told. They certainly seemed keen to charge everyone a fiver a week minimum. It was about fairness they said!

According to the 7th November 2017 Cabinet paper (agenda 10) the original proposal came to Cabinet in July 2017. In fact it was July 4th 2016. That paper proposed different charging options to go out to consultation in the summer of 2017. It duly went out. Can you imagine the hoo-ha! Acorn, the private renters' membership union, went into overdrive, so did the Greens with Carla leading, plus the Lib Dems and pretty soon many Labour Councillors too. The Mayor was riding a raging bull and had to stay on the ride until the consultation results came back and he could can the idea.

The Chief Executive in that fateful summer was Anna Klonowski, she of the Sept 2017 £98,000 pay off[61], I can't help wondering if any of this was connected.

And my role? I was a new Councillor when that first paper came to Cabinet (In fact I asked questions about trees that day). But by the time the consultation came out I was disappointed that a Labour Mayor could even consider this. Still, by 2017, it was clear the finances were pretty fragile, he had been told he had to consult and we would end up with more Green voters for sure.

The consultation closed and officers dutifully wrote a report saying that after due consideration the Council Tax Reduction wouldn't be changed after all. Puzzled by all this I looked back at the report in 2016 that suggested the different scale of minimum charges. It seems officers had drawn on an external report by Keith Ollerenshaw who compared the Council Tax incomes collected by different authorities from taxing the poorest at different levels. Using his figures I came to different conclusions than the officers.

61   see chapters B6 and B7.

In November 2017 I delivered my "counter report" to the Mayor in front of Cabinet and the cameras.

"The bad news is that I'm accusing your administration of wasting public money – the good news is that I'm not accusing you of anything worse.

My point is that all this information (about collection rates) was available in the summer before you engaged in this expensive consultation. The paper that went around in July had the same base data I have analysed but crucially used one different assumption. That assumption was a 70% collection rate of this "new money" you plan to collect, 70% assumed whatever the minimum payment.

It referenced the 2016 report by Ollerenshaw to justify this 70%. Yet that report doesn't say this, at Figures 3 and 4 it clearly shows an increasing level of non-collection the higher the minimum Council Tax charge, going from low levels for schemes like £50 a year to massive non-collection for those at £300 a year".

With Bristol considering high value options like five pounds a week it implied high rates of non-collection. It's hardly surprising if you try to tax people with no money what do you get? Yes you get no money, along with more bailiffs and homelessness.

Needless to say the Mayor wasn't best pleased, neither were his officers and I was invited to a meeting with them to be explained to. The officers already knew me as I'd tried to work out ways of increasing Council Tax[62] just a few weeks before; an idea that seemed a more likely and fairer way of bringing in money. That turned out to be non-starter, but at this meeting with the officers I didn't retract my analysis of Ollerenshaw under what seemed to me like an attempt to apply a little pressure[63].

You might want to ponder why officers were cooking up schemes to bring in more income. If I remind you of the situation it may help, funding

---

62   On home owners with low incomes, not pensioners, with cashable equity above £100k in those homes.
63   It felt that way, for example it was just myself surrounded by four officers.

cuts had been ongoing for a number of years and what with Brexit it looked like they might continue forever. Jobs at the Council were being lost and the Government, we were told, weren't looking favourably on the leadership of Bristol because we were the only remaining Core City to give one hundred percent Council Tax relief against Government's express wishes.

Update March 2020: Bristol's Council Tax Reduction Scheme is still fully funded and the City has one of the highest collection rates of Council Tax in the country; primarily because it doesn't tax those who can't afford to pay.

CHAPTER D13
FREEDOM OF OPPORTUNITY AND AVOIDANCE OF HARM – IT GETS COMPLICATED[64]

This is a small part of the story of how Bristol went from European Green Capital in 2015 to being rebuked by Government in 2019 for its inadequate response to air pollution. It wasn't just a simple telling off; there was the threat of legal action too.

In July 2019, with a brand new Prime Minister and everything focused on "No Deal Brexit", Westminster's gaze, like Sauron's eye, narrowed its focus and swung its attention onto Bristol; Bristol with its dreadful air, 300 premature deaths a year and many more young and old suffering from ill health, asthma and cardiac conditions. But Sauron didn't send forth an army of orcs, she wrote a letter.

This Government letter, published on 23rd July 2019 was toxic, more toxic than the air and more than the Party PR machines could cope with, certainly in the first few days. Government posted it on their website around about the 7th August. Here are some extracts...

"For the avoidance of doubt, I want to be very clear that your preferred

64   Written 11th August 2019

option must deliver compliance in your local area in the shortest possible time, and have a robust evidence base to support it. You have indicated that initial analysis has suggested compliance could be achieved by 2025, I therefore expect your preferred option to deliver compliance by 2025 at the latest."

This was at the same time that the Mayor's consultation was open asking the public for their opinions on two options; one to achieve compliance by 2028 the other by 2029.

And it continues...

"I would like to make clear that any delay or non-compliance with the September and December deadlines will result in me being forced to consider legal action against Bristol City Council which may include issuing proceedings without further notice."

The author tells Bristol's Mayor that he must add another option to the modelling, a Class D zone option, it would include diesel car charging as well as cleaning up the buses and taxis. The deadline given for modelling a Class D zone was 8th August[65]. That's not quite as bad as it sounds. The modelling had actually been done a year earlier, it's just that the Mayor had kicked it out as unfair on the poor.

The choice was harm the poor with charges on their cars and vans, or harm everyone with poor air quality. The choice was limited because the existing legal action[66] meant air quality must become compliant[67] in the shortest possible time. And because Government and Councils had delayed, delayed and delayed, partly due to broken promises from the car industry.

There is a whole industry around air quality modelling, trying to predict how the concentrations of the poisons in the air would vary if

---

65   The letter was published on 23rd July but presumably the Mayor had a draft earlier

66   Brought about by Client Earth. https://www.bbc.co.uk/news/science-environment-43141467 Actions to meet this would mean accessing Government grants.

67   Compliant means bring NO2 annual average concentrations below 40ug/m3 which by the way can still kill, just less people than if at 50ug/m3.

certain changes are made to vehicle performance and driver behaviour. Prediction is fine, except when you measure the actuals against what the expensive models forecast. This caught up with the whole industry with the Volkswagen emissions scandal; if only as much effort and money were put into making the air cleaner itself rather than building models.

So back to the letter, the author, Dr Thérèse Coffey, a Conservative, was appointed Minister of State at the Department for Environment, Food and Rural Affairs on 25th July 2019. She had been second in command there when she wrote her letter to Mayor Marvin on the 23rd. And unlike Sauron, her swift glance at Bristol was a benevolent one, to us inhabitants at least.

What was it that made the Mayor change plans sometime in late 2018 when all seemed to be on course for charging[68] drivers of old diesel cars and adopting the Class D zone? The Mayor was asked this on 18th June 2019 (38 minutes into the meeting if you want to check it on YouTube) about the two new options[69] presented to Cabinet now out for public for consultation. That was just one month before the letter from Government.

Councillor Jerome Thomas who has led the Green Councillors on an impressive journey on the topic of cleaner air for Bristol asked Marvin:

"Is it the case that Government is happy with you not including a Medium Class D zone in the way that we go about things?"

Marvin replied,

"Government is happy because they know [class D medium zone] doesn't reach compliance in the shortest possible time."

As we now know Government wasn't happy, they wrote to Marvin just one month later.

The Green Party's air quality campaign towards the end of 2016 was

---

68   A Class D zone means charging older diesel cars too
69   A diesel ban zone or a Class C zone charging buses, taxis and lorries (not diesel cars)

awesome. It resulted in thousands of people signing a petition, many writing statements to Council, masks put on Bristol's statues and a full, Full Council watching a specially prepared video prepared by the Greens and featuring Marvin himself and then most if not all voting for the motion "Clean air now for Bristol" proposed by Councillor Charlie Bolton and seconded by Jerome. This was on the 8th November 2016. Labour and Marvin were fully behind it.

So over three years later the air is still illegal in many locations. The excuse for this is not wanting to harm the poor the most, those with old diesel vans and cars. Actually statistics from UWE show that the very poorest often do not have cars of any type but they do live in the most polluted areas. So with this reasoning shot to tatters by one of the city's great universities what can be on his, or his PR expert's (the Assistant to the Mayor) mind?

a) It could be a true analysis. Early deaths due to poverty far outweigh the 300 premature deaths a year from air pollution. If charging those to use their cars will cause more deaths than those saved it might be a real attempt to minimise overall harm caused by primarily diesel vehicles.

OR

b) It could be a way of differentiating Labour's values over Green values.

OR

c) A reason not articulated at the time of writing.

In summary, a fairness principle of allowing people to be free to do as they wish (drive their diesel cars) but without causing too much harm (premature deaths from air pollution) and without harming the freedom of opportunity of others (the poor who would be unable to afford a car due to charges) can lead one to a number of better solutions[70].

---

70   One could be a charging zone, clean air or congestion charge and then subsidise clean energy buses, a scrappage scheme enabling cash to buy a bike, electric bike or bus passes for example. Car club facilities too. I'm not saying this is the answer I'm saying the fairness as freedom of opportunity helps offer wider options.

SUMMARY OF SECTION D

These five case studies illustrate what I mean by defining fairness as freedom of opportunity without harming others and not harming their freedom either:

The gas-powered generators right at the beginning and helping the residents fight their battles even outside my ward and making life better for future residents of that area.

Libraries to help people self-improve, bus subsidies focussed on the less wealthy to open up opportunities for them, keeping Council Tax low for those who can't afford it so not to limit freedom by throwing people into further debt, bailiffs and ultimately homelessness.

And the air quality example which illustrates the difficult choices to be made and proposes that using fairness equals freedom without causing harm actually creates a way through the options.

Now feel free to judge me and my new found value, "freedom of opportunity, unless you harm others including harming their freedom of opportunity".

In writing this book I've necessarily had to think further about this. For me life is a series of opportunities[71] and you have to decide which ones to take; being a good parent, following a religious route or undertaking university research, whatever your wants. That's what leads to fulfilment in my view. If so, then everyone should have freedom to take opportunities and not be socially stuck (lack of social mobility). And if society agrees then the economy should support this ideal.

Onwards to Section E and the economy: "It's the economy stupid[72]".

---

71   Viktor Frankel institute of Logotherapy. Tom Rippin Fellow of the RSA writes in RSA Journal Issue 1 2020 that Frankl would define meaning as having a cause to serve or a person to love. Presumably during life you can have a number of causes and persons to love.
72   James Carville, 1992, strategist for Bill Clinton during the successful campaign to win the US presidency. The US was in recession during 1992 and so it was deemed a weakness of their opponent the incumbent US President G H W Bush.

SECTION E
THE EXTRACTION ECONOMY

I n the last section we explored what fairness might mean (I developed my personal definition of it), now it is time to work out how we achieve an economy that meets this fairness (freedom without doing harm) criteria? This section draws much from my teaching[1] at the University of Bath, and shows how I applied these principles to Councillor work in Bristol. We will discuss the five[2] main economic players (the processors) and the situations when each does well or less well for us as consumers and members of society.

There are four[3] case examples applying these ideas at the end.

---

1   Which was based on an MBA from INSEAD Business School (Fontainebleau, France) as well as
extensive business and investing experience.
2   It's not just about nationalisation versus privatisation.
3   Across five chapters E8 to E12.

CHAPTER E1
@SAGEANDONION RIDES AGAIN

Welcome back to my alter ego[4] @SageAndOnion, this time we look at the economy. Earlier on you will recall (sections B and D) we considered the Mathematics of Power and why and how economies are made to work for the leaders and their friends: the people they owe their position to and need to keep happy to stay in power. That isn't fair, so we looked at what is fairness. We contrasted equality of opportunity, freedom of opportunity and meritocracy and I plumped for the middle of those three; it fitted my experiences best: defining fairness as freedom of opportunity, more specifically; freedom to do what you want as long as you don't harm others including their freedom of opportunity. You may or may not agree, but I think society needs to work this one out.

We now come to "how do you make an economy work to support freedom of opportunity as long as you don't harm others principles?" Good question. We will get to an answer I devised which formed the basis of advice and statements to the administration.

Again I need to take us back to first principles: In 1776 Adam Smith wrote *The Wealth Of Nations*. That was his second great book, the first being *Theory Of Moral Sentiments*. Mr Smith was an expert on morality and used the credibility built up from his first book to convince a sceptical readership that the emerging amoral economic system, free(er) markets, capitalism and the profit motive, all tempered by competition was "safe". Even though it is not driven by morality, he argued, it gives an honourable result. He raged against government-granted monopolies like the East India Company as reducing the wealth of his nation(s).

Adam's book has (at least) two great insights: The first is about the positive results from deals between a buyer and seller using the facilities of trading via a market[5]. The second is the wealth creating effects of specialisation and productivity. You may know of his description of the benefits of specialisation in a pin factory at the beginning of his book.

4   More accurately, perhaps, my inner ego?
5   Nowadays we might call this a platform

It is the division of labour that enables specialisation which enables improved productivity; meaning each human being can create more useful output per hour of work. The world's demand for pins (or most else) is satisfied with less person hours than before, freeing up and paying labour, so creating demand for other stuff. This specialisation helps drive technological progress and when innovation is applied to specialisation it too further improves productivity.

In this section we will focus on his first insight: if a buyer and seller are free to choose whether to transact or not, i.e. that they are free to close the deal or are equally free to walk away from it; if that holds, then if a bargain is struck it will always be a win-win outcome. The buyer wins because they have decided the product brings them more value than the money they spent and the seller wins too, the price was presumably higher than the cost and so seller makes a profit. As long as the management of that marketplace[6] where buyer and seller trade is fairly cheap to run and it doesn't distort the transaction then this principle works. To stop the seller charging outrageous prices, Mr Smith said, you need competition, plus free, unencumbered marketplaces to encourage it to be effective. If a seller sets prices too high, that will encourage competitors to come in and prices will fall.

So free in three senses of the word: the buyer and seller are free to choose, the market is free to participate in and competitors are free to enter and exit. Freedom cubed. You will note how we are back to that word freedom again. Free is not completely free though. Buyer and seller may need to pay for tests, or transport and tolls to get to the market place. The market might have some form of daily charge[7] for a stall and customers might have to pay to enter: for the set-up, facilities, land

---

6   A marketplace can be the town square market, or high street, or within a supermarket, it can be online, eBay, Amazon or more, or on a stock market, or a price comparison site for example. All these market places will have similar rules – so they are not totally free – they will have the law of contract, the support of the legal system and then any extra ethical rules. They might have quality or safety guarantees, testing, or random visits or inspections, price refund rules, rules governing the competition and the advertising. All this marketplace management is called regulation. We abbreviate the word marketplace to "the market". All free markets are regulated to some extent. A true free market is a wild west, ruled by the gun so that's not free either. In situations where the suppliers run the marketplace then they might introduce regulations for their own benefits, watch out for self-regulated markets.

7   A fairground operates along such principles, you pay for entry and pay again for each ride.

rent, entertainment and the clean-up at the end of the day. The owner of the market place will try to ensure that competition is managed in a balanced way, enough to keeps prices under control but not to drive prices too low or allow predatory behaviour, otherwise it would wreck the benefits to the sellers who then won't turn up in future and pay the stall charge. So it's (nearly) freedom cubed.

And trillions if not quadrillions of deals have been done since then. In theory each one leads to a win-win outcome. All these wins have contributed to national prosperity and individual earnings.

Except, and I will now argue that Adam Smith was describing a special case perhaps more prevalent in the 18th Century. Nowadays there are many instances when either buyer or seller is not free to walk away from the offer, often the negotiating power is unbalanced, for example if the buyer desperately needs something she is not free to walk away from the deal. And market places are usually not free, they are sometimes highly regulated and costly to enter; many markets lack effective competition and sometimes competition isn't even desirable[8].

CHAPTER E2
CAPITALISM, MARKETS AND THEIR FAILINGS (1)

Before we get to the list of exceptions to Adam Smith's neat theory, I will take the opportunity to try to describe the difference between capitalism[9] and markets. I sent this off to a Twitter contact in answer to a question of his.

---

8   A natural monopoly is when the size of the market is about the same size as the most efficient scale of the current technology, that means there is only room for one player: electricity and natural gas distribution are currently most efficient when sized for a national market and so are natural monopolies. This is due to the scale needed for the grid, it wasn't always like that; when coal and coal gas were the technologies in use, then supply efficiency was local. But without competition the business could seek to profiteer; that needs regulation. Safety, instead of cost, could be another desirable reason for a regulated monopoly; take air traffic control as an example, this needs to be regulated but a well regulated monopoly can be better than competition plus a market. Natural monopolies can be local like bus services in and around Bristol.

9   Capitalism is a political construct, about who can own what: private ownership of the assets and processors for providing parts of the economy is thought by many to be desired for society as a whole; whereas a marketplace is an exchange mechanism to facilitate trade between different owners. The market place can be privately owned or by the state.

"Dear Martin, capitalism and markets are separate things. You can have capitalism without markets, for example: in feudal times, more recently the buying up of state monopolies (in Russia) and still, in some countries, you can inherit land but not be allowed to sell it due to local laws. Nevertheless it is capital and you can extract rent from it. Another situation is when one can invest in an unlisted business (one in which the shares are not traded). This is all capitalism without a market.

Markets are also possible without capitalism, like the market for charity shops. A market by the way is short for a marketplace. Nowadays it's rarely in market square in a town centre; many marketplaces are online or on a car showroom forecourt or even in a supermarket where Marmite competes with Bovril/Vegemite and Daz with Ariel[10].

But often markets and capitalism are combined; I still find it useful to appreciate they are actually separate things."

Markets, with or without capitalism, work well in many situations, but there are times when markets don't operate so well; they have weaknesses, failings even. For example: when it comes to basic R&D and seeding start-ups (see Mazzucato[11]), or when there is harm done to the environment, or harm done to people (these two effects are often called externalities[12] by economists), for example air pollution caused by too many cars. And more: high rents cause homelessness, or foods that make you unhealthy (where the cost of sorting out the resulting medical problem is borne by the NHS paid for by us, the taxpayer).

---

10   Daz and Ariel are actually owned by the same company, Procter and Gamble (P&G). I have chosen those products as examples because they enable me to discuss internal competition inside a business. In preparing this book I looked for examples where cooperation and competition are used within the same organisation, P&G I thought was one. But as it turns out that is a bit mistaken. We shall come to this point later in a footnote to E7.

11   *The Entrepreneurial State*, Mariana Mazzucato, 2013 Anthem Press. I have written a letter to Mariana (Appendix 10).

12   Externality is often misunderstood as meaning external to the economic system, it's not, it's so named because the effects are external to the buyer/seller, demand/supply transaction. They impact third parties.

Positional goods[13] (as discussed in section D) rely on scarcity and status which often means that the buyer is a winner but the third party can be a loser. This is a form of externality too, but the very success of the positional good often relies on the third party loss!

Sometimes an externality can be positive when it brings benefits to other people who haven't had to pay anything, like neighbours getting benefit from the cherry blossom on the tree you bought, or car users getting the benefit of less congestion as you decide to use the bus.

Another market failing, one that Adam Smith identified, is when there is little or no competition or there is a natural monopoly this is sometimes managed by using an industry regulator to ensure the customer doesn't get ripped off. A monopoly is sometimes enabled by Government itself like the granting of a patent (and upkeep of the licence fees). It is argued this stimulates innovation. That's fine as long as the patent applications are for that purpose.

I've already mentioned this one, but it needs to go on the list (of when markets are known to not work well) is when the bargaining powers of the buyer or seller are very unbalanced, you see this particularly when businesses are supplying peoples' needs. If you need something, rather than just want it, you tend to be in a weaker bargaining position. On the first course I gave to the Bristol Green Party back in 2015 one of the participants, Tamara I think, a bright young cookie, challenged my thinking in a helpful way and gave me a stunning insight. But I only realised it a few months later. So if was you and if you are reading this Tamara, thank you, sorry I was a bit slow on the uptake. Tamara said it was all about the difference between needs and wants. I'd been taught that economics was about allocating scarce resources efficiently according to peoples' needs and wants; not considering needs as different than wants. But I now realise that needs bring up different dynamics. A need sometimes means the buyer has no option but to buy, breaking one of

13　Same footnote as D8. R.Frank, *The Darwin Economy*, 2011 Princeton University Press: in chapter five Frank develops the impact of the work by Fred Hirsch on positional goods. Position can refer to both location and status. Positional goods are limited in supply. Living in a house in a catchment area of a good school or having a Ferrari on the drive to demonstrate your social status. One argument being that someone buying a positional good (so increases their status or opportunity) deprives someone else. So a trade is win-win for the buyer and seller but third parties lose out.

Adam Smith's axioms; the one assuming transactions are via freewill. If broken then the deal is not always win:win; it could mean the deal is accepted but it is win:lose. This occurs for example when someone is having difficulty paying rent but they have to or else they will be evicted; that could lead to homelessness because they need to live in the area to hold down a job. Try negotiating a rent decrease with your landlord when there is an excess of people looking for homes. Any mismatch is made worse if there are high switching costs (see next chapter).

Markets care nothing about resource shortages either, but interestingly we rarely run out as the market mechanism means the price goes up in order to conserve the raw material, incentivise more supply and seek alternatives. But the price hike will impact on the poor quite often and have other consequences. Helium is an example, used in party balloons and in important medical equipment; the latter costs more to run as helium has gotten scarcer. You can still buy helium for party balloons; it's got more expensive too. That's how markets work with scarcity.

Markets (buying and selling through a marketplace) don't work when the good is a common[14] good like a park, police, defence and in the UK the National Health Service.

CHAPTER E3
MARKETPLACE FAILINGS (2)

Our list of marketplace failings[15] now includes:
- Basic R&D and seeding start-ups (see Mazzucato).
- Or for when there is a common good like a park, police, defence.
- Where the product brings benefits to others like planting a tree or taking the bus.

14   A common good is one which you benefit from even if you don't buy it; a classic example being defence of the realm. To defend your country, you normally need the military, they don't come cheap and have to be paid from taxes to prevent the free rider effect. This also applies to parks (unless they are private), roads, the fire brigade and more.
15   It seems to me that if a market has a number of failings then it gets pretty difficult to manage the downsides; one should then question whether it is most efficient for society to run it as a market at all.

- Where there is harm done to the environment, or harm to people (in economic parlance these are called negative externalities), including positional and status goods.
- Or where there is little or no competition (e.g. an oligopoly[16]) or a natural monopoly. Sometimes this is deliberately created by the industry (barriers to entry) or lawmakers for example incentivising innovation via patent protection rules.
- When the bargaining powers of the buyer or seller are vastly unbalanced: often a problem when markets allocate resources to supplying what are needs to some people and wants to others like homes, a home to live in versus a holiday home. It can also be an information imbalance perhaps due to false advertising or one party having hidden knowledge (e.g. about the state of a second-hand car they are selling).
- When a defect in a product or service takes a long time to become obvious (e.g. a pension)
- When the protagonists become too important to let them fail. Bankruptcy and fear of it is an important check in the capitalist[17] system. If they can't be allowed to go bust then maybe capitalism isn't the best mechanism.
- Or if switching[18] costs are high. This might limit the effectiveness of competition. Switching costs apply when it costs you time or money to change provider. It's often easy to move hairdresser but more difficult to change over your bank account or phone number. They can worsen the negotiating position for the buyer if the good is a need.
- And markets can cause[19] resource shortages. Actually this last one is also claimed as a benefit of markets. In a resource shortage the price rockets, usage falls and people are incentivised to use or develop

16   An oligopoly is where a few businesses dominate a market. Such a situation isn't necessarily bad for the consumer. Businesses can afford higher salaries and attract engineers and innovate, bringing lots of consumer choice as well as well-paid jobs; everything within balance.
17   Allow me a little latitude here; I'm talking about capitalism in this paragraph but relating to markets.
18   Switching, also called transaction costs. This is often something a regulator will push to reduce and encourage switching websites for example.
19   Rationing is another method, in fact using a market is a form of rationing, the price goes up and only the rich can afford it. Markets care nothing for fairness.

alternatives or substitutes. But this whole process can harm sections of society and the big example is land. This is discussed in detail in section G.

The problem, in my view, is when capitalism is allowed to interact with markets that don't work properly; usually in one of the situations listed above, a weakness (so it occurs quite often). The flaw in the market enables the capitalist to capitalise on it (word chosen deliberately) and extract excess profit. Sometimes this can be prevented by regulation, but managing the market place with regulation needs to be paid for. The European Union has many regulated markets and part of the membership fee is to pay for that marketplace management. Without a managed marketplace, the participants can then start to operate and exploit these weaknesses, extract extra profits and give the consumer and third parties a worse deal. And because the capitalist makes so much money from doing that they use some of the excess earnings to lobby and influence politicians so the weakness never gets sorted.

Provision by markets becomes unfair when capitalists home in on failings in markets. In the example in the text box below the failure is in the rental market for property in London and there is not enough supply[20] at the cheaper end. We cover this issue in detail in Section H (affordable housing). So capitalism does what capitalism does; shifting resources and people around;

Summary is from the Daily Express on 31st Dec 2019.

"Bradford foodbank workers have reported a rise in the number of low-income people from London and surrounding areas descending on Bradford in the hope of finding cheap rented accommodation to avoid becoming homeless. Josie Barlow, manager of the Bradford Central Foodbank, said: "Seeing so many people coming into the area from places like the South, to me, is a bit like social cleansing. These people have no family or friends here

---

20   The cause of this is complex including the ability of some parties to borrow money at low interest rates and tax breaks. This is developed further in *Rethinking The Economics Of Land And Housing* – see bibliography

but most don't have a choice". She added: "We're seeing them coming from affluent areas in the North too, such as Harrogate and York, where rents are much higher". A Bradford Council spokesperson said: "Councils have an obligation to make sure families can access housing suitable to their needs. In London this is becoming very expensive for Councils as rents rise. London Councils are therefore increasingly arranging accommodation for their residents in places outside London. Bradford Council does not receive any payment or funding if these placements are made and we are not responsible for finding the housing for these placements." Thanks to LGiU

There are at least two ways of considering the above article:
1. If there were a real free market for labour and rents, then these people would go to work for a pittance and live in slums. Our society doesn't work that way anymore. Some people say it should go back to how it was.
2. But in a newer fairer arrangement, the Government would manage the situation, invest and encourage those in Bradford to create opportunities for this influx of people, new openings to take up, perhaps subsidise adult education, retraining opportunities, childcare, free buses and new jobs; creation of and enabling better prospects; it would fit with the freedom of opportunity ideal that I have now adopted.

Therefore, in my view, the market mechanism which theoretically works to allocate resources efficiently often doesn't in real life, it sometimes does and sometimes doesn't. And when it doesn't, the capitalists work hard to ensure it stays that way.

This is one of the things that we need to unpick in order to fix the harm being done to our planet's future and create better freedom of opportunity. Capitalists are free to take their opportunity as long as they don't harm others but if the marketplace needs fixing they shouldn't stop its repair.

So our list of reasons for market failure is long, and when capitalism grabs hold of a market that isn't working well then the failures don't get fixed. Why? Because the capitalists (or their employed managers) use the excess profits they make to lobby, fund and advertise and make sure it doesn't get fixed. Thus they go on to form part of the friends of the political party in power (and if it looks like political change making sure the opposition is lobbied too). I have a name for this: it is grab-it-all-ism.

CHAPTER E4
EARNING A PROFIT IS NOT THE SAME THING AS CREATING WEALTH

Capitalist organisations including businesses normally exist to make profit. Does this profit motive improve the situation for the rest of us? Hopefully yes but not always. That leads us to the question as to whether a business making profit is the same as one creating wealth?

Wealth and profit are words that require a tighter definition so we can make progress. For this purpose, I want to reserve some words to describe the assets and resources of a nation or society and other words to describe the possessions of an individual or business.

My definitions are as follows: Wealth, prosperity and welfare belong to society or a nation; whereas profit, earnings, value and well-being belong to an individual. So in my terms one can't be a wealthy individual. Instead you have captured a lot of value for yourself and are well off or rich. Using this lexicon we can have individual well-being, but welfare belongs to society, an individual can have riches, retained earnings for example (the later expression is used for every UK company) but society has prosperity.

With these definitions we can now make progress.

National wealth consists of four things:

* Its stock of people and their knowledge: overall welfare, motivations and happiness.

- Its physical infrastructure: like roads, bridges, factories, power stations, railways, reservoirs.
- Nature: its forests, land, fertility of the soil, beauty of lakes and mountains, minerals too.
- And its social infrastructure: the legal system, its education and universities, its health systems, its government, money systems even and more.

These four types of national assets[21] are akin to headings in a national balance sheet. For any accountants out there, the true annual measure (akin to profit and loss of a company) of national wealth creation would be the difference in the national wealth balance sheet, the total assets less liabilities[22], and its change year on year. The current measure of a country's success, GDP, doesn't capture all of this. It measures most of the change in physical infrastructure, but not its depreciation[23]. It measures some of the country's services and output[24] during a year but doesn't measure whether the national stock of nature, peoples' wellbeing (welfare of the population) nor other aspects of its social infrastructure as to whether they are increasing or decreasing. So as many suspected, GDP is a false measure of change in national wealth, prosperity and welfare. I agree that GDP measures what currently can be measured but even that was after a lot of effort by Keynes, Kuznets and others responding after the depression of the 1930s. What GDP does measure is the paid-job aspect of the economy. Given the problem of those times was unemployment, it isn't surprising GDP[25] concentrated on measuring the output of jobs.

Wealth and prosperity can be increased[26]. This is done by converting some of the stock of wealth, resources, into other stock. For example

21   The economy we currently have allows many of these assets to be owned by individuals. Property ownership and private profits have been found to be important for improving the standard of living of populations. But there are downsides too and I think whole areas of private ownership need to be challenged and regulated: Land is an example to look at.
22   A liability could include levels of air pollution, student debt, worsening democracy and homelessness for example: Things that need to be sorted.
23   Indeed, one method of calculating GDP adds a depreciation allowance rather than subtracting it.
24   GDP doesn't include second-hand goods even though converting one person's throw-aways to another's useful goods is clearly subtracting nothing from one person and adding wellbeing to another.
25   I think I read somewhere that Keynes suggested that GDP be a temporary measure?
26   Sometimes in ways that might not be completely measured by GDP.

combine people, power plus minerals and you can build a bridge. If that bridge increases group well-being[27] by more than the inputs then wealth has been created. But if you use too many inputs or you pollute the area with discarded paint or metals then your new bridge[28] might subtract from national wealth. Another example: If you combine skilled people, power and technology you can make people healthier. The nation's stock of wealth, in this case of healthy people, has improved.

In many western countries we are told that wealth creation is the task of business. Some people even claim that the state destroys wealth. In my view these ideas are mistaken and sometimes downright harmful. Both examples I gave in the previous paragraph are things that business or the state could do. Indeed other types of processors could do them too, like a charity. So it's not who does the task that creates the wealth, it's how efficiently[29] it's done and what if any are the by-products, harm or side effects caused.

At this stage I'd like to add in some ideas from Martin Farley[30], Brighton Green Party, with whom I have discussed such issues since 2016. Martin recently presented his thoughts to over 200 people at an online conference and has helped challenge and develop my views about the processors and creators of wealth. People traditionally think of state versus business; but there are other processors too: social enterprise (including charities and philanthropy), the household[31] group and of course nature herself. Building a small bridge over a stream could be done by any one of these five processors. Depending on the size and complexity of the task a different processor might be more suited. (I

27   So for example it might increase productivity of farming by creating a route between two fields, it might improve family productivity by creating a quicker route to the shops or whatever.
28   This bridge example also illustrates another key principle of economics and that is diminishing returns. The usefulness of objects declines the more you have of them. Having two bridges is better than one but unlikely to be twice as good.
29   Different processors for different tasks, some will be better at increasing the prosperity of society than others.
30   And brave convenor of the Green Party England and Wales tax policy group which so ably came up with some coherent policies for the 2019 election. (Work started on them three years earlier.)
31   The household group being those who share in the jobs of everyday life. It might be a family and so one of the jobs, one of the most important, is bringing up their children. It could be people living say six to a house but they share in the chores of putting the recycling out, going to the shops. This increases the productivity and well-being of those people so they have time to do other things. I would include a commune as a household, albeit an extended one.

agree you would be fortunate if nature built you a bridge but it is possible if a tree falls in the right place). But neither nature, nor probably a household will build you a railway track[32]. Any of these five processors can add to national wealth and if annual prosperity is the change in that wealth then they should all be accounted for (somehow), GDP doesn't do this.

As business is the one processor traditionally thought of as the wealth creator, I will develop arguments regarding commerce a little further, fortunately it's the area I have most expertise in. When business undertakes activities it is normally motivated by profit; an individual goal for the owner and shareholders rather than the collective goal of wealth creation. A business will therefore minimise the use and cost of the resources it has to pay for; use free resources where possible. It will seek to maximise the profit from its output (bearing in mind competition should keep a check on this) and, apart from legal constraints, it probably won't worry too much about pollution, slag heaps or resource degradation as long as it's cheap or free and doesn't affect profit. In the interests of maximising shareholder value they should try to avoid paying much for such things unless there are side effects like their customers stop buying. So the activities add to wealth but if the side effects subtract from it then we don't know if overall wealth is positively or negatively affected. The earnings of a person or business is not necessarily linked to whether there is wealth creation to society overall.

Society consists of the business, their customers and everyone else: the third parties. Hopefully most of the time the business (the seller) is happy and the customer (buyer) should be happy too, they bought out of free choice, so far so good. But what about the third parties, everyone else external to the deal, that's why impacts on the rest of us, or on nature, are called externalities as it's us who they affect. If the effects are significant, then the marketplace that businesses operate in needs to be

---

32   Except a toy one: My father built me a fantastic one for an early birthday (6th or 7th maybe), one that folded back to the wall when not used.

regulated[33] to align earnings of the businesses to be in line with wealth creation for society.

The downsides when this doesn't happen are most easily seen when excessive earnings are extracted by a chief executive in charge of a business that has cleverly manoeuvred itself into becoming a monopoly. For shareholders the CEO is doing the right thing, this is what CEOs were taught in business school. A monopoly is one of the many forms of market failure, so prices of the output are usually higher, especially if it is poorly regulated or if harm, like pollution or ill-health, is not paid for. Then neither the earnings of the business nor the chief executive's dividends will correspond to the wealth created or destroyed by the business, despite the fact that the company's accounts show a good profit and it pays tax to government.

Too much profit extraction causes a drag on national wealth and at its worst can reduce overall prosperity. Here are four short stories taken from my ward and anonymised to illustrate exactly this issue.

CHAPTER E5
FOUR STORIES; THE ECONOMY ISN'T WORKING FOR ANY OF THEM

Here are four short stories of people I met in my job; it was quite clear that the economy was failing to provide their needs. You decide who or what is at fault:

1. Sleeping in a church doorstep "lives" a homeless man, he is a rough sleeper, one of about 500[34] in Bristol. We will call him Jack, he used to live with his partner, but after repeated rows, presumably quite heated, she kicked him out. He could not find somewhere else to stay that night

---

33 Much regulation at the moment is to protect customers, the buyers (second party), I am arguing that to align profit with wealth creation then regulation should protect third parties from harm too. Sometimes this is done. The UK's planning system attempts to do this. We will analyse why it fails in some cases in sections G and H.
34 About 500 have to sleep rough for at least a night over a year.

so slept out. The next day he discovered that as a single person the Council didn't legally have a duty to find him somewhere to sleep until he became "vulnerable". After sleeping on the streets, taking drugs and being beaten up he was interviewed by Social Services again and this time deemed sufficiently vulnerable to be admitted onto the Council's housing list. A couple of stays in hostels, more beatings up, thefts and he now feels safer sleeping on the steps of the church, calling on their alms and calling that place home. How do I know this? He came into see me one day and I asked him how he ended up living like this.

Comment: In the above example the Council is following the law to not owe him a duty of care (for housing). I'm told that the law was supposed to save tax payers' money by creating a disincentive to people so they wouldn't just "drop out" and become a burden on the state. It may work some of the time but what it also does is reduce individual health and national wealth as it causes much deeper social problems. A political/economic system that improved and supported his freedom to take opportunities, ideally earlier on, might work better.

2. Living nearby that church was an elderly couple; the man in his 90s had just been diagnosed with cancer. That very same day they got an eviction notice from their landlord, it was a coincidence I'm sure, but an unfortunate one. With something like cancer it's very difficult to get new rented accommodation as you are often asked about your health. Their savings were just above the limits for Council housing so their application to go on the list was rejected. They were actually faced with the thought of street sleeping. Fortunately their local Councillor was able to help persuade a Council officer how ridiculous this all was and they were offered and accepted Council housing in the North of Bristol.

Comment: An intervention by me and the officer managed to save what could have been death by homelessness before the big C got him. This was caused by a gap in the system; older people with health problems relying on rented accommodation would find it hard to move unless they have enough savings to buy a home. Such insecurity fuels the desire for homeownership and fuels the gap between old and young.

3. Jackie lives in a housing association flat, she works 30 hours a week and relies on housing benefit; she is financially helped out with universal credit payments. Now recovered from depression, Jackie wants to get a better job. She currently earns £240 a week. Looking around she has found a job paying £300 a week but it's a bit further away. She calculates how much that extra £60 a week will bring her. Take away tax and NI leaves her £40.80, her benefits are income tested and she will have a reduction in universal credit of £25.70 per week and she will have to pay more of her Council Tax (currently reduced) that will be £8.16 more. That job move would leave her with just £6.94 more per week. Not enough to pay the extra bus fares of £7.50 a week. So Jackie is stuck in her existing job and stays on a higher level of benefits.

Comment: This is about benefit traps. We looked at a similar case in chapter C2. The system supporting those on low pay, called in-work-benefits, actually incentivises Jackie to reduce national prosperity because she stays on a higher level of benefits, she could take a better job and probably improve her well-being. Either the benefit tapers should be reduced and/or bus fares be subsidised. An economic system based on improving freedom of opportunity might do just that.

4. George is relatively wealthy, lives in a £ million plus home over in Redland but now suffers from lung problems. His doctor thinks it's due to the air pollution from the nearby Gloucester Road. In fact air pollution went up in Bristol last year (2018) from an illegal 40 to an even more illegal 42 (ug/m3 of NO_2). The solution for him is to move out of the city to the countryside or coast.

Comment: The air pollution in Bristol is primarily caused by cars from commuters (shown vividly during the Covid-19 lockdown). If cars were less polluting and/or were used less, with more people working from home or using the bus or bikes then George would have a better quality of life, be able to help his adult children more and participate in charity work. His freedom to take opportunities is limited by the air pollution.

All these stories are within half a mile of one another. There are hundreds more. They illustrate that despite our nation's wealth, many still suffer the problems of poverty and in one instance air pollution. It reduces their freedom and our national wealth. These are some of the side effects of the way the economy works at the moment. These are due to externalities along with other failures like weak bargaining power, and are examples of the harm caused by poorly operating markets, poorly designed benefits to fill in the market failings and how they impact the vulnerable. You could say, "but this is what a Councillor is supposed to do, to plug the gaps," and to some extent you are right but there's just so much; because the markets, laws and benefits, the things that comprise the economy, have been badly designed or run.

But it's not just the moral conscience that's pricked. I will say this cold heartedly; the impact of these situations is a drain on the local economy. If you have to get hooked on drugs to get a home, or can't take a better job because benefits taper off so fast or you are unable to work in charity due to air pollution then removing these problems, making people healthier and able to take their opportunities increases national prosperity; it just needs to be seen that way. Then we would make sure Jack was housed before he became a drug addict and that George had clean air. Jackie would be able to take on that better job enabling someone else to take the one she is currently doing, more social mobility, reduced benefits bill and the elderly couple would be automatically provided with a home they are capable of paying for but outside the power of private landlords.

People need an economic system to give them the freedom to take their opportunities.

CHAPTER E6
ALIGNING PERSONAL AND BUSINESS PROFIT
WITH WEALTH CREATION

So how do we align business profit, state activities and other activities even those within the household to align with a goal of national wealth creation? The current measure, GDP hinders that; the household (whether a family or a group) is such a central part of the economy; bringing up children is one of the most important jobs any parent or carer could do. Yet its contribution isn't measured at all except through what they consume.

These are tough issues, I know some approaches being taken are going in the right direction. I was able to use some of these ideas and build them into statements and suggestions; they come later on in this section.

One approach is to properly price all inputs including wages, raw materials, land and knowledge and make sure the outputs are charged for too including slag heaps, pollution and ill health. Not easily done I agree but attempts are being made and one I like is called Social Value Accounting (similar to triple bottom line sometimes used in business). This is slowly being adopted in Bristol City Council and its suppliers. It is a national initiative. But even it doesn't include the wealth creating activities of the family within an economy (yet).

A second issue we face as a society is valuing activities that increase society's wealth but don't lead to higher individual earnings; so it's the opposite[35] of extracting too much. Many of you will see this in your payslip. Quite often persons who don't take much in earnings can still be adding to the nation's wealth. This was brought to sharp relief in the Covid-19 disaster where the low paid became relabelled as key workers, because? Well they are.

A nurse, who by his or her efforts, helps save a life or mend a broken bone; the output is a healthier person so adding to national wealth. That nurse has contributed to this but hasn't extracted much profit for his or

---

35   These are called the "fat cats", perhaps the key workers who aren't paid so well are the "slim cats"?

SOCIAL VALUE

The Social Value Act 2012, is a successful private members bill, congratulations to Conservative MP Chris White.

The way I try to explain this to people is as follows: When a Council makes changes, sometimes they will have knock on costs elsewhere within the Council's own services, even to the extent that the issue costs more than the savings in the first place. One lovely example is from 2017 when they cut the tree maintenance budget, this was reinstated in 2018 once the ramifications were fully understood (this is in the Appendix, 1 and 2, by the way).

With social value (as applied in procurement/buying) the Council is trying to ensure that side effects to society are either avoided, or costed in; sometimes opportunities are created for the disadvantaged or the impact on air pollution or CO_2 is costed. The potential suppliers not only have to demonstrate how good their product or service is (and for the price) but they also have to show how they can help improve a wider problem or create opportunity.

For example, employing more disabled people; or if the supplier is bidding to provide a carer service they might combine it with solutions to assist in solving the loneliness problem with old people. Or it could be just employing local people. These add-on activities are valued using a nationally agreed scale which can be used by the Council in its decision making of who to buy from, even if that supplier offers a slightly higher price. So it's not a decision based on just price and quality, there is a third factor called social value.

Local authorities are free to suggest extra criterion, Bristol has added CO_2 and there is a benefit associated (nationally verified) if a supplier proposes to reduce its CO_2 footprint (which might reduce their costs as well).

I think there is a long way to go and much more to add but it's a start and it's national. If it can adjust situations where profit doesn't align with wealth creation then that's an improvement.

herself because the regulation and competition around wages in the NHS limits that. That nurse's activities over a year might have added more wealth to the nation than the chief executive of a business exploiting a monopoly; he might take home 60 times as much as the nurse. This doesn't seem balanced. Economically it will lead to more greedy chief executives and not enough nurses, not the best for a healthy society[36].

Another example; a Council social worker with dedication and skill manages to help a family to stay together. The strife could be due to a "stroppy teenager", they are helped to stay in school. The quality support continues for another ten years perhaps and rather than a life of crime, the now adult contributes to society perhaps adding over a £1 million of wealth over their 40 plus years' of working. How much does that Council worker get paid out of that £1 million? Not much, yet this is wealth creation. It's by nurses, social workers and many more.

Wealth, therefore, is not just created by business and not just by high earners.

Implicit within Adam Smith's account of an economy of free markets and competition is the profit motive, self-centred motivation leading to non-selfish outcomes. It is the selfishness of the butcher and the baker combined with competition that makes meat and bread available at fair prices. Some people are very motivated by money. I was earlier on in my life, certainly much more than I am now. A lot depends on your upbringing and your choice of friends. For some of us the amount we earn defines our self-worth. Many grow out of that.

Other people are less motivated by money. Enough money for a comfortable life but valuing other parts of life and valuing what you do. A nurse, a Council housing officer, a tree officer, social worker, teacher, planner, stay at home carer, a cleaner, they are all adding to the nation's wealth by what they do. They don't grab it all for their own personal income; wage regulation and competition put a stop to that anyway but hopefully they feel good about themselves and how they contribute.

36   I would love to see a system where wages were linked to the social value a person creates.

TAKEAWAYS

Wealth and prosperity are the sum total of the nation's collection of resources; consisting of natural, human, built and social infrastructure. Wealth is created by processing these resources and creating more goods than bads. This can be done by business, charities, the state, nature and within households.

Profit and earnings are what an individual can and do extract for their activities. It often doesn't align with wealth creation. And the gap can get worse if it is a business operating in an unregulated sector where there are market failures they can exploit.

There are efforts to align activities better, to align profits to wealth creation. For example social value accounting and triple bottom line accounting. But we have a long way to go...

People doing these jobs are not predominantly motivated by money (as long as they have enough).

Where profit and wealth creation are easily aligned we can afford to have money motivated, greedy even, capitalists, ideally tempered by competition and regulation. Where profit and wealth aren't aligned then people with different prime motivations should be running the show, those who love to care, or educate for example. They should be in charge. Adam Smith described an amoral system to bring us all benefits and wealth. Where there are failures then the system needs some morality, perhaps a new subject, "moralomics[37]" to be taught alongside politics and economics?

So how do we balance what you take out as earnings with the wealth you create? That's for the next chapter

---

37   I think this is my word first used in one of my @SageAndOnion blogs. A quick Google search shows a reply to a blog on July31st 2017 using this. It referred to "Climate Moralomics" used as a pejorative term. I posted mine late in 2016 meaning it as a positive area of economics (perhaps one day) where market failures require leaders of organisations to not be motivated by just profit.

CHAPTER E7
WHERE WE HAVE ENDED UP WITH ALL THIS –
SUMMARY OF D AND E

Adam Smith reconciled the (selfish) profit motive as the creator of good and goods when businesses operate in fairly free marketplaces tempered by competition; no need for moral sentiments.

But, as I communicated in my lectures, and they followed what I had been taught in business school, the job of business leaders is to put effort into sectors where competition is less, because that enables more value extraction irrespective of whether it creates more wealth/benefit to society. In moderation this is not such a bad thing as it funds innovation and higher paid jobs[38]. But if it gets out of hand and/or there are serious market failures then profit extraction can be excessive, offensive even, because of the harm it is doing; examples being where workers have little bargaining power and are exploited or some undergraduate university education[39] (in the UK) where competition is not keeping a cap on price.

Contrast that situation with an entrepreneur who is truly creating wealth[40] with a product or service bringing improved productivity to a process, or better health and well-being to his customers; even better if they ensure that any pollution and harm is minimised and even paid for. They deserve (using my model) to earn a substantial amount until the business gets to the stage when there is a market failure. A really successful entrepreneur will want to grow their business as fast as possible and end up in a monopoly position. That's what the shareholders want to

38   This was of interest to many of my students as they had tuition fees to pay off, as did I from my MBA!

39   I put this one in to stir up the argument! Perhaps some vice chancellors have already learned the error of their ways?

40   The capitalist process means that the promise of high profits enables the entrepreneur to raise funds from investors to develop the business and its technology; the business may go on to be a financial success or it may fail, but technology has been moved forward and as this eventually becomes a social gain (knowledge) then wealth has been created in part. Booms like railways in Victorian times or the internet boom in 1990's led to legacies of railway infrastructure and the internet infrastructure and software long after the entrepreneurial companies had either gone bust or moved forward. This is the process of creative destruction first described by Joseph Schumpter also by Janeway and Mazzucato and many more.

happen. When that occurs then they slowly shift[41] from being a brilliant wealth creating entrepreneur to running a grabitall company taking advantage of a market failure. The regulators will struggle to catch up. Facebook, Google are current global examples of this phenomenon one that in the past has included: The East India Company, Standard Oil, Carnegie Steel and others.

There have been, I hear, attempts[42] to design a tax system where a young business is taxed low but rates ramp up as it matures. Tax breaks based on social value (wealth and prosperity creation) might be a better bet.

The profit motive doesn't motivate everyone. There are whole sectors of the economy where the managers, some directors even, are not primarily inspired by profit, nor should they be. These people are more suited[43] to running social enterprise, charities and trusts: care homes, schools, hospitals, Councils even. They need to keep an eye on costs for sure but care or service should be priority number one, not profit. Adam Smith didn't talk about a mechanism for not-for-profit businesses; sometimes competition encourages efficiency but sometimes it does not; we have an example coming up about two competing Councils. Cooperation seems a better approach. The final example of Children in Care is definitive in my view.

So I applied these @SageAndOnion insights (well I think they are insights, others are free to call them viewpoints) directly into my Council work. Just to summarise these are:

Freedom: I eventually dumped equality of opportunity for freedom of opportunity (to take opportunities). I still feel sad about this and comfort myself with adding "freedom to do as you like as long as you don't harm others including harming other peoples' freedom of opportunity" is not so far away as we saw in section D.

41 This process needs balance; in the capitalist system investors love the idea of high profits and low competition. Piling money in, giving the entrepreneur first mover advantage. If they thought that regulation would close off these profit opportunities too soon then they wouldn't invest. But at some stage the successful business (and let's remember that most fail) needs to be reined in.

42 It will be from one of those many think-tanks that churn out ideas like this.

43 It's a combination of the personality and values of the leaders in those sectors themselves along with what society wants as the key goal. Input into the economy and make money, input into the economy by providing quality and efficient care, input into the economy by providing good and efficient education etc.

Economy: I wanted to steer officers and Labour towards intervening in a small way to help the local economy deliver this freedom of opportunity goal more widely.

We viewed an economy as a social construct, one that can be and has been changed over the decades and centuries; indeed for thousands of years, it has really been about supplying the needs and most wants of the leaders and their friends. Others can just get by and support the system. How can this be reconciled with liberal values, opportunity and equality? Adam Smith was part right, combining the profit motive with free markets plus competition, does work in some situations but since then we have discovered many failings. And when capitalism gets to work on those failings people can extract immense profits and use the money to prevent lawmakers from closing the loopholes.

Mr Smith didn't address at all organisations driven by the care or public service motive. Organised cooperation is much more likely to work in my view. In fact perhaps the insertion of an artificial market mechanism might even be harmful? It could reduce cooperation if you try to use such approaches on social enterprise or authorities where cooperation is key? Lots of people in the NHS, or running the railways might concur. Someone somewhere may have a theory about when competition is best and when cooperation is. I really look forward to that[44]. Our nation's wealth and prosperity is down to the health and education of our people, the infrastructure, the natural resources and our social systems. Prosperity increases if each and every year we undertake activities that combine these resources in a way that improves the total.

---

44   I asked a long-time friend, who recently retired from Procter and Gamble, about the workings of their famous internal competition, brand management system where from the outside it seemed that the brand managers (e.g. One for Daz and one for Arial) would actually compete with one another. It seemed like it might be an answer to my question of when is it best to compete and when best to cooperate.
As it turns out, although the individual managers themselves compete (for promotion and recognition), the organisation itself made sure that this was within a strongly co-operative environment. A few years into their careers there are not enough jobs for all these young ambitious people to get promoted into. So some decide to leave and work elsewhere. That was the system. For most of business although we outsiders see it as competitive, it is cooperation working inside. This is healthy. Switching to shops and the high streets, one of the reasons it's difficult to boost and revitalise the high street is that the shops see themselves as competing with one another for trade. Whereas the companies that run the big shopping centres try to fill their units with complementary businesses so that as a shopper you have a range of experiences and opportunities there: coffee, food, entertainment and a range of purchases. Councils that "run" the high streets don't and possibly can't do this.

If activities reduce the total like habitat destruction or pollution then prosperity is reduced. We need to stop that and remove any incentives to do that.

A person's income currently comes from being able to extract earnings from activities, but sometimes in business (and in other sectors too) that activity may not create wealth. Earnings are not an indication of how useful you are. If you add in social value you are more likely to get a better picture of wealth (prosperity) creation.

So dear Alderman[45] Bev Knott, we never did have that coffee and apple cake; you left me to work it out myself. Do you agree with my workings? It only took me eight years!

I'll close this topic with a comment from the people of Britain. Maybe a revolution or reform could be on the cards, the *Observer* published (via LGiU):

17 Nov 2019, Voters open to economic reform: A YouGov poll commissioned by the IPPR think-tank suggests that voters are increasingly open to a radical change to the way the economy is organised. A survey of more than 1,600 people saw 60% in favour of the next government making "moderate" or "radical" changes to the way the British economy is run, while only 2% said the government should leave the economy as it was. Of those open to change, 29% backed moderate policies and 31% supported more radical reform. Looking at respondents' political allegiance shows that 59% of Labour voters back radical change compared to 9% of Conservative supporters, with 35% of Tory voters calling for "moderate" changes.

These next five chapters are examples of how I applied the points we have just covered to real local issues, illustrating examples of how I would like to see an economy work, one that supports the values of freedom of opportunity unless you are doing harm. Let's see if you agree.

45   I introduced Bev Knott at D4. A retired Councillor who has given enough (good) service gets to be called an alderman with appropriate pomp.

208

CHAPTER E8
COMPETING LOCAL AUTHORITIES

This illustrates what happens when the idea of competition and freedom run riot; two Councils competing against one another. Is competition the tool to encourage efficiency in this case[46]?

By way of introduction, around 2017 South Gloucestershire Planning Committee approved a retail expansion of the out-of-town shopping centre; Cribbs Causeway. Bristol City Council and our Planning Committee objected. It was clear it would harm Bristol's retail offer and national planning policies have long recognised the damage that out-of-town shopping has done to city centres. This permission was called in by the Secretary of State and eventually overturned once the harm to Bristol was properly considered (not really an important issue for South Gloucestershire Council). The SofS's report said, "It could threaten the vitality of shopping in Bristol City Centre, for example Cabot Circus which was described as vulnerable." Cabot is Bristol's central shopping district and links to the other two big central ones. If Cabot started to lose shops there were worries the retail offer could fall like a house of cards.

Fortunately the Secretary of State recognised the damage that could be caused by competition between the two authorities.

Development of South Gloucestershire is right on the North Western border of Bristol, thousands more houses are going up, which when occupied will bring lots of Council Tax to South Glos Council. Yet they are not planning to pay for transport improvements into Bristol. It feels like it's a game of poker. Understandably the Councillors for those areas of Bristol which will be most affected; more congestion and pollution are trying to get something done. They put a proposed budget amendment to Full Council. As you will now read, I didn't like it.

---

46   In theory it's one of the goals of a combined authority (Bristol as part of WECA) to make the LAs work more closely together. It's also written into Planning law too (NPPF). But as you can see competition goes on.

Clive's speech – Full Council 26 Feb 2019 on Conservative Budget Amendment Proposal.

I'd prepared and practised this one a few times. I wanted to hit home. The Conservative ideas were pure "fix the symptoms, don't worry about fixing the causes". I might have been more forgiving but they had been in power nationally for nine years. So with nervous anticipation I rose, pressed the button to start the microphone, checked it lit up, counted to two, made sure I stood straight, notes not blocking the microphone...

"Thank you Lord Mayor. Teamwork and cooperation in cities is my theme for today. So how does this amendment shape up? Leaflet fodder, that's what Carla called your proposal Mark[47], Carla how could you be so cynical about this? If Cllr Mark Weston gets elected as the MP for Bristol NW I'm sure he will be able to persuade the Conservative leadership to change its damaging ways... So Mark this is what you have to change.

"Don't rely on competition to improve efficiency. It often doesn't work. The problems you are trying to alleviate with the capital part of this amendment[48] are because South Gloucestershire Region and its Council are in growth competition with Bristol. South Glos have land upon which to build houses (good) and will get more Council Tax (good for them) when they are built, but they don't need to help with the transport into Bristol.

"And why not?

"Because they have the regional shopping centre up at Cribbs, more shopping and offices and of course more business rates. The dynamics are such that it is we, Bristol City Council, who will have to fund transport improvements into Bristol, because South Gloucestershire don't need to and we do need to.

"Two authorities in competition, leading to growth for one and relative decline for the other; a deadly dance, survival of the fittest game, played to rules written by the Conservatives. And unless it is sorted we will see more congestion, more air pollution, worse buses, worse retail...

---

47 This is Councillor Mark Weston again, leader of the Conservative group of Councillors back then
48 To invest in road schemes to manage the increased traffic from new homes being built just North of Bristol in the neighbouring authority of South Glos.

"Mark instead of tinkering at the edges with this extra £2 million, sort the politics out. You have a Conservative South Gloucestershire Council, a Conservative Metro Mayor and a Conservative Government. Same party, should be easy. But no, your party has completely lost the plot. You let Osborne and Cameron grind our country into the dust. And the new Conservative leadership are continuing with an equally impressive display regarding Brexit.

"So locally the arrangements around the new homes in Filton and its surrounds, which should be such a good news story, is likely to be a complete cock up arranged by the Conservative Party.

"But to fix this you will need to promote the politics and economics of cooperation and ditch the Tory dogma; free markets and competition, where it obviously doesn't work like two local authorities scrapping over a big bone. I must say I haven't much confidence that you can make this intellectual shift. If you do then it will be worth turning up my hearing aids for. I don't know how I will vote, I am so angry with your Party."

I got a round of applause from Labour as well as the Greens and the Conservative Amendment was voted down[49].

But that wasn't the end of it. The Bristol Mayor proposed that a large arena complex be placed just on the northern edge of Bristol. You might think he was out of his mind, many of us did. South Gloucestershire lapped it up but it was fully funded by the developers of the new homes in Filton, the ones in my speech to Mark Weston just above. An arena complex would make money and help justify the new infrastructure needed for the homes which will cost the Government millions and possibly increase the selling prices of the houses as long as it is all designed right. The Bristol Mayor bought the scam. He could now say he delivered on a manifesto promise to bring an arena to Bristol, for free and it freed up the originally reserved land for development. If you're interested in how this panned out then read the chapters in the Appendices (11, 12 and 13) on the Brabazon Arena.

Needless to say I hope I have shown with this example that

49   I suspect it would have been anyway.

competition isn't always the best answer especially between Local Authorities which are not even operating in an official marketplace. If they were then at least we could list all the market failures: like local monopolies, externalities, provision of common goods and more and put in appropriate regulation. Local authorities are surely one part of an economy which requires cooperation to solve externalities like homelessness, impacts on traffic, pollution, and the success of Bristol's centre.

CHAPTER E9
MARKET SHAPING IN ADULT SOCIAL CARE (1)

This second example is about the care home industry and how it is the Council's duty as their main customer to ensure the provision around Bristol is well managed; in my terms, a managed marketplace[50]. Using my approach I wanted to nudge the market for care homes away from potential domination by profit maximising businesses to one more conducive to charities and social enterprise instead. The care motive, not the profit motive should be tops.

Comment: I suspect that the nation's approach to care homes will be ripped to shreds by Covid-19. It already seems (at the time of writing, early April) that the arrangements have allowed a disaster to unfold. At this stage the country isn't even publishing death counts. I'm sorry to all the families who have had loved ones lose their lives to the virus accelerated by a poor system. If it does cause a complete rethink then I hope the ideas that follow can be added to the mix.

The analysis is simple. One of Adam Smith's two axioms is broken here; the deal between a care home and the Council is not one the

---

50   I think managed marketplace is a better term than a regulated one. Market places have been managed for centuries ensuring appropriate competition, sellers' terms, weights and measures, opening hours etc.

Council can walk away from because of external pressures. For example the national drive to reduce bed blocking in hospitals means that the Council has to find a place where someone can live safely after their discharge from hospital sometimes within a day or two[51]. Supply of care homes is limited and often there might be only one with necessary capabilities. Take it or leave it. Prices were increasing about 10% a year.

In section F (next) we will look at the "Bristol Price" which was implemented in 2018. The customer (the Council) will in future dictate the price, this was to stop the escalation of care home prices which was becoming unaffordable and already a major cause of 3.99% Council tax increases year on year. That new approach (which was how it had been done a number of years before) partially worked but the long term trend of higher prices and power over the buyers (Local authorities and public) is the theoretical attraction[52] for the private sector to further encroach into this market.

I argued this in a statement to Cabinet on 3rd September 2019 why allowing that to happen is a bad idea.

Agenda Item 9 - Proposed Pricing Strategy for Residential and Nursing Care for Adults with Long Term Impairments[53].

"Your proposal outlines a useful couple of steps on what needs to become a journey; a journey I hope that will shape Bristol's impairment care market and a number of others too, in order to make them sustainable.

The 2014 Care Act imposes a duty on LAs to shape the market (market is better described as a marketplace; shaping is leadership and signalling by defining the rules and behaviours of participating players). An LA can do this by using its buyer power as the biggest customer and it is allowed to do this too, it is even suggested how; you award grants. An example is shown to improve innovation especially to third sector providers. (See

51   During Covid-19 this was accelerated to within an hour or two, much more money was provided to do this, temporarily

52   Those of you who have been business trained will know of Professor Michael Porters 5 Forces. In this instance superior profits are obtainable due to market power over the customers. The fact that some are messing it up is because they overpaid to enter the market (see Four Seasons case study in the next chapter) so it may slow up but I don't think will halt the attractiveness of it.

53   I'm told that the word disability is the more accurate description but I use the word impairment as that is in the title of the Council document.

Government Guidance: Adult Social Care Market Shaping[54] *- Updated 14 February 2017).*

Your Cabinet report complains on p33,

"Currently providers offer to take placements at a price they determine."

This is what happens in a marketplace that is not led the way you want it. It is a symptom of a market being allowed to manage itself, not supplying enough services of the right type, providers dictating price over you; you the biggest customer. Don't blame them, they are often businesses trying to maximise a profit. That, according to current law, is their job in society. And they can do that by operating in a marketplace that is not being well managed by you for the customers' and tax payers' benefit. If it is not shaped then prices will continue to rise, profit motivated suppliers will enter and eventually you will have enough supply but at a higher price and with providers of the wrong motivation. I know as Chair of the Finance Scrutiny Group that the Council can't afford to let this happen, you know this too.

This begs the question what type of market do you want so that you can lead it right. I don't see any evidence that you know what you want it to look like. So although what you have done is a start, trying to put a break on price increases, getting information on costs and surveying the suppliers, but what next? Your pricing is still too high. And there will be a long lag before enough people are on the new rates to make a significant difference. And allowing a 7% return on land and property is too much. Oh the suppliers will complain, "profit is too low and it's too risky". The reality is many companies can borrow for much less than 7% when secured on bricks, mortar and land. Then they pocket the difference with an almost guaranteed return. Property yields are less than 5% now, but here you allow 7%. So this should give you a clue as to one of the next actions you need to take to begin to shape the market more to the favour of the residents of Bristol and their Council.

And you are also allowing a 5% mark up on the other costs of operating these homes. What level of return on capital does that bring the private sector suppliers of this service? Do you know? What is their average

---

54   Market shaping is a form of marketplace management. In some markets shaping might be enough.

working capital requirement? And how about charities, what do they do with that profit allowance?

Market shaping is key to long term sustainability here, the wider ASC sector and for children's care too. (By the way did you see those recent headlines about Private Equity buying up foster care agencies? Even the Government's worried).

The provision of residential and nursing care for adults with impairments costs Bristol City Council £35 million/year. It is just one of a number of care markets that BCC is the major customer of. In total they add to well over half of the Council's costs. You have to get a grip and decide what shape the market (marketplace) should become, even with the right actions it will take a decade to get these markets to become sustainable.

I said as much in my statement to Cabinet back in June 5th 2018. Immediately afterward I had a chat with the Director of Adult Social Care at his instigation. But I have heard nothing since on market shaping and there is little to see here. If you want to shape the market then let's discuss it seriously. Otherwise I fear that by failing to act you will create a big problem for future incoming administrations. So I'm happy to listen and talk. The big decisions are the ones where you are judged if you got it right or wrong in the years to come".

Do you think anything resulted from this?

CHAPTER E10
MARKET SHAPING IN ADULT SOCIAL CARE (2)

As it turns out a senior officer from Adult Social Care did contact me. Firstly I was sent a Market Positioning Statement that had been produced and sent out in the middle of 2018. I hadn't seen it before but it was a well-written description of the requirement of the Council that the market (business and charities) are being asked to fulfil. I call this the MPS (1) I digested it carefully and wrote back. That is detailed in the next section on ASC (at chapters F12 and 13) describing what an MPS (2) might look like.

In case you are wondering, these ideas haven't been plucked out of the air you know! During September of 2018 I was reading Mariana Mazzucato's brand new book, *The Value of Everything* and halfway through is a case study of the UK Care Home Industry. She starts by describing a market in the 1990's with care homes owned by small family firms or local authorities whereas by 2015 a substantial number were following a private equity model using financial engineering; some of them based in tax havens. She describes the Four Seasons business which used to be a small Scottish enterprise bought up in 1999, then sold on, sold on again, each time saddled with more debt and now it has so much that it costs about £100 per bed per week just to pay the interest. That business first ran into difficulties in 2015 as Local Authorities refused to pay higher fees at a time when their funding was being cut by the Government's Austerity Program. Since 1999 it doesn't seem to be an organisation where owners had care as their primary goal.

Here is some news from Four Seasons-run homes (thanks to LGiU).

On 11 Dec 2019, Four Seasons hands over 57 homes Crisis-hit care provider Four Seasons has been forced to hand over 57 care homes to rivals. One of Four Seasons' biggest landlords, HPH, has handed over the homes to rival providers Roseberry Care Centres, Belsize Healthcare and Harbour Healthcare. Four Seasons has been attempting to secure cheaper deals from the landlords of 135 of its 320 sites, and started withholding rent in September as a negotiating tactic. *Daily Mail, P: 70*

8th March 2020 – Break-up begins at Four Seasons Care home operator Four Seasons is being broken up with the sale of a group of specialist care hospitals for up to £100m. The firm collapsed last year and is being run by administrators Alvarez & Marsal, who have reportedly asked BDO to find a buyer for hospitals from Four Seasons' Huntercombe division, which cares for people with mental illnesses, learning disabilities and brain injuries. *The Mail on Sunday, Page: 105*

This is an example of capitalism working on a market with failings and thus being able to extract more profit than the wealth they create. The market failing in this case is supplying a need; which usually leads to uneven negotiating power, sometimes its due to a lack of freedom for the buyer to agree or to walk away. If the buyer is a person, they are in a very weak position to organise something whilst their frail parent is waiting to leave hospital, only the big local authorities who buy hundreds of bed spaces a year have enough market clout. Yet in Bristol, between 2015 and 2017, the Council was implementing a new procurement system that meant that care homes could bid prices up higher and higher. This actually reduced the Council's own power to negotiate. It has stopped now.

For the Four Seasons game of pass the parcel, the capitalists who gained were the ones who bought and sold the business after 1999, the one that failed was the final owner the one actually left carrying the parcel, more like a parcel bomb.

I leave you with this piece from the *Daily Mail* on 6th Feb 2020 (page 2) – reproduced via LGiU

> ***Private care home spending up 18% in five years*** *A report from the Office of National Statistics has revealed that the total amount paid out in care home fees paid privately has risen by 18.2% over the last five years – while the cost of state-funded care to the taxpayer rose by 12.6%. The report found private care providers "have experienced increased financial pressures, partly because of local authority fees being below full economic cost."*

Bristol's costs had risen much more than 12.6% in five years so were definitely doing something wrong. What that was is fully described in chapter F4.

COMMERCIALISATION: SHOULD COUNCILS GO INTO BUSINESS?

One of George Osborne's[55] wheezes, after the 2010 commencement of Austerity[56] and reductions to Local Government financing, was to get Councils to behave like businesses, take risks and make money. This was despite the fact that Councils are often a provider of services without competition, normally they do things that business won't touch because the activities are not profitable without support. They contract aspects of their services to business and keep the unprofitable bits for themselves. But the idea of commercialisation was taken on with gusto[57].

I joined up too and in 2017 Bristol City Council's commercialisation task group was set up. I watched and contributed as over a hundred ideas were sifted, some ridiculous, some massive, some risky, some unlawful and with one or two that might just make it. This was an activity I was familiar with for two reasons: I had been a private investor myself (not particularly successful) and also I reviewed student projects at Bath University along similar lines. Not quite Dragon's Den as it was for grades not bundles of £50 notes.

One idea I championed was for the Planning Department to add services to sell to developers and architects on top of their regulatory role (the granting and enforcement of permissions). Services like consultation with the public, a fast-track for planning (if you pay more) and reports prior to the formal application. I conveniently ignored the obvious conflicts of interest it would bring; where the Council could sell services to help speed planning application approval and then two months later it would be decided upon by the very same officers. Nevertheless it seemed an idea to offer good opportunities for profit and perhaps the conflicts could be managed like consultants do[58] when they audit their clients and provide advice as well.

---

55 Chancellor of the Exchequer 2010 to 2016, now editor of the London Evening Standard (April 2020).
56 Overall Bristol City Council's budget was held around £350 million for ten years. But there were wage rises to pay (minimum wage), demand pressures with an aging population, increasing homelessness and more. In cash terms care costs went up and everything else went down.
57 I got the impression that the primary driver was to bring in income to protect jobs. As you know the driver for business is to make profit for shareholders and not to protect jobs. I wonder if this difference in motivation led to some of the issues.
58 Something called Chinese walls. I've never been convinced.

Another opportunity I watched with interest was rat catching, now relabelled pest control. It had grown up as a service to Council housing (over 26,000 dwellings) was provided at low cost and with the obvious benefit that prevention of rats at one house stops the complaints coming in from nearby houses (a very positive externality). And not just rats but insects and other pests too. So that department put up their prices, bought new equipment and, well, wait and see...

Fortunately most of these commercialisation meetings were Friday afternoons so I couldn't attend them, they clashed with lectures I gave at Bath University. Coincidentally the classes I gave there included teaching entrepreneurship and writing business plans. I stopped teaching in 2018, the University wanted to increase class sizes for what seemed less money. I think it was a hint! After eighteen years I'd probably got too bolshie. So with Friday afternoons free I re-joined the Commercialisation Task Group hoping to hear about some thriving businesses and great stories.

This, of course, is a Council. They had done some good work whittling down the long list of a hundred ideas down to ten or so and deciding on what criteria to use to filter ideas further but there were some gaping holes. I didn't see an investment plan for anything.

I didn't see any embryonic profit and loss (P&L) accounts, nor forecasts and I didn't see anyone actually accountable for making each business idea work. Now this wouldn't matter so much if these new ideas were going to be extra bunce but the potential profits were being factored into budgets. And so the non-profits would soon show up as a variance to budget and that would then trigger cuts elsewhere.

Three of us "rebelled" in October 2019 we had a secret meeting (Green, Lib Dem and Tory) and decided the test of whether this was ever going to work was if the Council could write a credible business plan for the rat catcher. I sent an email.

"Come to me with a business plan for rat catchers in Bristol with a draft profit and loss, forecasts, someone accountable, explanation of the Council's competitive advantage, milestones, then that's something I can add value too."

A few weeks later I got a reply. I decided I needed to follow up immediately. I wrote:

"Thanks – I didn't make myself clear, apologies. I think the approach should be for all commercialisation not just micro businesses. For example: take the Harbourside, what is the Council's overall profit and loss, its turnover? Does the offer to customers split into revenue streams (moorings, rents etc.), which ones are highest margin and have opportunity for growth, who is the MD of "Harbourside Ltd" what is the competitive advantage of each of the revenue streams? I only used the example of the rat catcher business to see if such thinking was possible at all – it seems not. It may be because commercialisation via the public sector needs to take totally different approaches than the entrepreneurship I see in the private sector. I suspect not but I'm open(ish) minded. But what I've seen over the last two years doesn't encourage me. As it turns out I have a meeting clash tomorrow with Member Development. I'll be going to that one as I feel I have more to contribute. Kind regards – Clive"

No reply, except an invite to lots more meetings all the way through to summer 2020. One caught my eye; an afternoon tour of the Harbourside by boat. I accepted. It didn't happen.

Update, March 2020: I did see something on the rat catcher business a month ago before we all got sent home. There was one line called income £68,000 and it was predicted to become £100,000 in the year about to finish. I asked, "is this revenue or net profit?" Revenue meaning sales before the costs have been taken off and net profit being after costs have been taken off. "We don't know" was the answer. After discussion we decided it was probably revenue. So two or three years ago new equipment was bought and the activity of selling services to the public was increased. We don't know how many visits were made and what the cost per visit is. Is it making a profit? Who knows?

Stop Press, July 2020: I have just seen the first ever profit and loss, and it's for Pest Control. It took quite a lot of effort between Finance and IT, but it's worth it! It has so impressed me that I have delayed sending this to the printers to include the news. What it shows will have to wait. Ask me when you read this book

.

Summary: I like the rat catcher (Pest Control) example, it's an instance where Council officers can actually sell something, but we don't know if the results are good or bad. Possibly if all local authorities had software to run their small commercial operations then resources could be deployed better. George Osborne's notion came without any IT, just encouragement from outside bodies and the motivation of fear from the cuts and commercialisation perhaps being a way out. This illustrates poor Government (Section C) and should make us question whether this is something Councils should be doing at all because that's not their purpose. The bigger example of a Bristol cock-up and enormous waste of money is Bristol Energy in section C. There are many examples elsewhere. So many I have listed some in one of the Appendices[59].

If there is market failure so business can't make a profit from the activity and if the Government fails to act on that failure, then I think it is legitimate for a Council to consider action once it has shown there is enough social value to justify the investment.

Bristol's team have been successful in leveraging in grants for affordable housing, support for social enterprise providing services to the under privileged and reducing CO_2. All are adding social value, are not done by business and use grants available for the purpose.

But I question going into business to earn a profit to save job cuts in the Council. That puts a LA in direct competition with the private sector. I don't think a Council can compete usually. The rat catcher though is an example where the positive externalities (which are social value anyway) mean it might.

59   The examples in the appendix are about owning commercial property like offices and shopping centres. Things don't seem to be going that well for any of them; unless it is part of a bigger plan?

CHAPTER E12
CHILDREN IN CARE

Another failing of markets, yes the list is quite long, is when the quality of the product or service only becomes obvious long after it is bought. A car may have a fault that only shows up after a few months for example; the solution then is a warranty and the buyer can choose to pay a bit more for that at the time of purchase. But when selling insurance or pensions, poor quality may only show up much later and the only answer is the regulator or legal system. Still, at least they can offer some hope of redress, as happened in the pensions mis-selling where banks were caught out and had to pay back to customers, often decades later. In both cases the market and then the law (and regulator) have cobbled together a solution.

But what if the harm is irreparable? I don't mean death or physical disfigurement, they are bad enough, here my eye was caught by a BBC headline[60] where private equity were buying up children's care homes with plans to consolidate them into larger companies so increased buying power, economies of scale and thus more profit. The reason this caught my eye was Bristol City Council had been buying up homes for children's care to do just the opposite, reduce the scale to give a better family feeling for the teenagers and better outcomes.

Children who go into care do so for a number of reasons; it is a last resort by the authority. It might be brought about by a court order following a wrongdoing and the child is below the age of criminal responsibility, or it might be requested by the parents when they can't cope or may have split up, especially if one of the children was becoming unmanageable. Other times it might be due to a learning difficulty or disability that triggers a parent or authority to suggest a change in care responsibility. Abuse is sometimes a factor too. Whatever the case, the child comes into Council care and the Council has the responsibility to be a "parent" to them, we become the "corporate parent" and there are various bodies that ensure they are well cared for and educated. The

---

60   Private equity and foster homes: https://www.bbc.co.uk/news/uk-england-49450405

normal solution for teenagers is foster parents[61] or adoption if they are very young, fostering can be temporary as the original parents could apply to a court to have their child back if the situation improves.

Some children are so troubled that they need to go into a care home. Here they get lots of professional attention and time to turn things around to become a responsible adult in the external community. Many make that journey and authorities have duties up until the age of twenty five to assist the then young adult. Placement in the right type and size of care home is crucial, not just the home, but for the other children and the adult carers too. Bristol has found that the more serious the needs, the smaller the home, as it creates less "sibling conflict". The goal being to help the child work through their problems, get back on track in their education and head towards an independent, self-sustaining and happy future. If this fails which it does from time to time can you imagine the costs to the child and to society of the likely crime and in and out of prison and all the other services needed. If measured in money it comes to £ millions but it could also be measured in upset too for the victims, the carers and the child now often an adult.

So considering this kind of provision by business; can redress occur through the courts? Can a private company write a warranty? I would argue that this is an example where the private sector should not be allowed to operate at all. The ability to mitigate the harm that could be caused by the profit motive is just not possible.

The Government is helping local authorities in their attempts to keep families together. I'm told that the evidence is that in many situations[62] this leads to a better outcome. Bristol has done well in this regard and over the last few years has managed to reduce slightly the number of children in corporate care, bucking the national trend. The Government offers something called the Troubled Families Scheme[63] or Programme.

---

61   I am told by the foster parents themselves that being a foster carer is very rewarding and it's paid too. It should become a career option and considered a vocation with training and status. Foster parents are paid for by the Council, some direct and some via agencies (more expensive).
62   But not in cases of abuse of course.
63   Troubled families scheme: https://www.bbc.co.uk/news/uk-politics-50999083

6ᵗʰ Jan 2020, £165m boost for Troubled Families programme
The Government's Troubled Families project, which supports families
with multiple and complex social and health issues, is getting £165m in
funding to ensure it continues for another year. With existing support for
the project due to run out later this year, Communities Secretary Robert
Jenrick said the scheme, which has helped transform lives and relieve the
burden on public services, will be extended. The Troubled Families project
was launched in 2012 at a cost of £448m and revamped in 2015, with
around £920m spent since then, averaging about £157.6m a year. Analysis
suggests that since 2015, 297,733 families have "made improvements" in
regard to the problems that led to them joining the programme, with one
or more adults having moved off benefits and into work in 26,848 of these
families. Children's Commissioner for England Anne Longfield welcomed
the Government announcement but called for "long term and extended
funding commitments" in this year's spending review. BBC News

Comment on article above: Being on the Corporate Parenting Panel, I
wanted to know if this was new money or just a press release. I asked the
Council officer, they are all very good in this department. I got a reply
the same day:

"The programme started in 2012 for three years and then in 2015 the
government announced a further five year programme which is due to end
in March 2020. Last year (2019), under intense lobbying from the Local
Government Association and a detailed evaluation of the programme
the Government set out an aspiration to keep the programme going. Due
to the fact of Brexit/general election the Government decided to roll the
programme over for one year to allow the election to take place and then
facilitate longer term thinking.

This announcement is the anticipated one year roll over. In the
Government manifesto it has committed to a further troubled families
programme into the future and so proposals are going into the Cabinet
which is expected to be held in the summer to have yet another programme
albeit altered to some extent. Therefore some form of funding should be

available for several years to come. The detail has to be worked out.

In Bristol the grant has for several years paid for about 50% of our early help offer i.e. Families in Focus. We are very reliant on it to maintain our existing service. We were looking at a very challenging and significant reduction in our service but this roll over and future funding will enable us to maintain our existing service which is badly needed

I hope this helps, in a sense, it's not additional money but welcome money to sustain our existing service."

This scheme is so valuable to society that it's a shame that a longer term approach can't be committed to, still it's funded for now.

I'm pleased I could end this whole section with a positive story and in Bristol the care of its corporate children and approach to troubled families seems to be very good: A testimony to cooperation by people who are motivated by care. A sector that shouldn't let business within a million miles of it, there are sectors though where business[64] is best suited to serve and shouldn't let Councils or the state[65] get anywhere near, like cafés, perfumes, computer games and running shoes...and maybe[66] more!

> What's coming next in Sections F and G:
> Armed (so I think) with a coherent value system of fairness (equals freedom without doing harm) and knowing about market shaping, management and market failure I decided to wade in to the deep end and try to understand two of the Council's biggest issues: Adult Social Care, which is next and then Homelessness/Affordable housing.

---

64   UK 'has particularly extreme form of capitalism by Simon Jack, Business Editor: https://www.bbc.co.uk/news/uk-politics-50999083
65   Except for market place management (regulation) or market shaping.
66   I'm teasing my business school friends who will be horrified at being limited to just four markets. They will be pleased to know that I can think of another four markets that could be served by business too!

THE FUNDING BLACK HOLE OF ADULT SOCIAL CARE

INTERLUDE

So now to apply financial and economic views, fairness and attention to detail to two of the most pressing problems facing society: An aging population and homelessness.

Firstly to the care of the elderly (homelessness is in the next section, G).

Sometimes we Councillors have to behave like detectives, trying to wheedle out evidence of the causes of a crime; the "crime" in this case being always over budget.

This whole section is devoted to all those who work in adult social care (ASC), including the officers and the politicians and hopefully it will give you an insight into your own future prospects, assuming you are getting older[1], as well as show up weaknesses in the economic and political systems (as seen from the lowly level of an opposition Councillor in Bristol)

Adult social care is much more than putting people in a home, yet care homes are a major cost to the public and to Councils too. The costs are both financial and social; the system runs the risk of "out of sight, out of mind" and I fear that Covid-19 is going to expose this ruthlessly. There are other reasons why it's better to have the old and frail living within a fully functioning community with children, students, mums, dads, singles and dare I say it, even the homeless. The reasons are that often the older person wants to live in a place they can call home plus, usually, the costs to them and to the Council are less too.

In summary we have a system that relentlessly tries to place old people into homes and the Council is trying to fight this with a more humane system of enabling them to live at home.

"Now I am older, entering care, money worries now
Will you still be sending me into a home?
With strange people, leave me alone[2]"

INTRODUCTION

"Thank God Bristol is not Blackpool!"

Three-quarters of Blackpool Council budget spent on social care:
Reported on 31ˢᵗ January 2020: Blackpool Council plans to spend 76% of its annual budget on social care, up from 48% 10 years ago. The

1 Most of us are!
2 Apologies to Lennon / McCartney and my attempt at the second worst poetry in the universe.

local authority intends to invest an extra £14m in children's care from April. Council leader Simon Blackburn said: "It is absolutely right that we spend the money that is needed to protect and care for our most vulnerable residents but that does come at a price". The Council is planning to make cuts of £5m as it seeks to make savings of £19.6m. Up to 75 jobs will be lost, while Council Tax is expected to rise by almost 4%. BBC News The Guardian, Page: 32 Blackpool Gazette (Thanks to the LGiU)

This whole section is a case study about adult social care provision from the perspective of an opposition Councillor attempting to work with the administration to improve care quality and value for money. Believe me it is possible; just very difficult. It's a difficult political balance providing support to Labour, but also injecting analysis and criticism when appropriate. None of this made a good story for the press and my colleagues must have wondered if I was wasting my time. "Labour are the enemies, don't help them" You will be pleased to note that I have edited some of my statements and removed much of the jargon. It proves a good case study into the benefits of good scrutiny and is a helpful demonstration of how I'd make the economy work for people.

CHAPTER F1
ASC – BLOWING UP BRISTOL'S BUDGET – TASK AND FINISH

Most societies don't allow their old, frail or infirm people, nor those with severe disabilities, to fend for themselves; long ago in the UK what is now called social care was provided by the family or community, often church based. In 1601 the Elizabethan Poor Law formally made parishes responsible for providing this form of care to those whose family couldn't support them. Then came the Industrial Revolution; the population and cities grew, people became dissociated from their extended families, from their town or village of birth. Care for the poor became highly variable and there was a stage where it could mean living a life of work in the notorious workhouses; they had it solved, care for the elderly wasn't an issue then as they didn't live that long. This system got patched up but never really worked.

Things took a turn for the better; responsibility was transferred to Councils in the 1930s. Then the NHS was set up in 1948 but social care stayed with Councils and their prime aim was to help the aged poor. In those days life expectancy averaged around 65, it's now about 81 with many living well beyond 85. So as a percentage of population, the numbers of aged needing care back then was relatively low, now the numbers are already massive and growing fast; more older people with different and often more difficult requirements. Governments have avoided tackling this issue and the funding of it. No votes, I assume. So whilst the wealth of the nation has been growing, most of that growth has landed in the hands of a relative few, but the care needs of the country are growing fast and for the relative many. In Bristol the costs of adult social care are about 40% of the entire take from Council Tax and Business Rates[3].

Councils tend to employ their own social workers and occupational therapists[4], but often contract out work to physiotherapists[5], carers and care homes. So most of the tax payers' money spent is commissioning services bought in. In Bristol we have to be careful not to compete with neighbouring authorities otherwise wages and therefore costs go up for all. If they did, (and this is how capitalist markets work) then, in theory, more carers and physios would train up, but the costs would then be higher and so would the tax as it is required to pay for it all. Interestingly, fans of capitalism in these types of markets seem to forget the impact of

3   The City used to earn a substantial amount from business rates. Post Covid-19 we shall see how that changes.
4   Social workers assess the needs of the person entering or in the care system and write, organise delivery of and monitor the care plan to ensure the needs are provided. OTs as occupational therapists are called can do most of that but also produce a plan to improve the independence of the person so that they have reduced care needs and so reduced costs. OTs are therefore very good value for money. OT activities are briefly covered in a report by the Royal College of OTs:
https://www.rcot.co.uk/sites/default/files/ILSM Social Care report (Web).pdf
5   Organised differently across the country. Often some of these roles are provided by the NHS, sometimes the whole package is integrated like in Torbay.

price increases caused by markets causing rises in tax.

Care is means-tested and only those with assets of less than about £14,000 get it totally paid[6] for by the Council and often a deal is struck between the family and the Council to pay top ups. Typically living and care in a residential home costs £800 a week and care provided to someone still living in their own home can cost £200 or £300 a week.

Average Council care costs hit £5,700

On 1 Dec 2019, According to analysis of local authority data by the Labour Party, elderly and disabled people are paying an average of around £5,700 a year for Council social care. The party found that more than half of those eligible for Council-funded care, including care home costs and home care for tasks like dressing and washing, are having to pay for their care from their savings or benefits, with the total paid out coming to around £1.7bn a year. Under the Care Act, those with assets above £14,250 are liable to pay the full cost of their Council care, while Labour has promised to roll out free personal care, excluding care home costs, for all over-65s. The Sunday Telegraph, Page: 9

The article above, thanks as always to the LGiU, shows that many of the public are paying for some of their care even if Councils are supposed to pay.

Much of the famous bed-blocking that the NHS suffers from was due to the shortage of carers (to provide care for the person when they return home) but if their home wasn't suitable or if the delays were too long, then they transferred straight into an expensive residential home whether they needed it or desired it or not. That speedy transfer then costs the person and the Council (from tax payers) a fortune[7].

---

6   And if savings are around £24,000 or more then you pay entirely out of your own pocket.
7   This process was speeded up during Covid, the Government provided billions to make sure that NHS beds became free within minutes sometimes. The money was to Councils to pay the extra care costs this resulted in.

CHAPTER F2
THE SITUATION IN 2017

Some think that looking after old, infirm persons is the job of the NHS; others say they should be cared for by their own, now adult, offspring. Others say people should save up during their lives to afford to live their final year or so in a nursing home. But these three routes have big potholes: many people haven't saved up enough for a pension let alone care. And even if they have enough for a year's care costs that can be enough for their savings to run out. Or perhaps they have gotten sneaky and have gifted it away early to their now grown up children. Or their children don't want to look after them, or they don't want to be a burden on them? Private thoughts harboured of shipping the old folks out to Spain maybe or to some coastal resort nearer home? I certainly didn't know anything about this multi-billion pound industry before becoming a Councillor, premature thoughts of my own penultimate destiny were certainly not welcome.

The extract below, from 2020 shows some of the pressures, worse than 2017.

23 Feb 2020 - Care system could collapse in a decade
A report from the Centre for Economics and Business Research (CEBR) think-tank, shown to the Sunday Times, has warned that the care system could collapse within a decade thanks to the death of final salary pensions, cuts to Council budgets, and soaring nursing home fees. The report found that workers need to save an average of £574 more each month to fund growing care home costs in retirement.
The Sunday Times, Business and Money, Page: 12

So how did I become one of the Green Councillor experts in adult social care you may ask? Good question; it became clear to me that as Bristol City Council, like most other Councils, was haemorrhaging money each year paying for the care of 5,000 means-tested persons of 65 and over (usually 85 and over). Then add the costs of 2,000 at working age, but probably not working, adults often suffering from acute physical or mental disabilities. Costs rose so fast and seemingly out of control that, having participated in the 2017 Budget Task and Finish Group, I wanted to get onto the adult social care Task and Finish Group (why it was expected to finish I don't know), to understand where the money was going and why it was always over budget. This ASC group was a sub group of People Scrutiny.

I had a few preconceived and probably unfair ideas about People Scrutiny. It consists of Councillors who sit on the group, ideally to consider proposals ideally before sign-off by the Mayor and Cabinet. We have discussed scrutiny earlier in the book, if at all possible this is done long before Cabinet, but more often it occurs just before, even sometimes after. The Chair of Scrutiny has to be from an opposition party, but Labour had a majority of Councillors and so have a majority on each scrutiny group. If it ever came to a vote, say on a report from Scrutiny into Cabinet, then Labour would win it, unless one or two of their Councillors went maverick. This occasionally happens but that type of behaviour I'm told risks the wrath of the Labour whip.

Back to People Scrutiny; my initial opinion was that these are busy Councillors who care very much about the quality of care for the elderly, some might have parents in care themselves, another might be an ex-doctor for example. What I expected and found was little real interest in the costs of care provision. Their line of enquiry was always about the quality of care and not seemingly the value for money. People Scrutiny also covered children's care and education; three massive areas accounting for £600 million of costs in Bristol each year (education paid for direct by the Government). That's about 5% of Bristol's entire economy, scrutinised by 11 Councillors meeting three or four times a year.

So who did care about the value for money of adult social care? Indeed you could ask the same question in many of the big cost areas. And the answer is: Finance Department and the directors of other departments who were continually having their budgets cut because adult social care needed more money, and then more and then some more. And the

Mayor of course who couldn't get any initiatives past Finance because of the risks. I say risk. It wasn't really a risk, it was a certainty that there would be an ASC cost overrun.

All of those people who do care about costs, are the very ones who don't know the details about adult social care, nor children's care, nor education. A recipe for spiralling costs and that's what we got. Don't get me wrong, cost overruns were happening throughout the UK, and with an aging population and big business entering the care home market, the situation wasn't going to improve.

16 Feb 2020, Even richest pensioners will struggle to pay for care

Sunday Times analysis suggests that even wealthy savers who hit the £1.055m lifetime cap on tax-free money placed in a pension will not have enough income to pay for the cost of one year's old age social care. The average annual cost of a residential care home was £33,852 last year, or £47,320 including the cost of nursing care, according to figures from the not-for-profit organisation Paying for Care. Someone who converted their pension into an income for life by purchasing an annuity at state pension age would generate an income of £32,000 a year, figures from tax adviser Blick Rothenberg show. Even adding the full new state pension would only take the total income to £41,000.
The Sunday Times, Business, Page: 11

As I was already the Green Councillors' self-appointed financial expert, I decided to really understand what was going on so I joined the ASC T&F G (adult social care Task and Finish Group). This kicked off in 2017 and concentrated on one area; the 65 and over age group, the T&F group idea was an innovation for Bristol, started due to budget cuts and lack of effectiveness of the old scrutiny system. It was decided to stop the old-style scrutiny meetings and create a mechanism for detailed understanding; deep dives into specific areas. Topics were chosen; future of libraries, the Council's budget, adult social care and a few others. Rather than populate them with Councillors taken prorata from the parties, Councillors could attend if they were interested, sometimes there wasn't a Labour majority, usually all the participants were interested in making progress. Even then, the effectiveness of this new "pre-decision" scrutiny process turned out to be variable, but for me the ASC T&F G was a great success. I think it was too for the Cabinet Member who was sufficiently enlightened, confident and interested in the opinions of others, and she made sure of the quality and quantity of information coming to our meetings (approximately monthly). Her attentiveness made sure the officers were interested too.

It was helped by the fact that the Government had identified Bristol as one of the worst areas for hospital bed blocking. Termed delayed transfer of care (abbreviated DTOC) and they had kindly offered the Council some management consultants[8] to tell us what to do. So the quality of information went up a notch or two and we saw some comparison with other local authorities[9].

Bed blocking is when an elderly person who, having gone into hospital for example after a fall at home, can't then be discharged. This can be because their own home isn't suitable or there is a lack of a care plan or carers; if something can't be sorted quick then to free up the hospital bed they are whisked away into an expensive residential or nursing home. The process of discharge requires assessing their specific needs, getting the homes to quote a price and then the Council, family and outpatient all agreeing, this was while they were still occupying a hospital bed, not much time to get best value.

Given the nature of politics in the UK, antagonistic to say the least, I think it takes some political confidence to let opposition Councillors deep dive into what's going on. Well done Helen.

So having sat in and been allowed to question officers during that heady 2017, I felt equipped to start asking what I thought were useful questions about where was all this money going.

---

8   One problem was they didn't know either but they did improve the data and quality of thinking.
9   The Council used to buy in benchmark data, comparisons with other Councils, but due to the cuts this had been stopped.

CHAPTER F3
BETTER LIVES (FOR OLDER PEOPLE)

The program to improve care and reduce the costs to the Council of the 5,000 over 65s in care funded by the Council was optimistically called "Better Lives".

The following question to Cabinet illustrates the depth and complexity of the issues

Cabinet 3.4.18 - Question from Cllr Clive Stevens - (Better Lives, ASC)

Dear Mayor and Cabinet,

We are all aware of the six fold (maybe more) pressures on adult social care, three primarily due to medical advances: ageing population, longer time in care, more complex health issues, and three due to the economic environment: living wage increases impacting on care home costs, competition for scarce resources bidding up prices and family refinancing. This must seem an impossible combination to deal with, yet the paper submitted to Cabinet highlights some of the routes out:

More re-ablement, occupational therapy, assisted technology and mobile working for social workers.

My questions relate to two of those routes out and are primarily about bottleneck management:

1. Mobile[10] working: This in itself is a major project relying on our ICT support and new working practices. We are told that social workers are wanting the change. My concern is ICT resource and how is this to be managed. I would argue this project should be priority #1 not just for ICT but everyone should help.

For example; I see there is an ICT project for HR and Payroll delivering benefits of £450k. We haven't yet costed the benefits for mobile working ICT, it is surely higher than that, perhaps 10 x as much and so should surely take priority. But last month's paper didn't show any financially quantified benefits so we don't know.

---

10   Also termed agile working.

The fact that there were no financial benefits[11] was a hobby horse of mine. In this example there were no financial benefits costed out for a Cabinet spend of a million quid. By March 2018, more than a year after the Bundred report was released which had criticised just that. I was increasingly exasperated by the Council requesting spend without a cost benefit analysis. That led me to a mistake later on in 2018 regarding Colston Hall's business plan, you can read Appendices 1 through to 5 to get the full flavour of my frustration.

Back to adult social care....

Question 1: Could the Mayor ensure that social worker mobile/agile working takes a very high priority, maybe the highest within ICT's long list of projects please?

I then moved to the topic of re-ablement, which means enabling the person to live a life from home[12]. That means a better layout, equipment, perhaps a stair-lift, easier to use kettle and physio[13] to get the muscles working again.

Re-ablement: The graph isn't shown here but we saw it at Better Lives Task & Finish. It seems that Bristol has one of the lowest rates in the country of delivering re-ablement therapy (and occupational and physio), at least four times less than the national average. When we saw this statistic it seemed it might be a probable cause as to why we have such a high rate of elderly in residential or nursing homes. Assuming it is one of the causes I'm wondering firstly why the re-ablement rate is so low and then what are the bottlenecks that will occur as we try to increase it, not just doubling but quadrupling the amount of re-ablement delivered? Will there be a lack of trained carers, physios, or occupational therapists, or is it because social

11   Actually it was shown there was £10k benefit on print costs, a 100 year payback on a £1 million investment.
12   Primarily a task for the occupational therapists.
13   Physios were via the NHS. Technically this is called rehabilitation rather than re-ablement but the goal is to help the elderly person be as self-sufficient as possible.

workers haven't had the time to prescribe it?

<u>Question 2:</u> *Could the Cabinet Member please use her team's expertise to confirm that lack of re-ablement is one of the causes of Bristol's high residential care levels and if so what bottlenecks she anticipates occurring when we try to increase the levels of re-ablement?*

The answers were very instructive and when I last looked, still on video. Firstly on ICT, Helen, the Cabinet Member, seemed quite grateful that I had raised the priority need of this project in front of Finance (who look after IT). I got the feeling that ASC system development was the Cinderella of IT and so any recognition that it's key to improving value for money in the biggest cost area was gratefully received.

As to part two, it was explained that even if re-ablement performance was up to scratch, the next bottleneck would be not having enough houses or flats which can become homes that the elderly can move into; somewhere to call a home of their own and to be designed for the needs of the frail, infirm or even with mild dementia. If enough homes were available, called locally as extra care housing, then the elderly leaving hospital could enter residential care temporarily[14] while assessed and re-abled before moving into a "new home" of their own, to rent probably. "I want to live in a home of my own" is a frequent request, if that's what people want and it's less expensive than residential care, then surely it's not rocket science? That requires capital investment and it seemed to me that ASC was the Cinderella of the capital investment program too.

Anyone coming from a business background, and that includes me, knows that to improve value for money of a service or product you have to invest, often in IT, in capital and sometimes in product innovation. So it seems the same applies in Local Authorities. Additionally, you need to manage the bottlenecks. I recall that from the 1990's as part of my business education[15]. In ASC there were bottlenecks everywhere and

---

14   This facility now exists called a re-ablement centre.
15   *The Goal* by Eli Goldratt and Jeff Cox was compulsory reading for any manager in the company I worked for back then.

they moved much like a bowl of wriggling snakes. A new one pops up to bite you each month. The next story relates the story of a particularly big snake of the Council's own making. I estimate it is still costing Bristol's Council Tax payers £5 million a year, every year.

CHAPTER F4
THE BITE BACK FROM THE MARKET PLACE
MANAGEMENT SYSTEM USED FOR CARE HOMES

Buying up, adapting and even building homes for rent specifically for older people who need care is a good thing to do, but there is a time lag and the need to contain care costs was urgent; they were going up about £ 100,000 a month. One of the main problems was the increasing cost of a stay in residential and nursing care homes. If a market is being used when there is excess demand then prices rise, eventually supply should rise to catch up. With ever increasing demand, care home companies could dictate the price. Bristol City Council had taken a decision around 2015 to manage the market differently which invited care homes to do that and they did.

This was before my time as Councillor but the way I understand it is, that to comply with latest best practice in procurement, a new system was brought in to help decisions on placements (into homes) to run things as if it were an auction[16] like an inverted eBay whereby the buyer can take the best deal.

So for a new service user (as they are called nowadays, but I mean a person who is in need of residential care) their needs are carefully assessed and if it is decided they need to move into residential or nursing care it was then put out to competitive tender using this new

16   An auction is the way for a seller to extract maximum value from the marketplace, in theory a similar system taking the lowest price enables the buyer to pay lowest value.

system[17]. This was one or two people each day. That state of the art[18] thinking meant that care homes could up their prices each time a new person's needs were advertised and indeed they managed to increase prices by almost £10,000 a year, per person, before a way was devised to abandon the system and procure more effectively, throwing out the "market based" solution.

Abandoning it, good but not quick enough, it had the potential to cost the Council Tax payer £10 million[19] a year, every year; officers hurriedly, quite quick for a Council, went back to how things used to be done and created a buying price list, called the Bristol Rate which covered most requirements. They set buying prices (of residential and nursing care, with or without dementia care) at less than the current market rate by £5,000 a year but substantially higher than they paid two years earlier. To be fair on the care homes they were underpaid before and with the impact of minimum wage increases needed a higher rate anyway. But I couldn't help thinking how the private equity owners of some care home groups were rubbing their hands with glee as a way out of the mess they had gotten into by overbidding for care businesses.

By 2018, after four years of teaching, reading and comment I had come to a view on what I thought was a more efficient economic approach, rather than free markets for this sector. This was based on the research and teachings of Mazzucato, Stiglitz and many more with the odd tweak by me.

Below outlines how I would restructure the ASC market and who better I thought than to tell the Mayor and Cabinet themselves...

Cabinet 5th June 2018 – Questions – adult social care – Cllr Clive Stevens
The prices for adult social care accommodation have risen extremely fast over the last couple of years. The dynamic purchasing system that the

---

17   I also wondered if this led to delays and hence the bed blocking in the NHS. I never found out.
18   I mean this sarcastically. It frustrates me because this decision (and Bristol Energy) both seem, with hindsight, to have been so stupid and expensive, taken by a Mayor who was a business person supposedly. I wonder about whether better scrutiny would have improved things and saved Bristol Council Tax payers many millions per year.
19   With around 1,250 in some form of care home paid for by the Council and rates going up nearly £200 a week that equals close to £12.5 million, rounded down to £10 million.

Council brought in carries a lot of the blame, it has created something like an auction but where the provider wins. Over the same time quality of care might have increased but I don't think that's due to higher prices.

So setting a Bristol Rate and having it at £100/week lower than current rates has to be a step forward. But I urge you please not to make this a three year deal because I fear even at these rates it will irreparably damage the market and drive it towards for-profit providers funded by big business and I don't think that is going to be good for us, not for the older people nor for the charity sector.

Here are my two questions and then my analysis as to why I feel we need more detailed work on this issue:

Q1: Do you agree that we need to look deeply into the structure of the market and decide what type of offer we want for our older people before tying ourselves into a specific Bristol Rate for several years. If so, could the Bristol Rate be flagged up more as a stabilising level plus a strong future possibility of a reduction to deter a rush of undesirable private investment?

Q2: Could you undertake the market review I suggest below and do it as a cross party exercise drawing on all the skills we have at our disposal?

I also provided an analysis (see below) of the marketplace, it earned me a one to one meeting with the lead officer of adult social care. I'm told that this was a very rare invite for an opposition Councillor (I'm sure they checked it out with the Cabinet Member for People, Councillor Helen Holland, I can't thank her too much for her open approach to a strange type of Councillor that I must have seemed to be). If you aren't up to too much thinking right now, maybe you have a headache or it's late then feel free to skip the analysis below (Chapter F5) and jump to chapter F6 where I start "Oh Dear". But do come back to F5 another time, promise?

CHAPTER F5
MARKETPLACE ANALYSIS FOR RESIDENTIAL CARE HOMES

Analysis 5th June 2018 (summarised)

1) The first and most obvious thing to enquire about is experience from other Local Authorities, especially any that have set their own buying rate.

2) Demand management. It is nationally acknowledged that Bristol places far too many of its older people into care homes. All of 2017 was spent planning how more older people could live in their own home which is where we are told older people normally want to stay. This might now be working, the graphs shown (on page 190 of these Cabinet papers) show that our accommodation requirements for residential and nursing homes might have peaked due to this better demand management. The figures are only up to end of March 2018 and I have just seen latest data which also shows the same reduction. One bottleneck now I'm told is lack of availability of Extra Care Housing which is different than a residential care home. It is this ECH market we need to incentivise and via the private sector if necessary. Reducing demand and incentivising ECH is one of the keys to getting on top of this pricing issue.

65s And Over Placed In Residential And Nursing Care (Bristol)

September 2017	1,290
November 2017	1,275
January 2018	1,260
March 2018	1,200

Data above from the Cabinet papers of 5th June 2018

3) This "Bristol Rate" is £100/week less than our current average placement costs (thus saving BCC many millions once fully applicable and presumably not affecting quality). The first estimate of costs before the consultation process started was a rate even lower some £75/week lower than the Bristol Rate you have settled on, bringing us back to price levels of a couple of years ago plus allowance for the minimum wage and inflation.

Officers have recommended raising that rate by £75/week. (To put that into context that's a £1.5m/year saving[20] given up, just like that; enough to keep all the libraries open and more). The justification for some of that £75 increase is because the suppliers said those first estimates were far too low. What else are suppliers going to say?

4) I worry about our relationships with some of our care providers. Audit papers show that we have been overbilled by £176k by care homes after the resident became deceased and so far we have only recovered £51k of that. I am looking into this further.

5) Using the price benchmarks for 17/18 plus wage inflation, these Bristol Rates are pretty close to national ceiling levels. This signals that the Bristol Rate might still be too high.

Then I detailed some financial reasons as to why I thought that officers' maths was wrong.

Financial reasons the maths was wrong...

6) I agree with four of the six respondents to the consultation that the model's profit and return on capital assumptions are inconsistent; the good news is it can be easily corrected and should result in a lower price.

Here are four inconsistencies I can see:

• The model double counts profit allowing a profit factor for return on capital and another profit for return on costs. In all, the profit sums to a 10.4% return on capital. For highly geared (e.g. 50% funded by debt) private investors this can become 15% return[21] on equity; very nice return for this type of business. To stop a potential in-flood of private investment simply say this Bristol Rate is a stabilisation and expected to fall in the future, that should minimise further private investment and especially from private equity and offshore based businesses who are the last people

---

20   With 1,250 in paid for care and an average expectancy of staying in the home for two and a half years (some less some more) that means about 500 new placements will occur each year. If they are £75 a week more than needed that is about £2m cost increase in the first year (and a further increase in year two of course). But not all the placements will be in the beginning of the year so I made an allowance for that. If you are really picky you could knock me down to £1m rather than £1.5m!

21   A 10% return on capital will translate to a 15% return on equity if the business's capital is funded 50% debt (loans) and 50% equity (shares) and the debt attracts an interest rate of 5% per year.

we should be entrusting with adult social care.

• Return on capital is not a measure for not-for-profit businesses at all. They just need to make enough return to reinvest back into assets of between 2.5% and 4%. That's at least a 6% difference on the 10.4% for private enterprise which all other things being equal is why charities can still thrive at lower price levels.

• The model estimates the capital as the sales value of the business. That's got all sorts of problems associated with it and is not how it is usually done in business which would use a depreciated asset value. A 10.4% return on the sales value is generous.

• Another potential price reduction reason is because some of the costs in the model don't apply to local authority placements. For example some head office costs and even some general expenses will be marketing costs to attract new residents. There are no marketing costs in supplying BCC and other LAs. Indeed across the UK private residents pay on average £100/week more than LA residents. The extra costs of marketing and the weaker negotiating position of an individual explain most if not all of this £100 difference. If for-profit care home providers are allowed to make 10.4% return on assets for a Local Authority revenue stream[22] they will be making 14% or more on their private customer revenue stream. Averaging at 12% and their return on equity will be even higher. No wonder some for-profit investors are highly geared as this pumps up their return on equity to very high levels.

The impact of the four factors above means that at the Bristol Rate levels you have now set are at risk of creating a very profitable market for highly geared private equity and they will eventually take it over. Lower prices, within reason, keep the market more suited to supply by the not-for-profit sector. AND if combined with a more attractive market for Extra Care Housing will support our goals.

In and around Bristol, 40% of care homes are run not-for-profit, but

---

22 Revenue stream is business school jargon meaning sales into that particular sector of a market, so here we are looking at sales of places in a care home paid for by a local authority as one sector (revenue stream) and sales to the public direct (because they have enough savings) as a second revenue stream which incidentally is usually at a higher price.

nationally the figure is less than 20%. The Bristol Rate now allows very good profits to be made to the for-profit sector and so there is a good chance that business will buy up care homes thus removing not-for-profit (charity) suppliers. I don't want to end up with this result for Bristol.

7) The Care Act 2014 calls for efficiency. Efficiency comes through either economies of scale and technology (work processes or equipment). The former leads one to thinking of larger and larger homes. I don't think many older people want that. Technology is coming and I feel that not-for-profit providers are more likely to use it for true care rather than for replacing staff (which is the incentive for business).
So in conclusion.

BCC are in a 50% market share23 position as a buyer of care services, that's monopoly buyer power in most books, so we have a duty to shape the market. If we don't, it will be taken over by the for-profit sector. Do go ahead with this decision today but please don't fix the Bristol Rate for three years, do say that BCC will take a more strategic overview of the provision of care homes and need for more extra care accommodation. We have a unique opportunity this year before high prices ruin the market. We want to ensure a better quality provision by appropriate providers at a fair cost.

The acid test of course is what happened. I'm still waiting but there is news later on...

---

23   This means that the Council pays for about half of the older people in care. The remainder pay privately.

CHAPTER F6

OH DEAR. THE COUNCIL SAYS IT'S DOING LOTS OF GOOD THINGS BUT THE COSTS KEEP GOING UP

So by the Autumn of 2018, the Better Lives Program was investing in new mobile devices for Social Workers and other key staff (tablets, mobile phones and appropriate software). Although the business case was poorly written, it seemed the right thing to do. I reviewed the business case with the officer responsible for the quality of all business cases and they had identified some new savings in physiotherapist costs due to more efficient scheduling (and probably other care workers too) which apparently saved approximately[24] £100,000 a year. So at least this brought the published payback from 100 years down to 10 years. My point was that if they had known in March 2018 when it was approved that the main benefit was efficient scheduling of therapists (physio and occupational) then they would have chosen different measurements of success. But there you go.

They had already identified all the bottlenecks (except one – see later) and were working on them but the biggie, the lack of appropriate housing (extra care housing it is called) hadn't been addressed yet, not visibly to people like me anyway.

So we move on to September 2018 and I analysed the Council's accounts and they did not make pretty reading…

I'm not sure how welcome my running commentaries on the Council's finances were. Labour Councillors claimed they weren't told much and as it was my job to keep an eye on the finances for the Greens. I thought every once in a while it wouldn't hurt if someone explained the situation in plain English to everyone. So here we are with accounts three[25] months into the new financial year.

---

24   I have subsequently reviewed this and I'm told it's not true. Physio costs are paid for privately or by the NHS. I think this is an example of a finance person trying to help the ASC Officer justify their investment and simply not understanding things. Easily done.

25   So the "management" accounts are April 1 to June 30th and published late August.

Statement to Cabinet 4/9/18 - Agenda item 23 - P3 Forecast Outturn - Cllr Clive Stevens

These Period 3 accounts are forecasting a large overspend for adult social care (ASC) of £11.8m for this year, this caught me somewhat by surprise. I was expecting perhaps £6m or £7m but this has forced me to dig deeper into the figures and the variance now becomes slightly clearer. I also see this £11.8m is actually understated compared to the budget that we Councillors saw in February. The variance you are quoting is against an amended budget figure some £8.1m higher than the figure seen and voted on back in February. So ASC costs are forecast to be nearly £20m higher this financial year above the original budget. How can this be?

As it turns out most of the £8.1 million was money held in different pots: for wage increases and late grants from Government. This pot was called "Corporate" but it was not clear at all when we Councillors voted on that budget in February 2018. We weren't told, so a lack of transparency there. That was the same budget they hid the Special Educational Needs cut, the one that went to judicial review and we were told by the judge (in my words) we didn't know what we were voting for. I think ASC fits that too.

But there's still the £11.8 million cost overrun expected by year end[26] to look into. So what's happening? ASC placement costs are in two blocks: The Over 64s and secondly the costs of care for those people who are younger aged between 18-64 but have a disability of a kind that requires Council support. The costs for them have climbed even faster and both are now roughly the same amount at about £75 million each year each.

Over 64s - *Most of the process improvement work has been aimed at improving the service to the over 64s. More are opting to live in their*

---

26   This is in the budget year 2018/19, the 2019/20 was on target to be over £6m over budget before meaningful analysis stopped due to Covid 19. In February 2020 Councillors voted on the 2020/21 budget and analysis showed that ASC was underfunded by at least £10m. I came to the conclusion it was a plot by Local Authorities to show Government that ASC was underfunded (fair enough) and coming in over budget year on year on year was the best way of showing it. https://www.bristolpost.co.uk/news/bristol-news/10 million-blackhole-bristol-councils-budget-3883756

own homes rather than in residential or nursing homes and attempts are being made to use this reduced demand to put downward price pressure on care home pricing via the Bristol Rate. As long as the quality of care is maintained and staff are paid appropriately that seems the right thing to do.

I've done some calculations comparing the July 2018 metrics vs the January 2018 metrics and it seems that the progress in reducing numbers in homes so far would give a £1.8m[27] annual saving over last year. But with regard to the price reductions there is a lag for lower residential prices to kick in as those leaving[28] residential and nursing care were on a rate of say £650 to £700/week but new people coming into that service will join at £800 (or £750 if the Bristol Rate holds). So the placement price drop from £800 to say £750 will take a year or longer to work through. At the moment new people are coming into care at a higher price than those leaving. That means a cost increase this year of some £1.5m, it should start to decline in 2019/20. There are other cost increases too like pay rises. Additionally I see an underspend in the Extra Care capital program. This needs to be accelerated urgently as it is now one of the major bottlenecks. So knowing what I know now I can't see any big savings in ASC over 64s this year.

Social worker agile working I am told is being implemented effectively. All in all it seems you are doing the right things but not quickly enough for the finances. If implementation is being done as quickly as possible, and there are resource limitations and democratic and consultation issues then we need to make sure the 19/20 budget, which we start working on soon, reflects reality.

18-64s - *People in our care with disabilities. Costs continue to increase and the same quality of process improvement work needs to be done in this sector as has been done for Over 64s. Numbers continue to increase,*

---

27   A reduction of 90 people at £800 a week is £3.6m (halved as would average out over a year = £1.8m roughly). The price is £800 as the saving is from people not being placed in care homes because they can live at home or in extra care housing instead. The numbers are rough estimates.

28   In a public statement I have to be guarded but generally you leave care for one reason only, you have died.

placement costs rise too. Although I've not seen a cost allocation across the two categories I fear this service is tracking perhaps £5m maybe more than 17/18.

Overall: *Therefore I can't see a year-end cost of less that £144m[29] for this current year of 18/19. How to get the £150m down to that? There is a grant of £1.3m to allocate. There may be other Government funding, perhaps some recharge invoices to be sent out and maybe a need for some reduction from reserves.*

"We must bear in mind the probable need to consult on in-year mitigation actions too. That will delay cost mitigations but hopefully improve the quality of the decision making.

In summary - apart from the urgent actions highlighted above this confirms my and probably your view that local authority funding of adult social care is fundamentally unsustainable, government needs to stop dodging the issue and actually do some governing. Although I have dwelt on numbers of £, we are talking about individual people here each of whom needs a good quality of care and a national mechanism to ensure that is provided when they need it. In the meantime we are like the proverbial boy putting his finger in the dam and the water is rising and more holes are appearing."

What officers thought of me summarising a complex situation in a couple of pages, I don't know. They never said. If they believe in the goal of improving clarity so Councillors and Cabinet members can make informed decisions then they might even have thanked me: in my dreams.

But costs are still out of control and the bottlenecks are still to be addressed.

---

29   It ended up at £149m.

DIFFERENT TYPES OF HOMES FOR OLDER PEOPLE

A Cabinet paper was released a week in advance of the meeting on 2 Oct 2018. I was all over it as you'd expect. Finally the issue of building new (extra care) housing for older people who needed care was being addressed but was it enough with year-end predicted costs still escalating by £1 million a month?

Agenda item 9 - Extra Care Housing Scheme[30] *– Questions from Councillor Clive Stevens*

Dear Mayor and Cabinet,

Increasing the investment in extra care housing is as some people say "a no brainer". Not only does BCC save £400 or more per week if someone stays in extra care rather than in residential care but the impact on reducing demand for residential care will also support BCC's attempts to reduce the prices[31] *of such homes. So for example if one hundred people move into extra care rather than into residential care the prices for residential care might drop further even £50/week lower. Multiply that by 5 or 6 new people who need that form of care and who enter the system each week. Over a year you could imagine a saving of £2m in care costs and a further £400k in lower residential care prices and that benefit continues to increase over the years. (Your Cabinet paper p48 estimates a £28k saving per year per person seems right).*

And it seems residents prefer to live in this form of housing too, and their improved well-being seems to benefit their health. So a cost saving, a benefit in well-being, less hospital admissions and a delay into residential care = win-win-win-win.

So per home the financials work out as follows, say we invest £200k per home, BCC would get the rent coming in and save a further £28k

---

30   Extra care housing is similar to sheltered housing. The residents live in their own place, pay affordable rent from their pension, the buildings are designed to be accessible and carers can for example visit all in one trip. A couple of big schemes are coming on stream soon (but not enough).

31   By reducing demand for residential care there were hopes that the prices could be brought down too.

per year. That's a six year payback on property - wow! Even better than student accommodation and the difference is BCC get the payback.

My question is about whether you are planning enough capacity.

• I see we are already £1m behind plan in this year's capital budget.

• Your cabinet paper says there is a waiting list of 178 people plus we already have about 400 people in Extra Care Housing (ECH).

• There is a target[32] to reduce residential care numbers by 200 (and I think it's similar for nursing care). So that could channel perhaps maybe another 300 into to ECH.

• So the above numbers total about 900 people by 2021.

• Additionally we know that demographics are only going one way. The BBC recently showed a chart with the number of people aged over 90 predicted to go up 50% in ten years, increased lifetimes (even if they have stalled currently) will increase the numbers wanting this type of housing.

• Your equalities assessment states that the main users are the over 80s. Add 50% for the coming decade to the estimate of 900 that we already have and you get a need of 1,350.

• The vision[33] is for 968, the lead times for these developments are a fair few years.

• BCC saves money, the NHS saves money and it makes people happier.

Question. It seems you are doing the right thing, but maybe not enough of it. Could you arrange to have the numbers assumptions reworked and ideally come to scrutiny please so it can be assessed whether the 968 you have forecast is enough?

And here's the written reply received a while later.

Dear Cllr Stevens, Here is the written answer to the question you put to Cabinet.

1. The strategy for increasing the availability of Extra Care Housing across Bristol is part of the wider Better Lives Programme, which is being managed through a multi-agency Programme Board, of which Councillor

---

32 Cabinet papers Oct 2nd 2018 see Period 4 trajectory report p392
33 Vision is what the Council Officers called it. Targeting 968, I was saying build more you need 1,350.

Helen Holland is a member.

2. Officers are currently undertaking a full needs analysis for Extra Care Housing and will refresh the business case for our future need based on this and information from the soft market testing event that will take place in November.

3. However, we are also aware that Extra Care Housing is not the only choice available for older people and therefore we will also review the need for other housing options which avoid or reduce the requirement for residential care, such as sheltered housing or general need housing with home care and support. Through more qualitative research we will seek to understand the choices that people may make in the future to meet their housing and care and support needs and help people to understand the choices available to them.

4. We welcome an opportunity at Scrutiny to discuss our findings and aid the development of our strategy for Extra Care Housing and other forms of housing with care and support for older people in Bristol.

Helen also spoke about this at the meeting[34]. To translate the written stuff above, it means that more ECH is being looked at, which is good, but also I learn that Extra Care Housing isn't the only solution to be provided. For example there's a development going ahead where older people and students will mix in a community (based on a Dutch model I hear), some may prefer that to exclusively older persons' housing. Other people might wish to live in a "normal" environment with a mix of families, single persons and the like; that all made sense, and so the message was not to go mad on building one type of extra care housing because not everyone will like it.

But I couldn't help thinking that this should have started years ago. I couldn't blame the current administration too much, they'd been in power just over two years. The previous Mayor, an independent, had what's called a rainbow cabinet and Helen Holland had been cabinet member then too. Somehow the idea of building the needed housing,

---

34   For the answer given at the meeting, any supplementary questions and answers please refer to the recording of the live stream of the meeting at https://www.youtube.com/watch?v=wyrfd1JfJsE

rather than residential care homes was completely missed. I don't think it was just Bristol either, although I think we were late to the party.

> Instead of sticking old people who are entering the final stages of their lives into residential care homes, smaller homes and flats should be built, or bought and adapted, all within the community; homes of different types, where carers and neighbours can help. This would cut the demand for residential care altogether and probably some of the costs.

Central Government channelled so much of its Austerity program into local authority cuts. Many, including me, think this was ideologically driven, but cutting money without providing the answers is sheer incompetence (in my book). I saw the same lack of joined up thinking regarding IT strategy and university expansion. Indeed much of section C is about a Councillor's role and it is too often spent correcting Government mistakes.

So armed with Councillor Holland's insight about different types of Extra Care Homes I decided to enter the fray and find her £2 million myself to save the Council's (taxpayer) money and improve peoples' lives.

Next up is the story of the Green Budget Amendment number five in February 2019. Improving lives was an obvious win but saving money means that other Council services can be saved or cut less, like libraries for example.

CHAPTER F8
GETTING HELEN TWO MILLION POUNDS:
FEB 26TH 2019

This was my third speech of the day, the first was mildly critical of a Lib Dem budget amendment and the second was majorly critical of a Conservative amendment[35]. I was unlikely to get support from those quarters, so it was all down to Labour (Greens would support me hopefully, they had said they would, but aren't whipped).

Would Labour vote through a Green amendment to their own budget?

I had actually chosen the theme of cooperation for all three speeches. Though not just political co-operation; what I meant was that in cities I thought there is a need for more co-operation between all the stakeholders, between the public, business and the state; less blind competition and more working together to make a city function well.

The Lord Mayor said, "Councillor Clive Stevens", I wasn't using headphones yet so wasn't sure she'd called me, I looked across at the faces opposite who were all looking back at me. Perhaps I'd better stand up and start…

"And to complete my theme of teamwork and cooperation here is an example where we Greens think the adult social care team lead by Cllr Helen Holland could do with a bit more money. The idea isn't ours, in fact Helen already has £4m in the budget but the pressures on ASC are so severe that much more capital investment is needed. So we Greens are proposing it is increased by £2m to £6m. And actually I think that you might have to keep investing at this level for years to come.

This extra £2m is to buy up existing properties, kit them out to become homes for adults with severe disabilities either just coming into Council care or those already in a residential home who may wish to move out. Time and time again people say they want to live in a home of their own,

---

35 If you like Tory bashing and want to read it again it is chapter E8 the one about the two competing local authorities (and there's also the Freeport one as well at C3).

plus it's cheaper for the Council to provide the care and it can sometimes be to a higher level. So win-win-win, not a scenario we often see. I have spoken extensively to officers who support this idea and assure me the people who are offered these homes will be carefully selected.

And as I mentioned before, the idea itself is not ours but we Greens are helping bring it into the world.

One suggestion I had from a physio who specialises in old persons rehab[36] was that perhaps these homes could all be in the same locality, not next door but maybe down the street or on the same estate, so a cluster if you like. Social workers, OTs, physios and carers can park up and then visit a number of them by foot.

This amendment is hopefully going to be another example of cooperation across political parties, something our country needs more of, to get us out of this mess."

This wasn't to build new extra care homes, it was to buy some homes already built and perhaps previously had been lived in but now available to buy, to assess their suitability and purchase. Then, with a few in the bag, invite those coming into Council care to look around and decide if they would like a home of their own (to rent usually). It would of course need to be adapted to their needs. The result is a happy person in a home of their own.

We would also have a happy Council because this costs much less than if the same people were in residential care, in fact the annual savings were predicted to become £400k per year from that £2 million investment, pretty good payback, return on investment or whatever financial measure you choose, and of course the money is in bricks and mortar which means the investment will hold its value, possibly even increase.

As it turns out this amendment was passed unanimously, the other parties being quick to forgive. I recall the Tories being particularly keen on this idea? Still they have always been into bricks and mortar.

---

36 Rehabilitation of the muscles and joints rather than off drugs. Although many old persons take drugs too, but of a different kind.

WHAT HAVE WE LEARNED FROM ALL THIS? APART FROM LACK OF LEADERSHIP FROM GOVERNMENT

By we, I don't mean the Council, I'm referring to us, you and me. Throughout this section I have played the role of commentator, as an opposition Councillor. I don't take the decisions, the nearest to that was getting that £2 million amendment through, but that needed Labour's vote which must have come with Helen Holland's support. So I am a commentator with a bit of scrutiny and analysis added. Different than an official seat on People Scrutiny, complementary I prefer to say.

As a commentator I see a local authority really struggling with an immense problem, one facing all Councils that have ASC responsibilities. And that is the impact of an aging population, combined with the huge spending pressures that came from Austerity as Government cut grants to near zero. In fact Bristol now sends around £80 million a year to Government (from the Business Rates). No wonder businesses ask the question about what do they get from their rate payments?

I watched Prime Minister May suggest a different way of funding adult social care during the 2017 General Election, and become toast for it. There's certainly no votes for this type of thing, well only lost votes if you get it wrong.

The *Daily Mail* seems to be the most regular publisher of adult social care stories. They know their readership base no doubt. Here's a typical one (via the LGiU):

> *On 14 Jan 2020, Care fee divide widens:*
> *Analysis by Care England suggests that in 30 areas of England, Councils pay care home operators less than £500 a week to house those who need their bills covered because they have few savings or assets of their own. It means that those paying their own bills are now typically paying £125 a week to subsidise those unable to cover their costs.*

In Bristol, the Council pays £800 a week typically. Those paying their own bills do pay more, there are some extra costs like marketing to cover, it is partly an issue of bargaining power and having a constant load. If Councils paid more, taxes would need to go up and what would the *Daily Mail* say then?

Strangely, given their interest in the subject, they didn't pick this up but plenty of other papers did on 9th March 2020

> ### Over-40s face new care taxes:
> *The over-40s could be forced to pay a new tax to pay for their old age care, according to plans being considered by the Government. Health Secretary Matt Hancock reportedly backs the idea, which would see workers pay an additional 2.5% of their income as part of efforts to improve the country's social care system. The Government is preparing to kick start cross-party talks on social care reform and PM Boris Johnson is preparing to offer a "menu" of social care funding options, the Times reports. City AM, Page: 7 The Times, Page: 2 Daily Mirror, Page: 12*

CHAPTER F10
RE-RUNNING 2010

Looking back to 2010, it's easy to imagine the incoming Conservative and Lib Dem coalition coming into office knowing they had to cut government expenditure. All parties back then agreed that spending needed to be reined in; the issue was for how long and when should the Government decide to expand the public sector part of the economy again.

So they came into office in 2010 and one area of big cuts was local government, it was presumably a soft option because people tend to see closed libraries, bad buses, litter and the like and blame it on the Council, not the MPs. Maybe they also took a "free market" approach to Councils to let them sink or swim, and believed that pressure might stimulate local innovation to local issues?

adult social care provision and the related NHS bed blocking were (and are) such big issues, the same across England and Wales that we needed a national solution; not just funding, but guidance telling the NHS and authorities what they should do and giving them the powers and budgets to do so. It was never going to be cost effective to put those people leaving hospital and needing further care into residential or nursing homes, it was always going to be too expensive. I agree that some of the businesses that were buying up care homes with or without the underlying buildings could well have lobbied the Government - as we know that's how the system works[37].

The journey that Bristol City Council had to take was similar to other Councils also without Government guidance. I witnessed this in 2017 and have written it up for you, including the cock up of the "free market" procurement system implemented before then. It didn't work because demand out-stripped supply, so any supplier could virtually bid what they liked, and because the Council needed to place people so quickly to clear NHS beds, the Council had no choice and the tax payer paid. It is an illustration of combining poor government with market failure (in this case due to unbalanced negotiating power between a Council and care home when an NHS out patient needs to be discharged, quick). How is creating that situation in any way good government? It's brought pain to many families, those in care, carers, social workers, Council administrators, Councillors and Council Tax payers too as more and more of the money they pay for services has been sucked into caring for older people. So parks sold off, libraries and public toilets closed and so on[38].

Bristol did have problems of its own, with high land prices and so high house prices. In fact average property is ten times average earnings, higher than much of London. It is difficult to get "the market" to build affordable accommodation for the older people who need care. The costs are higher and the income lower, easier to make money out of building luxury flats. This lack of accommodation is one of the drivers for the high adult social care costs. But most local authorities had pressures too,

---

37 Back to the Maths of Power
38 Not all this in Bristol but has happened elsewhere

maybe not quite as high as Bristol.

You may decide to take away different learning from this. If you are a student of politics or economics you might even research the Cabinet documents from that time and read more widely. Alternatively you may simply adhere to party dogma. But hopefully many of you are open minded and will consider these facts as I see them and come to a similar conclusion to me following this ASC history at Bristol City Council. I think that this is an example of broken Government. It's not doing what it should to maintain a thriving economy and protect its people.

Here's the *Daily Mail* reporting again…

10 March 2020, MPs launch inquiry into social care funding:
The Commons Health and Social Care Committee is launching an inquiry into the social care crisis, to look at how much additional funding the Government will need to provide over the next five years to stabilise the system. Chairman Jeremy Hunt said: "This long-standing crisis comes with a huge cost to families and individuals who can't get the social care they need. But it affects us all when a lack of availability prevents people leaving hospital, contributing to increased pressure on the NHS. We'll be establishing an agreed figure that represents the extra funding that's needed in each of the next five years in order to fix this." He said the committee would also be "examining solutions to tackle staffing shortages in social care that would be responsive to workforce changes."

Throwing money at the problem won't fix it. And it's not just workforce changes and staffing shortages. Just give Local Authorities the directions and guidance they need.

If you are not able to do this Boris (the Prime Minister at the time of writing) then copy and paste the start of Chapter F11 into your consultation.

CHAPTER F11
FOR THE PRIME MINISTER – IT'S NOT ROCKET SCIENCE

Send this to Boris (or whoever is in charge, if someone is):

adult social care is structured differently across the country. Some areas are fully integrated with the NHS and where this works it cuts out some inefficiencies. Occupational[39] therapists are better used at all stages to assess the appropriate interventions to care for each individual, to help them become more independent and to minimise hospital admissions. Multidisciplinary working with social workers, physiotherapists, carers and support in a joined up way to help people stay at home in their communities is most desired and least costly.

The process should be as follows: Older people enter the care system either by self-referrals, via their relatives or when discharged from hospital. They should be assessed by occupational therapists (and social workers often) to see if they can return home assessing what aids, adaptations and re-ablement they need to promote their independence.

If it will take some time; allow the person to live in a short term residential home (re-ablement centre[40]) while they improve and their own home is adapted. If their own home can't be adapted then make sure you have enough capacity of extra care and other housing so they can move on to that fairly quickly.

Have excess supply and use IT to help the ASC staff to help the elderly person choose their future home; with their family too. Only, and as a last resort, should they go into a residential or nursing home. (And the market for that needs to be managed, see Chapter F12).

There is a need for better skilled and better paid carers, the current structure of using care agencies entirely is akin to running a school entirely with supply teachers. It is quite the wrong approach. This is the caring

---

39   The use of OTs is recommended because they not only assess the needs of the person but also prepare a plan to reduce their needs so they can be more independent.
40   This has been done in Bristol.

profession, a profession with training, support, professional development and career opportunities.

There is a need to work closely with the NHS, but not run by the NHS. It isn't really geared up for adult social care. It's more about fixing problems so we can get home and get back to work. Therefore a formal partnership is an option[41].

Social workers, therapists should all be linked with mobile working software and hardware to improve their efficiency and speed and quality of care. There should be strong links with the universities (and employee training courses) that provide these qualifications to ensure skills are up to date.

The best practice approach should be rolled out across the country. No ifs, no buts.

Finally you need a national funding approach. It is quite ridiculous that Council Tax and business rate payers pay for this. It is right to have a debate on funding but the above activities are equally important.

If you found this ASC section interesting and informative, then there's some more information below, including updates (not good news). Then chapters F12 and 13 cover my views on how to structure the market for care homes, and we end wondering summarising the success of the Better Lives program.

Three updates:
• The first thing is that the "Mobile/Agile working" program described earlier in the questions to the Mayor on 3.4.18 has been stopped. Bristol's new IT program has overtaken it and is getting rid of all the old legacy software some going back decades and moving onto a Cloud based package. This is costing £10 million and then another £10 million to run the "apps" once the foundations are in place. Who knows how much extra this is costing the Council in delayed efficiencies to adult social care. The benefits of the mobile IT was supposed to be a much faster diagnosis of needs and so a better opportunity to square the pressures of

---

41   In business terms you'd say "a joint venture between Council and NHS".

leaving hospital quickly, having your home adapted or a home you can move into of your own; plus the ex-patient re-enabled. Just one extra person a month who could live in their home rather than in a home saves £300,000 a year to the Council and thus the Council Tax payer. It wouldn't surprise me if the project could deliver ten times that much value.

• The £6 million of funding (of which my £2 million was the budget amendment) to buy extra care homes has been delayed due to the difficulties in adapting existing homes to the needs of adults with severe disabilities. The obvious answer is to focus the newly bought homes on those with less severe difficulties. I don't know if that has been done.

• And thirdly, in 2020 The Observer *published:*

23 Feb 2020, Bed blocking reaches highest level since 2017
The latest NHS figures have revealed that bed blocking has reached its highest level since 2017, reversing years of progress. The number of days lost to delayed transfers of care, with patients unable to be discharged from hospital due to a lack of availability of suitable Council-run care services, reached 148,000 in December 2019, 15% higher than in December 2018.

From what I saw of the figures Bristol has followed this trend...

CHAPTER F12
CHANGING THE MARKETPLACE FOR ADULT SOCIAL CARE IN BRISTOL (1)

September 2019: It was time to apply thinking to how the marketplace for adult social care should be structured using the @SageAndOnion principles I'd collected (I say collected because in reality I was picking the best bits from various thinkers and cobbling them together to give a coherent whole). This only describes the residential and nursing care side of the market. Check the footnotes for explanations.

"Dear XXX - Thank you for the Market Position Statement MPS (1). I haven't seen it before, probably because I don't sit on People Scrutiny. I like the document and it provides a good foundation for the following ideas[42] especially if you end up doing a second version, an MPS (2). Best - Clive

One form of analysis prior to an MPS (2)

A) Based on your MPS (1) looking for a sustainable solution is key. You identify the following:

-A national productivity issue which will mean less wealth generation than previously and those not earning enough will not be able to afford ASC and it will put pressure on national tax revenues too.

-Brexit risk assessments have identified labour shortages in ASC and probably wages will go up.

-The number of people over 85 is growing rapidly.

-Land prices are continuing to increase.

-Productivity in ASC provision isn't improving either.

The combination of the above shows that continuing with the current approach to funding, commissioning and gentle market shaping isn't long term sustainable. For-profit companies will be squeezed and have to cut costs and quality to compete or they will consolidate and use their market power to reduce supply and charge higher rates. Either scenario is not sustainable for Local Authorities.

B) Those issues you have identified in MPS (1), above, lead me to target on the following conclusions:

- You need to do something about land.

- You need to do something about supply and training of carers/support staff to address costs, productivity and the quality of care.

- You need to do something about the type of providers, too high a reliance on for-profit provision will lead to market consolidation or poorer quality.

C) The Three Tier model (one: help older people to help themselves, two: provide re-ablement help at their home, and tier three is live in a

---

42   To XXX the following are ideas, they are to stimulate further discussion and are no way meant to be the solution, I'm old and wise enough to know that! I have only looked at some aspects of older person's care just to give you a flavour of what I mean.

care home) looks good but how do you get more provision by people and organisations whose primary goal is better care (community, charity, faith based) and less provision by those whose primary goal is profit and for whom care is a means to an end?

D) A classic problem people associate with social enterprise/charities is lower rate of innovation[43] and efficiency? Innovation is traditionally associated with the for-profit sector.

E) As BCC is the largest customer in the Bristol Area (approx. 50% share) and BCC's duties to shape the market[44] come from the Social Care Act 2014, BCC can do a lot if we want to. So if you do an MPS (2) you might consider some of the following shaping approaches...

F) This is for the frail who come into ASC either via hospital discharge or referral by themselves or via their adult children. You might consider a temporary "assessment/re-ablement stay centre" if they urgently need to come out of their home. This Re-ablement Centre would unblock DTOCs and enable someone to stay for a week or two or more whilst experts like physios, social workers and occupational therapists decide on the person's needs, the suitability of their current home and if possible develop plans to adapt it (Possibly this Centre[45] already exists, in which case does it have enough capacity?)

G) On exiting the Re-ablement Centre, the user ideally follows a pathway[46] to a solution that means adaptations and re-ablement care packages into their current home or via Extra Care Housing (we know we need more ECH). Extra care housing is sheltered accommodation, like groupings of flats or bungalows rather than residential care where they pay for 24/7 support.

---

43   I'm not sure if lower rate of innovation is true but it is clear that the for-profit sector can suck in lots of funds to innovate if it can put a good case for long term excess profits.

44   I was delighted to discover that some of the ideas I espoused in Section E about market place management were in that Act dating from 2014. One of the issues I think is people don't understand what to do. I do.

45   I am now told it does

46   Pathway means route. Not a physical route but the way the person is routed through the system. The Council also uses the term front door which I think I've avoided. They would say "the service user is assessed at the front door to decide what pathway to follow". For a while I thought that makes sense, they are seeing if the house has disabled access and a wide enough door frame. But no, front door means the initial evaluation the user receives when they first contact the Council. It's also called Care Direct. Nobody uses the term back door but it would presumably mean the service user's death and leading down the pathway to the front door of a cemetery? We will all go that route one day.

H) If the pathway leads to Tier Three[47], then they stay in the Centre until there is room in residential/nursing care which offers CQC[48] "good or outstanding" at a fair price or placed temporarily in CQC grade "needs improvement". Currently BCC don't have enough supply of care homes of good or outstanding but bear with me please, as to how to get there...

CHAPTER F13
CHANGING THE MARKETPLACE FOR ADULT SOCIAL CARE IN BRISTOL (2)

My analysis continues, and explains what needs doing...

I) The market for Tier Three care needs to be shaped by BCC using the market shaping principles from Social Care Act (and its 14 Feb 2017 Guidance Note) so that social enterprise (i.e. community, charity and faith based providers) are advantaged because they are seen as more long term sustainable (see my argument above in para B third bullet point).

So you offer social enterprise (i.e. Not-for-Profit) the following package:

• Land purchase and lease back offers (maybe even the buildings too). BCC can borrow money cheaper and can make money on the rent. It provides much needed cash to a Not-for-Profit organisation to invest in quality, training, staffing, innovation, productivity and expansion. (It also gives the LA more control).

• Providers agree a long term agreement with Care Homes (rather like University of Bristol do with their providers of halls of accommodation) which would mean guaranteed supply of x beds, at a price scale as long as the home remains good or outstanding and contributes to and implements schemes of training and innovation.

• Innovation and efficiency are promoted via grants and the spread of best practice. Perhaps set up a group at UWE[49] (or wherever) who look at

---

47 Tier 3 is Bristol's term for moving to residential or nursing accommodation usually.
48 CQC = Care Quality Commission, a national body that checks on the quality of care (as you might expect).
49 UWE = University of West of England who include vocational education

best practice nationally, hold conferences and help disseminate best practice at Bristol's homes. Social Enterprise is less secretive about innovations and some will have signed up to your long term agreement.

• Price is to a scale and pays for quality of care e.g. CQC good slightly higher price than CQC graded improvement. But pricing takes account of the fact that BCC own the land and charge rent and provide a scheme of innovation and training.

• The agreement could also request open book pricing/accounting which enables bench marking of best practice and sustainable levels of price and internal reinvestment.

• The social enterprise sector is assisted with training, grants etc to get to CQC good or outstanding.

• BCC helps with training and qualifications for care home managers and staff.

• The same offer would, I presume, need to be made available for the "for-profit" sector but this is all carefully designed to ensure it appeals to Social Enterprise (Note: each provider is still in competition with the others but buying in major services from BCC, land, training and innovation)

J) In ten years' time most Care Home providers will end up as social enterprise providers (and so can concentrate on caring), many renting from BCC plus support to improve quality, cashflow, innovation and expansion within long term agreements.

K) I suspect an approach to encourage social enterprise in the care agency market might also bring benefits but I don't know enough about the structure of that market to make any suggestions. In any case I think the total cost of care homes is five times the costs of the agency providers and so higher priority...

These market shaping suggestions are driven by a desire to have the suppliers of services motivated by care and not profit. To then manage the market using the duty as empowered by government and using the fact that the Council is the major customer too.

To encourage and support social enterprise with land leaseback deals, innovation centres and grants in return for long term contracts, open pricing and participation in the innovation and training programs. This would be a package unpopular with business. It is my conclusion that this market is better served with less profit motivated business with more care motivated and cooperative social enterprise.

At the time of writing this I don't know if work is being done on a new market positioning statement MPS (2) and if so whether these ideas have been incorporated. We shall see.

SUMMARY OF SECTION F

Chicken or the egg? It's not clear to me whether my three years of concentration on Adult Social Care informed my understanding of the economy or whether it was my views on that that triggered my analysis of ASC. Whatever, it is clear to me that this whole study shows the value of "deep dive" scrutiny, working with political opponents and highlights the appalling lack of leadership from government.

It also supports my views on the economy. Many of these people have recently been relabelled from the "low paid" to "key workers". Key workers are the ones heavily involved in social value activities, it often means they can't extract the same level of pay as those in grab-it-all jobs. Some will argue that the tax payer wouldn't be able to afford it. I would argue that's because our economy isn't targeted on wealth, health and prosperity creation. Do that and we can. I hope, following Covid-19, that society looks long and hard at decides to reward key workers more.

And Bristol's Better Lives program? In a chart:

ASC Service Users aged 65 or more	In Residential and Nursing Care Homes	Living in their own Extra Care Housing	Living at home
Sept 2018	1,200	380	1,000
Nov 2018	1,185	380	1,000
Feb 2019	1,130	385	1,030
June 2019	1,120	400	1,020
Sept 2019	1,170	430	990
Nov 2019	1,160	430	1,000
Feb 2020	1,120	440	990

Above: The aim is to enable people to live in their homes or in extra care housing because that's what they say they want. The effective use of occupational therapists can help by creating improvement packages. This wasn't the only intervention of course. It was all going well up to June 2019 then a big, expensive hiccup! Three things combined: the NHS introduced a new policy of dealing with bed blocking but didn't work with the Council (or the implications weren't understood), secondly the carer shortage became more wide spread so that it was more difficult to get care to people living in their home and thirdly something as simple as a few key people on holiday at the same time. All three issues combined meant that most elderly people discharged in May 2019 went into residential homes. The two right hand columns show the number of users (clients) living in extra care housing and on the far right those able to live at home. These haven't grown as fast as desired, limited by the bottlenecks described in this section (extra care housing capacity and lack of carers). The total is about 2,500 people and has stayed fairly static despite the pressures of an aging population. The remainder receive other services to help them live independent lives.

Comment: When you have a broken system it doesn't take much to wreck it. The next section is about another broken system, the provision of affordable housing.

SECTION G
THE USE AND ABUSE OF LAND

INTERLUDE (2)
LAND AND HOUSING.

Ever wondered what it's like to be homeless? I have, many times, because of some of the people I have helped. By homeless I don't mean street sleeping. There are about 100 sleeping on the streets of Bristol in any one night[1]. Then there's about 1,900 who are not quite on the streets, sleeping with friends, in temporary accommodation, in vans or hostels. Plus there are 8,000 more who are somewhere but it's not suitable, they need to move but can't afford private rents. This totals 10,000.

---

1   And about 500 different people over the course of a year.

We start this section on the management of land with a story of one of the 1,900, sofa surfing in a friend's flat, her child having to live elsewhere.

But before that story a bit of background: land is special, it's the scarce resource in a city, especially one surrounded by Green Belt. Mark Twain (who was not a resident of Bristol) advised, "Buy land, they are not making it anymore". Those with enough assets have followed through on that and generally done well. Homeless people are the consequence of the way we allow land to be bought and sold with inappropriate economic and planning regulations. I think we need to change them.

As of March 2020, there were over 13,000 people seeking social housing in Bristol, those are the ones allowed to bid on the Council's home bidding system[2]. We should subtract about 3,000 already in homes for social rent wishing to up or downsize, that gets us back to the 10,000. Many more can't get on the list at all because they don't meet the criteria and are not owed a duty of care of housing by the Council (primarily single people without vulnerable dependants).

The Government's response is to get Councils to set a target for affordable home building in the official plans (called Local Plans) currently in Bristol that target varies between 20% and 40% depending on the location. The assessed need is nearly 60%. Let me spell that out. In Bristol the requirement for new homes is assessed at about 35,000, about 60% of them need to be affordable, that means that 21,000 need to be subsidised because the market won't provide them otherwise[3].

This is market failure of immense proportions. The market only provides 40% of current demand. That 40% comprises the wants of the people who can afford to buy or rent at market levels. The market provides close to 0% of the needs of people searching for affordable homes. To provide for the needs the "market" currently requires subsidies. It is getting worse and is unsustainable.

2   The allocation systems for affordable homes are currently suspended for the Covid-19 virus but will go back to the system I describe in this story.
3   I have rounded and moulded planning estimates to be as up to date as I can.

Unsustainable because: rising house prices mean rents go up; less people can get on the housing ladder therefore more people become tenants, that means more housing benefit is paid out (more people and higher amount); plus there are more subsidies to developers and land owners for affordable housing. This means that the system we have now is clearly long term unsustainable unless the tax payer is willing to fork out more and more.

Until recently the only route to affordable homes was via developer subsidies, within what's called a S106 agreement, that money enabled the delivery of around 20% of all homes being built to be affordable. They could be sold at a discount to a housing association for them to run. As prices of houses went up, the discount required became deeper and the percentage provided fell. In the centre of Bristol it almost reached nought percent.

I'm sure some developers thought they were being generous.

At the same time Councils couldn't build Council houses due to the new cap on borrowing and strict rules on the reuse of money from the Council houses they sold to residents through Right to Buy. As of 2020 Councils are beginning to build again, developers continue to subsidise some and are accepting grants paid for by the tax payer (local and national) to include more properties within their development that can be run by housing associations or by the Council.

Bristol's build target is about eight hundred a year; if achieved it will take twenty six years to reach today's need not allowing for future population growth. That assumes we meet the eight hundred a year so far we are half of that.

Affordable homes scheme receives extra £9.5bn

12th March 2020 the FT ran with, "The government has pledged an additional £9.5bn for its affordable homes programme, bringing the total amount to £12.2bn. The move should bring in a further £38bn in public and private investment over the following five years, according to the Budget. The programme, which helps *people in England into home ownership and assists those at risk of homelessness, is co-funded by the government and private investors."*

And where does this tax payer funded subsidy go? It goes to the developer/ builder so they can cut the price of some homes, the developer to pay the full price for the land and for building the properties. That subsidy therefore continues to feed the market for land, a market where there is no increase in supply, and so land prices go up. The tax payer funds the landowners' profits. These increased land prices fuel higher property selling prices and that means the discounts for affordable homes need to become even higher which is why you can't build as many into a scheme (for it to be profitable to the developer). The tax payer is paying for landowners to make profits each and every year.

Of course many tax payers are home owners themselves and gain from this spiral too as their house or flat price goes up. A windfall and during my life I have made nearly as much money on house (land) increases than I have savings from work income. But then we need to seek a way of transferring these gains to our children so they can afford the high costs of housing. The economy for land (in a city) is clearly unsustainable for those who rent. They are often key workers and those starting out in life. It stifles opportunity to self-improve. It might even be unsustainable for those who are buying now.

The Guardian reported…

21 Nov 2019, Affordable housing figures published.
Government figures show that 57,485 affordable homes were delivered in England in 2018-19, up 22% from the year before, the vast majority new-builds. However, just 37,825 new homes were built to be let at discounted rents last year, despite a national housing waiting list of more than 1.1m households. The number of new homes classed as social housing and available at the cheapest rents from Councils was 6,287, the second-lowest level in peacetime since Council house building began in earnest in 1921. The data came as a report from the charity Crisis warned that in a third of areas across England fewer than 10% of homes are now affordable to

welfare recipients. Meanwhile, insurer Legal & General has partnered with 14 housing associations to build 3,000 affordable homes annually".

To understand the fudges better we need to unpick that article (above) to start really understanding the problem. Firstly definitions: The Government defines anything that is less than market rate (to buy or rent) as affordable. So of that 57,485 quoted in the article, 19,660 were discounted to buy, often for first time buyers and 30,538 were rented out at levels above social rents. In Bristol the problem is lack of homes available at social rents (the ones usually run by housing associations or the Council). That corresponds to the national figure of 6,287. In Bristol (slightly less than 1% of the national economy) we need 21,000 of these in the next 15 years (so that would scale up nationally to 2.1 million as a future need). We have over 10,000 people on the current list which scales up to 1 million nationally, close to the 1.1 million in the article. Bristol's Council is aiming to get 800 a year built which if achieved and it's twice as much as current rates will take 26 years to get to 21,000. The detailed maths is covered later in chapter G13.

The market system is broken for millions of people.

Conservative MPs call for serious action on social housing

Former Conservative Cabinet minister David Davis writes in the Sun on behalf of 27 other Conservative MPs to urge the Government to take serious action to build more social housing, saying that while Right to Buy has been "a great source of stability and mobility for millions, and a triumph of Tory values," the net loss of thousands of Council homes each year is happening "while thousands of hard-working families sit on social housing waiting lists, desperate for a shot at the stability they cannot find anywhere else." "If our policies simply continue to provide only expensive new-builds for the already well-off, and almost unaffordable rents for the rest," he says, then people will lose their trust in the Conservative Party. He calls on Chancellor Rishi Sunak to use tomorrow's Budget to "signal the party is serious about tackling housing inequality head on."

The Sun, on Mar 10th 2020

Spot on David. But you will have to ditch your deeply held belief about a free market for land.

Before we get into the battles and sagas with developers to get more affordable (social rent) homes in Bristol, I bring you the story of one of the 10,000 homeless people in Bristol in 2020. This is the Law and the economy working in harmony to make many peoples' lives miserable.

CHAPTER G1
HOMELESSNESS IN 2020 (PRIOR TO AND POSSIBLY POST COVID-19)

Great news! The Government brought in a new duty, an Act no less, to prevent homelessness and they say they will be removing the dreaded section 21 notice which allows no-reason evictions. From a landlords' perspective many think if they can get a higher rent from someone else, then the tenant is at fault. That is a reason to many of them.

And so what happens with this combination of good news, the Act and proposed removal of S21?

I was happily relaxing one Sunday in October 2019, reading the papers, thinking they are pretty poor nowadays so I switched to my iPad and there was a new message in the inbox. Not the usual weekend complaint about a noisy student party, not even uncollected waste, but a plea to an MP copied to me. In summary it read: Help I'm trying to get away from an abusive relationship but Bristol City Council won't help me find a home. I wrote back saying that I was her Councillor and we are the first port of call for housing and I'd look into it on Monday. That was my Sunday relaxation ruined. It would have been the first I'd had off for a few months, still it's not as bad as being a doctor or emergency service or Prime Minister I suppose. But at least they think they are doing something worthwhile, all I'm doing is plugging the gaps caused by poor government.

Come Monday (actually Sunday evening) after a Twitter exchange with the very helpful Cabinet member[4] for Housing I got straight through to the right person, shortcutting the system by a day or more at least. And then the barrier: "Yes we have met her, she didn't turn up three times, we have offered assistance." Why I had thought it might be quick to fix I don't know. This is all head-banging stuff (and not in the heavy metal sense).

Next step?

I was soon in the library chatting to this smartly dressed woman, maybe slightly too smart for a library but that comment says more about me perhaps. At least I've now been trained to be aware that we all have our own subconscious biases. She told me how her marriage and subsequent relationships had gone sour, violence too, so much so that the police advised her to flee her hometown and come to Bristol (an English refugee if you like). But her money was now gone, she was sleeping on a friend's sofa, and her child was still in her old hometown living with a dad who is "being a bastard with custody rights". She's about to start a part-time job; is creative and determined and will clearly succeed if given a chance.

The Council by this stage had explained that she didn't qualify for Council housing as she hadn't been in Bristol for two years, and even if she had she wouldn't qualify as a vulnerable woman. I told them they were uncaring and they didn't like that.

Under the new prevention of homelessness duty, the assistance they had offered her was a five year loan to help with a rent deposit and first month's rent, but there were conditions attached. She must be able to prove the property is safe by showing them the gas and electricity safety certificates and prove it was an assured shorthold tenancy. She told me that landlords wouldn't supply the certificates, it was easier to find another tenant they said and the tenancies she saw were something called a lodger agreement. Assured Shorthold Tenancies are being phased out of this market, she explained, due to the future restriction on section 21 notices.

So to take stock: we have a vulnerable woman told to move here for

4   Councillor Paul Smith

her safety, currently sleeping on a sofa but with her child back in her previous hometown. The Council has this brand new duty to prevent homelessness and one approach is loans, but the conditions are so onerous that the first person I have had to deal with can't fulfil them. So how is it safer causing someone to become homeless than a flat not meeting the electricity and tenancy requirements?

It's safer for the Council officers, they don't get criticised in the press for encouraging people to sleep in substandard accommodation. Instead the "to-become-homeless" simply became homeless. Head-banging or what?

A tweet back to the Cabinet member: he recommended approaching a local charity dealing with protection and homes for vulnerable women. The charity is struggling due to lack of funding.

I rang them up. After a bit of verbal data dancing (data protection: I couldn't reveal the personal information of the lady and neither could they) we eventually discovered she was already on their books. I let them know what I knew which helped them I think.

They were very helpful and the caseworker helped her to fill out a vulnerable person's housing request form which could be discussed among the different departments who get involved, a process abbreviated as MARAC[5]. They decided she wasn't at very high risk as the threat to her safety did not originate in Bristol and as she wasn't sleeping on the streets or with a child in tow, she was graded level 2 which might mean she'd get a home within a year or two. But to do that she had to bid for affordable housing every week knowing she wouldn't get one but every week she participated meant she would go up the ranking.

That, I thought, was that.

5   Multi agency risk assessment conference

CHAPTER G2
HOMELESSNESS CONTINUES

2019, Boxing Day morning and I make a fatal mistake. Well not quite that dangerous. In fact what I do might have prevented a fatality. The mistake is I look at emails and there's one from her. In summary it says,

> "Help, I had a dreadful Christmas Day, on my own, so many miles from my child, trying to live on a sofa. I'm so fed up with trying to find a home where I can bring my son to visit that it's just not worth it".

A mention of suicidal thoughts too.

I know she's bright but like many struggling with the system. She has moved from the "homelessness prevention team" (HPT) to the "Council housing team". A loan of £1,000 would have got her into private housing but the HPT didn't permit it. The landlords wouldn't give certificates of safety. Nor would they give an assured tenancy, just lodger's agreements. So she's back sleeping on sofas and is now on the list for Council housing level priority two. You can wait two years for that. I don't tell her.

Her son is growing up and is more influenced by her estranged partner. I learn that some other man is out to get her too. That's why she has fled to Bristol. Although she has been re-accepted onto the Council's housing search engine, for some reason she can't get her bids in. An application for a home is called a bid. I guess it's a system modelled on eBay, recommended by the Government, except you can't see the highest bid. You have to blindly bid for up to three homes and compete with 13,000 others. The bidding doesn't involve money, it's your priority that counts which, apart from a number[6], you don't know. The round closes on a Sunday night and you get the answers on the Monday. No, no and no are the usual responses, you are told afterwards where you came on the list like position 25th on that one, 18th on that one....

On Boxing Day she won't get a response from the Council so I reply just to show her that someone cares. I also send an email to the generic

6   Priorities 1,2,3 or 4 in Bristol or A,B,C or D in South Glos.

email address to ensure she has her account number and password. She replies later on, much more positive. She says she has a new job too. Won't earn enough for private housing probably, and anyway she has no money for a deposit, nor first month's rent.

30th December: Council Housing officer replied by email. That's good. I try to phone to check they are open on Tuesday so if she needs to call then she can. The number I have is engaged and engaged. I ring about ten times, maybe more during the day. Then she calls me back; charming lady but just talks and talks. No wonder the phone is always busy. I email my sofa sleeping constituent saying what she needs to do. No reply.

31st, no reply, 1st, 2nd...still nothing

Then I get a reply, she's bidding and getting higher up the rankings. When she gets the results back, some are in single digits now. I tell her to note which areas she gets high rankings for and to concentrate her bids there. She says St Paul's. I think she has been accelerated up the priorities, maybe I helped.

A week later she's got one. It came back with 1st and she's off to the interview this very afternoon.

She didn't get to the interview. She got an email saying the flat had just been directly allocated to a vulnerable person a few hours ago. She's distraught. Isn't she vulnerable too? I have to agree. But if she got a first ranking she can get one again and she does. And she moves in and it's near where her job is. Outside my ward so I'm not her Councillor anymore.

I email a few weeks later. She is depressed again. She has no money, it costs so much with deposits on the gas, electrics, rent and more, she has 57p to last the week. She went to the Council's offices to talk about applying on the Local Crisis Prevention Fund, they couldn't help and pointed her to a food bank. I put her in touch with her new local Councillor to get this sorted. I chose one I knew well and had a quiet word.

So as far as I'm aware that's how we solved the problem of one lonely, vulnerable woman who had a job and was fleeing violence. Not all of the

13,000 on the Council's affordable housing list are fleeing violence but they all have their own stories.

We need more affordable housing, the situation is down to market failure and that causes huge harm and many externality costs.

The *Independent*, 25 Feb 2020, Unaffordable housing harming people – thank you LGiU

Housing affordability is negatively impacting the health and wellbeing of millions of people across the UK, according to research conducted by YouGov on behalf of the Affordable Housing Commission (AHC). One in seven (13%) said that their mental health had been negatively impacted by their housing situation, a figure which increased to a quarter (25%) for those living in "unaffordable" housing. Lord Richard Best, chair of the AHC, which was set up by think tank the Smith Institute and is funded by the Nationwide Foundation, warned: "We need a fundamental rethink and structural change to rebalance it and ensure it works now and for future generations.

CHAPTER G3
AFFORDABLE HOUSING – THE BATTLE WAS GOING LONG BEFORE I ENTERED THE FRAY

Property developers are a sensitive bunch. This is most obvious when they are asked to open their books and reveal how much profit they expect to make on a particular site they want to build houses on. They don't like doing this, perhaps they don't want their staff to know, or the taxman, or perhaps they are simply embarrassed? The only thing that brings this openness out is an attempt to protect their profits and justify why they can't build the amount of affordable housing that is needed.

As I write the state of the market in Bristol has led some to estimate a need for 58% of all the homes built to be affordable. (Source: Joint Spatial Plan). Given that current percentages have been running between 10 and 20% that target seems pretty steep and probably unachievable.

The opening of their books as part of the planning process is called submitting a viability statement. I tried to be the developers' nightmare on this, and achieved some success, but they got smarter. The next few stories illustrate the cat and mouse games we played. The developer pays an agent to submit a viability statement based on the price of the land, the costs of building and the fair profits due. Fair to who? The Council[7] then pays for an independent property agent to review this statement and give their opinion. That independent agent might represent the Council on one job and then represent a developer on the next. In fact on one development we will look at later the Council's agent was then recruited by the developer and suddenly all the numbers changed! That's ND6, We look at that one in all its gory detail in Chapter G7.

The fair profit margins allowed on affordable housing are much less, just six percent rather than 20% for market housing. The developer needs to sell that part of the block or site to a housing association who will then manage it and rent it out to those on lower incomes. The risk of disposing of affordable housing is much lower as demand exceeds supply; whereas the rest of the development is sold into the speculative market for housing. That brings risks of delayed cash-flows and the mega risk of trying to sell into a market when there is a recession, the houses could remain unsold or need a heavy discount to avoid bankruptcy. Big risks.

The term affordable housing is loosely defined in national planning policy. It can include houses or flats sold at 20% below market price, like a first time buyer incentive, all the way down to properties available at social housing rents which can be the equivalent of a discount of 50% off market price. In Bristol the need is at the lower end. The average house price is nearly 10 times average earnings. So if you are earning anything less than ¾ of average earnings (about minimum wage working 50 hours a week) and have a family and you are in receipt of housing benefit you need to be able to rent at £5 or £6,000 pounds a year. Market rents can be more than twice that. So Bristol has stuck rigidly to its need for supply at social rent.

---

7   The Council acting in its role as the Local Planning Authority, the LPA.

By 2019 there was more money going into supporting affordable housing, grants and loans as well as the process through planning judging the viability. So if we achieved 20% from viability it might be possible after permission is given to get this up to 40% or more[8] with all the extra subsidies. Still not 58% though.

And look at this, in the text box below. Government clearly missing the point; or maybe they just want to make sure that enough people need to be their friends (Mathematics of Power)? I just wish I weren't so cynical.

On 7 Feb 2020, New first-time buyer scheme could hit social housing

New homes will be almost a third cheaper for local first-time buyers under a scheme unveiled today by ministers. Housing Secretary Robert Jenrick's First Homes scheme could save those who are eligible nearly £100,000 on average. The 30% market discount rate would prioritise key workers such as nurses, police officers, military veterans and teachers. The discount would apply in perpetuity, so when a home is sold in the coming years the new local buyer would get the same discount. The discount would be paid for through the "Section 106" contributions that housing developers pay through the planning system to benefit local communities – which are currently used to help fund the construction of social and affordable housing. The Local Government Association warned: "It is important that this does not come at the expense of providing truly affordable homes for rent."

The Sun, Page: 14   Financial Times, Page: 3   The Times, Page: 13   The Daily Telegraph, Page: 6   Daily Express, Page: 8   Daily Mail, Page: 19   Daily Mirror, Page: 4

There is no doubt that many people want to buy their home, that's the culture in the UK and one that has led to riches, freedom and avoids the rent collector. The S106 contributions in the article are the ones

---

8   It is easier further out where land prices are cheaper. It is also easier to get higher levels with a few specialist social housing developers, but there are not enough of them.

referred to in the stories that follow, except that the ones I was involved in were always to subsidise social rented housing. If the S106 is diverted to subsidise houses to buy, not rent, then what happens to the supply of social housing? If people were guaranteed jobs that paid a minimum of £21,000 a year then perhaps it would be different. (See G13 for further analysis)

CHAPTER G4
VIABILITY STATEMENTS; THE DEVELOPERS' NEW WEAPON

Bristol's Local Plan (adopted in 2011) requires 40% affordable housing in central areas and 30% outside. If economic theory worked, the price of the land should have fallen so that it was financially viable for the developer to achieve such levels. But the pressure for getting houses built of any type after the economic crash of 2008/9 meant that lower affordable percentages were allowed. This meant that land prices didn't fall enough and in fact probably rose[9] to soak up the difference in profit.

Then in 2014 the Government brought in the viability statement system which institutionalised the ability to dodge affordable housing commitments. And by 2017 there were some areas of Bristol achieving zero percent. Ruses I have seen include: overpaying for the land (accidentally or deliberately), explaining how difficult and expensive the demolition is, the costs of the retention of existing buildings for heritage reasons, protecting a view of them, or that the market sales prices in that area are quite low. The best one is an allowance for stamp duty on flats to be rented when stamp duty isn't payable. A scam in my view but allowed; it deserves its own special write up and that's in G7 (second part, site ND6).

The rise in the price of land is predicted by economic theory. Bristol is surrounded by Green Belt so if someone wants to build in Bristol there is limited supply, with excess demand for all housing let alone

9   Land prices do this you know. Mark Twain was right.

affordable, land owners could name their price. Then Mayors looking for overseas investment in their quest for more homes probably made the situation worse.

Comment: The book, *Rethinking The Economics Of Land And Housing, 2017* published by Zedbooks written by Josh Ryan Collins, Toby Lloyd and Laurie MacFarlane, gives a marvellous explanation of the economic and social issues because of the way we allow the market for land to operate. I have used some of the points from that to inform my recommendations in the next section.

Because Bristol's public transport system was and is so bad, people need to live fairly close to work. Bristol is a popular place to move to and has some good industries. The final nail in the provision of cheap accommodation was the Government's lifting the cap on student numbers and University of Bristol expanding, adding the need for another 7,000 bed spaces. The housing market responded and provided lots of shared accommodation, so families and the lower paid either had to move out or were evicted, rents rose and students who could borrow seemingly infinite sums moved in. A perfect storm made by poor Government Policy and a misunderstanding of how processes work in a broken market economy.

The battle with the University is described in an Appendix. The chapters below describe some of the skirmishes with developers at the Planning Committees. We couldn't win the war but if we could get even 50 more affordable homes each year, then that was 50 families off the homeless register. Small fry as it was going up about a 1,000 per year but at least something.

So armed with a good maths brain, my calculator, a desire to make a difference, a sense of injustice and working most weekends I laid into affordable housing viability statements with gusto.

Number one was the Chocolate Factory, which was a learning experience for all.

CHAPTER G5

CHOCOLATE FACTORY 15/06400/F

Raw chocolate tastes slightly bitter they say, bitter is not strong enough to describe the taste left after the battle over affordable housing at the former Elizabeth Shaw site in Greenbank.

New Councillors and the Mayor were voted in May 2016, Labour were dominant. And although we didn't see eye to eye on everything, affordable housing was one where Greens and Labour sang the same song, slightly off key but nevertheless recognisably; "we shall not be moved". And so the fight to get more affordable housing and development to benefit all sectors of the community, not just the better off, was commenced.

First up, the former Elizabeth Shaw site; this came to Planning Committee in November 2016. It came with a viability statement saying that the developers could afford zero affordable houses. Zero in number and zero in percentage; inflaming Councillors, the community and probably officers too. The papers came out and soon after followed the viability statements, in those days they were only released to the Councillors. The timeline was as follows:

• 21/11/16 – Viability statements issued to Councillors. I get my calculator out.

• 23/11/16 (Wednesday) – I asked questions to officers about the viability statements, I thought I'd found a few errors. One I was especially proud of: the amount of space shown devoted to community use, and so couldn't be sold, was 5,000 sqft more than the amount required in the proposal. If converted into housing or retail that was worth an extra £600,000 in value. Another issue was reducing the amount of commercial property planned and increasing the amount of housing, which is more profitable and so would fund more affordable housing.

• 28/11/16 (Monday) – Answers from officers plus a revised viability statement which adjusted the bottom line by nearly £600,000 and reduced the amount of community space to what I had said.

• 29/11/16 – The developer makes an offer of 6 affordable homes which implies about £100,000 each of reduced profit per home. Totals approximately £600,000.

• 30/11/16 – (Wednesday) Committee (A) meets.

The Committee meeting was packed with protestors. Greenbank is near Easton, Eastville and other areas where house prices and rents were (and still are) rocketing. It also has a strong community and people didn't want to have to move out just because of rising rents (also termed gentrification). Statement after statement said it was wrong for officers to recommend approval and that the offer of six homes, less than four percent, was derisory. Planning policy for that area is 30%.

Having gone through the viability I knew that the developers did have extra costs protecting the heritage and fabric of the old factory, I also knew that this was the first time they had been subject to the new "we shall not be moved" regime of Green and Labour combined. That would be eight out of the 11 on Committee. It was though important that this site become a signal to all developers that times have changed. The electorate of Bristol want, no, need affordable homes and developers should stick to planning rules (set down in 2011's Local Plan).

As you can see from the timeline I found a 600 grand error which when corrected enabled the offer of six homes, I thought there might be more if they changed the mix between commercial and residential. They could have built fewer offices or given up the restaurant and added more homes which would have improved the profit and thus the viability of affordable homes. But if they did that and offered more affordable homes the profit would drop back to where it had been before[10]. No further changes came. I thought the process was all a bit slapdash and needed tightening up. That error had been past two Chartered Surveyors maybe more and the Council officers. Not good. And there were concerns from the Transport officers too. Should we reject this I was wondering?

About an hour and a half into the meeting, I saw Councillor Richard Eddy's hand shoot up. "Yes Richard" from a somewhat weary chair. Councillor Eddy talked about the need to get a move on and accept

10   This is one of the crazy disincentives of the viability system.

the six homes and approve. He then proposed a motion to approve. I was shocked. We all were. There was silence. It continued and we Councillors looked blankly at one another. Was anyone actually going to second this? With all those people in the room perhaps they daren't. But we aren't supposed to be intimidated by the public.

Whether we were or weren't it became clear that the rest of us didn't like Richard's proposal. My senses had recovered I waved at the chair, "Councillor Stevens" he said. I turned on my microphone

"Thank you Chair, I propose we defer this to consider the provision of affordable homes. If they can come up with six on the day before Committee then perhaps they can find more given time".

It was seconded by my Green colleague Steve and voted eight for, two against and one abstention. So the application was deferred for more work on the affordable homes.

Instructions were given to officers and the developer to go away and work on getting more homes that the locals could afford. The developer's profit was shown to be nearly 20% on this and by the time the houses and flats come on the market it would be more. It was going to be tough to pull off as the Council didn't have a huge amount of negotiating power and the developer could just run off crying to the Planning Inspector if they so wished. But would they? Or would they help us?

In the meantime…

CHAPTER G6

IT WOULDN'T MELT IN THEIR MOUTHS

The fact that the viability statements were visible only to Councillors was an anathema to the idea of "open and transparent" government. They were one of the few documents of commercial sensitivity that the UK Government allowed to be published at all, in the public interest. Even they realised the divisiveness of property developers and land owners hiding behind commercial sensitivity whilst the numbers of homeless rose. In Bristol it was some 8,000 households in 2016/17. And that didn't include single people to whom the Council didn't owe a duty of care (a legal rather than moral term).

In Bristol, the figure for permissions granted for affordable homes in 2015/16 was only 21% and, of those actually built, less than 10% were affordable. We needed 40%. And the most recent example, Chocolate Factory had offered less than 4% after we found that error.

So for the December 2016 Full Council we opened up a second front, Councillor Stephen Clarke proposed a motion (it was the Green's turn) to make some changes locally and requested the Mayor attempt to get something done nationally. I was to give the Green's second speech and most was drawn from the experience just a few weeks earlier regarding the Chocolate Factory.

"My Lord Mayor - One of the key things we are asking for is clear visibility regarding viability. I can attest to the benefits of this first hand. As part of my preparation for the same planning committee that looked and deferred the Chocolate Factory application I went through their viability statement in as much detail as I could muster and barraged the planning officers with question after question. And to what effect? I found £600,000 more money in the scheme which enabled the developer to offer 6 affordable houses, not enough, but less worse than nothing. Since then I've discussed the viability process and assumptions with a developer friend, described how it works and listened and learned and what a learning experience it has been. If I had known then what I know now then even more could be found. That's why these need to be visible to all. And another thing...Sure Government needs to do its part but we can do something in Bristol too. We are asking for innovative ideas. If we can reduce uncertainty we can remove some of the contingencies and delays (time is money) that developers face and in return get more affordable homes. Among the many ideas I've heard for incentivising a high % of affordable housing are:

• creating a fast track process for plans with a higher % of affordable housing say 30% +

> • *creating a task force to simplify the system,*
> • *offering infrastructure funded from the Mayor's allocation of 80%*
> *CiL*[11] *like cycle paths,*
> - *and the list could go on...*
>
> *It is clear the system doesn't work, even planning offices will privately agree it's broken. And I agree with them. Some of the change needed is outside our control but there is much we can do in Bristol with good leadership and targeted effort. If asked I'd love to help get the affordable housing process working again and if it needs banging a few heads together then I'm up for that too."*

The full text of the motion is on the Council's website for 13 December 2016 Full Council. In essence Stephen was asking that viability reports be open to the public well before the Committee meetings, that Council officers should continue to incentivise developers to have a mix of affordable and rental homes on housing sites, not just for sale. Additionally, that the Mayor should lobby central government to remove the borrowing cap on Council housing (nationally), improve the flexibility of use of right to buy receipts and to allow Council Tax to be charged on empty plots. There were two other requests which the Conservatives tried to delete and failed; one about devolving more power locally, and another about enabling more compulsory purchase orders.

Labour liked this so much they decided to support the motion so it got through un-amended.

Amazingly for a Full Council motion quite a lot happened locally and nationally. The Council house borrowing cap was lifted, right to buy receipts became a bit more flexible, Council Tax is charged higher on empty properties (but not unbuilt ones), compulsory purchase orders were a useful negotiating ploy, but hardly used in practice. Viability statements now come in soon after the planning application for all to see

---

11   CiL is community infrastructure levy and is a sort of tax on new buildings or floor area. About 80% goes to the Mayor's fund for key Bristol wide infrastructure. If some of that could be diverted locally it would enable the developer to offer more affordable housing. That idea wasn't implemented.

and the Council now even has its own property development company[12].

The Government changes were presumably because everyone was pointing out the same flaws.

So it seemed that battle number two had been won. Battle number one was still being fought, but we were winning, The Chocolate Factory was being renegotiated. Christmas was coming.

2017 didn't start well. Committee A (the one I'm on) was told on the 22nd February 2017 that the developers of the Chocolate Factory had gone to the Planning Inspector after all, arguing that Committee hadn't decided in time. It seems a deferral isn't a decision and they wanted a Government Appeal Inspector to decide the case instead. Surely we were going to fight this all the way.

Also early in 2017 Councillor Kye Dudd[13] and I wanted to bring a motion to Full Council about the unfairness of this whole system. Scheduled for the 14th March 2017 we went through the preparations, prepared speeches lobbied other Councillors and then with a few hours to go it was pulled. Although the Lord Mayor takes these decisions I suspect the Council's Legal Expert had something to do with it because...

The night before Full Council the developer's planning agent[14] wrote to all Councillors explaining why this was not a good motion. I'm guessing he wrote to officers too. It was never totally clear what the reason was for pulling it, but I think Legal were worried that any Councillor supporting the motion wouldn't be able to vote again in a Planning Meeting if affordable housing were the topic.

---

12   Called Goram Homes.
13   Labour Party Councillor, before he was promoted to Cabinet.
14   I will never forgive him. I appreciate it's what he is paid to do, but has clearly lost any moral compass in my book.

CHAPTER G7
BACK IN THE HOT CHOCOLATE

Surely we had to fight the Chocolate Factory developers all the way?

But my Labour colleagues on the Committee thought otherwise. They were desperate to avoid legal costs as the Council was at the height of its financial crisis and so they accepted that the Council wouldn't contest this appeal. I was so disappointed. But maybe they were right?

The Planning Inspector allowed the appeal and the Chocolate Factory development could be built with a low number of affordable homes. Not the six that we had forced out of them but none. Yes none. I argued that the Council should have contested and submitted the evidence about the errors in the viability and the late stage of the change. But Labour had desperately wanted a balanced budget and contesting and losing might have cost us more so that evidence wasn't submitted.

In the end it was my proposal to defer that lost us six affordable homes, the six I had found with that 600 grand mistake, perhaps Richard Eddy had been right at the meeting to propose we agree to the six we had been offered.

Update: April 2020. It's being built[15]. There are about 25% shared ownership homes, financed by grants after the event. The developer didn't have to pay anything and presumably made their 20% profit (or possibly not, depending on the impact of Covid-19). Speculative housing is very risky. That's one of the reasons they say they have to target a 20% profit.

If selling speculative housing could be made less risky, then prices could come down.

The cat and mouse games with developers and affordable housing continued at what seemed every other Committee meeting during 2017 and for a couple more years after that.

15   www.chocolatefactorybristol.com

After the December 2016 Full Council decision, the viability statements were made public. I attacked them like a maths exam (I like maths). Often there was a perceived weakness which I then sent straight to the officer responsible for managing the process. He then either agreed or, more often didn't, but when he agreed he took that point to the developer's agent and sometimes got us a better deal. Although I didn't keep track of the exact amounts I found, I'm guessing it was well over £2 million worth. The list of battlefields includes Redland High (Girl's) School, Old Brewery, L&G sites ND7 and ND6 both near Temple Meads, Redcliffe Quarter, Old Ambulance station (and why the lower part is a storey higher) and more. Success became thinner and thinner: land prices increased and developers' agents learned to make fewer mistakes.

Nevertheless ND6 (2018) is a site on Avon Street that deserves a special mention.

It illustrates (in my book) a turn for the worse. It adjoins the site ND7; both were being developed by Legal and General (L&G) to be flats in two blocks, not for sale, but for rent (individual flats). L&G had gained planning permission previously for the first site ND7. For that they had a viability statement justifying why they could only put in 10% affordable housing. The main issue behind lack of affordable housing there is that this is build-for-rent and so the property values of each flat aren't so high as build-for-sale. Bristol has a shortage of rental properties, even at market rents, so it was voted through.

Now we come to the sister site ND6, initially costed the same way, some of the detail of the viability is as follows:

The demand[16] for rented accommodation is higher and so it is less speculative. L&G can afford to run at a lower profit margin, not the 20% anyway. When you calculate the value of a building where the flats are being rented out, you have to take the annual rent and multiply it by the number of years[17] to break even. So if 120 flats could be rented out

16   Demand meaning in this context numbers of people, not the price.
17   Technically you divide it by the yield in this case say 4.25% which equates to 23.5 years. The end result is the same.

at a net rent each of about £11,000 a year (after service charges, which include the gym, wifi and more) the total annual rent is £1.34m a year and times 23.5 years (4.25% yield) gives £31.5 million value for the block. That's the number used in the viability calculation.

The idea of build-to-rent is good but the assumptions that go into the affordable housing viability calculation are quite new and I think well padded. Firstly there is profit in the rent (this might be rented out by a business). Secondly there is profit in developing the building itself and thirdly profit on the uplift in value of the land once planning permission is granted. And then profit on the service charge and the gym which was to be open to the public. All of these profits are allowed as fair within the viability appraisal and then any extra predicted profit funds the need to provide affordable homes. This is standard practice and approved by the Royal Institute of Chartered Surveyors (RICS) who have created the guidelines to follow.

The first viability statement for ND6 showed they could put in some affordable. Then they changed their agent and hired a new one, this new one was the same one that had worked for the Council! Game keeper turned poacher, as poacher and working with the developers they added a new cost, one not included in the sister site ND7 previously.

It seems that the proponents of the build-to-rent sector convinced RICS[18] that a notional stamp duty should be allowed as a cost too. When you sell a property it is the buyer who pays the stamp duty, a tax payable on property transactions (and on shares too as it happens). For the purpose of a viability statement, the buyer's cost is taken off the valuation of the price of property to be sold. But build-to-rent isn't for sale, it's for rent. L&G agreed to a 15 year rental clause (after then they could sell the block or flats). But still RICS allowed for stamp duty even though it was 15 years away or more (if at all). Resulting in more profit for L&G (and pension funds as shareholders) and less affordable housing. I was incensed, in fact most were and probably the officers too,

---

18   I imagine RICS will deny conceding to any pressure but as RICS consist of chartered surveyors who earn big fees from developers it's easy to think there was some influence one way or another. If RICS weren't influenced then it looks an even worse decision by them; simply reducing affordable home building like that!

who are human beings after all.

Forgetting all the other layers of profit, if stamp duty hadn't been allowed we would have got 23 affordable flats (19%), with stamp duty included it became four flats (3%). As a Committee we approved the scheme as long as they delivered 23, we didn't think the RICS Stamp Duty Guidance had been implemented by then and if it had, it stunk anyway.

Fortunately L&G were doing a big deal with the Mayor to develop the land that had been reserved for the arena in the City Centre. This decision surely wouldn't be appealed; they wouldn't dare put that deal at risk?

CHAPTER G8
THE CAPTURE OF THE PLANNING SYSTEM

Legal and General went to Appeal, the Planning Inspector said that as RICS had approved the stamp duty cost then it should be included. We were livid. I wrote to the Planning Inspectorate pointing out the error of their ways and explaining that the RICS advice had such an impact on affordable housing that it shouldn't be considered as valid. My reasoning was that because it had such an impact it should have been circulated more widely not just to RICS members (because the clients of RICS members are developers and the construction industry so they are biased). The Inspectorate replied saying that in this instance the RICS guidance did apply but it wasn't a precedent.

So only four affordable homes. A loss of 19, means 19 more homeless because L&G want to satisfy their shareholders.

By then I had lost faith in viability altogether within the planning system. A year later, I wrote to the officer responsible for managing the viability process as mandated by Government. This was regarding another development that came to Committee, which was refused, but not for the affordable housing aspect.

"You won't win with me now I'm afraid because I have lost confidence in the system of planning and affordable housing altogether. It doesn't just relate to this application but to everything. The idea of capitalism and free markets is supposed to maximise the welfare benefit to the population by the efficient deployment and use of scarce resources (from economics text books). It clearly doesn't do that when we are building loss making cinemas but not housing homeless people. The planning system and affordable housing viability are fundamentally just fudges attempting to fix a failing system. I'm considering whether I can sit on DC ever again. I hope I can just about keep an un-predetermined mind until I step down in 24 weeks' time."

(I was expecting to finish in May 2020). The officer wisely didn't reply.

But there is always hope, isn't there?

AFFORDABLE HOUSING

It should be clear by now that lack of affordable housing and especially social housing is causing great harm. Harm is the externality and if we continue with a market the cost of the harm needs to be passed on to the players who make the money from the housing market, like a special tax or duty. In this case probably onto the owners of land who are benefiting the most. It is arguable whether land in a city should be in a market at all. It is such a scare resource that markets are doing what they do well and price it higher and higher to ensure it is conserved. That's what's causing the harm to 60% of those trying to enter the housing market (most at affordable rent level). It is also clear that those who gain from this market failure continue to gain and ensure that the laws and rules continue to benefit them.

The viability system was at best a fudge and is now broken.

On 28 Jan 2020, *The Times* and *The Sun*; (thanks as always to LGiU for these clips)

Government plans 'radical reform' of planning laws

"The government is exploring plans to speed up planning permission which could lead to Councillors losing their powers to veto housing applications. Local authorities would no longer be able to stop buildings in their area or prevent shops being converted into housing, under new rules proposed in a report by the think tank Policy Exchange. Instead, there would be a system in which land was either approved for development or building banned. Developers would follow standardised rules that would be scrutinised by local planning officers. The report is being "seriously looked at" by the No 10 policy unit, according to the Times, which added that ministers are keen to pursue an early "radical reform" of the system that has largely been unaltered since the Town and Country Planning Act of 1947.

David Renard, the LGA's planning spokesman, said: "Councils and their communities must be able to oversee all local developments, to make sure they are of good quality, and to help build prosperous places." It is a "dangerous and misleading myth," he added, that "planning is a barrier to housebuilding."

Regarding the news clip above, do you think that the Policy Exchange think tank have got it right? Perhaps as a short term fix? And what about the LGA's response?

Back in section B we discussed how donations from a director of the Bristol Port supported the Conservatives. The Freeports policy that would directly benefit them is currently being proposed (and consulted upon during 2020). We have now seen here parties who, belong to and perhaps fund the Royal Institute of Chartered Surveyors, have benefitted from a policy (stamp duty costs) which reduces the amount of affordable housing they have to provide. Two examples, I suspect there are many more that other books and articles have uncovered that show how the Mathematics of Power plays out. We will pick this up again in the next section. This next story is an illustration as to how broken the planning system is...

CHAPTER G9
A TALL STOREY

Sometimes to get more affordable housing means building higher. I wrote an article that was published about developing on a plot of land that is on the left of the A4 as you travel east out of the city, just after the bridge on the left and before Paintworks. In this case I didn't support the development, voting against it, due to the inherent problems with the quality of life for those who will need to live in the flats. Many people objected due to the height of the building itself which is a separate, also valid, planning reason.

Article published in *Bristol 24/7* on June 25th 2019, by Councillor Clive Stevens

> *"I feel so sorry for Councillor Nicola Beech, Cabinet Member for Planning (Labour) she has worked so hard on her Planning policy and to have this happen at the very first hurdle is disappointing to say the least.*
>
> *But before we get into the story of her policy's demise it is worth noting that virtually all Councillors in Bristol are in favour of having more affordable housing so that those on the lowest incomes and often with children can live. Market rents are often double social rents; fuelled by land price increases, property speculation and government policies, all of which are driving homelessness and many of the related social ills that surround us. In fact Bristol needs every other home built to be affordable, yes 50%[19], but we are getting 20% at best. So we need it everywhere, almost, there are some places where affordable, social housing doesn't work well and that's where there is no public transport or in tall buildings. So what follows is an example of the folly of chasing numbers for their own sake.*
>
> *So on with the story. Tuesday 18th June. The Cabinet meeting was long into its third hour and we all were flagging, I heard a sigh of relief as we came to the very last agenda item, but I still had a question and so asked why a Corporate Risk had gone up 40%, specifically the risk of not meeting the Mayor's housing target of 2,000 homes (with 800 affordable) a year*

19   It's actually 60% of course.

by May 2020 which is only just over ten months away now. Councillor Paul Smith, Cabinet Member for Homes and Housing gave a wide ranging answer about all the things he and the administration and the Government, even, are doing and questioned why the risk had been increased at all. That risk assessment was down to the Council's newish professional Risk Manager, a job I suggested they needed some two years ago, and it looks like they heeded. Presumably she has some evidence to have made that decision. But according to Paul there is no problem.

So we move forward 24 hours to Wednesday's Planning Meeting (DCA) where we ten Councillors had to determine an application for a tall building, a fifteen storey one as it happens, on the A4 Bath Road beside Totterdown, just before Paintworks as you leave the city. It looked pretty ugly but perhaps that's a matter of taste, it had no children's play area at all and it was expected to house about forty five children. The training we Councillors have received is that tall buildings can be fine in the right place and if designed well; offices, hotels and flats for sale to those that can afford them are uses that can thrive in such environments. One of the key things is to be able to afford the high service charges and secondly to not need the facilities that say a family on low incomes would need. But this block was to have thirty affordable homes minimum and possibly as high as sixty if more grants could be gained.

Normally I'm all for affordable homes, I rigorously check the viability studies but such homes are for those on the lowest incomes, often on benefits even if they are in work; and often with children. This type of demographic is not appropriate for tall buildings and was one of the mistakes made in the past.

This brings us back to Councillor Nicola Beech's great work, the Urban Living SPD, a planning document which sets out guidelines for building homes and communities in Bristol and includes the controversial "Tall Buildings Policy". It shouldn't actually be that controversial because it carefully details the requirements for tall buildings and sets out needs like children's play areas and a healthy living environment. It also seeks design excellence for new tall buildings.

It doesn't take a degree in Urban Planning to see that the design issues regarding, let's call it The Totterdown Tower, don't meet the Urban Planning Guide. So applying planning policy it should have been turned down. But only two Councillors voted against, that's me and Mark Wright. Eight voted for: the two Tories and six Labour.

Why would Labour vote for a tower block that clearly fails their own (Nicola's) planning policy? Well to me it's clear. Go back to Tuesday evening's Cabinet meeting. It seems that the Council will do what it can to meet its housing targets even if it means permitting developments which all the evidence says will take risks with people's lives. You might also wonder why a political promise, one of housebuilding, has become a Council risk? So muddling up political risk with actual risk, that's another story (not storey) that goes to the heart of what's wrong with the current reporting structure.

So sorry Nicola, both Mark Wright and I read your policy and worked to it. I do hope that none of the problems predicted will occur, it will take a decade or more to find out. Will Councillors be around that long to be held to account if it all goes pear shaped?

Comment: If land prices are so high that tall buildings are needed, then the quality of home provided is even more important, especially if you are bringing up a family on low income. It is a personal value of mine and many, that society should be mixed and balanced rather than creating ghettos of poverty, wealth or ethnicity. It seems the fundamental problem is the price of land. If we were discussing another need, say water; if the price were so high that people were dying of thirst something would be done, the Government would take over for example. People are dying due to lack of housing and so we should do something fundamental.

CHAPTER G10
A SOLUTION? SUGGESTED IN 2017

In 2016 the Councils of Bristol, Bath & NE Somerset and South Gloucester voted to set up a "super authority[20]" called the West of England Combined Authority (WECA). To have its own Mayor, a budget and responsibility for housing, transport, economy and adult education. The logic being that so much of Bristol's economy was now outside Bristol City Council's region that more joined up thinking should be encouraged. So as a resident of Bristol I vote for a WECA Mayor, and a Bristol Mayor at different times in the four year cycle; And local Councillors too; Oh and I forgot an MP, but no MEP now.

The idea of having a Mayor[21] is to accelerate decision making and make it clear who is accountable. We have two elected Mayors, so do you think that makes things clear and accountable?

In 2017 a housing strategy was to be discussed at WECA. I thought I'd write in:

G8 – statement to WECA….30th October 2017 Councillor Clive Stevens, Bristol City Council
"Dear WECA

Bristol City Council used to have a housing problem, but now WECA exists, you have Bristol's housing problem – and good luck to you!

And the scale of your challenge: Bristol covers 11,000 hectares, take away land needed for highways (about 10%), industry (10%), downs, parks, shopping centres, rail infrastructure, university buildings, hospitals….and let's not forget the floating harbour leaves maybe 6 to 7,000 hectares. A housing density of 50 households per hectare allows for 300 to 350,000 households easily enough for everyone in Bristol and perhaps all the WECA region if the city was built to such a density. But it's not and it's not going to be because of the national policy presumption "in favour of

---

20   This was enabled by Act of Parliament, a referendum won by 13% to 11% in May 2012 (all other cities voted against in that set of referenda).
21   Sometimes termed a Metro Mayor.

development" reintroduced in 2012. That means that market forces take precedence over the plan as can be seen by the increase in appeals and success rates nationally[22].

Don't get me wrong, markets are great when appropriate and run to good rules set by Government. Adam Smith taught us that a marketplace properly managed leads to win-win outcomes for both buyer and seller, but back in 1776 he left out the impact on third parties (externalities).

So back to your problem of Bristol, land is getting tight, much development is on brownfield sites and there is plenty of wealth in the city. In many areas the market will prefer to build 5 x £600k homes nicely spaced out on a hectare rather than 20 x £150k flats on a brownfield site, simply for reason of profit and who can blame them. So another hectare is used up and it becomes less easy to house those who can't afford £600k homes. Since land is the scarce resource, the market will do what it always does and bid up the price of the scarce resource so people with less money have to go elsewhere, that's how markets work. The fact that the poorer would have to move out is a mere externality to markets but will have huge effects on the economy of Bristol and the whole region in the long term.

Your Joint Spatial Plan has identified the need to build 18,800[23] affordable homes in Bristol, that is 56% of the total build plan in the next 20 years. Currently Bristol achieves less than 20% affordable homes and as land prices increase so viability reports will mean even less affordable homes will be built (certainly on brownfield sites). That's the market at work. Building high in the centre might help but build costs go up per square foot as the number of floors increases and land prices rise once it's known that you can build high, that wretched market again!

So do you want to allow markets to reign free and continue to bid up the price of land with the consequent externalities? If you think no then you might consider the following:

1) Convince the Government that in some parts of the UK a presumption in favour of development has harmful consequences.

And

22   Town and Country Planning Association report 2017.
23   That was in 2017, when I last looked, the figure was more like 21,000

2) Make much more land available to be built upon and put in infrastructure so residents can access Bristol and Bath quickly and inexpensively. I don't mean concrete over the floating harbour or build on the Downs, but I mean land to build affordable and low priced homes dense enough for the occupants to have local amenities and can also access the jobs of Bristol and Bath quickly and cheaply. The cheapest transport[24] is cycling, the second cheapest (assuming the distance is more than a walk) is public transport. To solve your problem of Bristol's homes, I would imagine you would need to free up some 5,000 hectares of land outside of Bristol (to "flood the market") and insist that the build densities are high enough to support the infrastructure and cheap bus, tram and/or rail routes and free cycle routes.

And

3) You may have noticed from section 2 above that as well as being the cheapest transport infrastructure for new residents these choices are the lowest in carbon footprint too; so gentlemen[25] it's down to you. Focus on cycle routes, low cost bus and other public transport but first put in strong planning policies while the land is relatively cheap to keep it cheap and that way you can ensure developers schedule quality, affordable homes and associated facilities. Robust defendable planning policy, then built infrastructure to ensure you don't increase congestion and pollution and then comes the house building. You have to break the scarcity value of land.

These actions need to be your top priority. Thank you.

Councillor Clive Stevens"

So that told them! And that was back in 2017, I edited this piece and submitted it as evidence to the Raynsford Enquiry into planning later that same year. And what did they all do?

Assuming WECA has to follow planning policies which rely on

---

24   In and around a city, society's most expensive transport option is one that brings high negative externalities; the car, which needs space to park in (outside the house, at the shopping centre and at work), space to drive on and also brings the pollution externality killing those in the centre of Bristol and Bath and adding CO2. A simple analysis shows each car needs as much space as each person. With land scarce which is more important?
25   WECA in those days consisted of the three male leaders of the constituent authorities and the Metro Mayor himself.

a market mechanism and a presumption in favour of sustainable development, then their main option was to select land where it could be built on. It should be chosen to easily connect to sustainable transport like buses and safe cycle routes; then enforce planning policies for a high build density and high level of affordable housing provision. That way the land price doesn't rocket when the policy is announced because the constraints are quite onerous and so it's not very profitable to build, but just enough. That required a robust suite of planning policies starting with the Joint Spatial Plan JSP to cover Bristol, Bath and the authorities surrounding them. The JSP is a story in its own right.

That statement in 2017 was based on what I knew then. I still think it's part of an answer we can work through in the next section. But now we move to the Joint Spatial Plan, the saviour to be, or not to be.

CHAPTER G11
THE JOINT SPATIAL PLAN – 1/8/2019 – RIP?

We all received an email from Bristol's Director of Planning. The inspectors who have been holding the public hearings on the Joint Spatial Plan proposals have stopped them and canned the whole thing. Those aren't her words, she was more measured. She did entitle it WOE Spatial plan. Woe could mean "woe is me" or woah, all stop. She might have meant West of England but the first two are more accurate.

So what happened? Basically loads of people complained about building plans on the Green Belt. The WoE region had been instructed by Government to build another 110,000 homes in the next 20 years. To put that in perspective there are about 450,000 homes at the moment (203,000 in Bristol). So that's a lot of building, but plenty of the extra 110,000, excluding Bristol's 33,500, were not destined for brownfield sites. Not even in towns and villages, because those Councillors didn't want it, too much strife from voters. So build them on the Green Belt they said. But that idea fell apart, too much strife from the other voters who wanted to protect the Green Belt.

The Planning Inspectors called the problem "a lack of evidence" as to why the 12 specific large sites had been chosen. But that's planning speak for its bloomin' obvious why green field sites were chosen. Green field has other advantages too. They make it easier to get a higher percentage of affordable homes; the land might even come cheaper and there are no demolition nor clean-up costs typically associated with brown field (already developed) land. But green field homes come without bus routes, doctors and schools. A car is essential, so sustainability is out the car window.

So now what? Back to the drawing board on where to put these new homes. Plus delays. Most of Bristol's 33,500 was to be on brownfield sites so it won't delay building them, but it will mean that developers can be speculative on what and where they want to build to maximise their profit and not stick to new planning constraints as there aren't any new ones. And with that is the delay to Bristol's new Local Plan; the one to replace the 2011 document and is needed as it starts to control university expansion and brings in standards for new buildings, including carbon neutrality. All that good stuff will be delayed.

And will the housing targets be changed? One of the arguments for Brexit was the pressure immigration put on infrastructure, housing and services. Now it's been stopped perhaps the house building targets will be reduced? But then rumours go round that the target for new housing is to be increased to 116,000 surely not? And it's not just any new houses we need, it's affordable ones. I haven't seen a revised target for them.

I interviewed one of the officers about the history of the JSP process (going back to 1974), it didn't make the cut I'm afraid and missed going into an appendix too; it seems to have been a unique process for just the West of England Area. All Local Planning Authorities have to have a Local Plan. Our WoE JSP was to join up four Local Plans, but now it won't[26].

---

26   In June 2020 WECA agreed a process to create a Spatial Development Strategy; Essentially it is a JSP for the three authorities in WECA plus an agreement with North Somerset LPA. This will have new targets and need new consultation and should be ready by 2023.

With the JSP destroyed[27], Bristol's emerging Local Plan, which was supposed to come out some months after the JSP, had to be put on ice. That left some big gaps in policy. I'll focus on two.

Firstly, the control of university growth. Many of Bristol's existing homes were converted and then occupied by students and if that continued (which was likely under the expansionist policies of the University of Bristol) then it would cause a major housing crisis in other parts of Bristol. The plan was to house the extra growth in students in purpose built blocks built in areas that would benefit from the vibrancy and business growth that having students brings. But with no plan, these blocks can be built anywhere that developers can find less expensive, probably derelict land; near enough to one of the campuses and they needn't bother too much about the impact on rents on the current population. It doesn't matter to them and it isn't a planning consideration that the influx of students will encourage house owners, landlords and home owners, to convert their homes to houses of multiple occupation. The rents paid are higher. Profit, profit, profit. This reduces supply, rents go up across the board and people who don't earn so much need to move out. It's one of the causes of gentrification. The free market capitalist approach which says, satisfy the demand. If there's demand it is economically most efficient to meet it, but the harm is enormous. And that includes more homelessness as the process roles out. See next chapter for more on this.

The other really big gap is the carbon neutrality of new buildings. The 2011 Local Plan (still in force) only required 20% reduction in carbon emissions. The new one was to require zero carbon emissions, after all, Bristol, the whole city, was aiming for carbon neutrality by 2030 (see A9). With no new Local Plan carbon neutrality can't be required. As it turns out during the winter of 2019/20 the Government were actually consulting on whether to prevent Local Planning Authorities on setting

---

27 *Rethinking Planning for the 21st Century*, Policy Exchange Think Tank, Jan 2020 suggests regional planning policies (a bit like the JSP). https://policyexchange.org.uk/wp-content/uploads/Rethinking-the-Planning-System-for-the-21st-Century.pdf Additionally the terms of WECA (combined authority) require the Metro Mayor to come up with a regional planning framework. So now the JSP is dead long live regional planning and the SDS!

their own targets at all. Setting your own target was a power granted by Labour in the previous decade. I provided an argument explaining why LPAs should be able to set their own targets because it would encourage innovation and help some businesses meet higher standards required in key export markets. We haven't seen the conclusion to this. The carbon neutrality problem for Bristol is on hold awaiting the result of the Government's consultation.

But what about controlling university expansion?

CHAPTER G12
UNIVERSITY EXPANSION

This was nicely summed up on 30th January 2020 by one of Bristol's Local Democracy reporters Amanda Cameron: Why reinvent the wheel? Thank you Amanda.

University expansion 'partly to blame for Bristol's escalating house rents', Councillors say

Rent prices in Bristol are rising more than twice as fast as the England average.

"Bristol's growing student population is partly to blame for the city's rapidly rising rent prices, according to elected Councillors.

Last week figures emerged showing that rent prices in Bristol are rising more than twice as fast as the England average.

The city's student population has grown by more than 16,500 over the last two decades but the local authority has few ways to control that number.

Most of the extra 6,500 students in the city in past five years is due to the expansion of Bristol University, according to Council figures.

Bristol City Council formally agreed to tackle some of the problems associated with university expansion two and a half years ago.

But the issue has come under renewed focus with a report on the matter requested by a cross-party commission of elected Councillors. Information supplied by Council officers to members of the communities scrutiny commission showed that the authority lost £13.3 million of income last year because of student housing, which is exempt from paying Council Tax.

But the "deeper and often more tragic" harm done by university expansion is to the city's housing market, especially rents, Councillor Clive Stevens told the commission.

Students typically live in university halls of residence, purpose-built student accommodation, or shared flats in homes licensed as a house of multiple occupation (HMO).

Cllr Stevens said that, while purpose-built student accommodation "probably" drives up land prices through an impact on supply and demand, HMOs cause even more harm.

"Filling [existing homes] with students takes houses away from the market so reducing supply for everyone else and with increasing demand for homes," he said in a written statement presented to the commission on January 27.

"It is a cause of higher rents and possibly even homelessness. Hardworking but low paid people are displaced to poorer areas," he said.

Commission member Councillor Estella Tincknell said that in her ward of Lockleaze, student rents are driving up house prices in what is a traditionally working-class area.

"But we need to speak to national government because at a local level there's not much we can do," she said referring to Councils' limited powers to control the local housing market.

Chair Anthony Negus said that government policy had resulted in student accommodation becoming a "copper-bottomed investment" for developers while at the same time shielding firms from paying their fair share towards the cost of Council services to support students.

"The Council is picking up the tab," he said.

In a wide-ranging statement setting out many of the problems associated with the "unstoppable increase in student numbers" in Bristol, Cllr Negus called for a report detailing what actions had been taken since the Council adopted a motion on how to mitigate university expansion back in July 2017.

"Bristol City Council and its taxpayers, and most particularly those less advantaged citizens trying to find somewhere affordable to live, are losing out," he said.

Cabinet member for housing Paul Smith told the commission that the Council had done a lot of work at a local planning level and that issues that require changes in government policy had been raised at national level.

Discussions had also been held with Bristol University and the University of the West of England, he added.

The commission heard that the Council is trying to stop future conversions of homes to HMOs and ensure that all new students are housed in purpose-built accommodation.

The proportion of new student housing that is purpose-built as opposed to resulting from HMO conversions has climbed from 40 per cent to just over 80 per cent, Council papers show.

The scrutiny commission agreed to ask the office of city Mayor Marvin Rees for a progress report on work to mitigate university expansion.

The motion adopted by full Council in July 2017 called on Mayor Rees to "engage with the Government to highlight that the current approach to university growth is creating unsustainable pressure on Council resources" and suggested that "adequate funding arrangements will probably require changes to planning obligation and taxation advantages".

It agreed that the universities' masterplans needed to be updated to ensure "sustainable future expansion, housing and transport solutions".

And it asked the Mayor to instruct officers to develop a bespoke planning document containing "best practice" approaches to universities, require universities to support transport and housing projects for more than just first years, and set up an all-party commission to oversee the above work and liaise with universities.

The report sought by the commission is expected after May's Council elections."

The bespoke planning document requested back in 2017 eventually materialised as the HMO SPD which was being consulted upon in March 2020. If implemented it makes it more difficult to convert homes to HMOs and thus pushes demand towards purpose built student blocks[28]. But there is no sign of a planning policy where those purpose built blocks should go and developers are speculatively applying to get permission anywhere as it is an extremely profitable use of land.

TAKEAWAYS

Government policies are fuelling the land price problem. If you have a market where there is so much demand; enough people with the ability to pay the high rents that lead to high land prices of £15 million per hectare (about £6 million an acre); then if you need housing for people who can only pay half that rent level (social rent), the value of the land needs to be much lower say for example £2 million a hectare, maybe less. That might be ex-industrial land, disused warehouses and offices or failing shopping centres and if there are high costs of demolition and cleaning away contamination too that can really make land cheap. But those costs are accounted for in the viability statement and so affordable housing levels are still limited. But if you do achieve this and get social housing built instead of market priced housing then you create single demographic ghettos, which are harmful too.

Tweaks are not the answer. And neither, it seems, are office conversions, do read on...

---

11 Jan 2020, Office conversion rules hit affordable housing

"Thousands of affordable homes have potentially been lost across England due to rules allowing offices to be converted into housing without needing planning permission. The Local Government Association looked at the number of office conversions carried out under the permitted development right, and found that since 2015, there were 54,162 new homes converted under the rules. Based on Councils' affordable housing requirements for

28   If they get built.

new developments, the LGA estimates this has potentially led to the loss of 13,540 affordable homes. It added that while the total conversions amount to 6% of all new homes nationally, in some areas a significantly high proportion – up to 51% - of new housing is office conversions.... The Daily Telegraph, Page: 14 The Sun, Page: 22 The Independent, Page: 17 Daily Mail Daily Express, Page: 17 Daily Mirror, Page: 22.
Summarised by LGiU – thank you.

Comment on above: Empty office space converted to homes, potentially = good, but if without affordable homes = Bad.

CHAPTER G13

THE NUMBERS BEHIND THE LACK OF AFFORDABLE, RENTED HOUSING

Bristol has 18% affordable (rented) housing, 37,000 dwellings, but requires at least 25%. The maths for this is broken down in Appendix 19. Seven percent more doesn't seem much, it's approximately 15,000[29] dwellings but that's not allowing for population growth. Allowing for stickiness in the market, population growth and rounding the Planning requirement is about 21,000 to get to a 2036 figure of 58,000 (affordable homes).

The plan (was[30]) to get 35,000 new dwellings of all types (market, to buy, to rent and affordable) by 2036; of that 21,000 need[31] to be affordable; that's 60% of the market[32] The market can't even satisfy half of that. It is an illustration of a broken market, very, very smashed.

29   The 2017 estimates for the JSP were 18,800 for 2036 and it seems the targets have gone up.
30   I'm referring to the JSP here, the Joint Spatial Plan, the one that was rejected by Planning Inspectors (see G11).
31   I use the word need here in its normal sense. Planners use the word need as a substitute for the word demand. The demand for homes is 35,000 (in 15 years), for some of those it will be a need but they can afford market rates, those who need to live in affordable housing, it is a real need. Their only other choices are to move out of Bristol; that links to the Bradford story in Chapter E3 and would starve Bristol of its key workers.
32   The point is that only the developers' contributions accounting for about 10% of the 35,000 is provided by the markets (kicking and screaming) the rest are subsidies or provided by the state (Council homes). And after Covid-19 some of these schemes might be cut back.

This level of brokenness should be of no surprise to you following the analysis of reasons for market failure detailed in section E. Housing is a need (negotiating power imbalance made worse due to high switching costs) and it requires land which, within a city, is a scarce resource; those are two reasons for market failure. And not having enough affordable housing has externalities too, harm to society as well as to the people and families concerned. So three reasons for failure[33]; no wonder the market has expired. The system has gone to meet its maker. In fact the subsidies are just fuelling the flames. If the provision of affordable housing were a burnt dead parrot[34] not only has it kicked the bucket, but the system is using the bucket to pour petrol on the flames.

The 25% need figure is an estimate for Bristol (I think it's conservative). It is based on the average earnings and the distribution at the lower end and an earning's level where Housing Benefit is needed to top up. This needs to be compared with private rents and an assessment of affordability. A city with lower private rents or a higher average income will end up with a different percentage.

Councils can start to build their own houses again and this has to be financed from the rents of people living in Council houses. These are going up slightly faster than inflation. In 15 years it might just be possible to build 5,000 Council homes which will more than offset the losses of "Right to Buy[35]" But we still need another 16,000? The appendix shows how another 4,000[36] might be built using developers' contributions (S106) and Home England grants funded by the tax payer. And the other 12,000? Anyone got a magic wand[37]?

This is a national problem but worse in cities.

33   The Jan 2020 Report, *Rethinking Planning for the 21st Century*, would add a fourth reason for failure which is the dysfunctional regulation going back to the 1947 Town and Country Planning Act. It certainly is poor regulation, dating from a different time. Therefore it's not just the market that's failing, it's the poor regulation of the market failure too. If for example 50% affordable housing was rigorously enforced then, with other assistance, land prices would eventually fall. So I agree this much with the authors. It needs change.
34   Analogy inspired by *Monty Python*.
35   Right to buy: after a number of years a Council house tenant has the right to buy the home at a discount (but not cheaper than the building costs). So to buy a new home will cost the tenant a fair bit.
36   Generous estimates.
37   Bristol, for the first time in well over a decade, registered little population growth in 2019; it has averaged 4,000 a year. Why so low, nobody knows yet. If it becomes a trend then the planning figures will need recalculating which may mean less housebuilding overall but an even higher % need for affordable.

National figures were reported in *The Independent*,

16ᵗʰ Jan 2020, Almost 200k fewer Council homes since 2010

"Labour analysis of official figures shows that almost 200,000 Council homes have been lost since the Conservatives came to power in 2010. The number of homes rented from Councils has fallen from 1,786,000 in 2010 to 1,592,000 by the end of 2018 – a drop of 194,000, or 11%. A Government spokesperson said: "Since 2010 this government has delivered over 464,000 new affordable homes, including 114,000 social homes. In addition to this, the social housing waiting list has decreased by 40% since 2012."
Thanks LGiU

Appendix 19 shows that a minority of the need for affordable housing comes from people who are unemployed or on disability benefits, the majority are those working hard but not being paid for either enough hours or high enough hourly rates or for those on low pensions. Please note many of these people are key workers but due to our current economic system they don't get paid enough for private rental housing (and not to buy). Also many years ago "Single Mums" used to bear the brunt of the tabloids "Benefits-Britain" pieces.

This article summarised from the Independent describes the situation now:

4ᵗʰ Feb 2020, Single parents working longer hours to avoid poverty, from The Independent.

The Resolution Foundation has calculated that single parents must now work seven more hours a week than they did 10 years ago to avoid falling into poverty. The research says benefit cuts have "negated" the impact of rising employment on poverty rates, leaving only those with high pay or a lot of hours able to lift their families above the poverty threshold.

At the time of writing, the impact of Covid-19 on the private rental sector and unemployment is unknown but the prognosis is not good. With a dead parrot of a system that should come as no surprise. There might be an injection of tax payers' money but that won't fix the system.

Private rents in Bristol are more than double affordable ones, costing an extra £6,000 a year. Much of that difference is the need for profit (some is to offset risk) and also to pay the cost of financing land. In Appendix 19 we see that Councils can provide homes sustainably for £500 a month rent, the private sector requires £1,100 (or ND6 model at £900/month).

And the solution?

Appendix 19 at Q10 covers some stop gap measures within the broken system, Section H (next) suggests some longer term reforms.

SUMMARY – SECTION G.

So you can see we have to do something about the market and thus price of land.

And the fact we can't all live in affordable homes is because of the price of the land and the need for profit (to offset risk) which drives high rents.

In Appendix 18 we explore another planning example which further illustrates the madness of it all (to quote myself!). The planning system itself is not so bad but it is failing due to a few clauses in the NPPF (see H2) and the dead parrot market failures for land and the petrol pouring management of the marketplace.

So my dear revolutionaries or reformers, if you want to read the recommendations in H then they start up right now, next page.

SECTION H
CONCLUSIONS AND
RECOMMENDATIONS

DEAR REVOLUTIONARY (OR REFORMER)

I have been party to some sights and sounds over the four years plus more at Bristol City Council and been able to apply a business and academic brain, and my heart, to some key issues. It's not a unique insight but worthy of adding to other evidence. This section covers the lessons I have learned, how they might apply to the national picture and some ideas about what needs to be done.

We then consider the more difficult question of how it could be done given the Mathematics Of Power and the current political situation.

Below is part of my statement to Full Council on 19th March 2019 giving an insight on who benefits from the current situation:

> *Making millionaires out of a planning bonanza.*
> *"Every five years or so Bristol Council's Planning Authority awards millions of pounds to some lucky landowners.*
>
> *"The giveaway date was yesterday. Yesterday was when the new Local Plan[1] was issued for consultation showing new sites allocated for housing. Often the selected land is derelict, or ex-car parks, unwanted industrial sites and this time includes a number of car dealerships. The lucky landowners will receive a value uplift of maybe a million pounds per acre possibly more.*
>
> *This new money isn't coming from the Council itself but is at the expense of those needing affordable or simply reasonably priced housing and hinders the City's progress towards carbon neutrality because developers who buy the newly allocated, higher priced land will say "I can't afford to build cheap housing or be carbon neutral because the land price is too high". And national laws permit this excuse because the provision of affordable housing and carbon neutrality are subject to a viability test, which means if the land price goes up then you don't have to follow all the planning requirements."*

As it turns out I was half wrong, but with a glass half full mentality being half right is enough to make my point here.

In theory this uplift shouldn't happen at all. Not if the allocation or permission is for housing at least. The uplift is "taxed" by the affordable housing commitment (S106 contribution). In practice, according to a Parliamentary Briefing[2] the land owner gains about 50% of the planning windfall increase. Land prices also increase from the improvement in infrastructure around the land sometimes paid for in part by the

---

1   As it turned out, the Joint Spatial Plan was rejected by Inspectors and so Bristol's Local Plan is stuck. Nevertheless the new Site Allocations, which is the list of plots that can be reallocated to housing, remains and can be given some weight by Planning Officers. So those lucky landowners keep their prizes.
2   https://publications.parliament.uk/pa/cm201719/cmselect/cmcomloc/766/76605.htm the 50% is at para 30.

developer. The third reason for the land price hike is driven by demand[3] and the general increasing affluence of people.

The planning uplift part of land enrichment has attracted most attention both in that Parliamentary Select Committee and another report in January 2020 by the Policy Exchange think tank[4] who have been discussing ways of taxing it. But it's quite problematical if you frame the issue as unfair enrichment. As Policy Exchange demonstrated much of the unfair land price increase is due to infrastructure paid for by the developer so not unfair at all.

But if you reframe the issue as a market for a scarce resource that needs to be managed and this management needs paying for and any harm paid for too then you move to a whole new logic. Later in that speech of 19th March 2019 I said,

> "A national Land Value Tax has been proposed by many as a solution to this five yearly bonanza but while we have a Conservative Government that's unlikely to happen. Why? Because the system I describe benefits the very individuals and businesses that tend to vote for and fund that Party."

CHAPTER H1
THE PRICE OF LAND

We have so much to sort out and so little time to do it in. I've mentioned before that my experiences are city-focussed so let's deal with the major problem identified in that last page; the price of land. It needs to be brought down to allow for other development types that are not simply profit maximising; buildings that are more affordable, buildings that are more integrated with nature, even land for nature. If you need more facts then just read the story of Belgrave Hill (Appendix 18) to show the

---

3   Interestingly they didn't discuss (in the briefing in footnote 2 above) that in cities land is a scarce resource especially if it is surrounded by Green Belt. This will magnify the impact of increased affluence.
4   *Rethinking Planning for the 21st Century*, Policy Exchange Think Tank, Jan 2020 also refers to the desire-ability of reducing land prices. https://policyexchange.org.uk/wp-content/uploads/Rethinking-the-Planning-System-for-the-21st-Century.pdf

ridiculousness of trading in land under a cliff and what increasing land prices can lead to.

One thing I've considered and discarded is nationalisation of all land. The state would lease or license it out, for a fee. I've dismissed it as my experience is only city-based, I know little of the countryside beyond its beauty, hedgerows, farm smells and fly tipping[5]. But there is an intervention that might bring us most of the benefits with less of the hassle.

The idea of a Land Value Tax (LVT) has been kicked around for many centuries. Both left and right have advocated it from time to time. England even had it on the statute books for a couple of months in the twentieth century; some other countries have it, often combined with a local tax too, to pay for services like waste collection, parks and libraries.

So parking the question of how we get it onto the statute books, let's look at the benefits and I thank Andrew McQuarrie for writing this up following an interview with me and publishing it on Bristol Live on 1st July 2019. Andrew found out that I was on the Green Party Tax Policy Group which had just had three years' worth of work voted through as policy at Conference. I have edited his article to focus on the benefits of LVT

Councillor Clive Stevens of the Green Party, which aims to scrap Council Tax[6] in favour of Land Value Tax

He said: "We're increasingly becoming a nation of 'haves' and 'have-nots' regarding land ownership and we need to stop that over the coming years or eventually it will end up as a revolution of some sort or another."

Mr Stevens played a key role in ensuring the national Green Party adopted a policy earlier this month to abandon Council Tax in favour of Land Value Tax (LVT).

Speaking to Bristol Live, the former Bath University business lecturer described Council Tax as "completely not fit for purpose".

---

5   Which always seems to be on the news.
6   And scrap Council Tax, Business Rates and Stamp Duty on land purchases.

And what is Land Value Tax?

The system that Green Party members wish to introduce would see landowners paying a levy based on land[7] values.

What does Mr Stevens say?

Among the most significant effects of LVT would be that more homes would become available, Mr Stevens claims.

He said: "We would come in with a very low rate [of LVT] in year one and that means immediately, if you're sitting on land that hasn't been touched, you're going to suddenly be taxed on it and that's going to cause you to sell the land or develop it."

If more houses are built, the laws of supply and demand will mean landlords will find it more difficult to get away with putting up rents.

As a result, tenants will end up with more money in their pockets, which could improve the local economy as people visit shops more frequently.

Describing the overall impact, Mr Stevens said: "The tenant is better off and the landowner is worse off and the shopkeeper is better off and the owner-occupier[8] is about the same[9]."

Another advantage that LVT enjoys over Council Tax, according to Mr Stevens, is that it takes into account 'unfair enrichment' - which is when a property's values are affected by state spending.

Green Party Councillor Clive Stevens says Land Value Tax (LVT) would benefit the local economy

An example, said Mr Stevens, was the establishment of Redland Green School in North Bristol.

"Local property values jumped because it meant you didn't need to send your children to private school and that enrichment is caused by the state investment – but the taxpayer bears the cost and people living nearby get the benefit," said the Councillor.

If LVT were implemented, public investment which raises the value of

7   The value of the land; not the actual building on the land. That's not to say that the use of the building could be taxed too but that wouldn't be LVT. It can either be levied on the price of the land or the rental value. Each approach has its pros and cons.
8   I also checked with a leaseholder (of a flat, currently paying ground rent but owning the leasehold), it was beneficial, just one example I know.
9   I suspect the builder, tradesmen and even developers could well be better off too.

a site would end up benefiting the community through higher tax receipts, proponents of the tax argue.

In a further endorsement of LVT, Mr Stevens emphasised how easy it is to collect.

He said: "Wealth tax is very easy to avoid, as has been proven in a number of countries, but land tax you can't avoid because the land is here - you can't tow the land offshore[10].

"So even if your company is offshore you still need to pay Land Value Tax."

Mr Stevens said the agreement of other political parties would be required in order for LVT to be introduced, but he went on to express doubts about the likelihood of the Conservative Party choosing to back it.

"In my view it's not got onto UK statutes because the Conservatives represent the landowning classes and they're not going to do very well if they introduce a tax on their voters," said Mr Stevens.

Bristol Live made unsuccessful attempts to interview a number of Conservative Councillors on Bristol City Council.

You will have noticed that I have assumed that land is still treated as suitable for a marketplace mechanism despite the problems this causes (see chapter H3 coming up).

One of the main benefits of a tax on land is that a plot wouldn't be sat around idly doing nothing. It would be put to use. We would need a more robust, better planning system, so some plots could be designated for affordable homes, some for trees, highways, and parks. Once the land is designated, the land price drops (or rises) to a value that makes that use possible. And if the use is for housing you don't sit around not building, just waiting for the land price to go up further, not if you are being billed at £30,000 a year, you get constructing.

Additionally, if the Council or state puts in new infrastructure or a school and land prices jump then more tax is taken, helping pay back the cost to the general taxpayer.

And finally with LVT the price of land drops, more affordable

10   You could flood it I guess but that will happen soon anyway!

A WORKED EXAMPLE OF LVT

This one is based on land price, one of many approaches:

A block of 120 leasehold flats using 0.2 hectares of land valued at £15 million a hectare.

With LVT at 1% then the freeholder pays £30,000 LVT a year. The leaseholders would still pay ground rent, won't pay so much Council Tax and no business rates. The freeholder can try to increase the ground rents to compensate. Development incentives kick in to increase supply so that ground rents can't be increased (in the long term).

If the tenure were rental rather than leasehold, the LVT should definitely not be passed on to the tenants, so some temporary rent protection will be needed before there is excess supply.

The £30,000 a year is now a cost attached to the land and if land is still traded on a market that annual cost will reduce the land price by the yield. If we take a 5% yield which makes the reduction equate to 20 years' worth of LVT. That works out as a £600,000 drop in the land price, that's 20%. That's quite a lot, so even a 1% LVT would need to be phased in.

developments come forward, rents decrease (longer term) and more people can afford to rent on the market or even buy. In either case the tax payer doesn't have to pay out so much housing benefit (less people need it and the rent subsidies are lower). Also the need for state subsidies to provide affordable housing drops. And the bonus, money is raised through LVT.

Conversely, consider a future if LVT is not implemented: rising land prices mean rents go up, fewer people can get on the housing ladder therefore more people become tenants (this is already a trend in London, Bristol and perhaps elsewhere). That means more housing benefit is paid out; plus there are more tax payer subsidies to the house building companies (who end up paying the land owners) for affordable housing. Therefore the system we have now is clearly long term unsustainable unless the tax payer is willing to fork out more and more.

Implementing Land Value Tax requires a better and stronger Planning System[11] and we come to that next. In fact I'm beginning to wonder whether the Planning System should be completely re-purposed to make LVT work and thus bring down the price of land (in a city).

CHAPTER H2
THE PLANNING SYSTEM

The Planning System and specifically the top level document the NPPF (the National Planning Policy Framework) is constructed on a "you are free to do as you wish as long as you don't create harm. The harm has to have been pre-identified as a problem in the area". Given this is so close to my "freedom of opportunity unless you create harm to others" I was puzzled as to why such a good, in my view, principle can lead to such disastrous results. Is the concept wrong? Or are there problems in the implementation?

The disastrous results coming from the planning system are numerous and as follows: a 60% failure in provision of affordable homes; loss of nature; developers getting rich by sitting on land waiting for the price to go up when it is allocated for building; trying to cram more buildings in when we are full up; the need for 20% profit levels due to the risky nature of both speculative development and the precariousness of getting planning decisions; rents going up due to university expansion and other influxes of people (of which I was one in 1988 when I moved down from London); the perceived need to attract big money into the city and more...

There are hints of the problems in the National Planning Policy

---

11 For example if someone designates their land as a garden then it would have a lower value and attract less tax. The issue would be when they sell up and the next owner wishes to build on that garden. They would need to get planning permission and in one scheme of things perhaps pay some of the LVT accrued whilst it was a garden (that's for the experts to design).

Framework[12] itself. There is the presumption in favour of development, in practice that means granting planning permission unless the likely harm is so bad. But you can't simply predict harm. It has to have already been documented in the Local Plan and to do that you need examples that have already occurred[13] and are material planning considerations which link to an NPPF policy. This means we have to exclude harm of many kinds including some demographic imbalances, impact on land prices, harm of many sorts to other parties and currently even carbon dioxide emissions[14]. The NPPF and Local Plan can't adjust quickly enough.

There is also pressure on Local Planning Authorities (the regulatory body within the Council) to bring forward sufficient sites for building on, to keep the economy going, jobs and profits and thus not to provide for the needs of some people. In practice this means that land owners can offer their land to the Council to be reallocated from industrial to housing so the land available for building meets the targets. It doesn't mention that land owners become instant millionaires in the process, but that's what happens sometimes. And because the land price has gone up so much then a future developer can't make enough money to subsidise the needed affordable homes or connect to the heat network or plant enough trees.

There are good things too. Within the NPPF there are requirements to take account of market signals (at 31 and 60) to guide the next revision of the Local Plan. Market signals include changes in demand

---

12   Some of the NPPF 2019 clauses are at the centre of why I think the planning system is broken. Clause 11 says there must be a presumption towards sustainable development. That is interpreted as a presumption to grant if the harm is mitigated enough (via conditions explained in para 54). Harm depends on those defined in a LPA's Local Plan. To do that you follow para 16c which requires consulting businesses who often dilute the meaning of harm (Strategic businesses can effectively veto draft policy). At paragraphs 31 and 60 the Plan most respond to relevant market signals which is good but means if a new demand arises (like diesel generators) then to control it, it must go in the Plan first. And if there's nothing in the current Local Plan which says they bring harm then there's not much can be done. Clause 67 means LPAs need enough land identified for development to last 10 years. This means that land owners can volunteer up land that was for shops or industry and suggest it is used for housing leading to land price problems as discussed.

13   The reality of this means you can't predict a problem and put a policy into the Local Plan, you have to wait for the problem to happen, then document the harm, insert it into a new draft Local Plan, consult, deal with objections, moderate the mitigations required, re-consult, get it passed by the planning inspectors and then it's adopted. That is a 10 year process if you are quick!

14   Planning and Energy Act 2008: Government are considering (July 2020) whether this should limit LPAs to a 2050 deadline for buildings to have CO2 neutrality of if LPAs can set tighter deadlines (like Bristol's of 2030).

for land (less general industrial, more warehousing for example) and an aging population. You can't just ossify the city and watch it decline. Additionally much of planning is done in the public domain. The plans are online as are any objections, the officers write up their response and if it's a report to Committee then the meeting is in public too. I'm only aware of two applications (out of the hundred or more I helped decide) where I suspected the majority party had made their decision in advance. And in both cases a great deal of work had already been done to mitigate the harm.

But then there are the dreaded Planning Inspectors to whom developers run to crying if the Council's Planner, or more likely the Committee, has rejected their application. Unless it's a public inquiry then it's a paperwork exercise looking at the application, the site and the reasons for rejection. It is important to have an appeal system but it should consider people.

So to review the things wrong with the Planning System; one that sort of promotes "freedom to take opportunities without causing harm (that's been pre-identified)"? The bit in brackets is the problematic part. Here are three examples.

Firstly you will recall the diesel and gas generator sagas (in sections A and D) this was a type of harm not envisaged when the 2011 Local Plan was being compiled. The 2011 Local Plan is still in force in 2020. The NPPF 2019 says Local Plans should be updated every five years, yet the planning cycle seems to take more than five years.

University expansion was envisaged, but it seems the university's contribution to the 2011 Local Plan was written circa 2006 and it said it wasn't going to expand! Therefore there was no evidence for the LPA upon which to base policy in 2011.

Thirdly, a harm that was pre-identified was loss of tree cover, we had evidence too. In 2009/10 it was known that cities needed trees to mitigate the impact of climate change. I worked on that as Chair of the Tree Forum and the full story is in Appendix 6. So the 2011 Local Plan has the goal of increasing tree cover and some policies to protect trees and replace any trees that have to be felled. And the result? The measurements indicate tree cover has fallen.

So is there something wrong with the Planning system itself as a way of managing freedom without harm? Or are the problems primarily due to the market and price of land?

To me Belgrave Hill is the killer application, the example is in Appendix 18. Land under a cliff, bought and sold a number of times, then it gained planning permission, that ran out after three years and the appendix details the attempts to get new permission again. It was all driven by the land market, increasing prices and profit.

In this book I'm not into tweaks. I agree that's all you can do as a Councillor, but I want to seed the ideas of fundamental change. Some of the Planning System is good. But it doesn't serve its purpose (in cities, regarding affordable housing, nature, pollution and more). Why? It's because of the market we allow for land. Perhaps Land Value Tax would help? A high level could reduce land prices by 50%. I think we need to make land work for and benefit society as a whole, rather than just land owners, to an extent developers[15], and those wealthy enough to own their own homes. Something needs to be done about land prices[16].

CHAPTER H3

LAND: IS IT SUITED FOR A MARKET (WITH COMPETITION) OR SOME OTHER METHOD OF PROVISION?

We explored the benefits of using markets in detail in Section E, I somewhat unfairly left the business sector providing us with just cafés, perfumes, computer games and running shoes...There is, of course, much more that business can do (with its profit motive, tempered with

---

15   Occasionally I feel sorry for some developers. The system is designed for landowners and if the developer isn't the landowner they can get shafted too. But don't worry, this sympathy doesn't last long.
16   *Rethinking Planning for the 21st Century* (also footnote 2) has a section about a Development Tax (the commentary isn't particularly enthusiastic though). The proponents (Jamie Ratcliff and Reuben Young) have included more detail in an essay in https://policyexchange.org.uk/publication/planning-anew/ starting page 39. The money raised would be exclusively for affordable housing. I fear that will be ignored if other recommendations are accepted. Their approach might also be a block to development.

competition, the risk of bankruptcy[17] and all governed by marketplace management). Could markets ever work for land, in a city? Where land is scarce and surrounded by Green Belt (building on that Green Belt would cause harm). The NPPF spells out the priority of Green Belt quite clearly and poorly evidenced plans for building on the Green Belt is what did it in for the Joint Spatial Plan.

From Chapter E3: Our list of market failings include:

• *Basic R&D and seeding start-ups,*
• *Or when there is a common good like a park, police, defence...*
• *Where the product brings benefits to others like planting a tree or taking the bus (in economic parlance these are positive externalities).*
• *Where there is harm done to the environment, or harm to people (negative externalities), or positional and status goods.*
• *Or where there is little or no competition (e.g. an oligopoly), patents, barriers to entry or a natural monopoly.*
• *Where the bargaining powers of the buyer or seller are very unbalanced; often a problem when markets allocate resources to supplying what are needs to some people and wants to others, like homes: a home to live in is a need versus a holiday home is a want. It can also be an information imbalance perhaps due to false advertising or one party having hidden knowledge (e.g. about the state of the flat they are selling).*
• *When any faults in the product take a long time to become obvious (e.g. subsidence).*
• *When the protagonists become too important to let them fail. Bankruptcy and fear of it is an important check in the capitalist system. If they can't be allowed to go bust then maybe capitalism isn't the best mechanism.*
• *Or if switching (transaction) costs are high. This might limit the effectiveness of competition. Switching costs apply when it costs you time or money to switch provider. It's often easy to switch hairdresser, but more difficult to switch your job or home.*
• *And markets can cause resource shortages. This is also claimed as a*

---

17   If you can't go bankrupt, too big to fail, then the risk profile of big decisions is changed. Success and the directors win big time, failure and the public lose big time.

benefit of markets. In a resource shortage the price rockets, usage falls and people are incentivised to use or develop alternatives or substitutes. But this whole process can harm sections of society and the big example is land.

Let's apply the above list of known problems with markets to land (in a city).

Land in a city: it's a resource that's in short supply and constrained by Green Belt often, and worse there are few alternatives! Build up and the costs of building increase; build down, basements and similar brings lack of light. Build more densely, this is needed anyway to ensure public transport is more efficient and it means less space[18] for the car. So building more densely provides some positives[19].

This shortage of supply often leads to unbalanced bargaining power between buyer and seller, its high cost brings negative externalities especially to the environment (trees, parks) and to those who don't earn enough to afford the prices. The capitalist answer is these people should leave the city altogether or move to the outskirts and cycle/get the bus in. If only bus services were regular, reliable and inexpensive – yes, if only; or there were dedicated cycle paths.

The shortage of supply and consequent high price can also mean certain land locations lend status to the occupant whether a business or resident. Status (positional) goods can have negative consequences on others.

Switching costs: If you lease premises and you get an increased rent demand you can't up and move location easily. It's not impossible, but it's expensive. There's also stamp duty which can cost 5% or more sometimes.

So the main market failures are short supply (and so lack of competition); lack of alternatives; unbalanced bargaining power especially when dealing with homes which are a need; negative externalities, status and high switching costs. That's quite some list;

18   As space is the critical resource in a city it should be one key measure for most decisions, for example deciding which are better transport options, which one uses the least space per 1,000 people.
19   And negatives of course, especially if the design and public space elements are poor.

enough to indicate that a market will function poorly, or even not work at all (in a city). So if it has to be a market then it needs strict marketplace management to protect third parties and those who need land for their business. I have seen little in the way of market management; there is stamp duty (tax) and of course the planning system which creates those millionaires[20] and is never up to date. Both can make the problems worse.

The Government have, in some small way, recognised this market failure. They have created an organisation called Homes England. This is the one that gives grants to local authorities and developers to transfer properties that were for the market to become subsidised affordable homes. Homes England[21] is also intervening in the land market by buying it up itself to get more homes built. It is therefore operating as a land buying business and is effectively a supplier to the big builders. In April 2020 it announced £180 million of land purchases to unblock 19 sites around the UK, about 5,000 homes, and many to be affordable (to the Government's definition).

Bristol's site, Brislington Meadows, is 10 hectares to be 300 homes and 30% of them affordable. So how is it that such sites can become stuck? Councillor Paul Smith, Bristol's Cabinet member for Homes and Housing, explained to me that this one is a difficult site with a stream running through the middle and there is a desire by the LPA to create a high quality public space that links up to a park and allotments (already in existence). The main owners of the site were responding quite slowly and presumably didn't have the same objectives, although Paul didn't say this. I would imagine they were trying to maximise land value: public space and open streams don't do that. That illustrates the difference between homes with space and making a community versus housing which can try to pack 'em in like sardines.

I have heard it argued that some land sites in a city operate akin to a monopoly. For example, a particular corner site in a high street could

20   A land and property specialist revels in telling his clients how to make money out of land and planning: https://www.gscgrays.co.uk/2017/12/18/selling-land-for-development-optimizing-the-returns/
21   https://www.constructionenquirer.com/2020/04/15/homes-england-steps-in-to-save-19-stalled-housing-sites/
And: https://constructionreviewonline.com/2020/04/homes-england-signs-us-249-5m-agreement-for-housing-scheme-in-england/

be the best site for a key shop or restaurant. The rent for this site is higher because the footfall is higher. The harder the shopkeeper works then, in the long term, the higher the rent that he or she is charged. This is Ricardo's Law[22] of Rent (originally about agricultural land) at play. Another example is a landowner holding out for a higher price if it is the last segment needed to enable a major development. LPAs do have compulsory purchase powers as used on an ex-hotel recently in Bristol (to enable improvements to Temple Way). But do these examples make a case for the argument that a plot of land in a city is a monopoly? If they did, it would be a slam dunk argument for very tight regulation and possibly even nationalisation. I'm not sure. Nevertheless I think there are enough market failings to justify a tightly managed marketplace for land including Land Value Tax.

A managed marketplace involves having a regulator, rules and powers. The types of rules usually are to benefit the customer, so that would include the future land buyer and the land user (the tenant or leaseholder). Additionally it should include issues like harm from externalities (to nature and to the 60% looking for affordable housing), management of monopolies and land shortages. This might require that the market itself for buying, registering and selling land becomes more open and transparent.

Marketplace management would include extensive land purchasing, house building and involvement by the state (as a competitor to the private sector). We see in Appendix 14 that many Councils were and are purchasing retail and commercial premises. This could be a good thing if they are deliberately buying them up cheaply to then repurpose the land or buildings for new uses. The Council then becomes the landowner. It would create a more flexible market for land too.

Extra burdens on the land owner from the regulator could further bring the price of land down. That is a good thing. The taxation raised from land could pay for the marketplace management and so go towards sustainable transport and public realm improvements, bringing better environments for all and to enable those on lower incomes to get to

---

22　I have always thought it strange that economists call their theories laws.

their place of work, should such a thing still exist.

Regulation of the land marketplace is key, but could we make it work? Another solution is to nationalise it (technically it is all legally owned by the Queen anyway[23]) and lease out parcels. Reformers and revolutionaries you decide. But it's vital you don't let the economic management of this asset class slip back into the bad old ways.

COMMENTS ON LAND AND PLANNING:

Nationally, if we retain a market for land it requires a regulator with goals to minimise harm from all the forms of market failure. We also need Land Value Tax (in lieu of not nationalising land) to pay for the Land Regulator[24] and appropriate interventions.

Locally, the Local Planning system requires reform and needs to be more flexible about identifying some of this harm in advance and collecting evidence to support it. The Council can buy up land where it is cheap and is in need of regeneration, for example those shopping centres and offices that are clearly unsustainable. The Council should also help reduce the risk of developments in return for the developer accepting a lower profit margin and thus more affordable houses. Perhaps a faster planning process and a guarantee to buy the whole block in cash at near-affordable housing values if the developer can't sell.

Office conversions (to dwellings) don't currently need planning permission in England[25]. This is already leading to poor quality and low levels of affordable housing (see conclusion of G12). I would expect a rush to close offices and convert to homes which, if unplanned, will not end happily.

---

23 I remember learning this in my law studies. It's explained nicely here: https://www.highlandtitles.com/blog/this-land-aint-your-land-part-1/
24 To be called *ofland* perhaps?
25 Presumably, and Wales?

CHAPTER H4

AND WHAT ABOUT DEMOCRACY?

"Government of the people, by the people, for the people"

Gettysburg Address by President Abraham Lincoln, Nov 19th 1863. It seems to me we have gotten lost, both nations.

In this book we have covered the Mathematics of Power[26], the importance of scrutiny for getting good law and the need for open and transparent government. Even if the system means you need 51% of the vote to be leader you will still be tempted to favour some groups and so openness and scrutiny (being held to account) are vital. The other type of scrutiny, policy development, is also needed to ensure more people from a wider cross section participate earlier on to get better law.

Sections A, B and C covered examples where this is not working[27].

The ability of officers, Mayors and decision makers to hide information, all legally mind you, means that elected representatives don't know what's going on. If they don't know, how are the voters supposed to know?

The press work hard and since 2019 Bristol has two dedicated Local Democracy Reporters[28]: Adam and Amanda, both mentioned earlier. All paid for via the BBC as a condition of their charter.

Between the two of them they try to attend nearly every meeting and write them up, and add an attention-grabbing twist (that's not easy). They too are excluded if information is declared exempt (see Bristol Energy C6 and C7), but they do try to be fair to both sides of the story. What they write up isn't always published as the newspapers are businesses too looking to attract readers and advertisers. However hard you try, some boring stories just aren't of appeal, even if they are 'in the

---

26 Four examples I have seen are: Freeports (B3) and donations; Jenrick and his planning decision (B2) and donations; millionaires from land price increases with or without planning bonanzas (H intro) and RICS (G7 and G8) and their stamp duty on buildings for rent, so less affordable housing. With 30% of the vote and power for so many years (over the long term), this is what you get. It's not one off's, it's a consistent system favouring the supporters of the Conservatives, state capture.

27 At the end of this section I provide a list of issues I have encountered. I'm sure it's a fraction of the stuff out here that needs to be amended.

28 https://www.bbc.com/lnp/ldrs

public interest'. And the ones that are attractive and interest the public are often the ones the administration would prefer to keep secret. It's a tough job and you don't get thanks for holding regimes to account. In this sound-bite dominated world, mayoral advisors get touchy. The first announcement is often the one that sticks in the public's mind, but as Adam found out, journalists can get taken to task if they get it even slightly wrong[29].

Democracy has to start with a commitment to an open and transparent state. Whilst I agree some personal information should be confidential like medical records, I would challenge financial secrecy. That would be one of the 'costs' of doing business with an authority which is, after all, supposedly for the people. It's not private; it's ours (or should be). It is not impossible to design a process during procurement where Councillors can see what's being negotiated, input if appropriate and then once agreed it becomes public. This should certainly apply to advice from consultants. As far as I know it is not PwC's fault that the Council won't release their 2015 advice to the Mayor about prospects for Bristol Energy. One reason I was told was that the information is owned by Bristol Energy itself which is 100% owned by the Council. The reason changed to protecting shareholder value. Then an article[30] from a tax expert said that any prospective buyer wouldn't care about how well or badly the business had been run. Legal are playing games within that 1972 Act.

The same should go for salaries and leaving packages. The cover up over Anna Klonowski's payoff is purely down to trying to save the embarrassment of the regime and/or officers concerned. Poor Anna is innocent as far as I'm aware, she negotiated a payoff in good faith and presumably was contracted to keep quiet and has done so.

In conjunction with openness and transparency should also come good, early scrutiny. Whether that be by elected representatives or by expert members of the public, it should involve those from different walks

---

29   Adam Postans wrote an article about the new Council tip, the regime called it a reuse and recycling centre and took him to task during a June 2019 Cabinet meeting.

30   https://www.bristolpost.co.uk/news/bristol-news/warning-redundancies-bristol-energy-city-4217358

of life to give a better range of views. In Section C we saw the errors that occur because the people questioning early on, assuming they did, were not from a wide enough group. Citizens' Juries and Assemblies[31] have been used in some countries to do this better, most notably in Ireland regarding the national conversation and the referendum decision on abortion.

I want to come back to Citizens Assemblies later as they do require the citizens to be engaged, devote time and for the outcome to be worthwhile. These require a change to society and the current democratic system.

Another form of scrutiny is public consultation, but the way this is often done, at least here in Bristol, is a survey and selection of different options. It has a value but is normally done too late to shape policy, more to help shape the message. The footnote[32] refers to a recent Council Tax consultation. Although I agree with the base increase of two percent, the consultation framework was done because it is a legal necessity. I wonder what would have happened had a majority voted for zero percent?

Representative democracy was set up hundreds of years ago so busy people could get on with making money and send their chosen person to Parliament to defend their cash from the king who often wanted to spend it on waging wars. Or so it seems to me. Is it now time for people to get more involved in local decision making? Technology and spare time (on average) are progressing and we are warned that with the coming of robots many of us will be out of a job anyway. What better than using time released to volunteer for a charity, visit friends and

---

31   A citizens' assembly is a group of people who are brought together to discuss an issue or issues, and reach a conclusion about what they think should happen. The people who take part are chosen so they reflect the wider population – in terms of demographics (e.g. age, gender, ethnicity, social class) and sometimes relevant attitudes (e.g. preferences for a small or large state). https://www.parliament.uk/business/committees/committees-a-z/commons-select/housing-communities-and-local-government-committee/citizens-assembly-faq-17-19/

32   Consultation like the 2019 consultation about the 20/21 budget where the number one choice voted for was no Council tax increase. The votes for choices two and three added together came to more. (These were two percent and one percent respectively) and that combined tally was used to justify that the majority of people supported a Council Tax increase and so it was put up two percent (social care precept went up two percent as well). The Mayor needed two percent. If over 50% had voted for no increase would he have not put it up? Consultations like this lead to a very cynical electorate – what's the point?

relatives and participate in local decision making[33]. Appendices 7, 8 and 9 tell the story, starting in 2009, of a Council success in local decision making that they then managed to turn into a failure. Read it; the lesson I took from it was that local decision making depends on getting the mix right: quality of information, the right people and allowing it to have an impact, to things get done: dynamic if you like. Add too much formality and you kill the goose that lays the golden egg.

CHAPTER H5
BALANCING FREEDOM OF OPPORTUNITY WITH AVOIDANCE OF HARM

Life would be very boring and bureaucratic if freedom without doing harm were governed by documents like the planning policies we discussed earlier. There have to be less clunky ways of doing it. The good news is there is. There's the use of social value which we discussed in Chapter E5. Just to remind you, it is currently being used by some Councils and other government bodies to guide their purchasing decisions. For example, in procuring meals for schools there might be two competing suppliers: one uses factory farmed chickens, has workers on zero hours contracts and transports the products vast distances using vehicles powered by fossil fuels. The other supplier is more expensive and provides meals using free range chicken, has better employee conditions and employs and sources much locally so less food miles; it uses biodiesel for its transport. The second supplier costs the Council more but the extra social value[34] more than outweighs that purchase cost difference. Social value factors are set to a national framework, can be adjusted locally, but needs to be validated nationally.

How could such a system be used in the private sector? If the marketplaces were managed to some extent then regulators could check aspects of social value, for example that waste disposal companies have

33 Especially if paid to do it.
34 Which includes the externalities, positive and negative and maybe other market failure effects too.

picked up and disposed of items correctly, with certificates and paid their landfill tax. Those payments could then subsidise local re-use, refurbishment and recycling centres (not tips Adam[35]). Supermarkets could be asked to do the same for their food waste, and to rationalise the different types of plastic packaging used to keep produce fresh. It doesn't take too much imagination that where a marketplace is managed then the ombudsman, regulator or whatever we call them can put in schemes using social value to incentivise the reduction of harm to people, society and the environment.

I hear cries of, "but that will put our costs up", and indeed it will because the costs of harm to people and to the environment, which are currently borne by society and often the poorest, will be paid for by the industry: a form of polluter pays and consumers will pay the extra. You can choose not to consume a product, but you cannot choose if the pollution or fly-tipping is where you live. This alternative reduces costs to the state[36] of sorting out the waste, litter, air pollution and reduces costs to the NHS too. In both cases it's less burden on the tax payer. The cost is borne by the businesses and onto the consumer instead. As part of this brave new world the consumer would need to earn more either through wages, salary or some form of basic income.

Where it is less clear is whether harm that warrants action could be decided by Citizens' Juries, Councils or local partnerships depending on the extent of the problem. Perhaps the following might prompt further deliberation: for local problems like noise from pubs and bars and their general opening hours for example, they could be decided by a local committee; granted powers and guidelines by the Council (or even government) and guided by policies on how the issue might be managed: a charge, duty, a tax or an outright ban. It's going to be a difficult balance between bureaucracy, fairness and enthusiasm. It was bureaucracy that strangled the neighbourhood partnerships (Appendices 7 to 9).

Enough on mechanisms and back to principles: Oxford economics lecturer, Kate Raworth, published her opus *Doughnut Economics* in 2017,

35   This references footnote 29 a page or two earlier. It's an attempt at humour!
36   The state is funded by the tax payer remember.

which has gone on to be a best seller, and apparently it has been adopted in 2020 by Amsterdam as a sustainable framework for running the city. Kate describes the economy as something that should be run at a level that allows people their basic needs and more, i.e. their wants, up to a level that is sustainable within the local and wider environment. Normally I give these "Green Economics" books short shrift, mainly because they don't seem to allow for the more negative aspects of human nature (which includes some selfishness, greed, material goals as well as priority for your own children). But slowly Kate's book has grown on me especially in the terms of needs versus wants. In 2015 I had the difference between needs and wants hammered home by Tamara during a talk I was giving, I thanked her back in Chapter E2.

Kate describes a base level, she calls it the social foundation, it looks like it corresponds in my terms to needs. The ecological ceiling, she calls it, is what I call harm, increasing harm as you get towards it and if too much then break through into an unsustainable situation. Kate's ecological ceiling is environment based. But there are other things that can be harmed too like health, freedom of opportunity, housing and aspects of quality of life. But my social ceilings are semantics really, so I think I am broadly won over to *Doughnut Economics* and want to marry it up with the ideas of Mariana Mazzucato with her search for a theory of value. Roll them in with freedom of opportunity[37] to do what fulfils you as long as you don't harm others, including their opportunities and maybe, just maybe?

This is not for me to decide what we should do. It's for the population through a national debate. We can't trust our politicians to do the thinking for us. They got us into this situation. Only trust them if you want to return to how things were before Covid-19 which, apparently (according to Sky News[38] reporting on a survey by the RSA[39] on the 16th April 2020) only 9% of people want to do). Transformation will mean

---

37   As a passing thought. Economics is based on utility. I wonder what it would look like if it were based on Freedom of Opportunity and harm? Any takers?

38   https://news.sky.com/story/coronavirus-only-9-of-britons-want-life-to-return-to-normal-once-lockdown-is-over-11974459

39   RSA https://www.thersa.org/about-us ; is a not for profit organisation which looks to help society create a better future, I am a fellow of the RSA.

we will need to change the economic and political system (it is one large all-encompassing system, remember).

There are those with vested interests who want things to stay as they are. I have seen some of this first hand and we have all read about the way big business and rich people fund political parties, lobby them, sponsorship and the jobs politicians get afterwards and the peerage system too. It's worse because the good guys have to behave this way too. It is inherent in a voting system where 30% can select their leader, it's the maths. Add to that all the disinformation and it does make it difficult to see a way forward.

The political system in the UK allows a Government with the support of 30% of the electorate[40] (remember 25% don't vote). That's not as low a level of support as a dictator with military power, but it isn't an encompassing 51% or more. But some of us voters don't want change, better the devil you know, or they fear for their property if a radical government got into power. So whilst not liking the Conservatives perhaps they find the offers from the other parties even less appealing.

So how do we get out of this swamp[41]?

CHAPTER H6
HOW TO DRAIN THE SWAMP (1)

It's time for another story. This one illustrates a part of where we are now, which is a sorry state, and offers an option for where we could be; and if you want to get from here to there, where better place to start, than on the train.

This is a chronicle encompassing a little less than three hours on the campaign trail during the December 2019 General Election. I was not a candidate, but I was helping one out. I learned a lot from the experience and I hope you draw similar lessons.

The hustings, 5th December 2019 11:29am

40   Back to the Mathematics of Power chapter B1
41   If you think we are in one.

"We are now arriving at Filton Abbeywood", came the muffled announcement. The train started to slow in the usual, juddery way. Papers are all over the table and on the seat next to me. A slight panic, I gather myself and shove all my notes back into the bag. We stopped, with a final jolt just enough to knock me off balance, I still had my hat, iPad, coat, scarf and bag to grab and get down the corridor before people began to board the train. Thankfully my hat stayed on my head and my arms took the rest. "Sorry, sorry", I politely barged through, the door was still open and then …freedom. Well, the platform anyway and a bench to get everything on and into where it should be.

Preparation, so they say, prevents piss poor performance. So now where to go? North it had looked like from the map, the sun was out, presumably roughly south and to the west is a high fence and a housing estate. I knew from previous estates that if I attempted a shortcut through I'd get lost. I had already set myself a one mile acclimatisation hike without needing any extra distance.

Filton reminded me of parts of Essex where I'd grown up; sort of familiar in a way. I arrived at the College. Half an hour early, a very welcoming receptionist, and after signing in I went to the loo and was just about to go in when I met the Principal. "Ah, Mr Stevens, welcome, come into my office". I explained that I needed to go into other room first, he nodded.

Three minutes later, I'd given him a slightly wet handshake, I never could get them properly dry after washing[42] them. The Principal explained how the hustings were going to work. Each of the four of us would do a five minute introduction to the party's policies and then answer questions. I didn't hear anything after that. They hadn't told me about a five minute introduction, they being the Green Party. Actually they hadn't told me much, I was standing in for the candidate who had another appointment, I'd offered to help at the last moment. I've never done a hustings before, never, I didn't need to do one before becoming Councillor in 2016. Perhaps I should have watched some on television but I find them pretty boring, badly run and just arguing soundbites

42   May 2020 – I can now!

with one another.

The Principal was slightly surprised that I hadn't prepared an opening but allowed me 10 minutes to collect my thoughts. I had prepared, my god, I had prepared, just not an opening, I almost knew the manifesto off by heart, in fact I'd unknowingly helped write a small part of it. You may recall the mention of Land Value Tax. But I'd never expected our leaders to use it.

Filton and Bradley Stoke (abbreviated FaBS) is just north of the City of Bristol. I knew about some issues in depth, the likely forthcoming arena, the traffic problems, their worsening, the poor public transport, that it was 51% Remain and that major employers were sending strong messages to Government; some for Brexit, some I'm told with money for the party campaigns and some for Remain.

I skimmed my seven pages of notes, put rings around the points I wanted to say and then wrote some bullet points. Mhairi arrived. Mhairi, pronounced Vaari, she's Scottish and is the Labour candidate for this constituency. She was surprised to see me, Mhairi and I are both Councillors in Bristol and I have respect for what she tried to do locally for transport and saving street trees (see Appendix 1 and 2). I tried to signal to her that I was "on her side", we were joking about our scarfs, hers was green and mine was red and I thanked her for saving Bristol's trees about two years earlier.

The strategy that had been planned a few days ago was that I would attack the Conservative candidate Jack Lopresti, leave Labour alone. The aim was to leave a good impression of the Greens but ideally to influence Tory voters so they would consider voting Labour. Strange you might think but that's one of the by-products of a first past the post voting system. Greens got about 3% in FaBS before, we couldn't win but we could perhaps shift a few votes away from Jack the Conservative MP to Mhairi the Labour challenger who was just a few per cent behind. And so why didn't we stand down are you asking? Please don't ask because the logic inexorably shifts to why have a Green Party at all and that gets uncomfortable.

CHAPTER H7
HOW TO DRAIN THE SWAMP (2)
– UP ON THE PODIUM

It's now 12:30. I'm in front of maybe 150 people, perhaps 20 teachers and staff, most of the rest are students who profess to be old enough to vote. Although this was open to the entire College, it was primarily part of the students' politics class.

The chair is the Head of Politics and after a short introduction he said, "let's start with Clive". Here's a precis of my five minutes.

"First eh, Greens should always be first", a few laughed, it was enough to settle me down, "There are six key points I want to make; firstly Greens want to modify the economic system so that it recognises the guardianship of the environment and resources for the future and provides fairness of opportunity, an opportunity less linked to your parent's wealth. That leads us into a changed tax system with a universal income of £89 a week whatever you are doing: student, out of work, artisan, entrepreneur or wind turbine engineer. It takes pressure off you when looking for jobs and gives you more freedom, one aspect of fairness. In return tax will remain at 20% but start on income over and above the universal income level, most people will be better off. This will be paid in part from a fossil fuel tax which will incentivise use of renewable resources, reuse and recycling.

Thirdly we recognise that the first purpose of any Government is defence of the realm. We do question though whether in this age of wars fought in cyberspace and guerrilla tactics whether the nuclear deterrent is value for money. Fourthly we are strong on education. It should start at age six, preschool before then and be free all the way. The country needs people who are skilled in the renewable based economy, technology, fitters, inventors, entrepreneurs.

Greens, like Labour, have a new deal (modelled on Roosevelt's 1930's new deal for the USA), with exciting investments in new energy like wind, waves, solar, energy storage and perhaps hydrogen to be the solution for when the sun doesn't shine and the wind doesn't blow. Transport provision needs to be more cooperative, in the centre of the city we dread the idea of everyone having an electric car; the congestion and space used would be overwhelming. Active transport and more regular and cheaper public transport are the answers. Here in Filton you too need better public transport, as I am discovering.

And last but not least a democracy based on cooperation, a strength which has enabled human beings to be dominant on this planet. Proportional representation leads to cooperative government, we believe in the supremacy of parliament, the 650 MPs and that the prime minister and the executive are beholden to them. Better cooperation is key to a sustainable and exciting future."

There followed a round of applause so that helped my nerves too. Some questions came in, mainly aimed at the Conservative. I guess being at a Further Education College which has suffered huge funding cuts, plus an audience including teachers and lecturers, it would be tough to be a Tory. I managed to land a few soft blows on Jack too.

The first question was about why was so much food is available from New Zealand and other far-away places, motivated by concern about food miles. That was answered by Jack who said that the Conservatives want to encourage Buying British. I asked for the mic:

"Of course with a Conservative Brexit you will be getting many more free trade deals from far flung places and see even more food coming in from New Zealand."

Jack, without the mic, shouted out "and exports too", but he had lost and shown that aspect of Tory policy to be completely hollow. Louise the Lib Dem added that we were just a few miles from Wales who farm perfectly delicious lamb so why do we need all these trade deals? New Zealand versus Wales is always a good rugby match, we didn't descend into a scrum and anyway three of us piling onto Jack wasn't fair.

Jack then managed to get in his soundbite about Jeremy Corbyn being useless for defence of the realm, Jack has done a stint in Afghanistan and is active in supporting the arms industry so he knows a thing or two, but his accusation rang hollow. Mhairi was indignant and I looked to her sympathetically in front of a doubtful audience most of whom didn't believe Jack and those that did stayed silent.

I justified higher taxes on the rich saying that the first reason for Government was defence and law. The rich have many more assets and so should pay more for their protection.

But the moral of this story isn't about the reasons for the Greens and knocking the Tories, I have done that in previous chapters, it's about the principle of being in a General Election and having to have a strategy to not harm one competitor (indeed to boost them if I could), and to gang up on and harm the other competitor. I doubt if the Green voters of FaBS would want me to promote Labour, the Labour ones would. This is the bizarre consequence of first past the post voting system that as a Green I actually wanted to help Labour win.

But forgive me one final self-pat on the back. Right at the end the Principal asked each of us to sum up what our parties stand for.

Jack was first,

"Aspiration and opportunity",

he said, then Louise, Mhairi and me. I'm afraid I didn't listen, I was busy scripting my thirty seconds.

"Aspiration and opportunity",

I said with a deliberate short pause to let it sink in,

"Aspiration and opportunity based on a foundation where we protect the environment, resources and offer fair opportunity to all".

I got the biggest round of applause of the day, or so it seemed.

Hopefully, Molly in Stroud and Carla in Bristol West, the two Green candidates who stood a chance of winning in constituencies nearby would be impressed with that positive message full of hope.

Back to tactical voting and tactical hustings. I am writing this on the Sunday morning before the General Election of 2019. I should be out canvassing with my Green colleagues. It has just rained briefly. I'm looking for excuses to not go out. Here in Bristol West it's Green vs Labour, the Lib Dems have stood down. Two parties who agree on much (not everything of course) slogging it out. But the real enemy, in my opinion, are the Conservatives. I'm wondering if it is hypocritical attacking Labour in Bristol West when three days earlier I was trying to help them up in FaBS. Perhaps not phoney because it's the political system that forces this behaviour. Many can't vote for who they would like, much of the talk is of tactical voting and like in FaBS there is tactical messaging from candidates and their representatives too. It seems a complete mess and surely needs changing.

The result of my Sunday 8th quandary was: it continued to rain on and off, but the showers were heavy. I continued pondering, then I sent a text and after a swift lunch I was out canvassing for the Greens. I spoke to maybe 10 people that afternoon, most addresses didn't answer, either out or hiding. Nine were definitely going to vote Green, they said. I came back a little damp to the local HQ, took some tea and cake and chatted. It's good to canvas and talk to real people. It's good to be in the Green Party and having climbed out of my Green hole in Filton questioning everything, I was now nice and safe back in with the rest of my pals. On Sunday the 8th I was not leaving the Green Party.

The General Election was on the 12th and resulted in: Jack Lopresti holding his seat in FaBS, Molly and Carla not winning Stroud, nor Bristol West. And as you all know Boris Johnson increased his majority.

CHAPTER H8
HOW TO DRAIN THE SWAMP (3) ?

Thoroughly depressed by the General Election result, I nearly joined Labour. Why I didn't was down to the counselling and persuasion skills of our local leader, Councillor Eleanor Combley. I did produce a blog which, under lots of advice from colleagues, was never published. I have adapted it for 2020. It was originally scripted as a letter to Labour members to vote for a moderate leader. They did that without needing my advice. Here is an edited version that is relevant to Labour gaining power. I feel nervous sharing it with you, primarily because up to now the whole book has been based on evidence; first-hand experience of what I read, saw and heard. This chapter and the next are opinion and assumption. So with that caveat here's my opinion:

"Dear Labour Party,

In late 2024 or perhaps earlier around May 2024, after 14 years of Tory rule, Boris will call an election.

So what, my Labour friends, should you do between now and then?

Greens, Lib Dems, SNP and the Brexit Party (or whatever Nigel concocts this time), are all knocking on your door asking for proportional representation[43] (PR) for national elections.

Whether you accept PR or not at Conference, it would need to be adopted as policy and then probably a preferred form chosen. You can get bogged down for years in that. And some Labour activists will fight PR all the way. You see it would mean dropping their socialist dream. For them that dream is still possible with our first past the post voting system for MPs. To achieve it merely requires enough dissatisfaction with the Tories so that in 2024 Labour win say 35% of the vote with Conservatives down at 30%, that would be just enough to get a majority working with the SNP. If you live in that dream world, the one that looks forward to the Socialist

---

43   There's very good work done by a not-for-profit organisation called Make Votes Matter. If you are interested in knowing more and then would like to volunteer do get in touch with them. I have found them very good.

Utopia of the UK it seems wholly possible, especially with an electorate in 2024 having lived through so many years of Tory inequalities[44], more markets, NHS dismantling, rich people's donations, favours and more.

Those dreamers, a minority, but still influential, would fight PR all the way. You see if Labour embraces PR it would mean Labour needing to win a majority[45] in 2024 with the Scottish Nationalists, then implementing PR via a referendum and proceeding to give up the chance of "absolute power", never ever again getting an absolute majority and thus giving up on the socialist[46] mission forever. Which I think is against the founding ideals[47] of the Labour Party.

My message to Labour's dreamers is you can't achieve anything my comrades unless you get into power. So whether or not you adopt PR the key issue is how to get elected. This is my suggestion:

How to get into power in 2024?

And to inject a little humour into these sombre times; A Walsall[48] Pact, the very term surely warms the cockles of left winger's heart, a pact between all anti-Tory parties for 2024 where only one of the Pact will stand in each constituency: Them versus the Tories. So the SNP is unchallenged in Scotland, assuming Scotland is still part of the UK. Labour unchallenged in say nearly 500 seats, the Lib Dems in say 80 and Greens in say 10 or 15. Perhaps Plaid Cymru would join in too? The Walsall Pact, to be signed in the West Midlands, not Poland, of course, would allow the parties to fight like cats and dogs locally for councillors and Mayors but when it comes to national elections the 2024 candidates are chosen to maximise the "Pact" vote. This is similar to the idea of a Progressive Alliance but that is a confused idea; for many in Labour such an alliance is of left wingers,

---

44   And their Covid-19 response as well.
45   With the Scottish Nationalists who are not socialist https://en.wikipedia.org/wiki/Scottish_National_Party#Social_policies
46   On the basis it will take more than five years to implement. And in 2029 perhaps in Government but with the Lib Dems and Scottish Nationalists there may not be support.
47   The commitment to Socialism was officially dropped in 1992 (old Clause IV) but there will be plenty I'm sure who want to go back to the good old days. https://en.wikipedia.org/wiki/Labour_Party_(UK)#Ideology
48   I mean this as a joke but to make the point about needing to appeal to different segments within the Labour Party. Interestingly, Labour members have just voted for a PR system for their internal elections to their National Executive Committee. According to the article the left wingers aren't happy with that either. https://labourlist.org/2020/06/labour-nec-changes-voting-system-for-internal-elections-in-starmer-win/

whereas for the other parties it means left wingers who support PR. Such a mismatch of visions is doomed to fail.

Back to our Pact; it needn't even include a PR referendum in the manifesto, although that might be a request from the smaller parties wishing to join. But imagine a 2024 Government with 350 Labour, 50 SNP, 50 LD, 5 Green. Labour would have a majority. A majority! A vision to unite the Labour left, the Labour centre and right. You can all agree on that surely? Even if Labour got just 300 seats you could still form a Government with your friends.

And then in power, yes in power, you can discuss with your coalition partners whether to have a PR Referendum. If not you will need another Pact in 2029 or if you do implement PR you could stay in power as the major party potentially for decades.

So dear Labour, please unite around the idea of a national electoral pact and charge your new leader to negotiate it.

Although proportional representation would change the Mathematics of Power (so 51% of the vote is required) there is no reason why electors would vote for parties proposing it in a General Election. Some will be frightened. I think Labour need to get into power with a pact and then decide with their partners whether to have a PR referendum once in power. If it is a requirement of the Scottish Nationalists then as part of their post-election negotiations then that might be the deal clincher?

Comment: But what are the chances of that, of a pact working?

CHAPTER H9
FAILING ALL THAT

What if a pact can't be agreed? Tribal loyalties in politics do run deep, I discovered that myself, I was as group-think as the best of them during the three years from late 2015 to 2018. But I escaped that mentality, yes I really mean that word: escaped. It doesn't mean I'm not a Green. In fact I'm still not quite sure as to which party to be in (if any). But for the moment it's the Greens as they let me say what I think (within reason) and have great policies. But don't have much power.

I escaped by resurrecting my old network of friends who tested me in a friendly but challenging way. I read non-Green newspapers, courted non-Green conversation and thought non-Green thoughts. It made me better at scrutiny, and by 2019 I think it made me a better Councillor. But that's me, I've always been open to seeing many sides to a story; I fear the pact idea will be pretty much unacceptable to tribal Greens and Lib Dems and to Labour? Why should Labour change (their activists will say)?

In a blog[49] by Martin Farley, Green Party, someone whose ideas I generally like and with whom I have worked; he argues that in the 2019 election in constituencies where Greens helped Labour by standing down[50] it actually helped the Tories win! If that's true and if the Labour vote suffered in areas where the Greens stood down that really hurts the idea of a pact. I have asked Martin a few questions about his analysis but the answers require further number crunching.

So what's going on? In Bristol West, where Greens came second to Labour and the Lib Dems stood down, many Lib Dem activists switched to helping their candidates in other constituencies. They didn't help the Green campaign one iota, apart from not being on the ballot paper (which was a big help). As far as I'm aware in the places where the Greens stood down, the Green activists didn't help the Lib Dems either, they too went to other constituencies to fight, many came to Bristol West to help Carla's campaign. So thank you for that, the Green vote doubled from 2017 to about 20%.

Tribalism means you will rarely see Green activists campaigning for Lib Dems, nor for Labour. I think my hour at the hustings in Filton and Bradley Stoke was an exception (by me, out of the bubble) and it would be interesting to note if the audience got the message from me about,

49   https://medium.com/@martin_farley/labouring-under-a-false-pretense-how-stepping-aside-for-labour-helped-the-tories-and-hurt-the-5e829668e45e
50   So where Greens stood down, the main parties of choice were Conservative, Labour and Lib Dem.

"Like your Greens, but vote Labour"; maybe too complex?

You won't get Lib Dem activists supporting Greens nor Labour and definitely won't get Labour activists helping either of us. Yet there has been one example of tremendous cooperation by parties in my time. That was the 2016 EU Referendum. The night before the count I was out with Green colleagues dancing and singing along with Labour activists too, just outside Sainsbury if I recall. Carla was there, looking somewhat bemused at the behaviour of a then 57 year old. Remain lost. But we collaborated, campaigned and cavorted together.

That my Labour friends, is my hope if you can't agree to a pact: then let's stride into the 2024 general election as part of an alliance asking for people to campaign and vote for an alliance, with a separate name, so more than a mere pact. Just stepping down in constituencies is not enough but appearing on a ballot paper under a different name e.g. Left of Centre Alliance, or Reformist Alliance. Just like the Remain and Leave badges in 2016.

Without something like that I fear we will wait even longer, further letting down our voters. Remember that normally 50% or more vote "not Conservative". I would like to avoid a revolution due to the unintended consequences. Reform, if possible, is better.

So that's my dream, I worry[51] that it will remain a dream but let's get Brexit done, get Covid-19[52] done and let's see what can be done enthused by the fear of even more years of Conservative rule.

And if an alliance can't be formed?

CHAPTER H10
LOCAL INTERVENTIONS

Whoever is in charge nationally, whether pact or no pact, alliance or no alliance, please make use of the testimony I have presented in this book (and the appendices), add it to other evidence and do something.

---

51   For the futures of my children and their future progeny.
52   With huge sympathies to those who have lost loved ones to this modern day plague.

The problems I've described in this book are not just Bristol's, many are shared by the inhabitants of cities across the country, perhaps across the world. I think it's worthwhile if the leaders of the UK's Core Cities discuss some of these (plus other issues I've not touched upon, like discrimination).

Some of these harms might also be affecting rural areas. Sorry I haven't covered that, it's just not my area of expertise. I suspect openness, poor scrutiny and the maths of power apply everywhere. The harms from market failures might be less as people are more spread out. Except, I know that bus services are worse in your world. And as for freedom of opportunity?

But us city dwellers, if, for example, we are dissatisfied with the way the market for land in cities is run (or other markets like children's care homes), be open, get experts in (publish their recommendations), see where that takes us, work together and get things changed.

My city based suggestions:

Land prices: We have discussed before the need to do something about the price of land. Can anything be done at the local level, for example in Bristol? Here are three suggestions:

• Firstly reduce developers' risks of planning consent and then of selling so that a 20% profit isn't looked for (in Government guidance[53] it says between 15% to 20%).

• Secondly, put strong, enforceable planning constraints on land to require a high level of affordable housing, take care with mixed use[54] designation (which allows developers to hide profits).

• And thirdly buy up derelict or poorly used land cheaply, then give planning permission on it, or put in infrastructure, bus routes etc. on or near the land the Council now owns.

Noting that such policies through the current Local Plan system need to be consulted upon (three times); big landowners have a big say and can veto; then finally it all has to go to a planning inspector for approval who

---

53 www.gov.uk/guidance/viability at para 18.
54 Mixed use means a combination of retail, offices and housing.

will take account of the comments and possibly junk[55] the plan.

So apart from some tinkering at the edges, not much but not nothing: Ideas off the top of my head like "if you build one to sell then build one that's affordable" in return you will have a purchase guarantee from the Council for both (even in a recession). That would reduce risk as the developer would be guaranteed to receive say 75% of open market valuation for the package. Cash-flow support could further reduce risk. These ideas might be being considered already, I know fast tracking is; which is good.

Better and cheaper buses help widen access to jobs, training and opportunities to improve one's self. It's not the same as having a job or college nearby, but it is better than having to buy and run a car or rely on poor, expensive bus services. So using buses to give freedom of opportunity to those in outlying areas (where the land is often cheaper). This would need a congestion charge to raise the money and clear the roads.

In fact, transport is a really big issue in Bristol, it seems to me that the city doesn't have enough space for all the transport modes and as space is the critical resource in a city, transport decisions should be judged on surface area required. Use too much area and you pay extra, sort of applying LVT principles more widely.

Scrutiny: Early stage scrutiny as we have seen is key to good decision making. But it gets muddled with late stage (holding to account) scrutiny. To give a national example, the sourcing of protective equipment for the NHS looks like it was a shambles. The questions and an enquiry are examples of "holding to account". Whereas early stage scrutiny would have been on a public health committee reviewing the prospects of a pandemic some two or three years ago; assessing the big risks. A virus epidemic was always on the cards and ensuring that the NHS had secure PPE supply chains in the event of a global pandemic that would certainly create shortages. A global problem, just like the banking crisis in 2008,

---

55   I'm wondering that if it were framed well, about inclusivity and needing affordable homes and a "Bristol Deal" with developers whether the planning inspectors might see it as a way forward. In my dreams?

which caused systemic problems that pulled the funding away from banks.

Early stage scrutiny requires the Mayor and Cabinet to value it, in Bristol I think they do, but they seem to dislike the 'being-held-to-account' scrutiny. It seems like the two should operate separately and the early stage should be run by the Mayor and Cabinet as policy development groups according to a process agreed by all the parties.

Citizens assemblies and/or juries should be used more. It's a way of informing the public, building their trust and respect of local government too. As well as improving the input into policy development. I think this could have helped the Adult Social Care program as continues to try to squeeze through bottleneck after bottleneck.

This reliance on consultants and requirements for secrecy (exempt material) is hugely damaging to confidence and accountability. If you use consultants they must provide reports that are open to scrutiny. In fact there should be an open write up of the public interest test for any document that is considered for exemption and it should be challengeable.

The Council should consider when best to use markets, recognising their strengths and weaknesses. Markets need to be managed, a good example are those surrounding the provision of adult social care. Steer provision towards those motivated by care not money. Market failures are often the cause of environmental degradation too, there are opportunities locally to address this.

Social Value: Putting more emphasis on buying products, services and taking account of the indirect benefits of a particular offer especially if it will save money in other areas. For example a company (social or for profit) hiring adults with learning or other disabilities to make face masks for carers, to choose an example topical in 2020, or prepare food for schools would save adult social care costs as this type of demographic are often unemployed and dependent on council services. From what I can gather Bristol are a leader in this area, but the Social Value[56] journey has only just begun.

Consider other interventions based on increasing people's freedom of opportunity like the library example in D9.

And work with the other Core Cities who are facing the same problems, present the evidence, lack of transparency, need for better scrutiny, policy and holding to account, problems with land and adult social care.

CHAPTER H11
NATIONAL CHANGES (IF THE PACT / ALLIANCE DOESN'T FORM)

If there are any Conservative Party members still reading this book then well done. I have given you a hard time. I hope you noticed I did credit some Conservative progresses; some I applaud like the Social Value Act 2011 (E6), The Statutory Guidance on Scrutiny 2019 (B11), turning your (Sauron's) eye on Bristol's poor air (D13), getting the BBC to employ Local Democracy Reporters (H4) and there might be more.

Nevertheless there are serious issues[57] with the way you are running things: clear favouritism to your supporters and the insistence on using markets to solve most problems being just two of them.

I have heard that one of the reasons you behave this way is a fear of the catastrophe that could happen if another party gained power. If this is true (in your opinion) then you should debate this openly and intelligently. Ah, but the electorate aren't interested. You might well be right, in which case the question is how to encourage them to become more interested, to engage more, learn the facts rather than relying on their specific Party's dogma. All parties have their creeds because they rely on votes; most voters and many members don't have time to consider

56   One of the ideas I'm considering after finishing on the Council is to work with the Bristol Pound to transform it to become a Social Value currency. Something that's actually more valuable than normal currency. As a concept this fascinates me, whether it would work in real life is a different matter. Keep it quiet please, as I haven't discussed it with them. www.bristolpound.org
57   Occasionally I wonder whether the Conservatives feel trapped by the Mathematics of Power. They would like to improve the voting system but then get scared because of the consequences.

more detailed analysis. This plays into the hands of press releases and untruths. That has to be unsustainable eventually[58]?

In the future, as technology takes more job roles, we have an opportunity to fix this. Citizens will have more time. We may on average become poorer because of less work or you might design a UK where we can use that extra time to participate in local charities, spend better quality time with our family, become an active citizen and show more interest in local affairs. In which case, if, in the future, people are doing social value adding activities (it was your Act remember) then perhaps pay them a Citizens' (or Basic) Income to participate as a citizen? Engaging in local affairs could bring out an interest in politics (or aspects of it), result in better engagement with it (I'd prefer to call the subject: "political economics") and so begin to encourage a better standard of debate. That's my message of hope to any Conservatives reading this chapter. I fear for all our futures if you don't come up with a vision that can engage the whole of the UK populace. And if that vision is based around, "freedom of opportunity as long as you don't harm others and their freedom of opportunity", then it's even better in my book.

---

58   Tories might say it has served us well for 300 hundred years and will continue to do so. I say at what cost to everyone else?

APPENDICES TO THE MAIN SECTIONS

These first five appendices relate to the implementation of the Bundred recommendations and specifically the need for business cases for investment

BUNDRED AND TREES (1)

When I was little (and I mean very little), living in Essex, my mother used to take me to Epping Forest to play amongst the beech trees. I had a favourite old stump that was hollowed out, I could crawl in and my mum couldn't; my own private home. So from the very beginnings trees have been part of my life and my freedom even though I am now a devoted city dweller.

Some forty plus years later, before I became Councillor, I was a member of a group set up to defend Bristol's trees from the tree antichrist, yes you got it; the Council. This was around 2008, the Stump Wars period. Every time the Council undertook their statutory duty and chopped down a big tree we turned up, children in tears and the local press too. Eventually a form of truce was declared and the Bristol Tree Forum, as it became, morphed from "terrorising Council officers" into a discussion group. And chaired by me we worked with the Council and especially Councillors (there are votes in trees) to improve local tree policy, at one stage we had more than 500 members. Developers found they had to plant more trees for each one they felled, sometimes lots more, or stump up thousands for Council tree planting. The Council tree officers themselves had to change style too and had to inform Councillors before they felled a tree to enable a community response.

As you know I won my Council seat by just 10 votes, 1001 to Labour's 991 and as more than 10 Tree Forum members lived in Clifton Down ward I think it's fair to say, "it woz the tree forum wot won it".

Noddy Holder spelling aside, from time to time trees featured in my Council work, not just individual ones but working on Council policies to maintain all 50,000 or more on their land. And sometimes my detailed knowledge on trees, planning and tree preservation orders, was useful to illustrate systemic problems on policy making more generally. This example is from the last days of meaningful[1] scrutiny at Bristol City Council back in May 2017. And I used a bad decision on street tree maintenance taken in isolation by the Highways Department to illustrate that some of the lessons from the Bundred Report were far from being implemented.

The Bundred report had been commissioned by the Labour Mayor in the Autumn of 2016 to investigate why the Council finances were £30 million adrift of target. Steve Bundred was a retired senior Local Government Official. He uncovered evidence of a culture in 2015 and before of Council Officers of not telling Councillors and possibly not

---

1   After then it went through a series of experiments but never really got (or got back, before my time) to a stage where policy could be influenced at an early stage.

even the then Mayor bad news. The Bundred Report stopped short of accusing anyone of deliberate lying but that was one of the implications. 2015 was the year that Bristol was European Green Capital, the only UK city to have won this title. The Council's top officer was appointed to run it; she was still running the Council too. In addition there were mayoral elections in 2016. The Austerity cuts were biting deeply; funding was falling about £25 million pounds a year in real[2] terms, forcing cutbacks in public services. There were also projects for efficiency gains which meant the need for further redundancies; plus sharper rises in Council Tax. The report also suggested that in some areas this "hiding of bad news" was endemic and so the Council needed culture change. That prompted a complete clear out of all the top officers; as I write this in 2019 almost all the top officers are new compared with 2017. Has the culture changed? Well there are other chapters to read about that and you can draw your own conclusion.

I developed a simple "Bundred Checklist[3]" after a conversation with one of our local journalists. A one page form that made sure that the department had consulted with other departments on the change. I unveiled the checklist at Full Council a few weeks later and the journalist and I learned a useful lesson about the relationship of the local press with the Labour machine.

The Assistant to the Mayor is a PR expert. It seems that PR involves using communications skills of many kinds, including pressuring the papers from time to time about how they write up and depict news. I have had at least three journalists tell me about pressure coming from that quarter. So any aspiring local journalist has to be careful when criticising Labour, that's another story. Read on for a cock up tale.

---

2   After allowing for inflation and population growth.
3   Bundred's 12 recommendations included these five(number refers to the numbering in his report): https://www.bristol.gov.uk/Council-spending-performance/an-independent-report-on-our-financial-deficit-in-2016/17
3) acceptable business cases are required for savings projects,
4) reports should be clear and transparent and should include analysis and incorporate advice,
5) members should be less tolerant of poor quality reports,
7) opposition members should be properly informed and
8) better internal communication needed.

APPENDIX 2
BUNDRED AND TREES – (2)

Street Tree Maintenance – Question to Cabinet – January 2018 (A full year after the Bundred Report)

"A year ago an innocuous budget saving called RS02 was approved. It proposed to save money on Highways Maintenance. After the budget was voted we discovered in April that this included the stopping of planned maintenance for street trees. During the last year it was revealed the following:

1) The Highways Department hadn't consulted any other department about this idea, not even the Council's tree experts. (The Bundred report picked up on lack of cross departmental communication as a key weakness of the Council, so this proposal is an example of the Council still behaving that way after the Bundred recommendations were known about).

2) A business plan hadn't been done outlining the risks of injury, insurance claims, leaf fall, tree felling, pavement lift or house subsidence. Add these in and the £187k saving could well become a net cost to the Council.

3) The Legal Department advised that there should be public consultation on this, the Cabinet Member at the time also said there would be a public consultation on this, yet there has been none.

4) This problem was firstly in the portfolio of Councillor Bradshaw, then Councillor Craig and now Councillor Threlfall. All holding and passing on this hot potato with a potential to grow to Sheffield sized proportions and drag Bristol's name through the mud.

Logic would imply that if there was no public consultation and if somebody actually did the maths and assessed the risks that the decision would be reversed before too much harm was done, but I haven't been able to see that this is the case within this document.

So my question is, assuming that the cut to planned maintenance to street trees is carried forward a second year, can the Mayor please share with us the business case that shows that this is a good deal for the City and then consult on this with the public as has been promised so they can have a say too?

The impact of this saving was first discovered in Scrutiny in March 2017. Most months I was able to come back to this and illustrate that in spite of the Bundred Report's recommendations officers were paying lip service to it. By January 2018 the Mayor and/or his Cabinet Member had enough and reversed the budget cut. That £187k was so damaging to the Council's reputation. As you can see from this saga and the university expansion mitigation[4] story later you have to reframe the issue to get on to a topic that the leadership cares about. Let's be honest they didn't care much about trees, but they did care about appearing financially competent.

Apart from making sure that issues are framed to get noticed by a Mayor, the other thing I learned was to look at every business case to see if each change project, saving, improvement, investment or other was following the Bundred recommendations, many weren't.

This obsession finally got me into trouble when I raised the question of the Colston Hall refurbishment, a mere £48.8 million investment.

APPENDIX 3

BUSINESS PLANS AND COLSTON HALL (1) – APRIL 2018

Can you imagine how I responded to reading a Cabinet proposal for £48 million to refurbish Colston Hall[5] without having a business case. What was the point of getting Steve Bundred in and his 12-point plan only for his key recommendations to be ignored. So I read the documents, they referred back to a decision in 2017; those papers said a new business case

---

4   The reframing of university expansion was about loss of housing and increased rents. Both administrations seemed to not care about the harm done to residents but at least Labour switched on quickly when it was reframed onto the impact on housing.
5   It's the main venue for music in Bristol, a grade one listed building and owned by the Council. It needed some big works anyway, demolition was not an option. It is being renamed like many other references to the former slave trader.

was being prepared so where was it? I did more homework and asked the Scrutiny Officer at the time who said:

> *"It was originally on the Place Commission's work programme for last April but the report was pulled by officers on the advice of the CEX (Anna). They said that they'd come back to us and would bring it to scrutiny but it didn't happen. I think Jude English made it clear to XXXXXX at the time that she wanted the report but then the Commission didn't meet after last July anyway so it didn't – no. "*

When these Cabinet papers come out, you get less than 48 hours to respond, some of that time is used up sleeping and eating. And other things too, like attending Council meetings!

But I knew it hadn't gone to Scrutiny and I knew there was no Council business plan in either of the 2017 or 2018 reports. So confident of the facts I penned and circulated a draft question for my colleagues to comment on and this is the result that went to the Mayor five days in advance of the meeting:

Cabinet Question: 1 May 2018 relating to agenda item 13, Colston Hall: Councillor Stevens

> *Marvin – I really think you should look at this again. This paper is surely not ready for you to push the button on over £48m of further investment into improving Colston Hall. This £48m equates to a spend of £20,000 for each seat in the Hall, and that is after £20m of renovation works have already taken place in the foyer. The paper before us doesn't even show a business plan, it hasn't been to Scrutiny and yet it is proposing to take up to £22m of Council money. And not just the £22m, but it adds a risk that we will need to put even more money in, if things don't go to plan. Surely as an organisation we have learnt from the Bundred Report (that you commissioned) and its core messages of stronger governance of big projects, more member oversight and better business plans. This misses all three.*
>
> *Additionally I also believe that decisions as important and big as this should not be looked at in isolation – they need to take into account all the*

ongoing capital projects in our city and coming decisions; particularly the arena. I appreciate there is considerable momentum and vested interests in approving this item now but I am deeply concerned that the Council isn't yet ready.

Don't get me wrong, I hope the conversion of Colston Hall into a modern venue will happen. The growth in customer numbers and the consequent 68% increase in revenue since 2011 is impressive. But it seems that this is not ready for you, our Mayor, to push the button on May 1st. This paper doesn't give the people of Bristol, nor me, the confidence that we have done things right.

I have two questions please:

1. Can we please have sight of the business plan that shows on a risk adjusted basis that this is a good investment for the Council?

2. Assuming a business plan will be available, it surely needs to be properly scrutinised before this costly work is agreed to. Could the Mayor please assure me that any final decision on this project will be delayed until proper scrutiny has been done and that the final decision will take into account all ongoing projects in the city?

You might sense the frustration in these questions. This was well over a year after Bundred published his report. So that was done and I got on with other work. I was surprised to hear on Monday that BBC Local Radio wanted to interview me the morning of 1st May. That was unusual, normally what I ask about is of no interest to the press. "I wonder what that's about." It turns out lots of listeners had phoned in or tweeted their worries about Colston Hall overspend. The Council had a bad track record of project overspends including the recently completed bus tracks for Metrobus that in some places were built to the wrong width and there were rumours that the budget for the still-to-be-built arena was going up by the day too.

So I set my alarm clock ready for an early start.

APPENDIX 4

BUSINESS PLANS AND COLSTON HALL (2) – MAY 1ST 2018

Up early, I trudged down to the BBC studios and sat politely with headphones on waiting for my slot. I can't recall my exact words, but I probably rambled on about Bundred and the need for business cases and risk assessments; Bristol's track record on major projects and inability to judge risks was well known. In fact, it is such a common problem with big projects that the UK Treasury now insist on something called an optimism bias to be factored in to add an extra buffer to projects.

And works to a listed building like Colston Hall would be subject to risks like undiscovered asbestos, uncharted services, increasing labour and materials costs to name but a few. This was then posted on the BBC website, you can see it here[6]:

Later I received an email from a fellow Councillor:

"The commitment to the Colston Hall reflects our recognition that it serves the whole city, not just a part of it, through its diverse and inclusive programming and through the nationally recognised work undertaken by Bristol Music Trust (BMT) to promote and facilitate music education across the city. Without the Colston Hall and BMT Bristol's cultural scene would be very much poorer. While it is entirely valid to ask if we are getting value for money from public support for arts and culture, I think it is also important to point out that the sector brings millions back into the city. Colston Hall is an important part of the cultural economy.

Getting this far with the redevelopment has taken a great deal of effort and commitment. I would be very disappointed if this were jeopardised in any way, as I imagine would many of your other constituents."

It was beginning to get out of hand and off my original topic which was why was there no business case? And no scrutiny?

It was now clear that the problem I'd started was because the question

6   http://www.bbc.co.uk/news/uk-england-bristol-43969335

asked the Mayor to look at this decision again. And that became the news[7].

Walking down to deliver my speech to Cabinet I was asked for a local BBC TV interview which I duly gave, it was obvious both the Mayor and the Trustees of Colston Hall had briefed them so the interview didn't go well, fortunately that was all edited out – phew.

Then on into the Council Chamber. Usually I'm greeted kindly by Labour Members but not this time. A Green pariah, nobody gave their usual welcoming smile. Presumably it would wreck their careers showing the Mayor that you are friends with an enemy.

Anyway I had a few minutes to think. I completely rewrote my speech. Here's pretty much what I said,

> *"People have said I'm brave to ask this question. All I'm doing is my job as a diligent and hardworking Councillor. I've never met Steve Bundred. The independent you hired to investigate the causes of the £30m budget black hole, but I've read his report many times. He said we needed to improve governance of major projects, their cost overruns and subject items to more Councillor oversight. And do better business plans. I am only asking what Steve Bundred would have asked if he were here today.*
>
> *It's unfortunate that the issue is Colston Hall. Nobody wants to delay this project. But I do want to check it's done right from Bristol City Council's point of view. I'm just doing my job as a dutiful Councillor in asking these questions."*

Then I read out the written question; you have seen earlier. Answers came back from the Cabinet Member for Finance (see end of this theme). But they didn't make sense. He said that Colston Hall did have a business plan and that it had been scrutinised.

Although I had it in writing that it hadn't been scrutinised, I didn't want to risk someone's job (the current and previous years of redundancies meant a widespread fear for jobs and careers). I kept that quiet and asked the Chair of Overview and Scrutiny, another Councillor

7   An example of bad framing. I learned from this.

who was sitting next to me, he said he thought it had been. Damn. So I sat down.

But then the Mayor spoke.

"Do you mind Clive if I ask you about something?"
"No please go ahead",

I mistakenly replied.

APPENDIX 5

BUSINESS PLANS AND COLSTON HALL (3) – A GRILLING FROM THE MAYOR

So the Mayor grilled me, I think he asked me the same question at least three times in a row about the Bristol Arena (not about Colston Hall at all) and how it was that I had voted for the motion to build it next to Temple Meads station without knowing any of the costs.

He was trying to show I was a hypocrite. Fair enough, it's politics.

I calmly explained that the decision about the arena was for the Mayor to take. Full Council had voted that the best place to locate it would be next to Temple Meads, if he, the Mayor, decided it was to go ahead. It was an indication of the opinion of 70 representatives of the people of Bristol. The Mayor retorted that the public wouldn't understand the distinction between a Full Council view and mayoral decision making.

With hindsight, I can think of so many answers to that insult to the people of Bristol regarding their lack of understanding. If, after five years of mayoral power and two mayoral elections, the public didn't know that it was the Mayor's decision, then that was down to poor communication by him and his team anyway. Answers are always easier with time.

The Mayor replied with the same question again (I checked by re-listening to the video). "How could you vote for the arena without knowing the costs?" That confused me as I'd already answered that one so I said I couldn't hear clearly, which was true, but back he came back again, same question. (My confusion made worse with other colleagues whispering other answers in my ear).

That altercation was written up in the local papers too. "Colston Hall questions met with hostility" read the headlines.

A few days later I checked with officers what had really been presented to previous meetings. It turns out that there was a Bristol Music Trust (BMT) business plan, I read it, it's impressive, it was designed to get grant funding. Core to their plan is that Bristol City Council takes on all the risk of underwriting if fundraising doesn't go to plan and also all the building work risk. To this very day nobody has shown me a Bristol City Council business plan showing the financial costs, risks and benefits to the Council itself. This is termed a value for money report and if it had existed it would look at the value generated on behalf of the taxpayer.

Scrutiny did look at BMT's plan quite a while back but not at any value for money report because there wasn't one.

Updates: There was a first cost overrun of £3.2m which was admitted in 2019, this was due to delays and the impact of inflation. That overrun was paid for by WECA[8] (and therefore not directly by the Council Tax payers of Bristol). In June 2020 there was news of further cost overruns; more difficulties, including asbestos, other discoveries and Covid-19 caused delays; the latter could not have been predicted though. This new overrun is first described in Cabinet (Agenda 17) of July 14th 2020.

It's difficult to not draw the conclusion that the Steve Bundred Report was implemented for the convenience of the Mayor and when it's inconvenient not implemented as rigorously. Overall it has been beneficial, I'm sure. Financial control and Audit (which were criticised as weak in 2015) have gotten tighter and I've seen some better business plans but by 2019 perhaps the financial control pendulum had swung too far. Officers without the skills to write business plans have found they can't justify proposals and get things done at all.

8   The combined authority set up in 2016, covers Bristol, Bath and NE Somerset, and South Gloucestershire

Nothing is ever simple. You will also have noticed that the cultural problems of officer behaviour have not just vanished. The answer to that is openness, transparency and early scrutiny.

And the press? In January 2019 we greeted two new reporters paid for by the BBC. Called Local Democracy Reporters their job is to attend Council Meetings (amongst other things) and write them up for the public to read. This is a national initiative, so not just picking on Bristol. I think this has led to an improvement in the detail and seeking the truth. Still need glamorous headlines though, the articles still need to help sell newspapers, but the two reporters seem more immune to PR pressures.

ATTEMPTS TO INCREASE TREE COVER BECAUSE TREES ARE GOOD FOR US

APPENDIX 6
TREES[9] WITHIN THE PLANNING SYSTEM

I had an enquiry from a Green Councillor in Reading about the truth behind Bristol's promise to double its tree cover. This is the reply I sent him in March 2020. It's a history story.

"In 2008/09 Bristol were doing a mini Sheffield. The public fought back with help from the local press and our children were crying over tree stumps. 2010 they halted the policy, started engagement and we set up a group called the Bristol Tree Forum (which still exists). I ended up chairing it circa 2011 to 2014.

At the same time we pressured the Lib Dem administration[10] (who were pro-tree and also committed to doubling canopy) to add a new policy into the Local Plan (adopted in 2011/12) that gave more priority for high

---

9   In cities there are three dominant life forms (not including bacteria and viruses): humans, rats and trees. Rats seem to be able to look after themselves, trees look after humans and humans need to look after humans and trees. Are we the neglectful species?
10   This was before the first Mayor.

visual amenity trees. Additionally if trees had to be felled, then there was a schedule of multiple replacements depending on trunk size. The approved loss of a big tree could need eight replacements; it's called the Bristol Tree Replacement Standard BTRS, if they can't be planted on site, the developer must pay about £700 to the Council per replacement to plant on public land. This still exists and funded 400 new trees in 19/20. Having said that, the Council felled about 350 as they said they were getting too old and expensive to maintain. Bristol's Canopy cover was measured in 2012 using aerial surveys at about 14%

In 2014 the Council officers had to abandon their funding sources for tree replacements (except for the BTRS paid by developers) and the then new Independent Mayor used that funding plus sponsorship to fund One Tree Per (Primary) Child which planted over 30,000 trees in 2015 (Bristol; European Green Capital). That Mayor also committed to doubling tree canopy. This program has continued but was scaled back to 6,000 trees a year (working with children in Year 5 only). The Cabinet member overseeing this was a Green Councillor. It is true many will die but they are planted so densely that a one in five survival rate would be fine and imitates nature.

In 2016 we had a Labour Mayor. He eventually committed to doubling canopy too and through his One City Plan is urging other organisations in the city to do their bit, like the University, NHS and smaller business. And there are sponsorship schemes too.

In 2019 an iTree[11] assessment was done and came up with a canopy cover of 12-13% but as it was a different approach to the aerial survey in 2011 it isn't comparable (I wonder if this was deliberate?).

So in 2020 we have BTRS, we have One Tree Per Child (Year 5), sponsorship schemes and activities via the One City Plan. I'm not sure if this is actually increasing canopy but it's better than not doing these things.

The biggest issues are:

---

11   This involves taking a few hundred random squares of land and uses volunteers to survey all the trees. That is then totalled up and within statistical limits provides data on species and an estimate of tree canopy cover.

• *Public engagement and especially in areas where citizens see trees as a problem: leaves not cleared up leading to blocked drains and slippery pavements, blocking light and dangers of branches falling in parks and pigeon poo.*
• *Finding enough land!"*

And I need to add to that summary that another big issue is trying to modify the planning approach so developers don't dodge the BTRS. For example they might say they are going to retain all the trees, get planning permission, build the houses and then fell them a year or so later. In theory they would only need to replace one to one whereas admitting it earlier on could cost them one to eight. This is still being worked on as I write this in May 2020.

The Bristol Tree Forum still exists and fights to make sure trees are replaced, protected and planted. They are campaigning hard to get canopy cover increased which as you saw won't happen without changing policies. Do join them if you are interested in this goal.

A COUNCIL'S ATTEMPTS TO DEVOLVE DEMOCRACY (APPENDICES 7 TO 9)

APPENDIX 7

NEIGHBOURHOOD PARTNERSHIPS (1) – A NEW HOPE?

In the Autumn of 2008, Bristol City Council engaged in an experiment the likes of which hasn't yet been seen again. The Cabinet (no Mayor back then) divided Bristol into 14 areas and gave £15,000 to each one and effectively said, there you are, go organise yourselves and improve local wellbeing.

Different areas organised themselves in different ways, some with strong community groups hogged the money, but some engaged fully in this new found democratic freedom. The Council provided community engagement officers and facilitators to be shared across the 14. From where I was it was all quite exciting. I was a resident back then, keen on street trees and our local park; that group were just getting into a fight against Council incompetence. My children were both at primary school and I was helping out as a school governor. I was also on a local community group[12] as their "tree rep" and when they were asked for representatives to join a steering group to help design this new process I said, "I'll do it"; a friend volunteered too, plus a few others from across the area.

So with the help of the Council's democracy officers we organised a public meeting in November 2008, about 120 people attended. Then the steering group met, it included all the Councillors from the three voting wards and about 10 representatives from community groups plus some members of the public. We worked on a couple of projects that fitted the priorities that had been set. To spend £15,000 by March when you are already in November, despite being nearly-free of Council bureaucracy, still takes some doing. The two schemes were waste doctors and street trees. Waste doctors are employed people who would visit houses to help them understand Bristol's recycling and waste system so that it could be collected more efficiently, foxes wouldn't get at it and all in all streets would look better.

And trees; that one was mine, I said I would spend the winter walking the streets identifying where trees had been felled and never replaced. And so I started my "long march", 49 miles as it turned out, identifying about 70 sites.

We presented back to the public in February 2009 and they gave us the OK for the two projects and put in ideas for many more. Next year's money was to be £30,000 and in came suggestions for youth provision, scouts and brownies groups, zebra crossings, a farmers' market, signs in parks and much more.

About 40 trees were planted in April 2009 and the Waste Doctors project started soon after. We engaged with the local secondary school and presented to them the problem of dropped litter from six-formers

12　Redland and Cotham Amenities Society (RCAS)

(years 12 and 13) during their lunchbreak pilgrimage to and from the local shop. They came back and said, "but there are no litter bins", and we looked and indeed they were right, so we asked them to tell us where they should go, they did and three bins were bought, put in and the litter problem was solved. We printed a certificate for each sixth former involved.

We had a big meet up in September 2009 where we were allowed to give talks. Buoyed by the confidence from having achieved something in my talk I drew a little cartoon of a brave knight being stamped on by a dragon. The dragon wasn't an evil one, it just didn't understand. The dragon was the Council. And then in my story a load more brave knights turned up (we, the residents) and the dragon was tamed to do our bidding. A couple of Council officers were in the audience and horrified. One says she is still scarred by that thought and reminds me of that dragon when I bump into her in the coffee area, even 11 years later.

But aside from scaring officers, the effect let residents know that this was different. It wasn't just more Council stuff, it broke the ice too and what came forth was a flurry of more ideas for projects and priorities like zebra crossings, youth clubs, graffiti and litter bins, that sort of thing, oh and more trees.

Community groups started up, like the street scene group, inspired by the combination of getting things done, access to money, speed of response and lack of bureaucracy. Further forums were held with topic tables concentrating on how to get best wellbeing from the £30,000. A Bishopston Youth Club called Vibe was granted nearly £2,000 for better equipment to add to their offering and attract more youngsters. It was all too good to be true.

APPENDIX 8
NEIGHBOURHOOD PARTNERSHIPS (2) –
THE COUNCIL STRIKES BACK

In the Autumn of 2009, buoyed by all this success, the Council's Cabinet decided to devolve more money to these steering groups, now called Neighbourhood Partnerships (NP). £11 million eventually across the 14 Partnerships, but not evenly shared out. This was a different order of magnitude and the lawyers at the Council insisted on a proper constitution, controls and Council papers explaining the options to Councillors. This was all to start in April 2010 but the style of meetings started to change before that.

The local news magazine published this from me in March 2010

"This show is now on view to anyone from the three wards who wants to come and rather than being on a top table I feel more like being on view in a goldfish bowl. Of course many residents would prefer to stay in and watch Coronation Street or go to the pub rather than watch us. Indeed that is a problem."

The process had changed, it wasn't a conversation between equals anymore, there were us 10 reps and six Councillors on top table all being observed by an audience.

We did manage to liven it up, I was Chair and trying desperately to recapture the magic we had had a year earlier. So I decided to contact any group with a grievance and tell them to come to the next meeting and ask for it to be sorted. Parks groups were first and were able to explain how the Council didn't listen; we sorted out an unwanted fence and turned around the project to sell a rundown pavilion called the Ardagh (up in the north of our area) and said "shame on you Council". As it turns out the community group that complained back then are now running the Ardagh building and area themselves (although it took 10 years for them to break free of the shackles). Then came the schools, who wanted safer routes and we were able to put in two zebra crossings. Councillors must have wondered why so many people were complaining, I never explained that it was I who orchestrated this, so this is my little confession.

Now there were ward forum meetings to be held prior to the main Partnership meeting; four meetings to replace one. These became complaining shops and it was difficult to recapture the positive environment from before. There was no money, nor grants, so why would it attract the same type of people that wanted to get things done, the people who used to come? Some tried, but attending three forums in different parts of the locality and then attending the actual Neighbourhood Partnership Meeting to get your grant for a few hundred pounds was just too much for most.

And by July 2010, I was having to explain to residents why a grant application from an older persons' group, which had been put in for April and met all our deadlines, had to wait until July. The Council's Legal Department explained that because April's NP papers didn't give Councillors the authority to grant the money for the next municipal year (starts around May 10th) until they had actually agreed and voted for it. Then any grant requests couldn't go through until the next meeting. I said what if we simply make this a later agenda item in April? "No", they said. Legal were strangling us.

What's going on I thought? Things used to work pretty well? I managed to get a one-on-one with the Cabinet Member responsible for setting up these Partnerships. Why was he stifling it with bureaucracy?

Here is part of the meeting notes between me and that Cabinet Member on 18th July 2010. This was to me.

> "What this new process is not: It is not a mechanism to improve the well-being or happiness of residents beyond their ability to get small things done and not for a vast minority to be involved in decision making. It is limited to this scope:
>
> Areas for improvement (existing NP scope):
> • Communication of issues and decisions to be made and communication of local decisions made.

• New and improved engagement services e.g. The Forums are not working as originally envisaged. There is a need to communicate widely accurate information regarding a forthcoming decision e.g. pavement works, lighting. The Forums are to enable people to communicate their objections and comments locally. This is then summarised and used as an input to the NP to help them make a better quality decision."

So there wasn't an intention to involve the public in well-being decision making. They were there to comment on proposals by officers. What the Cabinet Member wanted was for the public to see decision making done locally. And it wasn't just me that noticed this change, the numbers attending were falling fast. There was one forum that famously had just one attendee and he was an ex-committee member I had bumped into on my way there and persuaded to come along. The Neighbourhood Partnership meetings were down to audiences of 20 if we were lucky. And paperwork was multiplying.

The Council had let the genie out of the bottle and were now trying to put it back in. And I wasn't having any of it.

APPENDIX 9

NEIGHBOURHOOD PARTNERSHIPS (3) – IS THE GENIE TO BE SET FREE AGAIN?

I hadn't given up the fight, and in 2011 I launched my "Cunning Plan" strategy which the other members of our Partnership, including the Councillors, eventually agreed to. The plan meant we had a pre-meeting to go through the officer reports and decide if they could be simplified, rewritten or even rejected; either because it was indigestible for the public or it was just wrong. This process was to improve report writing and make officers more accountable to their public. We started these pre-meets with officers down at the Council House and they hated them. A couple of times we rejected a complete paper as it was impossible to understand, even for us, let alone members of the public.

Our share of this £11 million of devolved money came to just over £200,000 a year and included funding for traffic schemes: local ones, pavement works and highways resurfacing. Very few Highways officers could engage properly with the public and it was quite obvious that most, but not all, felt it was a waste of their time and how dare they, the experts, be dragged in front of residents. But there were some with humility and humanity and in March 2011 and 2012 I spent an afternoon with a very helpful officer using Google Street View to translate all those words written by officers into pictures plus sketches to show what these schemes could look like in real life. Much easier for the attendees at the forums to comment on and for Councillors to understand what they were voting for. Oh I forgot to say one of the new legal restrictions with this new money was that only Councillors could vote, no votes for the public. To their credit they did ask our opinion first and usually took that steer.

By 2013 Highways told us that they weren't to help with picture reports anymore and that we should accept their documentation and not do our own. And the local magazine had this small piece of text in its publicity for the next meeting,

> *"Two reasons to come along to the Neighbourhood Partnership Meeting. Although previously likened to watching paint dry there are two issues which should cause lively debate."*

One of those issues was residents' parking. Yet another thing mismanaged by Highways.

I had been Chair for three years and had valiantly fought a rear-guard action, but failed. Time to step down; I wrote my resignation letter which included,

> *"As you know the main reason I am so committed to NPs is that I viewed my role as trying in some small way to effect cultural change within the Council, perhaps there are some green shoots but much feels like wading through treacle and tilting at windmills, both at the same time!"*

My last meeting was in June 2013, hosting the Mayor's conversation about the newly designed residents' parking zones. 200 residents turned up, mainly to harangue him or just to see the new Mayor, very few for the Partnership meeting. But in those last few weeks we still managed to save a park from having a play area rammed down its throat in the wrong place.

Before then, in March I wrote an article for the local magazine, being honest but also asking for volunteers. I'm not sure the ideas mixed well. Here is a severely edited version.

"I've been musing over why I got involved in the first place and reflected back to a presentation of September 2009 which I gave to about a 100 residents, just after this NP thing started. I suggested then that the Council was like a dragon, roaming the streets, out of control, stomping on and singeing people, as it is the nature of dragons to do. And those of us in the Neighbourhood Partnership are the gallant knights setting out not to kill it, but to tame it. Three and a half years later I still feel the analogy is apt for at least one facet of the Council's behaviour, maybe more so. I've learned the dragon's brain consists of different compartments which don't talk to one another and have different motivations. These aren't bad, it's just that asking us and then acting on what residents think is too onerous, "a waste of public money" I've heard it said.

This dragon has been given its powers over the decades by well-meaning Parliaments and judges, making sure things are done in the public interest but they didn't realise what they were creating. I have seen some hope, we might have tamed a claw or two. So I'm off to lick my wounds and recharge, maybe I'll re-join the fray one day. But I hope you will soon.

I am convinced that the strength of the Neighbourhood Partnerships is what is needed to take back partial control over some aspects of our lives, I urge each and every one of you (not just the RCAS Committee or community groups) to don your suits of armour and take up your swords for just an hour a week."

I closed by asking for volunteers to be street reps (the idea was each street would have a rep who would be able to bring issues into the NP). And amazingly a new Chair[13] did step forward!

And with that I went off to recharge.

By 2016 I'd forgotten what it was like to work with the Council and stood to become a Councillor. And worse, I got elected.

MARIANA DOESN'T KNOW IT, BUT SHE HAS REALLY INFLUENCED MY THINKING – THANK YOU.

APPENDIX 10

MY JAN 2020 LOVE LETTER[14] TO MARIANA (NEVER SENT)

Dear Mariana – I thought you should know how much your ideas have influenced me as a Councillor in Bristol and hopefully I'm soon to be an author too. But if I may, can I ask you some questions please?

I first got to know you through your book the *Entrepreneurial State*, the one that describes how Apple and its iPhone relied so much on USA state-sponsored programs, for defence usually. And as you rightly pointed out Apple's hypocrisy in trying to avoid paying taxes that support the very system that gave them the foundations for their profitability. Reading yours just after reading William H Janeway's book[15] on venture capital (which adds evidence to the proposition that venture capital takes over only after government schemes have reduced risk and increased opportunity) worked a treat. I see that's when capitalism gets to work.

Your latest quest is to answer what is value? You seem to consider wealth and value as similar things. I checked the Italian words ricchezza and valore, they look to have distinct meanings. In English (and the USA) I think we have muddled them up. May I refer to two books, you definitely won't have read one as it was never finished, maybe not the

---

13 Thank you Nick

14 Mariana – if you ever read this don't worry, my love letter style is artistic license. You are perfectly safe.

15 *Doing Capitalism In The Innovation Economy*, William H Janeway 2012 Cambridge University Press

other? Back in 1992, just after I was unceremoniously sacked from a job as production director, during the months seeking solace and new employment, I started on a book to be called *What Is Wealth?* It never saw the light of day as I couldn't work out the answer, I was looking for things outside profit and money, things to justify the priorities and values I held that part resulted in my dismissal.

Move on twenty years and an INSEAD friend of mine, Stuart Jackson, who is a partner in a leading management consultancy, published his masterwork, *Where Value Hides* in which he describes how businesses can extract (and create) value from economies of scale and scope. I'm told it didn't hit the bestseller lists, but it did influence my teaching of business at the University of Bath.

In that book, Stuart describes value as a private thing; superior profits, earnings and income. And with that I would like to suggest to you, my Italian goddess of economics, that wealth and value might be different things.

Value is what can be extracted from wealth. The process of extracting value would ideally be a subset of wealth creating activities, but value extraction can also occur if an enterprise is diminishing wealth. The ability to grab value (earnings) in return for one's activities depends on one's position within an organisation, access to capital, skills, competition, regulation and industry norms.

Wealth, on the other hand, relates to available resources: a wealth of educated labour, a wealth of minerals, a strong transport infrastructure, healthy legal systems. It includes the quality of those resources too: healthy, educated labour for example. And it includes natural resources both positive and negative. Wealth is reduced for example by pollution; value isn't unless the polluter is made to pay.

So wealth is the potential of all the resources available, whereas value is what a person, business or community can extract from that wealth. Wealth can be created (food, inventions etc) or destroyed (e.g. pollution). Wealth can be without monetary value, like a wealth of nature trails. In that example, value could be extracted from wealth by fencing off the walks and charging people. Although this may or may not destroy the intrinsic wealth provided by the nature trails it would increase value to those who fence them off, charge for access and reduce value to those who cannot now use those trails in future.

So why have I had to think about this? Well Mariana, I joined the Green Party in 2015 and was elected a Councillor in Bristol in 2016. I found that the Greens espoused new economics by the dozen, but little I could actually apply to Local Government, so I have had to cobble together a qualitative set of opinions using your theories, those of Robert Frank (I plan to write to him too[16]) and other mainstream economists like Joseph Stiglitz and even Mancur Olsen. These opinions have helped support my analysis of Council and Mayoral decision making and to intelligently (I hope) challenge (and sometimes support) the decisions of the local administration.

So I thank you and I offer you a draft copy of my book *After The Revolution* for free, hoping you might get someone to review it, but only hoping. It's a present for you as you helped me and are indirectly helping the people of Bristol.

Yours sincerely – Councillor Clive Stevens

NO STORY ABOUT LOCAL POLITICS IN BRISTOL WOULD BE COMPLETE WITHOUT THE STORY OF THE ARENA (11 TO 13)

APPENDIX 11

THE BRISTOL ARENA AT BRABAZON (1)

Tuesday 3rd March 2020 – I don't think I've ever worked so hard before a meeting, I had a headache, presumably due to reading over 1,000 pages of Council reports, or did I have coronavirus? I consoled myself that I had none of the other symptoms. In fact, I felt quite jaunty as I sauntered down to the gym to work off the stresses of the morning and then at 11.51am it all fell apart.

---

16   Haven't quite got round to this yet.

Eleanor rang me. She's the empath of the Green Councillors (our Counsellor Troy for those who remember Star Trek back that far). She's also our group leader, of 11 Councillors and very capable at that too; knowing what to say at the right time, assertive but not too much and most of the time can get us to work together utilising our different strengths. Eleanor knows that I like to do my own thing but if I get my teeth into something then a thorough analysis will be the result.

The phone call went as follows,

"Sorry I have some bad news, you may not be able to vote on tomorrow's committee because the Greens have put in a statement that says the Green Group of Councillors object to this application. Gary Collins thinks you might be pre-determined."

Gary is the Head of Planning, he seems omni-capable of managing Bristol's planning decision system: walking a tightrope between judicial challenge if process is not followed; sanguine if decisions are overturned on appeal and with the added pressure of being in an organisation structure that reports into the Mayor (the main man who very publicly wants this arena to go through). Sometimes the stress is visible, maybe a slight dampness of the skin or a paler than usual complexion, these are symptoms of being under a hot limelight.

Back to Eleanor's phone call. I said retract it, I know nothing of that statement, I've worked so hard on this that I'm going to get my say tomorrow.

Pre-determination is the ultimate no-no for a Councillor on a Planning Committee. It means having made up your mind beforehand. Case law says Councillors can be biased or predisposed towards a view, after all we are members of political parties and sometimes the development is in our ward, but we mustn't be totally decided in advance. That also is a wee ridiculous because if you have read 1,000 pages of stuff and have been well trained in planning, you will come to a pretty firm view on what's going on in advance. It's an incentive to not read the documents! I jest.

I continued on to the gym and whilst on the running machine I considered whether I could vote for, against or for a deferral; the three options. As the breathlessness began, that's after three minutes nowadays, I could imagine voting against or for a deferral but what about voting for? Umm... I think, if new information came in about the out-of-town shopping centre, the one that competes with Bristol's Centre, if that were favourable, I could conceivably vote for the application. So I wasn't predetermined. Back in the office wolfing down a cheese sandwich a little too quickly I answered the inevitable email from Gary asking for clarification about my status (and that of Stephen Clarke too, the other Green Councillor on that Committee).

Eleanor and Jerome (he who wrote the statement) ate humble pie faster than I was eating my cheese sandwich and said that the statement was a drafting error, retracted it and replaced it with a personal one from Jerome. Phew, five days of effort wasn't wasted and I could attend Committee the next day.

APPENDIX 12

THE BRISTOL ARENA AT BRABAZON (2)

It has history. You could go back to the noughties and find proposals for an arena on the old diesel depot, which was on a site next to Temple Meads railway station. This land was eventually purchased for building an arena and planning permission for a 12,000 capacity (standing) and 10,000 (seated) was granted in April 2016. The land was then named Arena Island and a bridge was built, locally known as the bridge to nowhere. The arena was to be in the south and a patch of land on the north of the Island was to be a car park.

We start this section of the arena story in 2015 which recent discussions have revealed that's when YTL, the developers of the housing up in Filton, had conversations with the Council. Coincidentally the University of Bristol commenced discussions with the Council about developing land neighbouring Arena Island as their second campus. The

Mayor of that time says he didn't know about either and so presumably it was discussions with officers. Come May 2016, a change of Mayor and later that year the Bundred investigation into the financial "black hole" of £30 million. Bundred uncovered a culture of officers not telling Councillors, nor the Mayor, the whole truth.

In my opinion this culture didn't just affect the financial side of the Council, but was much more pervasive. The scope of Bundred didn't cover that.

We move to 2017, when the University of Bristol decided they needed more land for their second campus and negotiated with officers, with the knowledge of the Mayor, to buy about a third of the former diesel depot land (Arena Island). That was approved by Cabinet in March 2017. The officer named on that report went on to work for YTL and at the time of writing is now at the University. I must say I am not accusing him of any wrongdoing, but it is illustrative of a system that looks after people on the inside.

In 2018 the Mayor was wanting to abandon the idea of an arena on Arena Island and got some consultants to show it wasn't good value for money and that a private developer, YTL, had a better idea to resurrect the Brabazon hangers next to the disused Filton airfield about four miles north of Bristol's Centre.

What followed were special days of scrutiny, lots of evidence, claims about free trips, meals funded by business as the Mayor toured Malaysia and China seeking investment for Bristol. And although it wasn't disproved that an arena on Arena Island wasn't value for public money, the maths were much better for Filton. There were though huge concerns about traffic, congestion and diverting retail business away from Bristol Centre to an out of town site which would be right next to the "deadly enemy": Cribbs shopping centre, Cribbs: the out-of-town site which was trying to expand and thus threaten Bristol's vitality. Cribbs is in South Gloucestershire and brings in business rates for them. South Glos gains a lot from Cribbs.

We had lots of huffing and puffing at scrutiny. I was caught up in all the excitement, did a lot of work and probably did a better market analysis than the consultants who I imagine were billing £1,000 a day. This also became a Full Council debate and most Councillors and the Mayor voted that Arena Island was the best location for a city centre arena. The very next day the Mayor, at Cabinet, cancelled the plans for an arena in the centre!

The saga continues as planning permission was granted for the University accommodation for over 900 persons on Temple Island (can't call it Arena Island anymore, no arena); this is on the north part where the arena car park would have been. Then we heard about negotiations with Legal and General for offices, homes and a conference centre on the rest of Temple Island. That in itself was controversial as the Mayor tried to avoid procurement rules regarding a sale and lease agreement. It was hidden from scrutiny as long as possible; but enough on that one.

Back to the Brabazon hangers and to consideration of the planning application for the Filton site rushed through before the 2020 election.

APPENDIX 13

THE BRISTOL ARENA AT BRABAZON (3)

The documents came out on Wednesday 26th February 2020, the meeting was the following Wednesday. They came to 406 pages, additionally there were 301 pages of Environmental Statements and Analysis and if you wanted you could study another 300 or so on air quality modelling. As this was effectively my last "important meeting" of my Councillorship, I wanted to put on my best show. It was also an extremely important decision for the people of Bristol especially retailers and those relying on the roads of North Bristol for transport. This was back to the rivalry between Bristol and the vitality of its city centre versus South Gloucestershire and their attempts to build up their offer in the south of their area, grow their economy, but at the expense of Bristol.

Bristol had won round one when the Secretary of State refused South Glos its attempt to expand Cribbs shopping area (Cribbs 2 as it was called). This was round two, but with the potential to devastate[17] Bristol in the long term. This would also be referred to the Secretary of State and that was my ultimate hope. The Labour Mayor was behind this, he needed to deliver an arena to meet a manifesto promise from 2016. Labour Councillors occupied 6 out of 11 Committee seats. I needed to persuade one or two to defer OR I myself needed to believe that the mitigations (expressed as planning conditions) over 200 of them, was enough to approve.

"They are missing something here," that was ringing around my head by the Friday; the elephant in the room. The impact on shopping at Cribbs hadn't been assessed and neither had the impact of all that extra traffic on the M5. The officer's report addressed neither. And then Highways England illuminated the elephant just in time but in doing so accidentally killed the blocked motorway arguments all at one and the same time.

The Highways England report came racing out that Friday afternoon. They lifted their stop order and replaced it with yet more conditions; their main worry was blocking the M5. At least someone had finally recognised the issue. Or part of it anyway. Parking at Cribbs is free. That's a major attraction in itself. Park there, shop or eat there and then walk to the future arena. Highways England called this informal/ rogue use. To me parking at Cribbs is common sense and the cheapest transport option too if it's too far to walk or cycle to the arena. But by lifting their stop order and listing so many conditions including when the arena could hold events (not before 20.30) and afternoon events must finish before 15.00 during the week they had given the go ahead for Cribbs to become the future major retail area of Bristol, perhaps.

Maybe the consultants who pulled all this together for Bristol's Planning Department had done that analysis, the retail impact assessment on Cribbs. Would a competitive leisure and retail complex just a mile away, harm or enhance Cribbs? I didn't know. I had suspicions because of the informal parkers, as Highways England call them. There are 6,900 spaces at Cribbs, all free. If the arena benefits those shops, they will open

17   This is one where I will be so, so happy to be proved wrong.

later and allow later parking. There is nothing Bristol can do as it's in South Glos Council's jurisdiction.

4th March 2020, the meeting was televised. I put my headphones on confident in my analysis and all the planning policies and issues. I was asked if I was predetermined and no I wasn't, I was confident that someone must have done an impact assessment on Cribbs. There weren't many public statements, most for. One ex-RAF type adding a twist of lemon to his speech with an old stereotype of Greens wanting to live in caves. I smiled sweetly.

The officer's presentation (one actually given by the consultants) went on for two hours. We then questioned and debated. I asked about an impact assessment for Cribbs. No it hadn't been done. The Chair interrupted me, "you do know that Cribbs is not in Bristol, Clive?" That irritated me and as I write this, the day after, that's the whole bloody point – it's not in Bristol, that's the problem. Even the Conservative Government frowns on out-of-centre sites because they are so damaging. The consultant said that in his opinion there would be no impact on Cribbs. His opinion, where's the data? Planning of this importance has to be evidence based.

Each Councillor gets a chance to sum up. The developers and their colleagues had done a great job on the site itself, it looked wonderful, it would be a massive draw and there's the problem, the traffic and the impact on Cribbs and Bristol's Centre. I suggested a deferral. The looks on Labour Councillors' faces told me within half a second that there was no chance of that. "OK", I thought, move to damage limitation. The consultant showed that the average distance a car driver would be going was twenty miles, just twenty miles, surely entrepreneurial coach companies could pick up the slack. But there was only parking for ten coaches so that's say 600 people. That's about four percent with 65% driving in. I asked if this could be increased, that request wasn't accepted. And the vote went through. Labour and Conservatives eight for, Greens one and Libs Dems one both against and I abstained.

I am predetermined now, today, the day after the vote. This will be a great arena and such a good use of those old hangers where the

Brabazon (a massive plane, a flying white elephant, as engine technology progressed to jet engines) was built. But it could be so damaging for Bristol's retail sector. It will also mean more road schemes too, more public money spent on them when it should be used to solve the bigger problems we face: poverty, children's care, education, adult health or climate change and so much more. Now, just build more road schemes.

There is one ray of hope. This has to go to the Secretary of State, as this is an out of town complex, he or she needs to approve it. They turned down Cribbs 2, as it was called. Perhaps they will turn this down too. And I'm contemplating writing to him/her. They are bound to be a better audience than those Councillors eager to please their Mayor and help his re-election chances. Should I write[18]?

COUNCILS' BUSINESS SUCCESSES FROM AROUND THE UK

APPENDIX 14

COMMERCIALISATION AROUND THE UK

This appendix is an extension to the Council Commercialisation chapter E10. It's not just Bristol that's having difficulties with earning money from running businesses; each clipping from the newspapers (thank you to the LGiU), deals with retail and commercial property. Failed investments in Energy Companies were covered in Chapters C6 & C7.

1st March 2020, Councils' retail investments leave them exposed to big bills
Analysts have warned that investments by Councils into retail properties, as they look to fill gaps left by cuts in central government funding, has left them vulnerable to financial shocks as the sector struggles. Councils spent almost

---

18   I did, but not an objection; it was a concern that the impact of the benefits to Cribbs hadn't been taken into account. And therefore the traffic projections couldn't be trusted. They wrote back saying they were letting the decision go through. Time will tell.

£7bn on commercial property in 2017-19, with many sites a long way from the buyer and bought purely for income rather than regeneration purposes. Surrey is seen as the 'epicentre' of local authority borrowing to invest, with three of its borough Councils – Spelthorne, Runnymede and Woking – in the top five local authorities for commercial property deals, according to CoStar data. And Surrey County Council's £74m acquisition of Malvern Shopping Park in Worcestershire in 2017 raised eyebrows among industry insiders. "We think this will all end in tears as local authorities have a patchy record when it comes to investing taxpayers' money in commercial property," warns Mike Prew, an analyst at Jefferies. The Sunday Telegraph, Business, Page: 7

On 13 Feb 2020, Soaring Council property investments 'raise alarm bells'

According to a report from the National Audit Office, local authorities have increased their spending on commercial property by a factor of more than 14 over the past three years. Councils spent £6.6bn on commercial property between 2016/17 and 2018/19, including £2.3bn on retail properties and £759m on shopping centres, with the investments intended to help boost Councils' income to compensate for falls in central government funding. However, the NAO warned that the increase has seen Councils take on more debt, with some seeing "significant increases in the amount they owe and the cost of repayment," and that the investments could run into trouble as the growth of online shopping pushes down retail property values. Meg Hillier, chairwoman of the Commons public accounts committee, said the increase "raises serious alarm bells," and urged the Ministry of Housing, Communities and Local Government to review the framework that governs local authority borrowing. The Times, Page: 2 The Daily Telegraph, Business, Page: 1 Daily Mirror, Page: 13

4th Feb 2020, Private firms allowed to access Councils' website data[19]

Analysis of Council websites by anonymous web browser Brave has found that local authorities are sharing information about users of their sites – including when they seek help with a benefit claim, or with a disability or alcoholism – with dozens of private companies. More than 400 Councils were found to be allowing at least one third-party company track individuals who visit their sites. Critics have argued that Council websites serve a public purpose and should not let outside firms monitor their users' activity. The Guardian, Page: 22

On 24 Nov 2019, Treasury clamps down on Council borrowing

A surge in Councils borrowing to buy commercial property in the hope of generating rental income has spurred the Treasury to increase the cost of borrowing from the Public Works Loan Board[20] by 1%. Sources tell the Telegraph there are concerns the borrowing could become unsustainable and Councils could be left stranded with declining assets. But Pantheon Macro economist Samuel Tombs said the Treasury's intervention means borrowing costs have "skyrocketed" and has jeopardised "many capital projects that local authorities had planned". Local authorities have bought up one in five shopping centres sold since 2016. David Bell, director of finance and transformation at Hull City Council, said the rate increase was in response to "a perceived problem with authorities operating in a grey area" by borrowing to buy commercial property. He added: "An unintended consequence is that it's affecting everyday activity. It could potentially impact the ability to fund services." The Sunday Telegraph, Business: Page: 3

Having included this list of concerns about commercialisation, I agree that there are arguments for buying up retail or commercial land when it's cheap. It means that it can be repurposed and redeveloped for

---

19   I am making the assumption here that this access is granted for a fee. Whether it is or isn't it could well be breaching data privacy laws.
20   This 1% increase has reduced the ability of Councils to borrow to fund Council house building

building (perhaps even affordable houses) in the coming years. If that were the plan, then I'd be more comfortable with such an approach.

THE NEGATIVE IMPACTS OF UNCONTROLLED UNIVERSITY EXPANSION (15 TO 17) AND ATTEMPTS TO CONTROL THEM.

APPENDIX 15

IS BRISTOL FOR ITS PEOPLE OR FOR THE UNIVERSITY? (1)

In 2013 the Conservative and Lib Dem coalition took the cap off student numbers. Some universities including University of Bristol expanded by 30% or more, this was after a similar growth spurt just a few years earlier. Although First Year students usually live in halls they then move into rented accommodation for their second, third and sometimes fourth years. So one thousand new first years creates the need to house over two thousand more as they progress into second and third years. And the same Government increased tuition fees and created a student finance system so that the students could borrow, borrow and borrow with, as it turns out, a less than 50% chance of having to pay it back; a phenomenal way of placing them temporarily in a position to be able to outbid almost anyone else in the rental market.

Before I stood for election in 2016, and certainly through that campaign, there was a section of the population who were quite bitter about the quantity of students in the area. Some roads and localities had over 60% students, with perhaps a third of the houses packed to the rafters. Before 2011 anyone could convert a home for a family into a house with six students without needing planning permission. Before me, Councillors had managed to change the planning rules locally by putting in place something called an Article 4 direction[21] for this type of conversion from a family home to an HMO[22] so that after 2011 you then had to apply for permission. But the Local Plan rules were as such that virtually everyone got permission. And earning £6,000 each and mortgages at 1.5% on a £500,000 house it was money for old rope for wannabe landlords.

The problem with the old rope, young people embarking on lives of their own, was that they had parties until four in the morning and couldn't understand Bristol's litter and recycling system. Potentially a PhD in astrophysics, but can't follow the different bin colour codes and collection dates.

And by 2016 the residents were organised and had a North Bristol community association called ABC, action for balanced communities, with very, very capable leadership. Many Councillors including me were a bit scared of this type of people power especially as we had little power ourselves to actually do anything about it.

The previous Mayor, an Independent, seemed to ignore the problem and with my election came a new Mayor, one from the Labour Party; a party renowned for its care and attention for the well-to-do middle classes. So into the valley of death walked I.

Three years on and I was invited to address ABC at their AGM, April 2019, this is the story I told ABC.

"I'm standing down next year but progress on the University Expansion problem will, I feel, be one of my achievements.[23]

Nothing is achieved alone and Councillors Anthony Negus*, Nicola

21   An article 4 direction is a planning tool which means that something normally permitted without needing permission at all like turning part of your front garden into a driveway or building a small extension needs to go through the planning process (Don't assume on the basis of what's written here that you can convert your garden or build an extension, contact your Council).
22   An HMO is a house of multiple occupation with three or more unrelated people sharing some facilities like a kitchen or bathroom and often with six, seven or more living there.
23   Anthony (LD) is a long standing Councillor of a neighbouring, similarly inundated ward, Nicola (Lab) is the Cabinet Member for Planning and Paul (Lab) the Cabinet Member for Housing. I like all three of them despite any implications otherwise in the book. Same goes for Mark Weston the rogue in chapter B3! In fact I think that goes for all 70 Councillors in Bristol at that time. A camaraderie, fellowship even, against the vicissitudes waiting to see what can be thrown at us next.

387

Beech* and Paul Smith* deserve real credit too, possibly in effort terms more than me. But I will bag credit for a couple of critical bits of the thinking.

The expansion of the University shares a feature in common with the Expansion of the Universe. It is unstoppable. You just have to make the best of it.

The first issue I tackled in 2016 was to frame the problem away from middle-class residents complaining. That holds no truck in a Labour administration. In fact it was tough to get the Greens to agree to anything critical of students who have been big supporters of our party. But for some reason or other my colleagues trusted me.

As an ex-economics/business teacher I have the laws of supply and demand running through my blood stream (when markets are at work). More students mean more need for housing, and students can afford the rent because they borrow and pay back on the never, never. That must be affecting the housing market I thought, and so it was. My speech to Full Council in January 2017 reframed the problem from loss of Council Tax and bad behaviour to being one of ever increasing rents and one of the causes of homelessness. Labour woke up, the University was planning to expand further into other parts of Bristol and with potentially devastating consequences to communities. And students were also complaining about the high rents; the Greens woke up too.

This speech in January 2017 triggered a cross party working group, all four parties, and we reported back in the summer with a motion to Full Council that was carried unanimously (I was on holiday when this happened so my Co-Councillor Carla Denyer carried the torch). The motion called on the Mayor to take some actions to mitigate the impact of university expansion.

This set off various strands of work. Some of which I will speak about today".

APPENDIX 16

IS BRISTOL FOR ITS PEOPLE OR FOR THE UNIVERSITY? (2)

The strands that were started in the summer of 2017 are listed in the box below. Mainly for the planning geeks, for non-geeks just move straight on!

THE STRANDS OF WORK AS OF APRIL 2019:

– Introducing controls on HMO conversions including new Article 4s in 16 areas as far apart as Avonmouth in the west to Brislington in the east. Plus requiring new-build student accommodation to house all future growth in student numbers (and have affordable housing requirements, ideally with retail or cafés on ground floor).

– HMO Licensing in 12 wards for properties with three or more residents. At a cost of £1,000 (over five years) and onerous requirements if the HMO is in a state, we hear some landlords are giving in. I worry about non student HMOs, they are an important part of the housing mix and normally for the poorer in our city.

– Cumulative Impact Areas (noise and late night venues): A call for evidence closes on 30th April. If the evidence can prove it then a CIA will be reinforced and following further consultation an extreme result could be no new licenses for a particular activity.

– Anthony and I got onto the UofB Court and we both spoke at their AGM in November 2018 direct to the top dogs about the harm the University is doing. The University have granted greater powers to their enforcement team to clamp down on parties and anti-social behaviour (increased fines even a letter of apology from the students). We were then kicked off the UofB Court, as coincidentally, it was restructured and downsized.

– We gained a better understanding of the lost Council Tax issues (not quite as bad as it seemed). Also the CIL (developer tax) is actually higher on new-build student accommodation and the costs of providing students with Council services isn't as high as some

---

other sectors funded by Local Authorities.

– Bristol University and UWE participated at the Bristol Forum to listen to the city's needs and find solutions. I spoke about less congested roads and support for buses. UWE to be fair had also expanded in size in the early two thousands but had informed the Council so it could plan. The University of Bristol just did it and sod the consequences.

Welcome back non geeks. My talk to ABC continues:

"Of course it's not all sweetness and light but this list is evidence of progress. Each one of those advances has a story in its own right and if you have a couple of hours I'd be happy to go on and on and on.

This morning, your meeting is about the Local Plan Consultation. The Local Plan and its university expansion policies need their story to be told too.

Throughout the second half of 2017 Pat (Chair of ABC) and Anthony were banging on about needing an SPD[24]. I wasn't, I believed the officers, they said that all that was needed was a practice note, that was adequate and enough. Nicola Beech, the Cabinet Member for Planning believed them too. But sometime, early 2018, in Redland Library, one of the ABC members, who is an ex-Planning Inspector actually took the trouble to clearly explain the difference and finally I boarded the SPD train but Nicola wasn't on it (yet).

About the same time and listening intently to Planning Officers their reasons for not having an SPD didn't seem logical as they dipped, ducked, dived and dodged and came up with seemingly different explanations each meeting, so I decided to put in a budget amendment to give Planning

---

24   An SPD is a supplementary planning document that supports policies in the Local Plan. The previous Local Plan didn't have any quantity based policies to control university expansion and so it seemed an SPD wouldn't work. But the SPD is written to quantify the expression "harmful concentrations" (of HMOs) which is in the old Local Plan. I think Nicola Beech did such a good job in negotiations with the University about stopping future expansion that they agreed for the first time to take a responsible approach. It took a new Vice Chancellor as well. It targets HMOs as in Planning you deal with the type of building not the nature of the occupants.

Department £25,000 in April 2018 to gather some evidence and data to support an SPD.

But Nicola, on the advice of her officers, didn't want an SPD so a few days before the budget, and I was on holiday in Lisbon, beer in hand, on the balcony I had to make a phone call to Nicola to agree the wording. Beaten into submission, knowing the Planning Department had got at her, I basically said, "Nicola you do what you think fit, Practice Note or SPD or other, just get the data".

APPENDIX 17

IS BRISTOL FOR ITS PEOPLE OR FOR THE UNIVERSITY? (3)

"The budget amendment for £25,000 was voted through unanimously and I subsequently found out that Finance changed the source of the funding to come from increased planning fees, so Planning were paying for it themselves. As it turned out rightly so!

At the same time Anthony and I got ourselves put on the Local Plan Review Group[25] with 10 other Councillors looking at all aspects of the draft Local Plan. I think the others had fun with us because all the student stuff was always saved until the end of the agenda so it wasn't given much time. To Anthony it was a red flag to a bull. I ended up being a peacemaker. (And secretly, although he might suspect this, I was briefing Pat all the way and getting her feedback. I would never put that in writing). Pat had one or two meetings with Nicola and put forward the case quite forcefully.

Lo and behold sometime during the summer of 2018 another iteration of the draft Local Plan came out and it had the letters SPD written in it. You could imagine I had to stop, check I was reading the right document. When it came to the review meeting I asked and yes they had found a new source of data which meant the policies in the Local Plan and thus SPD are evidence based. So my budget amendment unblocked a crucial aspect.

The 2019 version of the Local Plan went out to consultation. In overview the University will be adding another 6,400 students over the next 5 or

---

25 A form of policy development scrutiny, the type I like.

so years. As I said the Expansion of the University is unstoppable, this number is about one third of Bristol's population increase in quite a short timeframe. By 2036 Bristol needs to have added another 33,500 homes for about 60,000 people. So in the longer term the extra 6,400 keeps the ratio of students at about 10% Bristol wide.

But the extra students will be, we are told, quite different. The University are expanding by adding Master's Degree courses (1 year mainly) and targeting overseas students. UoB has a good international name and can sell such courses for £20,000 or more rather than the measly £9,250 for a UK student. We are told that Masters' students from Malaysia or China for example have different accommodation needs[26] and the plan is for all of them to live in new purpose built student accommodation across a number of areas of Bristol.

So in theory new growth in student numbers will mainly be Master's students with different accommodation requirements and so purpose built accommodation blocks will be best for them. HMOs in the 23 areas will have quantity limits (called threshold requirements) for the first time and detail will be in the forthcoming SPD.

And before I hand over to Pat, the reason why I am not standing again, from the horse's mouth. The original reason was an affair of the heart. But my girlfriend and I split up this Christmas (2018). She lives in Norway so it was going to be difficult to continue being a Councillor. This January I briefly considered whether I should stand again, but no, firstly a new candidate had been selected for Clifton Down and secondly I decided I didn't like politics, not the UK's First Past the Post kind. It changes the behaviour of people who are mainly good people and locally almost always good people just wanting to make a difference. But you have to continually get in the press so people notice, make claims for yourself which were really down to teamwork and over simplify issues and statements on things that are very complex.

We have made much progress on student expansion. Anthony, myself,

---

26   We are told this is part culture but also because they tend to be older, sometimes sponsored by business and paying more. It seems they prefer to live in a purpose built block and not share a house with 5 or more other people. It doesn't apply to all so is a generalisation.

Nicola Beech and Paul Smith, my individual contributions were to reframe the arguments onto housing and rents, to get the £25,000 for the evidence and build a constructive working relationship with Nicola.

What you have before you is not perfect and I'm sure Pat[27] is about to explain why!!"

Pat took the microphone, said thank you Clive and then went on to explain why it wasn't perfect.

IS THE PLANNING SYSTEM AT FAULT OR THE MARKET FOR LAND?

APPENDIX 18

THE BATTLE OF BELGRAVE HILL (THE CRAZINESS OF PLANNING?)

Two hundred million years ago my ward was awash with dinosaurs[28].

Nearly 200 years ago part of it was a limestone quarry and the Bristol Dinosaur was dug up, only the fourth dinosaur to have been found in the world. It is now in Bristol's museum.

The quarry then had cottages built under the cliff the quarrymen had dug out. The quarry was then abandoned, houses built in and around the area. One area of cliff with remnants of the cottages remained and became totally overgrown. It was in need of maintenance and would be a liability on any owner. Such is Bristol's housing shortage, the original land owner was able to sell this patch of land just four metres wide sandwiched as it was between the pavement and the 25m high cliff. The land was then sold again at auction, planning permission applied for three houses and rejected, it was sold again, the latest landowner applied for permission to build two houses right up against the cliff, partially to stabilise it. I imagine a Council officer probably breathed a sigh of relief.

The locals objected as they would, but a Planning Committee

27 Pat was the Chair of this combined residents group ABC (Action for Balanced Communities)
28 Thecodontosaurids.

approved it in late 2014 with conditions that included needing adequate insurance, archaeological inspection and monitoring by a structural surveyor; all good ideas, but it was a bad decision[29].

So the developer started work clearing the scrub and brambles, a few rocks fell down but they continued. The archaeologists moved in, dug about and found things[30], they finished their work. By summer of 2017 the actual development itself hadn't started partly due to long waits and partly due to needing to satisfy the pre-commencement conditions like insurance. Developments must be started within three years or else planning permission runs out. So in an intense race against time the developer tried to get all the preparatory work done and provide appropriate evidence to the Council that all conditions had been complied with.

In the meantime relationships with the locals had become somewhat fractious, falling rocks and broken sewers didn't help. I think even the police were called.

Time ran out on our sorry developer and a few months later he got a response from the Council saying he needed to reapply for planning permission and he duly did. It was a formality really because he'd been given permission in 2014.

The application came in, was duly complained about, I was asked by residents to help their cause. I often wouldn't do this because as I was on Committee it was better to remain open minded, not predetermined as the parlance goes, that way I could be one of the 11 votes. But this time it was different. To me it seemed bonkers to build houses so close to a cliff that seemed to be falling down already.

So the hearing was set for November 2018. We had arguments about loss of parking, inability to maintain the cliff, loss of heritage, room sizes too small, difficult access for fire engines and the like. Other reasons too, but would any of them stick? One of the residents told his tale of being stuck in an ambulance on the way to hospital because parked cars

29 There are claims it was a hurried, tired decision. The meeting considered seven applications that day, this was number six.
30 We weren't told what they found.

had blocked the road. This was corroborated by his daughter. One of the Committee members had gone to visit the site and nearly got his car wedged in between two parked cars as well. Another Councillor was really concerned about the inability to maintain the cliff face with houses right in front blocking access.

The decision was to defer awaiting further information on access by emergency vehicles, room sizes inside the proposed homes and insurance.

Back it came in Feb 2019, still recommended for approval. The officer, in my view, weasel worded the room size arguments and the emergency vehicle access was ridiculous. Highways had recommended extending double yellow lines, taking out eight or more parking spaces (there were only about 60) this was so a fire engine could reverse in to get near enough to the new houses. (All the existing ones were OK, just). And, wait for it, this is a residents' parking area and so putting in new double yellow lines would have triggered a parking review which because everything was all so squashed up might have resulted in another 12 or more lost spaces. So possibly 20 spaces lost, residents having to find new spaces where there are none, the Quarry area of Clifton Down is already one of the most densely parked areas of Bristol. And yet Planning officers still recommended this application. Common sense is not a material planning consideration. Fortunately we have Councillors on Committees who between them do have common sense and the creativity to find reasons that are within planning rules.

The application was turned down, unheard of! And it should become a case study for all students at Planning School. The developer is stuck with this land, now a liability, at the time of writing has the opportunity to appeal to one of the Secretary of State's Planning Inspectors who may or may not agree with the Committee and its use of common sense. The cliff looks a mess, fencing to protect the public and no resolution for months if not years.

Update April 2020 – New plans have come in for one three bedroom house. Right up against the cliff, no garden, but the room sizes meet the criteria. I have called it in[31] and so await a date to start the process again.

Update June 2020 – The application came to Committee, officers recommended approval. They couldn't think of any planning reason to turn it down. The Committee turned it down, one member saying, "what's the point of having a Committee if all we do is rubber stamp officer recommendations". Indeed. The developer has a right of Appeal. He might win that. That's when the trouble would really start.

THIS APPENDIX IS A BIT LONGER AND DISCUSSES THE REASONS WHY BRISTOL NEEDS SO MUCH AFFORDABLE HOUSING. IT FEEDS INTO CHAPTER G13.

APPENDIX 19
THE MATHS OF AFFORDABLE RENTED HOUSING (IN TEN QUESTIONS)

As of April 2020 the City of Bristol had approximately 203,000 dwellings for its 464,000ish population not counting those living in Filton, Bradley Stoke and other parts of South Gloucestershire who think they live in the City of Bristol but don't. The adjusted JSP[32] figures evidenced the requirement to build approx. 35,000 more dwellings to house the expected influx of people moving to Bristol[33] as well as dealing with the demographics of births, people living longer and living in smaller accommodation. Out of that 35,000 the city needs to build around 21,000 affordable rented[34]. The other 14,000 would be broadly at market rates; some for sale, some at a discount for first time buyers (subsidised by the taxpayer), the others to rent at market rates and some at slightly discounted rates.

31　Called in to Planning Committee means the decision is taken by 11 Councillors and not an officer.
32　Joint Spatial Plan
33　Approx. 10% are students but they can be accommodated in purpose built blocks.
34　There is absolutely no chance of achieving this and that's what's led to my challenge of the whole system, especially viability but whether land is suitable product to buy and sell via a market mechanism at all. My conclusion is in H3.

I'm splitting this chapter up into ten questions, plus some answers.

Q1 – How much is the need for affordable and social rented accommodation? (I mean as a need not a want, people want it because it's cheap, but some people need it).

Please note that many of my numbers are estimates[35]. I'm reasonably happy I have done cross checks and it is therefore sufficiently precise to paint a picture[36], but if anyone wants to research the exact numbers please do[37].

Firstly some history and trends…

Tenure	2001 (Census)	2017 (QoL)
Owner occupied	63%	53%
Private rented	12%	29%
Social/Council rent	23%	18%
	Remaining 2% was other[38]	

The table above shows us the situation according to the 2001 Census, 63% of Bristol's housing was owner-occupied, 12% lived in private rented (market rate) and 23% in social rented (of which 19% was owned by the Council and 4% by housing associations) and the remaining 2% lived in "other" which includes living with your parents.

Sixteen years on, in 2017, a study indicates that private rented in Bristol has now risen to 29%, with 18% socially rented and 53% owner occupied. That 2017 estimate is taken from Bristol's annual quality of life survey. So the private rented sector has grown fast. Its increase of 17% over 16 years is due to the decline of owner occupied by 10% and

---

35   As a Councillor I can request information pertinent to doing my job. But writing this book is not my Councillor job and so I refrained from asking officers for the exact data. Councillor Paul Smith was very helpful in giving the general numbers.

36   More of an impressionist painting rather than a precise line drawing.

37   I'd be happy to help analyse the data and with assistance from Revenues and Benefits department check the assumptions.

38   I don't know if other includes van dwellers and which categories of homeless (if any).

social rent down 5% (plus or minus some rounding[39]) and of course new dwellings.

Of most interest here is the social sector decline from 23% in 2001 (37,000 homes) to 18% in 2017[40] (36,000) as there was almost no building of Council houses, in fact Council house stock was lost due to right to buy and any extra affordable housing (for the social sector) paid for by developers didn't quite keep up with that loss.

National figures were reported in The Independent, 16th Jan 2020, Almost 200k fewer Council homes since 2010

"Labour analysis of official figures shows that almost 200,000 Council homes have been lost since the Conservatives came to power in 2010. The number of homes rented from Councils has fallen from 1,786,000 in 2010 to 1,592,000 by the end of 2018 – a drop of 194,000, or 11%. A Government spokesperson said: "Since 2010 this government has delivered over 464,000 new affordable homes, including 114,000 social homes. In addition to this, the social housing waiting list has decreased by 40% since 2012."
Thank you LGiU

---

39 Sometimes the figures are for dwellings and sometimes for people. The average size of rented dwellings might vary from owner occupied but not by much especially if you allow for HMOs and purpose built.
40 Population grew by approximately 70,000 over that time (ONS) requiring over 30,000 dwellings. But the need would have been more due to the demographics of smaller families. (of that 30,000 at least 10,000 should have been social housing to keep up with demand). Even in 2001 I expect there was not enough supply of social housing.

Current social and Council housing stock and increase needed

Current Council houses	27,000
Current social houses (via HAs)	10,000
Current net waiting list	10,000
Sub total	47,000
Demographics and Pop Growth	11,000 (maybe 13,000)
Total requirement (by 2036)	58,000 to 60,000 (approx. 25% of 240,000)

In 2020 Bristol's social rent sector included about 27,000[41] Council houses; plus a further 10,000 houses at social rent (see later for rent levels) managed by housing associations. That's actually a slight improvement on 2017's estimate[42]. These 37,000 exist, they are the 18% of the 203,000 dwellings that are here in Bristol.

The net[43] waiting list for social housing is over 10,000 people and families all bidding for social and affordable rented. We need to add population growth and demographics adds to around 58,000 to 60,000. The 15 year plan[44] was to get another 21,000 social/Council built. With total dwellings going up to around 240,000, then (if achieved) that would make the social/Council sector become 58,000 so around 24% to 25% of all Bristol's housing by 2036.

Comment: 25% supply of dwellings needs to be at social or affordable rent. This is a key figure for Bristol and I shall attempt to verify using other data whether these planning estimates are true.

41   On some measures this is 28,000 depending on whether you include leasehold or just rented.
42   Which probably implies some small errors in the data collection and/or rounding issues in both figures.
43   This excludes the nearly 3,000 already in social or Council housing who are looking to move to a bigger or smaller house. That "blocking" is a problem and although they are on the housing list they are not actually homeless.
44   JSP to 2036

Q2 – If I want to check Planning's data can you verify this "25% need" in other ways?

We will now look at two different[45] ways of assessing this need. Social provision of housing is lower cost (rental usually) for those on lower incomes. And without it they can't afford a home at all and a home is a need. Renters in general aren't just the poor, sometimes people choose that form of tenure to assist in job flexibility. As you have seen from the 2017 data 29% of the population are in market rented (private sector) and 18% in social or Council rented. In the private sector rents can be double the social sector, maybe the occupants don't know that!

So two other ways of assessing demand to justify why 25% need affordable (mainly social) rent are:

a) Basing an estimate on the average (and spread of) salary of Bristolians; the mean is £28,000 gross per annum. The latest data from the 2018 Quality of Life survey shows that the bottom 25% of earnings have gross (i.e. pre-tax) incomes of £21,000 or less. If your earnings are at that level, or less then you can't afford to buy[46] a home (unless your parents pay much of it) and private sector rent could easily be at levels of £10,000 a year (about £800 a month), so that would be over 50% of your net income. Therefore to rent privately, people share, marry (or civil partner), or whatever, in order to split paying the rent or mortgage. But then if you want to bring up a family or you separate or one of you loses a job and you are down to one earner then to stay in the private rented accommodation you will need an income much higher than £21,000 a year. If you are on that or less you will need affordable housing (social, Council etc) or risk becoming homeless.

So 25% of people in Bristol are on gross earnings of £21,000 a year or less. That kind of level or below it means you probably need affordable housing (unless you have a load of cash from your parents, for example).

b) Another sensibleness check is to look at the situation of two key workers working zero hours contracts on £8.72 per hour minimum

45 Rather than planning data.
46 The same survey showed the bottom 25% of house prices (to buy) are £210,000 or less, a £210,000 flat is pretty unaffordable on £21,000 income a year, this is the 10 x earnings figure coming up again.

wage. They could well struggle to bring in £21,000 a year in total as often some weeks the hours aren't there. Whether single or a couple they would be eligible for Universal Credit[47]. (In fact a single person in private rented accommodation would require income of just over £30,000 gross before Universal Credit[48] benefits become zero. For a couple with no children, both working, they would need to earn £15,200 gross each before UC becomes zero). Such people are often key workers, carers of the elderly for example or in the hospitality trade and many of these jobs are on zero hour's contracts and/or minimum wage.

Covid-19 has taught us how appreciated these people are (we clapped for them every Thursday night). Why they earn so little is explained in section D. We need to do something about it. They are not benefits scroungers, some work the longest and most antisocial hours possible; increasing the minimum wage helps a bit as long as hours aren't cut.

Therefore given these two cross checks based on earnings data I am happy to say that broadly, in Bristol, social and affordable rental accommodation should be for those earning £21,000 or less. This is about 25%[49] of the population, I am discounting students as their loans are specifically designed to be able to rent student accommodation or share in a house. Without students these estimates mean about 25% of over 18s (including their children) which will be about 120,000[50] people (working age and pensioners, not-students) will require around 58-60,000[51] affordable dwellings (which is what the Planners said we needed).

The percentage who need affordable housing will be different in different cities depending on the range and average of earnings, and the

---

47 Including the housing part of it.
48 These state benefits paid by the tax payer are going into the pockets of the landlords.
49 Demand at 25% give or take 2% but certainly much more than the 18% affordable housing supply we have now.
50 In the 28,000 Council homes live about 60,000 people. So if you are looking to house 120,000 you need about 56,000 homes. Slightly lower than the 58,000 but close enough. Obviously some people in social housing earn more than £21,000 a year. That is a tenure issue.
51 I agree there's a lot of estimate in this: the average size of dwelling (this is still declining on average), the number of people who are in Council houses who now earn over £21,000 a year (but because of the leap up to private rents prefer understandably to stay in lower rents or buy their Council house). As a policy in my view Right to Buy is not necessarily bad. It's the discount that's given and then the limits placed on Councils to be able to replace those sold that is harmful.

level of private sector rents/house prices. In Bristol it seems that this figure is about 25%.

Now the answer to a related question; why do so many people need social and affordable rents? This is twofold; they simply don't earn enough. And/or the price of land is too high. Tackle both, that means tackling the market system for setting wages and for the price of land.

Q3 – OK, I now believe in the 25% need, how will we get there?

Back to supply. How to get up to 58-60,000? I've said that the city has 37,000 in 2020 and needs at least another 21,000. The first thing to realise is Bristol will lose some Council houses through Right to Buy[52]. We know the market won't provide enough affordable housing subsidised by developers; that was running at around 20% and fell to around 10% to 15%. To achieve a higher level needs subsidies to the developer.

Building 35,000 more homes of which 14,000 will be at market prices[53] would naturally bring in about 2,000 affordable[54] under the S106 scheme but the city needs 21,000. That's an extremely broken market. The net gap is 19,000 homes. Housing is a need and it requires land which within a city is a scarce resource. Not having housing has huge externalities, harm to society as well as the people and families concerned. Therefore for all those reasons of market failure it's not surprising that the market is broken.

This is not an answer, it just scales the problem.

Q4 – Another question I'm asked is, because social rents are so cheap, can we all get one?

Understandably access to social housing is rationed. To even get on the list you need earnings of less than £40,000 a year, savings less than that too and you need to have lived in Bristol for two years or more. That

---

52 In a 15-year period this could easily be 2,000 homes. These need to be replaced.

53 It's primarily the developments sold or rented at market rates which trigger affordable housing obligations.

54 So being generous, 17,500 homes at 20% affordable gives you 14,000 market priced homes (as per the JSP) and 3,500 affordable. The right to buy losses will be around 1,500 in that time period so it's a net positive 2,000 affordable. Historically affordable housing via developers contributions has just about kept up with right to buy losses (of Council houses) so this 2,000 is an extremely generous estimate.

gets you in a position where you can bid. You will probably go into Band 3 or 4. You need other circumstances to get you up into a band where there is a realistic chance of a home. These criteria[55] are being consulted on in 2020 so may change.

Tenure which starts with a 12-month introductory tenancy and then secure for the rest of your life means some people are in Council housing who don't meet the bottom 25% earnings rule of thumb. They did but their situation has improved. They are faced either with staying at low rent, or buying their house at a deep discount (Right to Buy scheme) or paying twice as much rent in the private sector. Not optimal. But as the system is broken changing this won't fix it, it might help a bit.

Q5 – Back to supply, what is the current approach to getting more affordable homes?

Nowadays there are new subsidies to support more affordable homes. In Bristol these are budgeted[56] at £72m total over the next four years, so £18m a year. £52m of that £72m is from borrowing and the interest on the loan will be borne by the local taxpayer. The £72m will increase the affordable housing levels by about 500 hundred in total over the four years; keep that going for sixteen[57] years and that's 2,000. But we know Bristol needs to close that gap of 19,000[58]. To set this in context the £18 million a year could also deliver free buses to tens of thousands of people to ferry them to and from homes where it is much cheaper to build (but is not permitted, as it would be Green Belt land usually).

We are way short on the numbers, the gap was 21,000; Q3 showed via S106 and accounting for Right to Buy "losses" it has come down to 19,000. Here with Homes England subsidies it is now 17,000 (required social/Council homes by 2036). We need a plan to close this gap further, it part relies on building more Council houses. Let's learn about that.

---

55   Vulnerability to harm from other people is one of the main criteria.
56   2020/21 budget. The cost of public subsidies range from £100k to £150k per affordable home. I have taken £144k as the price of land is likely to increase over the coming years (based on past experience).
57   Technically I should use 15 years (to align with the JSP data).
58   This could be achieved by £180m a year in subsidies (rather than £18m) but that would bankrupt the Council, maybe the government too and would stoke up the housing market and the price of land. Some of the strain could be taken up with Council house building, see later.

Q6 – Tell me more about affordable rents and just how high are private rents?

If you work through the maths which we are about to do you can see that the cost of private rent is caused by the way the economy has been structured over many, many decades.

In Bristol in 2020 the average[59] level of private rent at market based prices is approx. £1,100 per month, next level down is what's confusingly called affordable rents set at the housing benefit rent at £697 per month (63% of market rate), social rent (run by housing associations at 41% of market rate) at £450 per month and finally Council house/flat rents at £340 per month.

If you are on the Council's housing list you can apply for any of the three cheaper options. If you bid for a home at affordable rent you will pay a bit more but the chances are you will get one quicker (or less slowly).

The first thing you notice is the massive discrepancy and unfairness in this system for those who pay market rents, but for the moment put that to one side and dig deeper. When developers allow for affordable housing in their viability studies required under the S106 scheme, it can vary from a 30% price discount to as much as 55% and this often depends on the location, with the higher discounts in the centre where land prices are higher. This discount averages out to enable a housing association to buy and provide a mix of social rent and housing benefit level rent. (The developer will sell the properties to a housing association, which will run it, for about half of the market rate; if the developer has paid full price for the land that will hurt[60]).

Council houses are unbelievably good value to rent at £340/month. Council houses are not subsidised by the public, each Council runs their portfolio of properties as if it were a business (at breakeven) with an accounting treatment called a ring fenced housing revenue account, HRA. The Government has enforced rent decreases of 1% per annum

---

59   These are all averages provided to the Budget Full Council Meeting on 25th February 2020.
60   Not half as much though than someone made homeless, sleeping on the streets and being beaten up in the middle of the night.

for the last four years (to 2019) which has undermined the ability of Councils to use tenants' rent to pay to improve the buildings[61] or build new ones. That straight jacket has now been released and rents are going up with inflation plus 1% (still less than market rent increases in Bristol which are about 5%).

Q7 – How does a Council housing business model break even on £340 per month rent and yet private businesses need £1,100 per month?

There are four essential differences: firstly Council housing is unsustainable at £340 a month. Then we have three issues due to private sector involvement: the need for a profit, the price of land and new building costs.

For Council houses, we need to allow a Council more income to plough back into new building, insulation and better maintenance. To do that I estimate the rent would need to go up to about £500 a month to be truly financially sustainable[62]. Council rents could well get close to this level over the next ten or so years if they are allowed to go up with inflation plus 1%. This sustainable margin will also fund energy efficiency, fire safety, refurbishments and the new building program.

The three remaining differences between a sustainable Council house rental value of £500/month and £1,100/month[63] in the private sector are:

1) Developer's profit,

2) Financing the cost of land (which includes the landowners' profit)

3) And thirdly building costs which include the fact that on average developers provide 10% of what they build at a huge discount to sell as affordable dwellings to a housing association. So build 100 flats, get the rent from 90 and sell the remaining 10 to a housing association potentially at below cost.

61   Even cladding removal was difficult to afford.
62   CIPFA (The Chartered Institute of Public Finance and Accountancy have just emailed Bristol Councillors (9 July 2020) saying they have a calculator called CIPFA Housing 360 which a Council pays to use, £2,000, enters the data and out pops a calculation for the financial sustainability of their Council housing model. Whether it allows one to model the rent increase required I don't know. If it does I'll be fascinated to find out if it is near £500 a month.
63   The £1,100 is at 2020 rent levels whereas the £500 / month for a Council house is around 2030 levels. So the situation is worse than I show here.

We can account[64] for profit (point 1) at 20% so £220/month for all the various profits they make (see G8 for why) and for point 3 by taking off 5% of the average rent (£55/month) for the affordable housing via S106 that on average developers have to factor in. There might also be a higher cost of building private homes than Council ones. I haven't factored that in. Factors 1 and 3 bring the £1,100/month down to £825/month rent. Just £325 difference, which I claim is mainly due to financing the cost of land[65].

Council houses are built on Council land which can be cheap to finance if not free. Private rental property is built on land which can cost £10 million/hectare sometimes more, like £15 million in the centre and that's just Bristol's prices. A fairly high build density of 200 dwellings per hectare results in a land cost of £75,000 per flat, funding that at 4% is £300 per month accounting for nearly all the difference in rent between a private home and a Council home, that's in the centre. Further out with land at £7.5 million/hectare and say a lower build density of 100 dwellings per hectare at 4% interest also comes to £300 per month; so you can see that most if not all of that £325/month difference in rent is due to the cost of financing the land, and I haven't allowed for paying back the original amount borrowed (called the principal).

A Council which borrows more cheaply than the private sector and builds on land it might own which is valued less, or even free, can run a profitable, sustainable business with rents at £500/month whereas the private sector market rate needs to £1,100/month to be financially sustainable.

Q8 – That doesn't tally with the ND6 figures I saw in Chapter G8?

Correct: Purpose built private rented sector blocks like ND6 have a different cost structure because the flats are smaller[66], there is more use

---

64 In the financial meaning of the word. These are of course rough averages.
65 I'm treating it as an ongoing cost as the whole comparison on rents is annual costs per year.
66 This is a risk in the ND6 business model, Covid-19 might trigger minimum dwelling sizes, we shall see.

of communal areas and there is a service charge. The smaller size makes the land finance charge less because the density is so very high, they also take less profit percentage as the risk is less, but added stamp duty (thank you RICS – see G7 and G8) and minimal affordable housing means they can make a profit at £900/month rents.

I am not arguing that we should all live in Council houses, I am pointing out that the high costs that many of us bear for a market-based approach to housing is driven mainly by the price of land, its financing and the need for profit which is driven by risk. On top of high rents, our taxes (and part of our rents) are used to subsidise housing for the poorest 25% who don't earn enough[67]. And why don't they earn enough? I have covered that in section E. Our economic system favours those in occupations which can exploit weaknesses in markets. Additionally you might want to find out what happened to the trade unions and the history of relative negotiating power between employer and employee.

Q9 – So how much of my private rent (and tax) supports profit and land prices?

Back to those in private rented accommodation; renting at £1,100 a month, they (maybe you) are subsidising affordable homes at £55 (on average), paying £300 for the interest on the land, contributing £220 to the profit of the developer[68] (and perhaps the landlord too) and additionally you will be paying Council Tax of which £18m (about 8% or £140 a year) goes into financing the subsidies of 125 social rent homes to be built each year. That's a huge amount of money. And what's worse because many private renters can afford all this means that the cost of the land increases over time as developers bid up the price of land (which, as we know, they are not making any more[69]) to make more money from building on it and so make the problem worse.

---

67 Which finances the profits of business, some of which are structured so they don't pay much UK tax.
68 And the landowner's profit on the land uplift.
69 Imagine the land were a large flat canvas painted by Constable. Very expensive only painted once and people keep bidding more for bits of it.

Q10 – So what's the solution?

One solution is to buy your own property[70] and ideally the land too, but that is getting less and less easy and is probably not a long-term sustainable solution for society (in a city) as a whole.

Another short term solution is to share a house with others; live in a house of multiple occupation (HMO). These types of dwellings have been the answer in the past to those just moved to an area (like me in 1988), for young professionals and for those who can't afford to rent a flat or bedsit and aren't eligible for social housing. In Bristol there are about 12,000 HMOs housing maybe 50,000 people.[71] The main increase in demand for this type of property recently has been to satisfy the expansion[72] of the universities; the University of Bristol[73] in particular. You can see with all these issues going on, uncontrolled university expansion hasn't helped which is why I am so upset about it.

Another solution is higher income taxes to support more subsidies but that creates higher land prices too.

Council house building is being ramped up now rents can increase. We left Q5 with a gap of 17,000 social homes. G13 looks at 5,000 new Council homes by 2036. But we are left with a gap of 12,000. With all this effort and public money the gap in 2036 will be 12,000 and in 2020 it is 10,000. Something has to change.

Maybe you've already read the other options discussed in Section G?

---

70   This isn't all it's cracked up to be either as I've discovered as the rain is now coming in and I need a roofer.
71   Estimates vary widely from 7,000 to 14,000.
72   At the last count over 15,000 students were in this type of property. With this increase in demand one would expect an increase in rent levels, many students are paying £500 or more a month just to have one room in a shared house. That kind of level is unaffordable to many in work, students can "afford it" as the loan system enables them to borrow and maybe not even have to pay it back if they choose a low paying career.
73   The real problem is that this growth was uncontrolled. If the expansion had been planned for and purpose built accommodation built in areas that needed regeneration (this did work in the Centre) and the conversion of homes had been protected then many of the downsides would have been minimised. The University (in many people's view) just went for it, all that glittery money at £9k a student plus rent and even more for overseas. So, so harmful...

AND FINALLY IF ANY POLICY MAKERS HAVE GOT THIS FAR THEN HERE ARE SOME REFORMS YOU MIGHT CONSIDER.

APPENDIX 20

A SUMMARY OF THINGS THAT NEED CHANGING (OTHERS ARE IN H10)

This is for my good friend Matthew. He complains that once he's read a book he can't remember much about it to discuss in his book group. Well Matthew here's a summary of many of the issues raised and some of the things that need changing. But please don't just read this appendix, do read the whole book and no you're not getting it for free!

A2 – Future Generations Bill – to make sure new laws consider the people who are as yet unborn. It exists in Wales and might be coming to England.

A4 – Confidentiality as Director of the Port – the law allowing confidentiality agreements trumps the requirement of Councillors (representing the Council on a body) to be open and transparent.

A5 – If there are no planning policies you can do anything if you have the money (e.g. Biodiesel generators polluting the centre of the city). So there's a need for a more flexible approach.

A7 – Councillors' Code of Conduct and Member Officer Protocol: In June 2020 the Local Government Association sent out a "Model Members' Code of Conduct[74]" – good. Each Council won't have to re-invent the wheel. Its clause four is about the impartiality of Council officers. That's so, so important and missing from Bristol. Let's hope it's adopted.

Section A closes with a short story about Extinction Rebellion. I explain

---

74   https://www.local.gov.uk/sites/default/files/documents/LGA%20Model%20Member%20Code%20 of%20Conduct.pdf

why I have left the climate emergency to them because if they fail I have real fears that our democracy won't be able to cope. That's why we need a better democracy.

B1 & 2 – Introducing a concept called "Mathematics of Power" and how this helps explain why our rulers have to behave the way they do (to stay in power) and the impact on who the economy works for and doesn't work for. Perfectly illustrated by the behaviour of the 2020 Housing Secretary – thank you.

B3 – Example of Freeports (probable legislation to come), illustrating the funding of political parties and the Mathematics of Power.

The impact of the Mathematics still applies even if 51% of the vote is needed to win power. That's why the organs of the state (including Councils) need to be open and transparent to ensure everyone is treated fairly within the economy.

B4 & 5 – SEND (Special Educational Needs) Judicial Review – illustrating the requirement of openness and transparency in this case so Councillors know what they are voting for.

B6 – Organisation structures – How a change in organisation structure (three top officers reporting into a Mayor) can poison the trust between officers and Councillors. Some structures shouldn't be allowed (see A7 above, I hope the LGA look into this).

B7 – Legal Privilege – A centuries old privilege to lawyers meaning anything they write can be deemed confidential. This is fair when advising private clients but when an in-house lawyer in a Local Authority uses this to keep advice to the Mayor (or anyone else) secret it is not open and transparent and thus bad for democracy.

B8 – Member Officer Protocol – presumption of openness but see chapters

B11 and C6 and C7 where there isn't.

Scrutiny: Given the nature of power and if information can be made available then it needs to be analysed and discussed. This is called scrutiny.

B9 & 10 – Local Authority Scrutiny is a legal requirement but is primarily aimed at pre-decision scrutiny rather than policy development. The former can be made to work with two examples.

B11 – Policy development (the type of scrutiny that really adds value) and how it could be improved. It shows the value of public involvement.

C Introduction – It's the House of Lords that do effective scrutiny of national laws. It is they, the ones who are unelected and undemocratic.

C1 – Typical Councillor problems and inability to do much permanently about them. Skips vs containers (Planning), fly-tipping, cycle racks (insurance, street widths, parking...). It introduces the idea of different laws for cities compared with rural areas.

C2 – Universal Credit (taper, five week delay) – The IT wasn't up to it. These issues should have been solved years ago, problem with scrutiny and relying on markets.

C3 – Tale of two caps – University growth cap lifted. Borrowing cap stops building of Council houses. More bed space needed and less built. And how is it joined up thinking? Borrowing cap now lifted but borrowing rates higher, still losing affordable rented housing via Right to Buy (at a discount), and limitations on using that money from Right to Buy sales (receipts).

C4 & 5 – Licensing Act – Unfair process for residents and Councillors vs two Legals and no access to information.

C6 & 7 – Bristol Energy – Mistakes of this scale need to be shared nationally (to learn) yet the Authority hides behind LGA 1972 Sch 12a Part 1, clause 10: (Likely cause of this is the Localism Act 2011 allowed the setting up of businesses but the LGA 1972 wasn't amended?).

C8 – IT – This is what Government could do to improve Local Government efficiency.

C9 & 10 – Bus Services Act 2017. Still protects business from Local Government competition so maintaining monopolies and poor services.

C11 – Post Legislation Scrutiny – examples and whether it works.

Much of a Councillor's work is dealing with cases of unfairness, sometimes by the private sector (like rents, buses) and sometimes by Government and the Council. Why is fairness important and what is it?

D1, 2 & 3 – We see an example of fighting off a planning application for a mini power station in the centre of a city; in 2019 with the need for carbon neutrality. But the Government's Energy Policy EN1 dates from 2011, allowing gas generation, Bristol's policy BCS13 is out of date too.

D4, 5 & 6 – Comparing different types of fairness (Equality of Opportunity, Freedom of Opportunity without doing harm and Meritocracy) – Suggesting it might be useful for society to one day agree on this point; perhaps via a national Citizens' Assembly?

D7, 8 & 9 – The economy is a manmade construct, not a law of nature and if it is not working for enough of us we should change it.

D10, 11, 12 & 13 – Examples of possible changes to the local economy based on improving freedom of opportunity to all: libraries, buses, Council tax and clean air (the last one showing the unintended consequences of case law).

E1 – Markets were a good invention, a social tool to help trade but like all tools work well in some circumstances and less well in others. Where markets fail is where you see the unfairness in capitalism; either regulate, manage the market or provide some other way.

E2 & 3 Examples of market failings. Also considering whether Adam Smith's logic which applies to organisations with the profit motive work if the organisation's prime motive is care or education?

E4 – Align wealth creation with profit extraction. Don't allow grab-it-all-ism.

E5 – Four stories of economic failure – Homelessness Reduction Act 2017 (This law needs post legislative scrutiny), impact of benefits tapers and polluted air. These are all holding back the economy.

E6 – Social Value Act 2012 – Perhaps an answer. It would mean environmental and other harms are properly costed in. Additionally key workers should be paid more and those extracting lots from the economy without creating wealth should take less.

E7 – Profit is OK when aligned with society's goals.

We then consider where things go wrong if politicians create a market when there shouldn't be one. And if a market is the right tool how to manage it. Our leaders need to think more and not cling to dogma.

E8 – Competing Local Authorities – Planning introduces a duty to cooperate but they still compete.

E9 & 10 – Care Act 2014 (& 2017 Guidance) – A local authority should shape the market(s) for adult social care to bring better benefits (versus a "free market" approach).

E11 – Commercialisation – Should Councils be going into business?

E12 – Children in Care – Most definitely keep business well away.

Sections F and G look in depth at two of the areas I chose to focus on: the pressing problems of: (F) adult social care and (G) affordable housing.

F1, 2 & 3 – ASC – Blowing up the budget (not funded properly). People Scrutiny (quality not costs), covers 5% of Bristol's economy, ASC pressures (aren't going away).

F4 & 5 – Market place management goes wrong – Market approach to procurement: dynamic purchasing system, too much demand and poor negotiating power. Marketplace analysis (of costs within the Bristol Price) BCC has a 50% market share, Care Act calls for efficiency and tasks the Local Authority with achieving it. But we don't.

F6 – Budget 2018/19 (ASC costs misplaced), costs and bottlenecks.

F7 – Different types of homes: Extra Care Housing, in communities, shared blocks and more.

F8 – Getting £2 million more for ASC in the capital budget.

F9, 10 & 11 – Lack of leadership from Government, Rerunning 2010 – broken Government and it's not rocket science, what needs to be done.

F12 & 13 – Market shaping (Care Act 2014) shaped by the care motive.

Intro to G – affordable home subsidies

G1, 2 & 3 – Homelessness – Qualifications (2 years), duty to prevent homelessness (failings), bidding system (like EBay) market based to get an affordable, rented home. Government definitions of affordable (to buy) and latest initiatives may reduce grants for affordable rent.

G4 – Getting developers to pay – S106 Viability statements (also transport can be the solution).

G5, 6, 7 & 8 – Chocolate Factory site – We found £600k, deferred the application to find more. Affordable housing motion goes to Full Council, but the motion was pulled. Planning Inspector intervenes; speculative market "needs" 20% profit; Royal Institute of Chartered Surveyors (RICS) don't help, planning system capture by landowners. So the maths of power played out for long enough means landowners win.

G9 – Tall buildings – Compromising quality to hit the numbers.

G10 – Just buy the bloody land first.

G11 – Joint Spatial Plan and Green Belt, only one can survive. New policies are severely delayed.

G12 – University growth was uncontrolled and has done damage. It requires a Supplementary Planning Document, hopefully coming soon.

Interlude... Office conversions bring more homes but more harm!

G13 – The maths of affordable housing – The gap is still 12,000 homes.

We have arrived at section H, the big issues covered in the book that need fixing (there are many other issues too but not covered in this book, discrimination as an example). The ones I cover are the market for land and the sorry state of our democracy.

H1, 2 & 3 – Sorting out land – Millionaires made by the taxpayer (more maths of power), the price of land, Land Value Tax, problems with the planning system (too slow, cumbersome, too easy to veto and the many market failings that apply to land). If land remains a market then it needs different regulation.

H4 & H5 – Sorting out democracy – The maths of power means we will get this type of behaviour from politicians. The voting system causes that. How to get people more interested? Citizens' Assemblies perhaps, paid, robotics will lead to more "leisure time". A national consensus on fairness, ways to manage harm.

H6 & 7 – The hustings; tactical voting and tactical campaigning.

H8 – An electoral PACT (do that first, worry about PR later)?

H9 – Defeat tribalism with a new joint cause, an alliance?

H10 – List of actions that could be done (in part) locally.

H11 – And if we have to work with the Conservatives.

BIBLIOGRAPHY

Just some of the many works that have influenced me; a big thank you to all the authors. Its' not easy writing a book!

Adams, M. 2105 – *Land, A New Paradigm For A Thriving World*, North Atlantic Books

Akala, 2018 – *Natives*, Tworoadsbooks.

Anderton, A. 2008 – *Economics 'A' Level (5th ed.)*, Edexcel

Bregman, R. 2017 – *Utopia For Realists*, Bloomsbury

Byrne, E. 2013 – *Unbuilt Bristol*, Redcliffe Press

Cassidy, J. 2009 – *How Markets Fail*, Penguin

Cato, M.S. 2009 – *Green Economics*, Earthscan

Cato, M.S. 2011 – *Environment And Economy*, Routledge

Chang, H – *Economics: The User's Guide*, 2014

Christensen, C.M. 1997, 2016 – *The Innovator's Dilemma*, Harvard Business Review Press

Cottam, H. 2018 – *Radical Help*, Virago Press

Detter, D & Folster, S. 2015 – *The Public Wealth Of Nations*, Pallgrave Macmillan

Diamond, J. 2005 – *Collapse*, Penguin

Doyle, W. 2001 – *The French Revolution*, Oxford University Press

Frank, R. 1988 – *Passions Within Reason*, WW Norton

Frank, R. 2011 - *The Darwin Economy*, Princeton Press.

Frankl, V.E. 1946, 2011 – *Man's Search For Meaning*, Penguin Random House

Freeland, C. 2012 – *Plutocrats*, Clays

Gladwell, M. 2008 – *Outliers*, Penguin

Graeber, D. 2011, 2014 – *Debt The First 5,000 Years*, Melville House

Grayling, A.C. 2017 – *Democracy And Its Crisis*, Oneworld

Greenfield, S. 2016 – *A Day In The Life Of The Brain*, Penguin Random House

Greenhouse (Blewitt, J & Cunningham, R editors) – *The Post-Growth Project*, 2014

Hardman, I. 2018 – *Why We Get The Wrong Politicians*, Atlantic Books

Harford, T. 2017. – *Fifty Things That*

Made The Modern Economy, Abacus

Jackson, S. 2006 – *Where Value Hides*, John Wiley

Jackson, T. 2009 – *Prosperity Without Growth*, Earthscan

Janeway, W. 2012 – *Doing Capitalism In The Innovation Economy*, Cambridge University Press

Kahneman, D. 2011 – *Thinking, Fast And Slow*, Penguin

Lawson, G. 2019 – *Anatomies Of Revolution*, Cambridge University Press

Lloyd-Robers, S. 2016 – *The War On Women*, Simon Schuster

Lucas, C. 2015 – *Honourable Friends*, Portobello Books

King, A & Crewe, I. 2013 – *The Blunders Of Our Governments*, Oneworld

Machiavelli, N. c 1516, 2003 – *The Prince*, Penguin

Mason, P. 2019 – *Clear Bright Future*, Allen Lane

Mazzucato, M. 2013 – *The Entrepreneurial State*, Anthem Press

Mazzucato, M. 2018 – *The Value Of Everything*, Penguin Random House

Mcgarvey, D. 2017 - *Poverty Safari*, Luath Press

Norfield, T. 2017 – *The City*, Verso

Olsen, M. 1982 – *The Rise And Decline Of Nations*, Yale University

Olsen, M. 2000 - *Power And Prosperity*, Basic Books.

Peston, R & Knight ,L. 2012 – *How Do We Fix This Mess?* Hodder and Stoughton

Piketty, T. 2014 – *Capital In The Twenty-First Century*, Harvard University Press

Polanyi, K. 1944, 2001 – *The Great Transformation*, Beacon Press

Porritt, J. 2005 *Capitalism As If The World Matters*, Earthscan

Poundstone, W. 1993 – *Prisoner's*

Dilemma, Oxford University Press

Raworth, K. 2017 – *Doughnut Economics*, Penguin Random House

Ridley, M. 1996 – *The Origins Of Virtue*, Penguin

Rolleston, E. 1881, 2015 – *The Land Monopoly; Or Land, Taxation And Pauperism*, Forgotten Books

Rosling, H. 2018 – *Factfulness*, Sceptre

Ryan-Collins, J, Lloyd,T & Macfarlane, L. 2017 – *Rethinking The Economics Of Land And Housing*, Zed Books Ltd

Schumpeter, J. 1942, 2011 – *Capitalism, Socialism and Democracy* (2nd Edition), Martino

Schumacher, E.F. 1973, 1988 – *Small Is Beautiful*, Cox and Wyman

Slack, P. 1990 – *The English Poor Law 1531 – 1782*, Cambridge University Press

Smith, A. 1776, 2012 - *An Enquiry Into The Nature And Causes Of The Wealth Of Nations*, Wordsworth Editions

Stevens, C. 2008 – *Business Processes For Engineers*, (Course book – Bath University)

Stiglitz, J.2012 – *The Price Of Inequality*, Clays

Surowiecki, J. 2004 – *The Wisdom Of Crowds*, Abacus

Tavris, C and Aronson, E. 2007, 2015 - *Mistakes Were Made (But Not By Me)*, Mariner Books

Thiel, P. 2014 – *Zero To One*, Random House

Varoukakis, Y. 2016 – *And The Weak Suffer What They Must*, Penguin Random House

Verkaik, R. 2018 – *Posh Boys*, Oneworld

Wilkinson, R & Pickett, K. 2009 – *The Spirit Level*, Penguin

BOOK REVIEWS – BY STEVENS, C, 2016

Smith, A – *An enquiry Into The Nature And Causes Of The Wealth Of Nations,* 1776 (**957 pages**)

Review: Although nearly 250 years old this book (five volumes) feels quite modern. There are two thrusts to Smith's argument. The first is that although making money is inherently a selfish activity when linked with division of labour and competition it creates an efficient system for improving standards of living. WofN follows hard on the heels of Smith's other tome, a theory of moral sentiments, which I haven't read – sorry. I understand that at the time there was a great debate about how the embryonic system of capitalism which is fundamentally selfish could fit with humanity's higher morals, plus ca change... In WofN, Smith's second argument in the later volumes criticises monopolies as they reduce wealth creation for all. Because a monopoly lacks one essential factor within the wealth creation system, namely competition, then that essential check on excess profits and driver of cost reductions and innovation leads to a worse situation for all. The main monopolies in those days were those granted by the Crown. Smith argues that allowing competition in would benefit all including the Crown itself from greater growth overall. The same arguments are pro free trade.

WofN is a great book and so much of it is now in everyday parlance without us knowing. The trickledown effect, free trade, markets, invisible hand. And also so much has been conveniently forgotten especially by the free marketers; for example Smith berates businessmen taking excessive profits and explains that a natural price consists of a fair profit margin on top of the costs of labour and capital (stock in his day) plus rent. The fair profit margin reflects the political risk in a country and in the UK with most stable system (then) a fair profit would be 5 to 10%. Yet he explains market prices can be more if there is a deficiency (in supply or extra need) or where there are wealthy buyers. Prices will gravitate to fair prices if there is competition and so the market is self-regulating.

Olsen, M – *The Rise And Decline Of Nations* 1982 (237 pages)
Review: Special interest groups can stifle innovation and change in an economy. Groups like cartels, industry associations, unions, lobby groups and more they can use their power to extract extra profits from their industry by lobbying for trade protection, subsidies, import protection and delay market adjustments for example. Groups with a small number of players form more quickly than bigger groups and eventually over decades this can start to redistribute sizeable amounts of money and thus distort the economy. This was one of the theories used by the Thatcher Government to diagnose the "English Disease" as it was known in the 1970s and hence the battles with vested interests most famously the unions but also the merchant banks and other cartels. The lesson I take from this is to recognise this effect and Government must stop all lobby groups getting too powerful.

Olsen, M – *Power And Prosperity*, 2000 (199 pages)
Review: Written for the USA right wing surely? Olsen chooses the analogy of a bandit extorting money as comparable with Government taxation. It is enlightening and he shows that if the Government (or bandit) represents enough of the population then the incentives to support growth, defence and public health because a thriving economy means a thriving tax take, take too much and the economy dives and there is less tax. There is so much in this book to recommend including the analysis of how Stalinist Soviet Union was so successful at supporting state activities and how the system eventually broke down due to corruption which was an inevitable consequence of a system combining central planning with human frailty.

I draw a hypothesis from Olsen with a special interest group, he would call bandit, benefiting from lower than optimal levels of tax. They take more because tax is low others suffer due to lack of public services. A bandit extracting wealth...I hope to get someone to develop this as a separate thesis

(And I did, I wrote *After The Revolution* in 2020)

Wilkinson, R & Pickett, K – *The Spirit Level,* 2009 (311 pages)
Review: Not an economics book. Presents impressive medical evidence of the correlation of public health problems with inequality of wealth. Graph after graph showing this correspondence. Potential causation not just correlation is explained by showing how anxiety raises cortisol levels which are not healthy if this continues in a person for a long time. This is them linked to consumerism, status and marketing by companies. I was convinced. But the last third of the book proposes some economic solutions which were well put but not convincing at least not to me.

Frank, R - *The Darwin Economy,* 2011 (222 pages)
Review: Frank starts from the philosophical viewpoint of liberalism that people should be free to do what they like unless they harm others by their actions. Moving to economics he explains how markets give that freedom to consumers and suppliers for goods and services that bring an absolute benefit to the consumer. Basics like food, housing, clothes etc. The world of Smith's "wealth of nations". There are other types of goods where the benefits are shared like defence, police, parks and these are public goods and need to be provided by a tax on the whole community. He then explains there is a third type of goods which he calls "competitive" or "positional". Goods which give status or rank to the buyer and therefore reduce the status of everyone else around him or her. Examples given are mansions, schooling, impressive birthday parties for your child. Every time someone buys one of these goods then others lose and unlike the win-win that markets bring buyer and seller for absolute goods (ignoring externalities), markets for competitive goods bring a win, win, lose for buyer, seller and third party. If the harm (loss) is so much then that trade actually reduces overall welfare to society, not what markets are for at all.

When competitive goods are a small part of the economy then that's fine but in rich countries he posits they are the major part of the economy and the harm done to others through diminishing their rank because they can't afford the status goods can be quite high. Advertising nudges us all to buy these goods appealing to our status needs which is why we get a temporary buzz from our new car or pay increase but when we hear someone has done better we feel bad.

The same effect applies in sports for example wearing safety helmets. Players would never voluntarily wear these until mandated by the sporting authority. So like sports bodies, governments should do something about the markets for competitive goods to reduce or mitigate the harm to third parties.

Of course we all need to fulfil our esteem needs and Frank finishes off with two suggestions:

• Firstly that Adam Smith's book describes the special case of absolute goods and the invisible hand actually doesn't benefit society regarding positional and status goods.

• Secondly Frank suggests that if this type of good were taxed higher (e.g. higher VAT) the esteem value of the good would actually increase as less people could afford it and the tax revenue could be used to help deal with the harm caused indirectly due to the market system we use for our economy.

Stiglitz, J – *The Price Of Inequality*, 2012 (363 pages)

Review: In the capitalist system there exists a fundamental tension between the role of business in general which is to provide benefits to the public and the role of each business in particular which is to benefit shareholders. In order to manage this tension there must be market regulation. Regulation that is going to be most effective is incentives where social returns from business are aligned with the private benefits to shareholders. Towards the end of the book he explains how this might be done by taxing those business profits or activities that benefit shareholders but don't benefit the public as a whole.

Stiglitz offers examples of many activities that benefit shareholders but not so much the public. His list includes: lobbying, tendency to achieve monopoly positions, patents, unbalanced negotiating power, unions and more. In all cases (except unions) the fact that the activity achieves a higher return for the business means it is more likely to achieve more investment which will cause other businesses who compete for that investment to get less. Overall this distorts the optimum balance of the economy and moves away from the provision of maximised total welfare.

Government, he submits is needed to iron out these distortions including investing in basic research and education as examples. Much of this book is framed in the US political struggle between the Anti Government, Free Marketers and the rest. Stiglitz strongly argues that the state has a key role to play in ensuring business brings benefits to society which is why the market system exists in the first place.

Janeway, W – *Doing Capitalism In The Innovation Economy 2012* (283 pages)
Review: Janeway made a lot of money in venture capital in the USA. Initially trained as an economist this book shows his observations over his career spanning five decades. It is an interesting life story and has many lessons for venture capitalists (VCs). The main point relevant to us is that he observes that the main gains from VC over that period were in the Biotech and IT industries both of which were initially financed by Government funded R&D. There were other winners in other industries but overall VCs lost money. But in biotech and IT VCs made money as they were de-risked by Government. The conclusion is that for a state to be a leader in a new industry the state must fund basic R&D.

Mazzucato, M – *The Entrepreneurial State* 2013 (198 pages)
Review: Written after Janeway and referring to it, Mazzucato presents an argument as to why big corporations should pay taxes even though many in the US deny this! To have an innovative economy you need government investment in basic and applied research to approximately 2.5% of GDP. That is enough to take out uncertainty (differs from risk in that uncertainty can't be calculated) to a level that risk can then be calculated and the markets for venture capital can then take over. She takes a chapter to analyse all the technologies in iPhones and shows that 12 of them are spin offs from Government research. She notes that the US spends about 2% on R&D whereas China spends 6%. Note: The UK

is 0.5% and puts us very low and if you buy into Mazzucato's thesis this leaves the UK with little new industry in 20 or 30 years' time.

EPILOGUE

A short follow up on four announcements from the Summer of 2020 as seen through the lens of the Mathematics of Power:

a) Adult Social Care being transferred to the NHS. This was reported in the *Guardian* on 28th July. The Government denied it.

Comment: There is certainly a need for closer working and coordination between Local Authorities and the NHS. And if the NHS took over and received the £22.5 billion annual budget then they would be able to "unblock beds" faster and save money from that. The devil is, as always, in the detail and I would like to see whether it meant the NHS favoured care homes (and thus private business) for social care instead of trying to maximise re-ablement for care at home or in extra care housing. We shall see.

b) Planning Reform. The LGiU newsfeed on 2nd August said:

Major planning shake-up announced

Writing in the Telegraph, Housing Secretary Robert Jenrick outlines the Government's plan for the biggest overhaul of the planning system since the Second World War. New homes, hospitals, schools, shops and offices will be given an automatic "permission in principle" in swathes of the country as red tape is cut to produce "simpler, faster" processes as part of a "once in a generation" reform of the system. It currently takes an average of five years for a standard housing development to pass through the planning system but the Government believes it can reduce the process by up to two years. The country will be divided into three types of land: areas designated for "growth", and those earmarked for "renewal" or "protection". Additionally, money from developers will be used to give discounts of up to one-third off the cost of a house to local people. Councils will be able to prioritise housing for key workers such as police, nurses and teachers. As part of the reforms, Mr Jenrick is planning a "digital transformation" that would allow residents to view proposals for their area on interactive online maps.

The Sunday Telegraph, Page: 1, The Sunday Times, Page: 2

Comment: Criticism of this came the very next day. Headlines like "creating the slums of the future". Then there was another report detailing the secretive lobbying going on in this sector ranging from major conflicts of interest to downright bribery; And in another newsfeed from the LGiU, on the 6th August and covered widely:

"The Royal Institute of British Architects (RIBA) described the proposals as "shameful" and said they would do "almost nothing to guarantee the delivery of affordable, well-designed and sustainable homes".

Planning is certainly in need of a shake-up, but in cities the main problem is the price of land. Cutting red tape could mean smaller rooms, more money into the system and thus further land price rises. And who benefits from the land price increases and who suffers from the smaller rooms?

c) On 31 Jul 2020; some scrutiny on Universal Credit

Lords urge £8bn Universal Credit overhaul

The House of Lords Economic Affairs Committee has said Universal

Credit (UC) needs an £8bn overhaul to make it reliable for those who will depend on it as the COVID-19 crisis grows. The committee said public support for UC is "seeping away" because of multiple design faults, the inadequacy of benefit rates, and lack of specialised support for claimants. Proposed reforms include a catch-up increase in the generosity of benefit rates: "Universal Credit should be set at a level that provides claimants with dignity and security," the Lords say. The Guardian & Daily Mirror – Thank you LGiU

Comment: Covid-19 will test UC to the limit. Apart from the amount paid out, a large proportion is for housing benefit which as we have seen is often due to the price of land. The other issue is tapers which isn't addressed but locks people into relying on UC and low paid jobs rather than seeking opportunities for advancement.

d) And finally may I leave you with this from the LGiU newsfeed from 3rd August

Freeport benefits to business are 'almost non-existent'
Research by Sussex university's UK Trade Policy Observatory suggests that Government plans to build a network of freeports to boost post-Brexit Britain will have a negligible impact on the economy. Financial Times.

That was just three weeks after this announcement:

On 12 Jul 2020, Planning overhaul and tax cuts planned for 'freeports'
Under Government plans for a post-Brexit economic revolution, Chancellor Rishi Sunak is preparing to introduce tax cuts and an overhaul of planning laws in up to 10 new "freeports" within a year of the UK becoming fully independent from the EU in December. Mr Sunak will use his autumn budget to invite bids from towns and cities to become freeports, where tax and regulatory changes will be introduced, including research and development tax credits, generous capital allowances, cuts to

stamp duty and business rates, and local relaxations of planning laws. The Government believes the policy can transform ports into "international hubs" for manufacturing and innovation.

Comment: Umm... I wonder why Government are progressing this? Negligible impact on the economy and yet tax cuts and relaxation of regulation. Who benefits? I rest my case.